DAILY
Guideposts
2005

❋

*I will be glad and rejoice in
thee: I will sing praise to thy
name, O thou most High.*
—Psalm 9:2

IDEALS PUBLICATIONS
A DIVISION OF GUIDEPOSTS
NASHVILLE, TENNESSEE

ISBN 0-8249-4631-6

Published by Ideals Publications, a division of Guideposts
535 Metroplex Drive, Suite 250, Nashville, Tennessee 37211
www.idealsbooks.com

ACKNOWLEDGMENTS

All Scripture quotations, unless otherwise noted, are taken from *The King James Version of the Bible*.
Scripture quotations marked (AMP) are taken from *The Amplified Bible*, © 1965 by Zondervan Publishing House. All rights reserved.
Scripture quotations marked (JB) are taken from *The Jerusalem Bible*, © 1966, 1967 and 1968 by Darton, Longman & Todd Ltd. and Doubleday & Company, Inc. All rights reserved.
Scripture quotations marked (NAS) are taken from the *New American Standard Bible*, © The Lockman Foundation, 1960, 1962, 1963, 1968, 1971, 1972, 1973, 1975, 1977. Used by permission.
Scripture quotations marked (NEB) are taken from *The New English Bible*. Copyright © The Delegates of the Oxford University Press and the Syndics of the Cambridge University Press 1961, 1970.
Scripture quotations marked (NIV) are taken from *The Holy Bible, New International Version*. Copyright © 1973, 1978, 1984 International Bible Society. Used by permission of Zondervan Bible Publishers.
Scripture quotations marked (NKJV) are taken from *The Holy Bible, New King James Version*. Copyright © 1997, 1990, 1985, 1983 by Thomas Nelson, Inc.
Scripture quotations marked (NLT) are taken from the *Holy Bible*, New Living Translation. Copyright © 1996. Used by permission of Tyndale House Publishers, Inc., Wheaton, Illinois 60189. All rights reserved.
Scripture quotations marked (NRSV) are taken from the *New Revised Standard Version Bible*. Copyright © 1989 by the Division of Christian Education of the National Council of the Churches of Christ in the U.S.A. Used by permission. All rights reserved.
Scripture quotations marked (RSV) are taken from the *Revised Standard Version of the Bible*. Copyright © 1946, 1952, 1971 by Division of Christian Education of the National Council of Churches of Christ in the U.S.A. Used by permission.
Scripture quotations marked (TLB) are taken from *The Living Bible*. Copyright © 1971 by Tyndale House Publishers, Wheaton, IL 60187. All rights reserved.
"A Very Present Help" was written by Carol Kuykendall; "At the Foot of the Cross" was written by Julia Attaway; "God Sightings" was written by Elizabeth Sherrill; "He Leadeth Me . . . " was written by Roberta Messner; "The Mysterious Gift" was written by Marilyn Morgan King; "Simple Gifts" was written by Karen Barber; "When Lightning Strikes Again" was written by Marci Alborghetti.
"Reader's Room" by Terrie Becan, Nila Benci, Jeannie Berger, Joanna Bordner, Wanda E. Brooks, Lee Ann Fuller, Mary Hinkel, Rosemary Hoberg, Wanda Humphrey, Shirley Imerti, Carol A. Talvola, Marla Williams are reprinted with permission by the authors.
Gina Bridgeman's photo is copyright © 2002 by Michael Norton. Julie Garmon's photo is copyright © 2002 Jeff Von Hoene. Oscar Greene's photo is copyright © 2001 by Olan Mills, Inc. Edward Grinnan's photo is by Julie Skarratt. Rick Hamlin's photo is by Lilly Dong. Pamela Kennedy's photo is copyright © 1996. Cover Look Inc. Van Varner's photo is by Steven Boljonis.

Cover photograph © by Dennis Frates   Artwork by Cecile Schoberle
Cover design by Marisa Calvin   Indexed by Patricia Woodruff
Design by David Matt   Typeset by Planet Patti, Inc.
Design adaptations by Holly Johnson   Printed in the United States of America

TABLE OF CONTENTS

TABLE OF CONTENTS

THERE ARE TIMES in all our lives when we seem to be looking down from the mountaintop, our hearts overflowing with joy: when we realize for the first time how much God loves us; when we step onstage to receive a diploma; when we set off to work on our first job; when we hold a newborn baby in our arms. Those are times when praise and thanksgiving seem as natural to us as breathing, and it seems as if the very next step might take us into the presence of the Lord.

There are other times, too, when we seem to be looking up from the floor of a very dark valley: when we face illness; when we lose a loved one; when we've lost a job or failed a test; when we can't seem to find any good news in our daily papers. Those are times when we feel powerless, when prayer can be an effort and God can seem far away.

But we know a marvelous truth: Whether we're up on the mountaintop or down in the valley, we're always in the hands of God. And through faith and trust in His loving care, we can hope to share in His glory. And in that hope, we can always rejoice. So our theme for *Daily Guideposts, 2005*—our twenty-ninth edition—is "Rejoicing in Hope."

We invite you to spend the coming year with our sixty writers— friends old and new—as your daily companions. They're ready to share their own joys and sorrows with you, and show you the ways the Lord has helped them to rejoice in hope.

Discover how the seeds of hope planted over a lifetime can burst into flower just when they're needed, and how God's comforting presence can shine out from the heart of a trusted friend, the words of a familiar hymn or the face of a stranger. Travel with us from a frozen lake in Alaska to the muddy waters of the Amazon, from a country cabin to the midst of a bustling city, and find signs of God's love everywhere you look. Every day, as you share a story of living faith from our *Daily Guideposts* family, you'll find your own step growing lighter, your own heart filling with praise.

This year, we have seven special series to help you cultivate the seeds of rejoicing in your own life. You'll start each month with Elizabeth Sherrill as she shares "God Sightings" that restore her spirit when hope seems hard to come by. In the middle of each month, Roberta Messner's "He Leadeth Me . . ." will show you how God changes lives when we listen for His leading and follow that insistent voice.

Sometimes we don't truly understand the depth of our faith until it's tested. Join Carol Kuykendall for three days in February as she discovers the glimmers of hope that shine through even the darkest night. And during Holy Week, spend some time with Julia Attaway as she follows Jesus to the place where Easter truly begins: "At the Foot of the Cross."

Last year, Marilyn Morgan King experienced a series of events that are so improbable they border on the miraculous. As you read her series in June, you'll be touched by the deep truth that God acts in our lives in stunningly mysterious ways. In October, Marci Alborghetti discovers the God Who is stronger than any storm in "When Lightning Strikes Again."

For Advent and Christmas, we've got a wonderful present for you: Karen Barber's "Simple Gifts." As you get ready to celebrate the birth of Jesus, join Karen for a reminder that the best gifts we can give each other are the simplest ones of all.

You'll hear from cherished friends like Fred Bauer, Marion Bond West, Oscar Greene, Pam Kidd, Ruth Stafford Peale, Fay Angus, Carol Knapp and Dolphus Weary. You'll also make some new friends: Debbie Macomber of Port Orchard, Washington, who searches for a New Year word from God as she confronts the illness of her beloved father; Sabra Ciancanelli of Pawling, New York, who shares a Christmas memory of a little boy, a battered toy car and a gift from the heart; Rebecca Kelly of Coral Springs, Florida, who learns a vivid lesson about the boundless generosity of God and the beauty of a giving heart from her lively six-year-old; Pablo Diaz, who will tell you about the angel in the form of a seventh-grade teacher who made all the difference in his life; and Karen Valentin of New York City, who finds a new way of witnessing to her faith while leafing through her photo album.

Even as we welcome back our old friends and say hello to new ones, we must say good-bye to a cherished member of our *Daily Guideposts* family, Drue Duke of Sheffield, Alabama, who died on September 4, 2003, at the age of eighty-four. Drue joined *Daily Guideposts* in 1979, and over the years we came to love her for the faith, courage and simple down-home goodness that shone through everything she wrote. We rejoice in the memory of all she's given us, even as we hope to join her someday in our Father's house. Please keep Drue's family in your prayers.

All of us who are a part of *Daily Guideposts*—readers, writers and members of the Guideposts staff—have a very special reason to rejoice. As we begin another year of grace, walking together through the days in fellowship and prayer, we thank God once again for making us part of this wonderful family. Bound to one another in love by the God Who is the source and summit of our faith, this day and every day, we rejoice in hope.

—THE EDITORS

January

Be of good courage, and he shall strengthen your heart, all ye that hope in the Lord. —*Psalm 31:24*

SAT
1

"*Therefore, however you want people to treat you, so treat them. . . .*" —*Matthew 7:12 (NAS)*

BACK IN 1896, Charles Sheldon wrote *In His Steps*, in which the pastor of a church challenges his congregation to do nothing without first asking themselves, "What Would Jesus Do?" Ever since, this question, often abbreviated to WWJD, has become a familiar reminder.

As my New Year's resolution for 2005, I've determined to make WWJD my principle every time one of my pet peeves raises its ugly head.

For example, a pet peeve surfaces when the phone rings at 3:00 A.M. and I answer, "Wolseley residence," emphasizing *residence*, and the caller asks, "Is this the medical clinic?" (The clinic's number is one digit different from mine.) WWJD? He'd undoubtedly remind me that people who call the clinic at that time of night usually have some serious medical concerns.

Then there are those requests, "A donation is greatly needed. Even five dollars will go a long way." So I send five dollars and subsequently receive innumerable mailings, which use up the entire five dollars, plus more, in postage. WWJD? Probably tell me, "Give in secret so people won't see how much you give. God knows." Good point.

But my most maddening pet peeve is the misspelling of my first name. Half my mail is addressed to "Isobel," the other half to "Isabelle" or "Izabella" or whatever. WWJD if His mail came addressed "Geezus"? Would He bristle? Would He quote the Golden Rule? Or would He be glad to know that people are calling for Him, however they spell His name?

Please be patient with me, Lord. And I'll remember to ask, WWJD?
—ISABEL WOLSELEY

SUN
2

LOOKING FOR AND HASTING UNTO THE COMING OF THE DAY OF GOD. . . . —II Peter 3:12

TAKING DOWN A Christmas tree can be the most disheartening of tasks. The season is over, the presents have been opened, the celebration is done. All that remains is to put the ornaments in boxes, strip the lights off the branches, and take out the tree. As a kid, I remember starting to count the days until Christmas would come again—360, 359, 358. Contemplating the end of it was just too sad.

In such a mood, I took down our tree last year. No carols on the radio to carry me along, no one to help either. Just me and a tree so dry that at the merest touch the needles fell to the ground like hail. One more thing to add to my task: vacuuming. The pile of needles grew into a mountain at my feet, the tree a shadow of its former glory.

But as the needles fell, I noticed something that had been completely hidden when we bought the bushy pine. It was invisible when the tree was sparkling with lights and balls and stars and angels. Now, though, that the tree was bare, I studied it in disbelief. I reached in between the branches and pulled it out: a nest. A well-made home for some mother and her chicks back in Vermont where the tree had grown.

I laid the nest in a bowl on the piano. I promised to keep it there until the crèche returned again, along with the candles we put in the windows, and we bought a new tree. The first ornament for next year. My reminder that Christmas was only . . . 357 days away.

I live in hope, Lord, because Your day is coming and has come!
                                                                —RICK HAMLIN

GOD SIGHTINGS

"WHEN HOPE SEEMS hard to come by," says Elizabeth Sherrill, "I remember what I learned from my friend Jean Nardozzi. Anytime God seemed far away, she said, she'd pray that in her own everyday experience—past or present—He would show her Himself. These insights she recorded in a notebook that she'd titled *God Sightings*. 'Reading them over always sends my hope soaring,' she told me."

Following Jean's lead, Elizabeth began to record her own glimpses, both of God and of the kind of relationship He wants with us. At the start of each month this year, Elizabeth shares some of her own special God sightings.

—THE EDITORS

THE FACES OF GLORY

MON

3

So God created man in his own image. . . .
—Genesis 1:27

THE SNOW STARTED Wednesday afternoon and didn't stop for forty-eight hours.

The storm was widespread. On Thursday my husband phoned from Chicago to say O'Hare International was closed and he wouldn't try to get back before going on to Phoenix. Snowbound and alone, I reminded myself how much I had to be grateful for: plenty of food on hand; phone and electric lines intact; warm and dry while a blizzard raged outside.

Sunday morning dawned dazzling bright on a pristine white world. And oddly, this was the hardest day of all. Church services were canceled—I couldn't have gotten out of my driveway anyway—and the feeling of isolation was like an ache. *Where are You, God?* I prayed. I told myself not to be silly. God was just as near me here at home as in church. Why did He seem so far away?

The road crews were slow to reach our street. It was already dark on Monday afternoon when our plow service got through and cleared the driveway. Cabin fever propelled me into the car and through streets tunneled between six-foot white walls. The grocery store parking lot was jammed, the lines at the check-out counters twenty carts long.

I pushed my own cart down a crowded aisle; I didn't care which one. I wasn't looking at the shelves; I was looking at people. A woman's face framed in a blue scarf. A man's face, ruddy beneath his woolen cap. I was listening to voices: ". . . . shovel a path to the bird feeder." I was watching gestures. A mother lifting a child from a cart, a teenage clerk loading shelves.

I was seeing God.

God in every face, every voice, every action. God in the people I so seldom really look at, whose glory it had taken a snowstorm and five housebound days to show me.

Show me Yourself, Lord, in Your human likeness.
—ELIZABETH SHERRILL

EDITOR'S NOTE: Throughout this new year, we hope you'll take time to jot down the "God sightings" in your own life. You'll find space for them on the "Seeds of Rejoicing" pages at the end of each month.

TUE

4

TRUST IN THE LORD WITH ALL THINE HEART; AND LEAN NOT UNTO THINE OWN UNDERSTANDING. IN ALL THY WAYS ACKNOWLEDGE HIM, AND HE SHALL DIRECT THY PATHS. —Proverbs 3:5–6

ONE OF MY FAVORITE cartoons depicts a hardhearted Manhattanite glaring at a tourist who is sheepishly asking, "Can you tell me how to get to the Statue of Liberty or should I just get lost?"

I am just the opposite. I love giving directions. And I don't just give vague, generalized directions, either. I like to be as specific as possible and sure of my information. The more exact I can be, the more satisfaction I take in rendering assistance and the more confident I feel that the person will get where he or she is going.

This all amuses my wife to no end, perhaps because she's spent so many hours sitting in the passenger seat of a car while I drive around completely lost, yet refusing to get directions. "Why can't you just stop and ask someone?" she'll demand. But that would be too easy. It isn't a matter of stubborn male pride—or at least I don't think it is. It's more a sense that I want to figure things out for myself. There is, of course, a point at which I should just admit defeat and ask someone for help. But that point doesn't come easily for me.

All of which leads me to ask myself a question: Am I like that in my prayer life, too? Always giving directions—"Lord, grant me this" and "Father, help me to do that"—instead of seeking them? I listen to myself pray sometimes and it's more like I'm placing an order. So here's my New Year's resolution: Ask for direction.

That's me, God, the guy who's lost and still won't ask You for help. Next time I am in a bind, I'll try asking for direction instead of giving it.
—EDWARD GRINNAN

WED

5

"I WILL SHOW YOU WHAT HE IS LIKE WHO COMES TO ME AND HEARS MY WORDS AND PUTS THEM INTO PRACTICE." —*Luke 6:47 (NIV)*

EVERY NEW YEAR'S DAY I ask the Lord to give me a word to focus on for the next twelve months. It doesn't always come to me right away, but I keep my mind and my heart open and wait. Generally, within a week or two the word presents itself. Instantly, I know it's the right one, and I ask God to use it to teach me the lessons I need to learn in the coming year.

This year as I prayed, my heart was heavy. My father has been seriously ill for a long while and was recently placed in a nursing home. My prayers were clouded with worries about what the future held for him and for my mother. Then it came to me that my word was *surrender*. The Lord was asking me to surrender my father to Him, to give Him all my worries and fears. It wasn't the word I wanted.

As I drove to meet my walking partner for our morning walk, my eyes clouded with tears as I tried to imagine life without my dad. But as I drove past the Sun Trust bank, I blinked in amazement. Through my tears, the sign outside seemed to read SON TRUST. I stopped the car. Now I was sure God was asking me to put my trust in Him, to surrender my will to His. It wouldn't be easy, but I knew that He would provide the grace required for the task.

Oh, Father, how grateful I am for Your promises. I surrender myself to Your precious will. —DEBBIE MACOMBER

THU

6

FOR WE KNOW THAT IF THE EARTHLY TENT WE LIVE IN IS DESTROYED, WE HAVE A BUILDING FROM GOD, A HOUSE NOT MADE WITH HANDS, ETERNAL IN THE HEAVENS. —II Corinthians 5:1 (RSV)

GRACE CHURCH, A NEW YORK CITY landmark, sits like an oasis amid the restaurants, music stores and movie theaters of my Greenwich Village neighborhood. Walking past the church's quirky, ornate buildings, glancing into the fairy-tale garden they enclose or letting my eye follow the slender, slightly crooked stone steeple up into the sky, I always feel as if I'm being given a glimpse into a place apart.

Apparently I wasn't the only person who had noticed the steeple's slight list. Last year, the church set about correcting it, as part of a general renovation project. Boards and scaffolding rose up around the church, and without thinking about it, I started to take another street home most nights. I wasn't much interested in seeing the twenty-first century overtake the little church.

A couple of weeks went by. Then, one misty night, walking home from the gym on my old route, I stopped in front of Grace Church and looked up. There, caught in the beam of a light set atop a building across the way, was the steeple, covered from base to tip in a delicate lattice of scaffolding. The geometrical squares of metal and plastic and the familiar stone structure visible beneath them blended into a single, wonderful image. An image that, to my surprise, didn't destroy the message that the church had always suggested to me, but underscored it. Beneath the surface of this world that seems always to be changing, improving and modifying itself, there lies another, deeper one, immune to all improvement, because it is perfect already.

Lord, thank You for Your enduring presence, which is always close at hand. —PTOLEMY TOMPKINS

FRI
7

AND GOD SHALL WIPE AWAY ALL TEARS FROM THEIR EYES; AND THERE SHALL BE NO MORE DEATH, NEITHER SORROW, NOR CRYING, NEITHER SHALL THERE BE ANY MORE PAIN: FOR THE FORMER THINGS ARE PASSED AWAY. —*Revelation 21:4*

THE PHONE RINGS AS I'm washing the dishes for the 900,000th time. My daughter runs for the phone. My daughter is twelve years old and addicted to the phone.

She answers it, then brings it to me. It's an old friend who always makes me laugh. Not this time.

This time he's calling from the hospital where his daughter is dying. She got hit by a truck and broke everything you can break. She just had a baby. He is holding her new son in his arms at the hospital. The boy is two months old.

I remember when this boy's mama was two months old. She slept in the top drawer of a rickety bureau. Her folks had about seven cents when she was born. All these years later they don't have much more than seven cents, but they had three more children after Julie. "We are rich, rich, rich, rich," my friend would say, grinning. And he meant it, too.

He hangs up and I pray helplessly into the sink, into the bubbles and apple peels. I pray for my friend and his family to be rich, rich, rich, rich and not rich, rich, rich. I pray down into the cups and forks and the crusts of pizza my children refuse to eat. I say, "Rich rich rich rich" aloud to the soggy crusts, which makes me cry, and I wash off the crusts and dry them and carry them out to the grass for the crows to eat for some reason I don't understand that has everything to do with praying for Julie.

Dear Lord, tell me again that You will take care of the broken ones. Tell me that every day. —BRIAN DOYLE

SAT

8

REST IN THE LORD, AND WAIT PATIENTLY FOR HIM. . . .
—*Psalm 37:7*

MY FIRST EXPERIENCE of God's presence in my life occurred when I was six years old. My mother had put me to bed and gone downstairs. Lying quietly on my cot, I suddenly sensed an unusual peacefulness settle around me, and I began to hum a song I'd learned in Sunday school. As I hummed, I felt a love so profound that it removed all fear of anything bad ever happening. Everything seemed at peace in my heart and in my world. That loving presence stayed with me until I drifted off to sleep.

From that time on, whenever I felt the need for solitude, I would crawl onto the tall pile of quilts folded on a chair in the corner of the bedroom and sit with my back against the wall. At that age, I couldn't have explained it in words, but somehow God was in the stillness of that little room, gently making Himself known to me.

Now, as a busy adult with lots of responsibilities, it's hard to make time to quiet my mind and wait for that presence. Sometimes I wish I could crawl back up on those quilts and sit with my back against the wall, listening to the rain on the tin roof of our house, and hear God speak to me in every peaceful drop. Stillness doesn't come as easily as it did when I was young and distractions were fewer, but if I want to know love, patience, tolerance and forgiveness of myself and others—if I want to grow spiritually—I have to make the effort to rediscover that quiet within.

Father, thank You for always joining me in the quietness and speaking sweet peace to my soul. —LIBBIE ADAMS

SUN

9

O GOD, THOU HAST TAUGHT ME FROM MY YOUTH: AND HITHERTO HAVE I DECLARED THY WONDROUS WORKS. —*Psalm 71:17*

FOR LONGER THAN I can remember, my wife Shirley has wanted a player piano. Not just any player piano, but an old one with character. Well, we recently found a turn-of-the-century (the twentieth century) instrument that filled the bill, and now it sits grandly in the living room of our Pennsylvania house. And *grandly* is the right adverb. Not only are its dark oak finish and hand-carved appliqués beautiful to look at, the piano must weigh a ton. It took four men and a boy to move it!

Though I pretended to be uninterested in this purchase, in truth I'm pleased to have it, because one of my fondest church-related recollections centers on a player piano. When I was a boy growing up in Ohio, I often went with our church youth group to the country home of our leaders, Everett and Juanita Miller. The Millers had no children of their own, so they adopted all of us into their family. They owned a player piano, and whenever we visited their place, which was often, someone invariably put a roll of music into the machine and began pumping the pedals. Within seconds, a dozen or so of us would crowd around to see the words as they scrolled by, harmonizing on such standards as "Down by the Old Mill Stream" and "In the Good Old Summertime," and hymns like "Do Lord, Oh, Do Lord" and "When the Roll Is Called Up Yonder."

Gone are those days and the player piano that helped me bond with young friends who formed one of my early church communities. But such memories! And what a debt many of us owe to people like the Millers, who helped shape our positive attitude of the church and its importance in our lives.

Thank You, God, for people who work with youth,
Who by words and deeds reveal Your truth.

—FRED BAUER

MON
10

HE THAT HATH A PERVERSE TONGUE FALLETH INTO MISCHIEF. —*Proverbs 17:20*

I LIKED THE FIFTH GRADE. There were field trips, parties and even minor triumphs such as making A's in spelling. But when I think back to that time, it's Donnie's jacket I remember first.

Although he kept to himself a lot, I liked Donnie. He was the kind of boy who would stop to pick up a book you'd dropped or step back to let you in front of him in the library checkout line. He was neither the fastest nor the slowest boy in class, but everyone knew he was the poorest.

At first, it didn't seem to matter that he always wore the same jeans and shirts or that his shoes were awfully worn. Then winter came, and we found out that Donnie didn't own a coat. At recess on the first really cold day, I noticed him standing in a patch of sun, bare-armed and shivering.

"How can God let Donnie go without a coat?" I asked my mother that afternoon. "Before winter's over he'll freeze to death!"

The next morning, as my mother drove me to school, she pointed to a package that lay on the seat between us. "Take this package to your teacher as soon as you walk in the room," she said. "I called her last night and she's expecting it."

"What is it?" I asked.

"It's a new jacket for Donnie."

The next day Donnie arrived at school as warm as toast. All morning long he wore the jacket proudly. Then at noon, disaster struck. I was standing a few steps behind Donnie in the lunch line when a curly-headed girl approached him.

"Where did you get that jacket, Donnie? I know someone gave it to you. Your parents are too poor to buy a jacket like that." Donnie's head dropped in shame, and my heart fell all the way down to my toes.

My mother's kindness and a little girl's thoughtless cruelty taught the best lesson this fifth-grader ever learned.

Father, let me respond to the needs of others in Your merciful-mother style, never forgetting that we all need both warm coats and kind words.

—PAM KIDD

TUE
11

AND THE LORD, WHOM YE SEEK, SHALL SUDDENLY COME TO HIS TEMPLE. . . . —Malachi 3:1

AS A CHILD, I lived about twenty-five miles north of New York City. No trip to the city with my parents was complete without a visit to St. Patrick's Cathedral. We'd enter the darkened church, bathed in the flicker of candlelight. I felt so small beneath the towering archways and enormous stone columns that line the side aisles. Passing dozens of solid wooden pews, we'd pick a spot near the altar to pray. I'd say a simple prayer—"Help me to obey Mom and Dad"—then look up in awe at the tall stained-glass windows beneath a ceiling that seemed to reach to heaven.

I recollected all of this one January day when my family visited Flagstaff, Arizona, north of Phoenix. Driving outside town on the road to the Grand Canyon, we spotted a small wood-and-stone chapel, framed by snow and nestled among the pine trees. Walking through the unlocked front door, we breathed in the cold, fresh air and the scent of earth rising from the dirt floor. Bright sunlight streamed through the window behind the stone altar, and beyond, the snow-covered mountains stood as if reaching to heaven. We sat on an iron bench to pray.

My prayers are still simple—for health and a productive new year. Yet in the rustic beauty, and in the notes and prayers visitors had tacked to the bare walls, I sensed God as near to me as in any of His grander houses. And He seemed to be telling me that the house itself is not important. What matters to Him is that I visit often.

Heavenly Father, be with me in Your house, wherever that may be, for there I feel most at home. —GINA BRIDGEMAN

WED
12

FOR THE WORD OF THE LORD IS RIGHT; AND ALL HIS WORKS ARE DONE IN TRUTH. —Psalm 33:4

MY NEPHEWS AND I own some land in the eastern slope of Colorado, far from where any of us lives. It's not worth much; once we hoped that it could produce uranium, but that was just a dream. We dream a lot about it, as though it had a magic all its own, almost like the way it came down to us.

It must have been about 1919 when a man appeared at my grandparents' place in Indiana asking for Carson Hamill, my grandfather. My grandfather came to the door and, to his surprise, recognized the man as a murderer and an escaped felon.

"Please, sir," I imagine the man saying, "I mean you no harm. I want to give myself up, and I want you to help me." He was remorseful. "I have lived in the wilderness and have found God, the same God Who tells me you are the one, sir. Please."

My grandfather was the prosecuting attorney who had convicted the man. Now, twenty years later, he was a corporate lawyer of some renown and being asked to defend the same person he had convicted. Of course, he accepted the challenge and, of course, the man—in a blaze of national attention—was freed.

The man paid my grandfather in land, the same acreage that was passed to my mother, and on to me and my nephews. I wonder if their children, and their children, will dream as much as we have.

Father, You know the man. You guided him to do right. —VAN VARNER

THU
13

AND HOW DELIGHTFUL IS A TIMELY WORD!
—*Proverbs 15:23 (NAS)*

IT WAS TURNING OUT to be one of those dreaded "Can't I do anything right?" days. An important letter was returned to me, unstamped. In the grocery store I discovered my shoes didn't match, even though both were brown. Outside, I tried valiantly to unlock the door of a car that looked amazingly like mine.

Later, at the red light, I drummed my fingers impatiently on the steering wheel, but when at last the light turned green I couldn't remember where I was headed. I roared off anyway, so no one would guess my dilemma. After several blocks, I remembered where I wanted to go. Feeling almost smug, I pulled up at the dry cleaner. My victory was short-lived, however: I'd forgotten the clothes.

Back at home, I gathered up all my courage and phoned our insurance company to straighten out an unpaid claim. I concentrated intently as I punched the endless numbers that I hoped would connect me to a live person.

The lady who finally spoke to me was smiling; I could feel it all the way down in Georgia. Sweetly, she suggested, "Let me get you more experienced help. I'm new here."

"Oh no, please don't go," I said near tears. "You are so—nice—and patient and kind. Please help me." I didn't tell her that sometimes fast-talking people, especially short-tempered ones, scare me.

She laughed like a next-door neighbor. "Okay, then." She took care of my problem, and when we finished she said, "Have a blessed day. We're always home for you."

Lord, just a few kind words, even from a stranger, have changed my entire outlook. Help me do the same for someone. —MARION BOND WEST

FRI
14

AND HE SPOKE MANY THINGS TO THEM IN PARABLES. . . .
—Matthew 13:3 (NAS)

TEXANS SPEAK A colorful language, full of sayings that spice up conversation and lodge in the memory. Yesterday I heard someone refer to a rather wealthy but frugal man in our community as "having short arms and deep pockets."

Recently I conducted a graveside funeral service for Lois Reynolds. Mrs. Reynolds lived in Texas all of her eighty years. Married to a country-and-western musician, she had heard nearly every "Texasism" and invented a few herself. One of the things she taught her grandsons when they were little was "Don't run with socks on your feet and toothpicks in your mouth." Those words often slowed them down when life became too fast and frantic. She also promised them that she would "Dance at your wedding with cowbells on." Her colorful sayings will stick in their minds forever.

Jesus knew the power of colloquial words and folksy sayings. He taught His disciples through the use of homespun parables and graphic imagery: "Don't talk about the sawdust in your neighbor's eye," he said, "when you've got a two-by-four in your own!" (Matthew 7:3). These were the words of a down-to-earth carpenter. They've never been forgotten.

Share the best you have to offer with those you love. Give them your stories, your memories, your humor, your unique self. One day when they gather and remember you, they will rejoice and "dance with cowbells on!"

Father, the best gift I can share with others is the unique self that You have created. May the laughter in my voice, the twinkle in my eye, the wisdom of my years be wholesome and contagious. Amen. —SCOTT WALKER

READER'S ROOM

ON NOVEMBER 1, 2002, I had a heart attack, and on January 8, 2003, I was scheduled for tests to determine where I would start exercising at Cardiac Rehab. When I read Shari Smyth's January 7 devotional and read her words, "You can do it. Just take the first step," it was as if God was speaking directly to me. I knew that He would be with me through the weeks of rehab. I was not in this alone.

I'm now finished with rehab, and I'm doing well. It just amazes me that God would use a story written long before I had a heart attack to help me through a most difficult time in my life. —*Wanda Humphrey, Camden, South Carolina*

SAT
15

FOR TO HIM THAT IS JOINED TO ALL THE LIVING THERE IS HOPE. . . . —Ecclesiastes 9:4

I'M CURLED UP ON the sofa, cuddled with the kitty in my afghan, gazing out the window at a lone bob house on the frozen lake. This plywood cubicle on skis accommodates a power auger, a lawn chair and a hole in the ice the size of a dinner plate. Nothing more. But the bone-cracking temperatures and icy wind don't deter my brother Dennis.

Bundled in bulky clothes, he sits inside his shack and waits. Occasionally he emerges to check his fishing lines outside the bob house, then returns to the shack to wait some more. I tuck my fleece collar under my chin, sip scalding tea and contemplate his "recreation" in that shack, a brown speck on a vast white frozen slab.

What's the lure of ice fishing anyway? It couldn't be for escape; Dennis lives alone. His lodge-style home with knotty pine walls and a wood-burning stove offers much more comfort. The catch of the day? Not necessarily. Dennis is content to return home empty-handed, and he could easily buy whatever fish he wants. No, it's something else.

As I watch him check the lines that disappear beneath the thick ice, I think of my prayer life. There are times when I feel chilled to the bone with worry—paralyzed, really. Comfort and protection seem far off indeed. As I pray and pray for God's help, all I need is a hint of a promise, faint as a tug on a line or a silvery flash beneath the ice, to keep me at it.

Like my brother, I know what it is to live on hope.
Light of the World, warm me in the winter of my discouragement.
—GAIL THORELL SCHILLING

HE LEADETH ME . . .

WHAT HAPPENS WHEN we sense God is nudging us to do something and we follow that insistent voice? How is our life changed when others listen, too, and follow that urging?

For years Roberta Messner rationalized that voice away, assuring herself that those little things God was asking her to do couldn't possibly have much meaning in the big picture. Then someone ministered to her, explaining that she did so at God's guiding. Her act of encouragement was tailor-made for Roberta. Since then Roberta listens a little closer and finds that God's nudges are gifts from Him, a way He brings hope and healing to His children. Join Roberta each month as she shows how those who say *yes* to God's nudges truly take part in a master plan. —THE EDITORS

TO SAY THANKS

SUN
16

FOR IT IS BY GRACE YOU HAVE BEEN SAVED, THROUGH FAITH—AND THIS NOT FROM YOURSELVES, IT IS THE GIFT OF GOD. —*Ephesians 2:8 (NIV)*

I WAS ATTENDING a luncheon when I spotted someone I hadn't seen in many years. An inner voice urged, *Go over to Mrs. Oxley and tell her how much she meant to you all those years at Seventh Avenue Baptist Church.* Just the thought of my childhood church flooded my mind with memories of caring people. And at the center of them was Mrs. Oxley, the pastor's wife, who welcomed me the Sunday morning I joined the church.

I was ten years old and didn't think I could make it all the way down the aisle to shake Pastor Oxley's hand. Mrs. Oxley sensed my shyness and draped her arm around my shoulders, making me forget my fears. Seeing her again reminded me how much I loved her. So I pushed away the doubts that the middle of a luncheon was the right place to thank her and spilled out my gratitude as she ate her green beans.

But it was what happened later that made me know there was another reason for that nudge. As I was finishing my pie, Patty Dawson, another member of my childhood church, came over to talk to me. She had overheard my conversation with Mrs. Oxley. "I wanted you to know that I, too, was overjoyed the day you came forward to make your profession of faith," she said. "When I had you in Sunday school, I never could seem to make you understand about God's grace. You kept asking, 'All *that* is free? How can that be?' The day you walked down the aisle, I knew you finally understood."

Thank You, Lord, for the people in my past who pointed my heart to You.
—ROBERTA MESSNER

MON
17

HERE THERE CANNOT BE GREEK AND JEW,
CIRCUMCISED AND UNCIRCUMCISED, BARBARIAN,
SCYTHIAN, SLAVE, FREE MAN, BUT CHRIST IS ALL,
AND IN ALL. —*Colossians 3:11 (RSV)*

EVERY YEAR, National Public Radio replays Martin Luther King, Jr.'s "I Have a Dream" speech. They may have last year, but we wouldn't have known it—the local NPR station succumbed to Pittsburgh weather and went silent for a while.

Undaunted, our seven-year-old daughter Grace asked my wife Sandee if she knew the speech. Sandee said she did, and it made her cry every time she heard it.

"Me, too," Grace said.

"Oh?" Sandee asked. "You heard it in school?"

"Yeah. But I heard it when he first said it."

Sandee paused. "Well, Martin Luther King, Jr. gave that speech when *I* was a little girl, so I'm not sure how you heard it."

"I remember it," Grace insisted. "I heard it when I was with Jesus and the angels."

Listen, I can't make this stuff up. Thing is, I'm not sure Grace can make this stuff up either. I wasn't in heaven in 1963—I was too busy terrorizing my parents—so who's to say? But wouldn't it make sense that they would have paused to listen? Imagine all the heavenly hosts gathered around as one man on earth made a simple, simply amazing request: that his four little children be judged not by the color of their skin but by the content of their character.

I have it on good authority that Jesus and the angels liked that line.

Lord, today let me pause to listen to Dr. King, and then let me help make this world a little more like heaven. —MARK COLLINS

TUE
18

ESTABLISH THE WORK OF OUR HANDS FOR US—YES,
ESTABLISH THE WORK OF OUR HANDS.
—*Psalm 90:17 (NIV)*

EVERY TIME I TAKE out my mother's rings, I can see her hands. They were elegant hands, with long fingers, the nails perfectly shaped ovals. She painted them with brightly colored nail polish—usually red—that chipped and wore off so that the spots of color that remained were like ruby islands floating on her pale pink nails.

I look at my own hands and remember that I could only write a little after she was diagnosed with lung cancer late last fall, and that my pencil stopped when she died the following January.

Close to the end, I see my hands moving tentatively to lay a cool towel on her forehead. I see my hands lying on the arms of the recliner where I slept next to her bed.

Suddenly I laugh when I remember my daughter Lanea's young hands fussing over her grandmother, moving with twenty-something rhythm to find music to comfort her or putting my mother's favorite movie into the video player.

Finally, I feel my son Chase's hand on my shoulder, keeping me steady and reassuring me while he and I sang "How Great Thou Art" at her funeral. His hands were no longer a little boy's hands; they were big and strong enough to keep me upright.

When I'm done reminiscing, I put the rings away. I grab my laptop computer and begin to work. The hands I see before me are my own. They are alive, and they are strong—just like my mother's hands.

Lord, thank You for generations who comfort, teach and strengthen one another. —SHARON FOSTER

WED
19

BEHOLD, WE COUNT THEM HAPPY WHICH ENDURE. . . .
—*James 5:11*

A FEW WEEKS AGO, my wife Tib and I returned from a trip where we'd been guilty of too-much-food and not-enough-exercise, and I had a bad case of the flabs. When it came time to pick up my exercise routine, going to our local cardiac rehab center suddenly seemed like too much trouble.

Then one day, before I could cancel my membership, I was standing in a long checkout line at the grocery store when I ran into a slim, healthy-looking fellow I knew from rehab. "Hi, Daniel," I said a little guiltily, hiding a package of sausage behind a carton of orange juice.

"Haven't seen you in a while," Daniel said. I told him about the trip and how I wasn't all that interested in coming back.

"Oh yeah," Daniel said, "I used to hear that a lot when I ran a fitness program." I remembered now: Before his genes caught up with him and he had a heart attack, Daniel had been employed to manage a corporation's executive gym. Many men and women, Daniel went on to say, would begin an exercise regimen, then stop. Perhaps they were "too busy" or maybe just lazy.

"But I found a way to get them started again," Daniel said. "I asked one question. 'When you're out of shape, what's the most important exercise you can take?' They'd name various regimens—StairMaster, treadmill, bicycle. Then I'd say, 'It's none of these. The most important exercise is the *next* one.'"

Daniel's comment struck home, and I renewed my commitment to rehab. I took the principle a step further, too. Not only had I become lax in taking care of my body, but I'd also become spiritually flabby. I hadn't gone to church or read my Bible much while we were away.

Thanks to running into Daniel, I have applied his wisdom not only to my physical life, but also to my devotional life.

What is the most important spiritual exercise any of us will ever take? The next one.

Thank You, Father, for speaking to me in the most unlikely of circumstances —even while standing in line at the grocery store. —JOHN SHERRILL

THU
20

FOR GOD DOES SPEAK—NOW ONE WAY, NOW ANOTHER—THOUGH MAN MAY NOT PERCEIVE IT.
—Job 33:14 (NIV)

"PLEASE, GOD, just let there be a parking space for me!" That had been my morning prayer for weeks, ever since I started physical therapy for my arthritis. The drive from downtown meant I couldn't get to school until nearly noon, and parking was scarce. After a twenty-minute hunt, I realized there wasn't a spot to be had. I headed home, dreading having to cancel my meeting with my research adviser, angry I would miss my classes.

At home, I sat in the car for a few moments, wondering what to do. The therapy was helping, but the schedule was interfering with my work. My health was improving, but at what cost? Would I have to drop out of school? Would I ever make progress in my research at this rate? Then my gaze settled on my bicycle, a dusty blue cruiser, unused since I moved off campus the previous year. A crazy idea began to take form. Shaking my head, I muttered, "I can't ride that thing all the way to school!" I shuffled toward the bike, still stiff from the morning's workout. The tires were a little soft, but everything seemed in working order, even the lights. I dusted off the seat and rolled it out to the driveway. *Maybe once around the block*, I thought. I pushed off, and before I knew it, I had looped the block twice. I grabbed my backpack from the car and pushed off again, this time to school.

God's answer to my parking space prayer that day was "No." Instead, He led me to something better. In the two years since I started commuting by bike, my health has improved by leaps and bounds, in part thanks to medicine and exercise, but also by the grace of God, Who gave me hope I might make it to school on that dusty, blue bicycle after all.

Thank You, God, for Your wise and generous answers to my prayers.
—KJERSTIN EASTON

FRI
21

THE LORD SHALL PRESERVE THY GOING OUT AND THY COMING IN. . . . —*Psalm 121:8*

LIKE MANY OTHER PASSENGERS, I was changing planes in Chicago and hurrying to catch my connecting flight to Philadelphia. Out of breath, I arrived at the proper gate only to find that my plane was late. I found a seat in the waiting area and piled my tote and carry-on bag around my feet, not only to keep them out of the way but to discourage anyone from taking them. When I was a little girl, my mother had cautioned me to keep an eye on my belongings, and I still followed her instructions.

I had a magazine to read, but I kept looking at my wristwatch. I was tired and longed to go home. Then I noticed that a young woman sitting across from me kept looking at my watch. It's not a great watch; it's a copy of an expensive one. But, I thought, maybe she didn't know the difference. I looked around, but didn't see any security guards. Even if I did, what could I say to them? "Somebody's staring at my watch"?

Suddenly, the announcement came: The plane was ready for boarding. I gathered my luggage and hurried toward the ramp, but the young woman caught up with me. She touched my arm and said, "Excuse me, but your watch is unfastened." I looked down at my wrist and, sure enough, the clasp was undone and the watch was about to fall off.

I was embarrassed by my earlier suspicions. "Thank you!" I said. "Thank you so much!" There was no time to say more. We boarded the plane and sat in different sections.

Quietly, I offered a prayer of thanks. The world can be dangerous, and it makes sense to be careful. But when I let my fears get ahead of the facts, I can make it seem a darker place than it is.

Lord, help me not to be a captive of my fears. —PHYLLIS HOBE

SAT
22

THE LORD WAS MY SUPPORT. HE BROUGHT ME OUT INTO A SPACIOUS PLACE. . . . —*Psalm 18:18–19 (NIV)*

IT SEEMED TO BE TAKING awhile for my son to take his first steps. A fast crawler, Solomon had turned into a leaner, walking in endless circles around the coffee table, holding my hand and keeping a pinky on the table. It was obvious that he could carry his own weight; the only thing holding him back was uncertainty about his footing. He still needed someone to lean on.

We were at my mom's for brunch one cold January morning when Solomon leaned on a chair and picked up his boots. A small snow boot in each hand, he stood up, and in a moment took his first solo step toward me. "One, two, three," a roomful of my relatives whispered along with me as Solomon made it across the living room rug. In eight steps, he reached me and put his boot in my lap, unaware that he had let go of the chair. For the next few days, Solomon walked—but only with his hands full and outstretched, as if the things he held gave him grounding.

Solomon had found his balance, but I know he still had Someone to lean on, holding those boots, leading him step by step.

Lord, thank You for being there to lean on when I launch out into the unknown. —SABRA CIANCANELLI

SUN
23

HE GUIDES ME ALONG RIGHT PATHS. . . .
—*Psalm 23:3 (NLT)*

MY GRANDMOTHER WAS dying of cancer. She looked so tiny, so frail as she lay in the hospital bed, so unlike the strong, self-reliant woman I'd seen on so many mornings, sitting at the kitchen table with a steamy cup of coffee.

I spent a few minutes talking with my mother and sister, then offered to stay in the room while they went downstairs for a break. Grandmother had had a restless night, and I knew that they were both exhausted from tending to her.

I pulled a chair close to the bed. Grandmother opened her eyes wide and looked at me, unable to speak. *Does she know who I am?* I wondered. I spoke to her quietly, but my words only seemed to upset her. *Lord*, I prayed, *give me words to calm her.*

I took Grandmother's hand and began to pray out loud the first words that came to me: "The Lord is my shepherd, I shall not want. . . ."

By the end of the psalm, Grandmother was completely relaxed. Her breathing was quiet and even. I gently placed her hand back down on the bed. When my mother and sister returned, they were relieved to find her resting.

"What did you do?" Mom asked.

"Well, I didn't know what to do, so I recited the Twenty-third Psalm," I replied.

My mother looked surprised. "Did you know that the Twenty-third Psalm has always been her favorite Scripture?"

I didn't, but the Lord did.

Lord, when I have no words to speak, thank You for giving me Yours. Amen. —MELODY BONNETTE

MON

24

Fear thou not; for I am with thee: be not dismayed; for I am thy God. . . . —Isaiah 41:10

SOON AFTER MY HUSBAND Keith and I moved into our new house, our gray and white cat Pi got out through a badly fastened screen and vanished. Naturally, I panicked. For hours I went around the neighborhood calling her name, looking under cars and under bushes with equal scrutiny. When it got dark, Keith made me come home, but I was in tears that something terrible had happened to her.

The next day we made up flyers describing Pi and offering a hundred-dollar reward for her safe return. We went from door to door in our cul-de-sac and several of the streets nearby, passing out the flyers and telling our neighbors how much we really wanted our cat back. No one had seen her.

Two days later, Mary, who lived three houses down from us on the same side of the street, showed up at the door with Pi in her arms. "She was hiding in my backyard, and I found her when I was pruning my bushes," she said.

I snatched up Pi and ran for my checkbook.

"No, no," Mary said. "I'm happy I could return her to you."

I insisted that I wanted to give her something.

"Just be my friend," she said. "That'll be more than enough."

I hugged her and thanked her for bringing back Pi. And then I hugged Pi and thanked her for my new friend.

Lord, thank You for bringing good out of the things I fear.
—RHODA BLECKER

TUE

25

"See, I am doing a new thing! Now it springs up; do you not perceive it? . . ." —Isaiah 43:19 (NIV)

ABOVE MY DESK at home is a picture of a hundred-year-old South Dakota grain elevator. It was sent to me by a friend whose father-in-law moved it to his property and worked for more than thirty years to turn it into a beautiful home. It's an amazing place that sleeps ten, has a dining car, and a third-floor soda fountain complete with counter, spinning stools and authentic fixtures.

My friend sent me the picture in response to the anxiety he heard me expressing over the change and uncertainty that came into my life this past year. He said, "Imagine you are that old elevator. You've had a good life of service holding grain for years. Then along comes this guy with saws, nails, paint and sandpaper, and plans to make big changes. I bet you'd want to say, 'Leave me alone! That hurts! I want to be what I am, not what you want me to be.' Now guess who the carpenter is in your life."

Trouble is, I know the answer. The carpenter in my life is Jesus. I know He has dreams for me I can't even imagine, but they require some changes in me before He can fulfill them. I'm not nearly as useful to Him without the transformation, the "new thing" He wants to do. But the tough part is, unlike the grain elevator, I have a choice. And He's waiting for me to say *yes*.

Lord, help me to see the changes in my life as part of Your master design. Let me accept them even if they hurt, so my life will be fruitful in Your service. —ERIC FELLMAN

WED

26

THEY CALLED ON THE LORD AND HE ANSWERED THEM. —*Psalm 99:6 (NIV)*

A FEW YEARS BACK, with sons in and approaching their thirties and Bill and I our sixties, I wrote in *Daily Guideposts*, "I pray often for our yet-to-be-seen daughters-in-law, whomever and wherever they are."

Well, many of you joined me in hoping and praying, and during that same year, as you prayed, three of our four sons, Tom, our oldest, John, the next in line, and David, "the baby," introduced us to Susan, Courtney and Matti.

The next year, David was stationed in Korea, and Matti was able to get a teaching job near his base and live with a friend there. On Thanksgiving Day, they called home from Korea—engaged! Six months later, they were married in a sweet ceremony in Colorado Springs, Colorado.

One Sunday two months later, John called us from just over the mountain. "What are you up to?" I asked him.

"Not much. Well, actually, I'm here with my fiancée—" My shriek drowned out the rest of his sentence.

That December, in Rome, Tom knelt on a stone at the Coliseum—where seventy years before his grandfather Tom Rogers had proposed to Marian Spencer—and asked Susan to marry him. Six months later in Atlanta, Susan became our second delightful daughter-in-law. Four months after that, at a Virginia hunt-country inn on a glorious autumn day, Courtney became our third.

So now, thanks in no little part to your prayers, I am the "Naomi" to some very wonderful "Ruths." I know my sons Tom, John and David thank you, and Susan, Courtney and Matti do, too! Now, guess what you can pray for next? . . .

Thank You, Lord, for the joys of a growing family—and for those who pray for others' needs and hopes. —ROBERTA ROGERS

THU
27

JERUSALEM WHICH IS ABOVE IS FREE, WHICH IS THE MOTHER OF US ALL. —*Galatians 4:26*

I HADN'T HEARD the patter of little feet coming down the hallway, hadn't noticed when Mary slipped into bed beside me. My four-year-old has had a string of nightmares lately, so I've been up a lot at night, and tonight I was tired enough to sleep through her entrance. Mary slid under the covers, snuggled close, and my arms folded around her instinctively. I never even woke up.

Even a wisp of a thing like Mary takes up space, though, and eventually I tried to shift positions and discovered she was there. "Mary," I whispered groggily, "it's time for you to go back to your own bed."

After a few tries, Mary heard me. She tumbled out, mumbling, "But I want to be near you!" I heard her feet heading toward the door, rolled into the warm space left by her body and was asleep.

Some time later I had a nightmare of my own. Fully awake now, I got up to go to the bathroom and nearly stumbled over something on the floor. *Someone*, actually: It was Mary, who wanted to be near Mommy so much that she'd come back, curled up and fallen asleep on the chilly, uncarpeted hardwood next to my bed.

I took a pillow, gently placed it under my daughter's strawberry-blonde head, tucked a fleecy blanket around her to keep her warm and climbed back into bed. Snug under the covers, I reached down to touch Mary and prayed:

Lord Jesus, make me yearn for You as wholly as I wanted my mommy when I was little. —JULIA ATTAWAY

FRI
28

GET THEE OUT OF THY COUNTRY . . . UNTO A LAND THAT I WILL SHEW THEE . . . AND THOU SHALT BE A BLESSING. —*Genesis 12:1-2*

I ATTENDED SEMINARY IN BOSTON, and I had come to love the city's rich history, its cultural resources and the fast pace of city life. After graduation, I started a church, established roots and bought a house on Eastland Road. It was a dream come true for me and my family.

Despite all that, I loaded all our possessions into a fourteen-foot truck and headed for Irvine, California. I'd gotten a job offer I couldn't refuse, and I was excited about moving to a warm climate and facing new challenges. Yet I was sad to leave our friends in Boston and move even farther away from our relatives in New York. *Am I doing the right thing?* I thought. *Is this really the best thing for our family?*

The challenges were more demanding than I'd anticipated. For one thing, my new job wasn't quite what I expected. And it wasn't easy to make new friends or find a welcoming church home. Life in California was turning out to be less than idyllic, and I was beginning to regret the move.

Then one evening over coffee, my wife Elba said, "Pablo, God finally has your attention."

"What do you mean?" I asked her.

"You're not running around trying to save the world the way you did in Boston. Instead, you have time just to sit quietly with God."

Elba was right. In Boston, I'd become so busy with ministry, church and community activities that I'd neglected my daily prayer time. Here in California, things were different. While we were waiting to find our place in the community, a space had opened up that I could fill with prayer. It had been a long haul across the country, but it was worth every minute.

Dear Lord, help me find time every day to give You my attention, as You give Yours to me. —PABLO DIAZ

SAT
29

A HOT-TEMPERED MAN STIRS UP DISSENSION, BUT A PATIENT MAN CALMS A QUARREL.
—Proverbs 15:18 (NIV)

I LIKE SHOPPING for clothes, but it's hard to find a good place to shop for them. Store merchandise is often disordered, and there is little help out on the sales floor. When you find something, the clerks often behave as if they are doing you a personal favor by ringing it up.

I went to buy a sweater at a local department store and ended up standing in a long, slow line. The girl at the counter was training another clerk, so everything took three times as long. The people waiting soon became impatient and started verbally harassing the trainee. She in turn began making mistakes, and the line slowed down even more.

Remembering my own days as a trainee clerk, I turned to the woman behind me and in a loud voice said, "The first time I worked on a register, I hit the wrong button and charged seventy-five dollars for a pack of gum. Did that ever happen to you?"

"I couldn't remember how to make change," she admitted. "I would beg people for exact change so I wouldn't have to."

The man in front of us turned around and glared.

"How about you, sir?" I asked, mentally crossing my fingers. "Did you ever work a register?"

"At a fast-food restaurant," he said rather reluctantly. "Those picture buttons always confused me."

We kept talking, and some other people in the line who overheard us brought up their bad experiences. The grumbling slowly stopped, and the trainee clerk stopped feeling so nervous and was able to work a little faster.

Lord, help me to learn from my mistakes and not to resent others for making them. —REBECCA KELLY

SUN
30

How can I repay the Lord for all his goodness to me? —Psalm 116:12 (NIV)

AS I DROVE TO CHURCH that January morning, I was still stewing over the financial reports I'd received earlier that week. Seems my 401K had seen yet another abysmal quarter. My investments were shrinking faster than a cheap blouse in hot water!

When I walked into church, an usher handed me a white envelope. "Your giving report for last year," he said. I tossed the envelope into my purse and settled into a pew near the back. While I waited for the service to begin, I scanned the bulletin. So much was going on! A Bible study for women was beginning on Tuesday night. The teens were holding a fund-raiser for their mission trip next summer. The singles were having a dinner after the morning worship service. Indoor soccer was starting for children ages six to twelve. A new transportation ministry was being formed to serve anyone who needed a ride to church or to doctor appointments.

Music swelled as the choir filed in and the opening anthem began. And as the congregation—many of them visitors and new members—began to sing, I glanced down at the contribution report sticking out of my purse. Not *all* of my investments had done poorly last year. Some of them had yielded a hundredfold!

Father, in difficult financial times, give me wisdom. And help me never to neglect the surest investment of all—Your kingdom.

—MARY LOU CARNEY

MON
31

"BE STRONG, ALL YOU PEOPLE. . . ," DECLARES THE LORD, "AND WORK. FOR I AM WITH YOU. . . ."
—*Haggai 2:4 (NIV)*

IT WAS ALREADY after noon, and I hadn't been able to sit still and focus for more than fifteen minutes. How would I ever get in a good day's work with all there was to fret about? First I worried about the world situation: Was anyone safe anymore? Then I turned to finances; I needed that tax refund this year more than ever. That reminded me of a health insurance claim I needed to fill out. I sorted through some papers, talked on the phone awhile and finally took a walk around the block.

The exercise helped a little. Back inside, I opened my Bible and turned to the short book of Haggai. Hadn't I marked a verse once for a day just like today? Something to help settle my thoughts so I could work:

"Work. For I am with you."

That did the trick.

Lord, Your very presence settles me. —EVELYN BENCE

SEEDS OF REJOICING

1 _____

2 _____

3 _____

4 _____

5 _____

6 _____

7 _____

8 _____

9 _____

10 _____

11 _____

12 _____

13 _____

14 _____

15 _____

16 _____

17 _____

18 _____

19 _____

20 _____

21 _____

22 _____

23 _____

24 _____

25 _____

26 _____

27 _____

28 _____

29 _____

30 _____

31 _____

February

I wait for the Lord, my soul doth wait,
and in his word do I hope. —*Psalm 130:5*

GOD SIGHTINGS
SEEING THE DANCE

TUE *My times are in thy hand.* . . . *—Psalm 31:15*

1 THE GREAT AMERICAN BASS Jerome Hines was in New York City, singing the title role in *Boris Godunov* at the Metropolitan Opera House, and he'd granted my request for an interview.

He met me at the door of the apartment where he was staying, even taller than he looked onstage, and I spent a rapt hour listening to his reminiscences of a long career. What I remember best, though, is the first thing he said. "Thank you for fitting me into your day," I'd begun as we sat down. "I'm sure you have a very crowded schedule."

"Crowded?" he echoed. "Not at all!"

Earlier in his life, he went on, it was different. With a daily practice regimen, new roles to learn, a performance schedule on four continents and endless charity appearances, in addition to the demands of family and friends, he'd run himself ragged. The change came, he said, when he learned to stop before saying yes to any commitment and pray about it. "God will never assign us more than we can do gracefully."

Now, anytime he found himself hurried and harried, he knew he'd taken on something outside God's will for him. "Chances are," he added, "that this 'something' wasn't right for other people either." Once, for example, he said, he'd accepted a dinner invitation without pausing to pray—only to have to cancel when there was a change in a rehearsal schedule.

"Even over the phone I could hear the hostess' sigh of relief." Her cook had quit, her husband had been called out of town. She'd been wondering, she told him, how to get out of the evening without offending him.

"When I let God set my agenda," Jerome Hines said, "my schedule mysteriously meshes with everyone else's."

It was a lesson I needed badly—I still do. But more than that, it was a God sighting. A glimpse of the One Who keeps all our lives at once in His perfect oversight.

Teach me to move to Your graceful rhythm, Father, in step with You and with those around me. —ELIZABETH SHERRILL

WED **2** DO ALL THINGS WITHOUT GRUMBLING OR DISPUTING.
—*Philippians 2:14 (NAS)*

MY FIRST JOB in advertising was as a copywriter working on a photocopier account. The hours were long, and the assignments I got to work on were the ones no one else wanted. Whenever there was an extra moment, I'd sit around with the other writers and art directors and complain about the agency.

My second job was for an agency that had so little work, I wondered why they wanted to hire me at all. Sometimes I would go more than three weeks without a single assignment. I didn't like sitting there without anything to do, so I'd complain.

My third job was as part of a team assigned to create a TV spot for a toothpaste company. One year and a hundred storyboards later, the toothpaste company had still not chosen a commercial they liked. Can you believe that? Of course, I complained.

When my fourth job was offered to me, my bank account was so low that I was desperate to have any job. It was an obvious answer to prayer, and I decided that I wasn't going to allow myself to complain about it. From the moment I took the job, I found quite a few things not to like about it, but when I got home to my wife, I said, "It's going great!" When friends asked about the job, I said, "Good! Couldn't be better!" I've been on the job for months now, and it's funny. When I try to remember what it was that I didn't like about it at first, I just can't seem to remember.

Lord, help me focus on what's good instead of what's not.
—DAVE FRANCO

THU

3

THE PATIENT IN SPIRIT IS BETTER THAN THE PROUD IN SPIRIT. —Ecclesiastes 7:8 (RSV)

THE TELESCOPE STOOD in the living room, a top-of-the line model, its beautiful blue tube gleaming in the sunlight. I'd ordered it months ago and had worn the carpet bare waiting for it to arrive. At last it was here, and the door to the heavens was about to open.

As a boy, I had owned a rickety reflector with a dusty mirror and a rusty mount. Still, by simply aiming and looking, I had seen breathtaking sights: the rings of Saturn, the phases of Venus, the mountains of the moon. Now, with this superb optical instrument, I hoped to uncover even more wonders, to enjoy more fully the glories of God's creation.

But when I hauled the telescope outside and pointed it toward the stars, all I could see was blackness. Puzzled, I turned the focusing and aiming knobs this way and that. Finally something swam into view, an unfocused blob of light. *No star should look like that!* I thought. There was no doubt about it: The telescope was broken. Brokenhearted, I went inside and confessed my failure to my wife and children.

The next day I was ready to return the telescope, but my wife urged me to give it one more try. After a half-hour of frustration, I suddenly realized that I'd been flipping the magnifying switches in the wrong order. Beginning from scratch, I stayed up for hours, growing thoroughly acquainted with the telescope's mechanisms. Just before dawn, I saw the Pleiades sparkle in the eyepiece like the crown jewels of paradise.

As the sun rose, I headed into the house for a hot cup of coffee, having learned that God's creation is always available, but that sometimes a bit of patience does wonders to bring it into focus.

Lord, help me to take the time to see Your many gifts.
—PHILIP ZALESKI

FRI

4

WE WAIT FOR THE BLESSED HOPE—THE GLORIOUS APPEARING OF OUR GREAT GOD AND SAVIOR, JESUS CHRIST. —Titus 2:13 (NIV)

WHILE SITTING at the dinner table at the Billy Graham Center in Asheville, North Carolina, I had the privilege of listening to an eighty-plus-year-old woman tell her story. "I'm on the evangelism team for Billy Graham," she said in a strong voice, "and I usually go to a city a few days before we hold a big event there." Her job, she said, was to help counsel people who were making a new profession of faith. Demanding work! *At her age,* I thought, *she should be retired.*

But then I sat riveted by the rest of her talk. *Thank goodness she isn't retired!* I thought.

She gave me something to think about. No matter how old I get while waiting for the blessed hope, there is work to be done. Like the woman that night, I, for one, will keep busy.

Lord, while I grow older, help me to have a spirit like hers.
—DOLPHUS WEARY

SAT
5

JUDGE NOT, AND YE SHALL NOT BE JUDGED. . . .
—*Luke 6:37*

THE FIRST TIME I saw the Lost and Found room at work, I was dumbfounded. I ran my hands through the mounds of stuff, saying, "How can people be so careless?"

There was a huge box containing a Kitchen-Aid mixer attachment, a bottle of spray perfume, seven pairs of gloves and thirteen individual gloves, three unmatched shoes, a baby blanket, seven pacifiers, four stuffed animals, seven pairs of eyeglasses, six pairs of sunglasses, and eleven umbrellas, seven of them black. All we were missing was a partridge in a pear tree.

"I can't believe this!" I insisted. "How can someone lose a shoe in a bookstore? And how can we throw all this stuff out? It's so wasteful!" I was in fine form, judging people for being careless and us for being wasteful.

"Oh, we don't throw it out," my co-worker said, apparently shocked that I should think so. "We give all the glasses to the Lions' Club, we donate the pairs of gloves to the homeless shelter, along with the T-shirts. And the baby stuff always goes to the crisis nursery."

"And what about the umbrellas?" I asked.

"We put a big barrel of them near the front door when it's pouring, and tack a sign on it that says, 'Free. Take one.' People are very thankful, believe me."

"I believe you," I said. "I just don't understand how people can be so—"

"What?" he asked, hearing me stop abruptly.

"Nothing," I said quickly, but then admitted, "I just spotted my plaid folding umbrella with the wooden handle. Guess I got so involved in reading the last time I was here that I forgot to take it with me." I gathered some of the baby stuff together. "Here," I said, "let me help you take this batch to the crisis nursery."

Lord, let me look at my own faults before I criticize another today.
—LINDA NEUKRUG

SUN
6
FOR THEREIN IS THE RIGHTEOUSNESS OF GOD REVEALED FROM FAITH TO FAITH. . . . —Romans 1:17

RECENTLY, I HEARD a story about William Randolph Hearst, the famous newspaperman and collector who filled his mansion with art masterpieces. One day he learned of a painting that was supposed to be especially valuable and commanded his scouts to search for it. At last, one of them came back and reported that he had located the painting.

"Buy it!" commanded Mr. Hearst.

"You already own it," replied the scout. "It's in a crate in one of your warehouses."

My initial reaction to the story was amazement. How could Mr. Hearst lose track of such a treasure and not put it to use? Then I remembered the restless night I'd spent in a hotel the week before, worrying about the keynote speech I was to make the next morning at a conference. *Had I prayed about the speech?* No. *Had I asked for God's support and placed my faith in Him, so I could relax and get a much-needed good night's sleep?* No. *So where was my faith, my greatest treasure of all?* Locked up, I decided, in some dusty warehouse.

I resolved right then to get my faith out of storage, polish it up and put it to use.

Heavenly Father, today and every day I put my faith in You.
—MADGE HARRAH

MON

7

REJOICE IN ALL THE GOOD THINGS THE LORD YOUR GOD HAS GIVEN TO YOU AND YOUR HOUSEHOLD.
—*Deuteronomy 26:11 (NIV)*

MY FATHER WAS ASLEEP in the city, unaware that his children were secretly reuniting in my sister's home in the suburbs to plan his surprise party. Diane and I picked up our brother José from the airport that night, then anxiously waited for our sister Tilza and her family to pull up in Diane's driveway. They arrived after midnight, yet once they walked through the door the house exploded with excited squeals, long hugs and a storm of kisses.

The next day we marched down the supermarket aisles like a mini-parade, filling our shopping cart with avocados, bags of chips and bottles of soda. We spent the day preparing party details and enjoying one another's company. Mundane tasks like unloading the groceries or making guacamole became moments to remember. Long into the night, my brother's fingers danced over the guitar strings as we practiced the Puerto Rican folksongs we would sing for my father.

The day of the party passed in a flurry of activity. Decorations, Scotch tape and tablecloths swirled around us in sweet chaos. Finally, that evening, the food was cooked, the guests arrived and the candles were lit. There was nothing left to do but wait for my father's entrance. After we yelled, "Surprise!" the party moved as quickly as the festive music.

Soon this wonderful celebration filled with old photos, singing and delicious food came to an end. The decorations we'd placed so carefully came down in minutes. Yet as we all pitched in to clean the room, I knew it wasn't just the party I'd remember in the years to come, but all the joy and laughter I shared with my family as we pieced it together.

Heavenly Father, remind me to treasure not just the joy at the end of each journey, but Your daily blessings along the way. —KAREN VALENTIN

TUE

8

A MERRY HEART MAKETH A CHEERFUL COUNTENANCE. . . . —*Proverbs 15:13*

I LOOKED AROUND on that chilly February day at my fellow travelers. It was evening rush hour on the New York

City subway. Even making the homeward trip, this is nobody's favorite place to be. The lucky few were seated, and the rest of us clung together like stranded seamen. All around me were frowns heavy with strain. There were circles under a frail woman's eyes, and a heavyset man snored in the corner seat, his hands tightly locked around his backpack. The faces were blank, cut off from the world by earphones or weariness.

I began to wonder where the blessings of the day and the light of the Lord were hiding in this scene. *Where is Norman Vincent Peale when we need him?* I thought ruefully. *This subway car could do with a large dose of positive thinking.*

Then I noticed two women, both I guessed in their thirties, holding on to the same pole, moving with the train as it swayed. They were deep in conversation. I could only hear the odd word: "terrific," "thrilled," "let's go," "then he said. . . ." It was obvious they were friends; their faces lighted up with laughter as they struggled to hear each other through the din.

Their happy, mostly inaudible chatter was strangely contagious. I found myself smiling with affection for two total strangers, who brightened the world that day between the 33rd Street and 14th Street stations.

Thank You, Lord, for leading the way to small joys when the daily routine seems dark. —BRIGITTE WEEKS

WED
9
GOD . . . WILL NOT LET YOU BE TEMPTED BEYOND YOUR STRENGTH. . . . —*I Corinthians 10:13 (RSV)*

I HAVE A CONDITION that can be very painful, fatal even, if I don't stay on a strict diet. For months I was a disciplined wonder. Then yesterday I was fixing myself some pears and fat-free cottage cheese, when I saw in the refrigerator a huge piece of Dutch chocolate cake with white fudge icing. I closed my eyes and saw before me a piece of the cake topped with two scoops of rich vanilla ice cream.

Temptation talking: *What's the big deal? It's one piece of cake. You deserve a treat. Who's it going to harm?*

Sanity's reply: *For starters, this could trigger a new wave of pain and even kill you. Not to mention that trip your wife's been counting on.*

All of this is true, and I am a man of prayer with a lot of education. So how do I respond to the voice of reason?

"Okay, okay, you're right!" I say. "I won't have but *one* scoop of ice cream on top." And I reach for the cake.

Temptation can kill my body and grieve the Spirit of Christ within me when I let it into the driver's seat. The only way I've found to avoid the suicidal succumbing is to stop the instant I see the cake—before fantasy begins. I close the refrigerator door and:

1. Turn to God immediately. "Lord, I am powerless over temptation without You. Please help me now."
2. Repeat some Scriptures and prayers.
3. Thank God for my better days, and eat my cottage cheese and pears.

Lord, You know how powerless I can be. Thank You for forgiving me when I fail. —KEITH MILLER

THU
10

My soul thirsts for You. . . . When I remember You on my bed, I meditate on You. . . .
—*Psalm 63:1, 6 (NKJV)*

I KEEP A GLASS of water by my bed to sip during the night and first thing in the morning when I wake up. By doing this faithfully and by drinking more water during the day, I think I stay healthier and succumb to fewer viruses.

How I long for water in the morning! After gulping down the glass by my bed, I head to the shower. The forceful spray rids me of my sluggishness. My stiffness fades, my lethargic mind awakens and begins to burst with ideas and enthusiasm for the day ahead.

Morning prayer has the same effect on my soul's thirst. Recently I told my pastor that I yearned for more time to pray in the morning and regretted how long I snuggle under the warm comforter before I get out of bed.

"Use that time when you're still in bed," he advised. "When you first awaken, begin praying. Turn your thoughts to God right then and there. Offer Him your day and talk to Him about any anxieties you may have. Whatever thoughts come, turn them to God."

I've been following his suggestion, and what a difference it's made in my "soul health"! Like my first sips of water, that initial groggy turning to God often quickens my sense of thirst for His presence. And when I get up early enough to have a longer time of prayer before the day's work begins, that morning prayer is like a long shower—cleansing, refreshing and invigorating my soul.

Dear Lord, help me be more faithful to prayer each day. Thank You for quenching my thirst and washing me with Your living water.

—MARY BROWN

HE LEADETH ME . . .
TO GIVE GENEROUSLY

FRI

11

TEACH ME TO DO THY WILL; FOR THOU ART MY GOD. . . . —Psalm 143:10

ONE FEBRUARY AFTERNOON, I telephoned to check on Gerry, one of my patients at a treatment center several hundred miles away that specialized in post-traumatic stress disorder. I listened to Gerry as he told me about the fellow Vietnam War veterans he'd met there, one of whom he'd actually been stationed with during the war. It had been an extremely emotional reunion, and it had brought on even more intrusive combat thoughts and nightmares for Gerry.

Gerry had the kind of heartache that no one could break through, so I switched to a more practical mode. "What can I send you from home?" I asked.

"This is going to sound crazy, Bert, but what I really need is a needle and thread. The laundry here sure is rough on buttons."

I bought him a sewing kit with little spools of thread in assorted colors and a tiny pair of scissors in a pocket-sized plastic case. But as I prepared to wrap it up, my gift seemed so small in proportion to Gerry's pain. "Surely there's something else I can do, Lord," I prayed. "Those guys have wounds I can't begin to imagine. Be with them as they sew on their buttons. Whisper to their hearts that You can heal any wound."

Then an idea hit me: *Send them the biggest box of Valentine chocolates you can find.*

A few days later Gerry called. "Got your package, Bert. And when I passed around the candy at group and told them it was from one of the nurses back home, you wouldn't have believed it. Some of those big, strapping men had tears in their eyes. All choked up over a box of candy." There was a long pause. "I have to admit, Bert, it got to me, too."

Dear Lord, when I pray, You tell me how to touch hearts. Thank You.
—ROBERTA MESSNER

SAT
12

INCLINE THINE EAR, O LORD, AND HEAR. . . .
—*Isaiah 37:17*

CAROL AND I weren't in New York City the day the World Trade Center was attacked by terrorists. We were in New Hampshire, delivering our son William to his boarding school. Instead of seeing those horrible events from my office window, I watched them on TV. Like everyone else tuned in to the news, I was horrified. The rest of the day, in this placid New England setting, I could only think about what was happening back home in New York. Was anyone we knew trapped inside those buildings? Was everyone at our office okay? Our younger son Tim was in school in New York that day. I was sure he would get home safely with friends. But how would he feel? The lines were clogged, and we couldn't reach him or anyone by phone.

During an orientation meeting I could barely concentrate. "I have to go outside," I told my wife, and slipped out. I paced on the sidewalk and did the only thing I could think of: I prayed. *Jesus Christ, have mercy on us. Make haste to help us. Rescue us and save us. Let Thy will be done in our lives.* I must have repeated that prayer a hundred times before I felt some peace. No answers, just a measure of peace. I went back inside and arrived in time to hear the school minister leading the parents in prayer. More of what I desperately needed.

Driving home that afternoon, Carol and I listened to whatever radio stations we could pick up. Reporters gave updates, statesmen made comments. Someone invoked the name of Abraham Lincoln, president the last time there was warfare on American soil. Things must have seemed as bewildering to him back then as they were to me for the moment. How did Lincoln find hope in the midst of that terrible conflict? Where did he turn for guidance? Then I recalled something he once said: "I have been driven many times upon my knees by the overwhelming conviction that I had nowhere else to go." The only reasonable thing to do.

Let me never forget to turn to You, God, when there is nowhere else to turn. —RICK HAMLIN

SUN
13

"*I AM THE GOOD SHEPHERD AND KNOW MY OWN SHEEP, AND THEY KNOW ME.*" —*John 10:14 (TLB)*

OUR CHILDREN'S CHURCH is always lively. A small group of kids run to the front of the sanctuary and sit on the steps leading to the altar for a short sermon and prayer time. Recently, Pastor Warren's topic was "The Good Shepherd." "Sheep obey the shepherd because they know the shepherd will feed them, give them water and keep them safe," he said. "They trust the shepherd and follow him without question, don't they?"

Makayla, who has had experience with her friend Danielle's sheep, thought for a moment, then said, "Well . . . except for the sheep that have an attitude!"

We all laughed. In our rural community almost everyone is familiar with the traits of farm animals.

"Sheep do have an attitude," Pastor Warren told Makayla. "They can be stubborn, some wander off from the flock, and some butt you away when you try to help them."

Makayla's observation and Pastor Warren's response hit a sensitive spot in my heart. Just like those sheep, I often "have an attitude" that keeps me from listening to God. I make plans, then expect God to bless them instead of waiting for the Shepherd to walk ahead and reveal His will. I let other voices crowd out His gentle words. I forget that the Shepherd has other sheep not of my fold. He loves them and expects me to do the same.

How thankful I am that Jesus loves all His sheep . . . even those of us who sometimes have an attitude!

Good Shepherd, let me hear Your voice and follow Your lead every day, in every way. —PENNEY SCHWAB

MON
14

LET US PRACTICE LOVING EACH OTHER, FOR LOVE COMES FROM GOD. . . . —I John 4:7 (TLB)

OH BOTHER, I thought, *I forgot to get cards!* It was late in the evening of February 13, and I had no Valentine cards to place on the breakfast table the next morning. Fortunately I am a keeper; I have pictures, clippings, and a hoard of greeting cards sent to and received from various members of our family, all carefully saved in cardboard boxes.

Brilliant, I decided, *I'll just dig out some old cards and recycle love!*

I was up into the night, rustling papers and sorting Valentine's Day out from Christmas, Easter, birthdays and anniversary greetings. The largest card in the stash was from my husband. It had silk roses surrounding a white lace heart with the words, "I always dreamed I'd find you."

There were hand-drawn cartoons from our son, early on with stick figures and some letters printed backward. His art improved in later years, and the letters were done right, but the spelling had me wringing my hands! From the time she could color, our daughter used vibrant colors and an all-over-the-page look. Later this became a sophisticated, "To my *classy* parent," and a card with the surprise note, "Look in the dishwasher!" There I had found an air fern in a small hand-painted pot. A heart-shaped card from my husband's sister up in Spokane had the P.S., "The temperature dipped to eleven degrees last night, the coldest for this time of year since 1911."

Selecting dozens of cards from family and friends, I put them all over the house—on the piano, in the bookcases, on top of the valance above the curtains, in the bathroom, the kitchen, and some in surprise places like closets and in the glove compartment of our car. (It was weeks before that one was found.)

We spent days mulling over and giggling our way back through all the remember-whens of my recycled love. Forgotten cards? Nope. These were the best ever!

Thank You, Lord, for the love and laughter that are the joy bells of our hearts. —FAY ANGUS

READER'S ROOM

THE DAY BEFORE YESTERDAY, while applying grout to my first mosaic project, I got a few splinters of tile in my finger, and it was very painful. But then I noticed that the splinter was starting to work its way out, and marveled at the amazing power of our bodies to gradually expel things like that. My mind was carried away to the problems my teenage daughter has been going through lately, new and difficult emotions that need to work their way through and out, and that God has given her a soul every bit as wonderful as her body. And a new level of trust and acceptance came to me. I was happy to share it with her.
—*Terrie Becan, San Antonio, Texas*

TUE
15

HONOR SHALL UPHOLD THE HUMBLE IN SPIRIT.
—*Proverbs 29:23*

BACK IN THE 1950s, my friend Charlie was an electrician's helper at the Boston Navy Yard. Extremely quiet and modest, Charlie was always studying engineering books. He completed a difficult yearlong course and received a diploma, which his wife had framed and mounted on the wall. As I examined the new diploma, my eyes were drawn to another framed document. It was Charlie's degree in electrical engineering from a nearby university!

In 1960, things slowed down at the Navy yard and Charlie was laid off. He looked for another job as an electrician's helper, but found nothing. Then, unexpectedly, a civilian engineer with the U.S. Coast Guard told Charlie he had submitted his name for an engineering position. Charlie was hired. But the engineering officer told the man who had recommended Charlie, "I'm hiring him, but I'm doubtful. You say the man graduated in 1937 and has never worked as an engineer?" He didn't consider the barriers that had kept African Americans out of the profession.

Charlie had remained steadfast in his love for engineering. He had refused to be defeated by negative attitudes or the lack of opportunity. By the time he retired in 1977, he was the section leader of his department.

Father, through patience and hard work, help me to build my life on a foundation of rock. —OSCAR GREENE

WED
16

O LORD MY GOD, IN THEE DO I PUT MY TRUST. . . .
—*Psalm 7:1*

I'M SITTING in the El Paso County, Colorado, juror waiting room, hoping with all my heart that my number won't be called. I've never served on a jury and under other circumstances I'd be glad to do so. I think the experience would be interesting and educational. But not now! My children and grandchildren (some of whom I haven't seen for nearly a year) will be arriving tomorrow, and I've been looking forward to their visit. The last thing I want is to be tied up with jury duty while they're here.

But I've learned in my seventy-two years that when I turn my concerns over to God, things really do tend to work out for the best, regardless of whether I get my way!

So right now, this moment, I'm letting go of hoping my number won't be called, knowing that whichever way it goes, God's higher purpose is at work. As I release my desire to control the outcome, my neck muscles loosen and an involuntary sigh escapes my lips. And for the first time since arriving here, I find myself noticing the gorgeous view of Pike's Peak with the American flag on the courthouse roof superimposed on its face, framed by the window I had ignored in my self-concern.

In this and all things may Your will be done, Omniscient One.
—MARILYN MORGAN KING

THU

17

HE WHO GATHERS MONEY LITTLE BY LITTLE MAKES IT GROW. —Proverbs 13:11 (NIV)

I LOVED COMIC BOOKS when I was a young boy. I loved my younger brother, too, but I would have traded him for a good comic book any day. Not just any comic book, of course—only my favorite, *Superman*, and it had to be in mint condition.

My father decided to give me an allowance when I was ten years old. "A dime a week," he announced. "It's never too early to start saving." His admonition was completely lost on my ten-year-old mind. What I did know was that a comic book cost a dime, so I bought one every week until my dad discovered that I was squandering my money instead of saving it. My argument—that I was buying only *Superman* comic books, or an occasional *Batman* to be traded for a classic *Superman* at a later date—was completely lost on his forty-year-old mind. He revoked my allowance.

Years later, my father developed heart disease. I called him every morning to check up on him for the last three years of his life. We had a lot of great conversations, but we never discussed finances. When he died, I wondered how his eight children would pay the bills I figured he owed.

Well, I was wrong about Dad. He had saved a lot of dimes in his lifetime. I bought my wife a safer car with my inherited share of those dimes. And I was also able to set something aside for my own sons. Now I know that my father never asked me to do anything with my money that he wasn't already doing with his. It's a lesson not found in a comic book, and a lesson not lost on my fifty-year-old mind.

Dear Father, help me to teach my sons, just as my father taught me.

—TIM WILLIAMS

FRI

18

THEN THE SPIRIT SAID UNTO PHILIP, GO NEAR, AND JOIN THYSELF TO THIS CHARIOT. —Acts 8:29

I TURNED LEFT at the four-way stop instead of continuing straight ahead toward home. I hadn't seen my eight-year-old friend Cynthia recently, and this chilly February evening seemed like a good time.

Cynthia was entertaining her best friend Hayley, whom I had never met. The girls pleaded with me to drive them to their school book fair, which was taking place that night. Being a book lover myself, I did.

We spent a wonderful time browsing through all the selections. I offered to buy them each a small item. Hayley chose a poster of cats captioned "Best Fur-riends." Then we checked out the science projects on display and ate a snack in the cafeteria.

Just a month later, Hayley died in a traffic accident. Cynthia's mother and I shared the difficult task of breaking the news to her, then drove to Hayley's house to be with her mother. There, Cynthia was asked to choose a special keepsake in remembrance of her friend. She chose the "Best Fur-riends" poster from our night at the book fair.

Who could foresee the tragedy to come when I made that sudden left at the four-way stop? I only know that God had put a desire in my heart to see Cynthia, and that gave Cynthia a last treasured night with her friend and put me in a position to comfort her.

Lord, teach me to heed the promptings from Your Spirit within.

— CAROL KNAPP

SAT   *THE LORD RECEIVES MY PRAYER.* — *Psalm 6:9 (NAS)*

19

EVERY MORNING I SAT DOWN in front of my computer with eager anticipation and pressed the "send and receive" button for my e-mail, waiting to hear from our youngest son Glen and his family, who live way out west on Vancouver Island. Had they tried the recipe I'd sent them for old-fashioned cookies? Had they chuckled at the joke I'd forwarded? Did the children explore the Web site I thought would be of interest to them?

No response.

Oh, they're probably just so busy they haven't got around to answering yet, I tried to console myself.

Several days passed. I sent them a few more e-mails. Still no response.

I began to worry. Maybe they were all sick in bed. Worse yet, maybe there'd been an accident. Maybe . . . well, you know how mothers are.

I picked up the phone. "Hello, Glen?"

"Oh, it's you, Mom. Say, what's happened to the e-mails? We haven't heard from you in a dog's age!"

"You haven't? But I've sent all kinds of messages. I was wondering why you weren't answering."

That was the day I learned that just because I send an e-mail message doesn't mean that it arrives. After several phone calls, our Internet service provider discovered a glitch in the system. My messages were being intercepted and scrapped as junk mail ("spam" in computer jargon). The very idea!

Once the problem was cleared up, it didn't take long before Glen was responding.

"Yum . . . the cookies turned out great."

"Check out this Web site."

"Here's a funny for ya."

How grateful I am that there are no glitches in God's system. When I send Him a prayer, He not only receives it, He responds. He always gets the message.

Thank You, God, that none of my concerns are "junk mail" to You.
—ALMA BARKMAN

SUN
20

FOR YOU HAVE BEEN BORN AGAIN . . . THROUGH THE LIVING AND ENDURING WORD OF GOD.
—*I Peter 1:23 (NIV)*

ONCE A WEEK, I stop by Mom's house for a cup of coffee and "Granny Hour," when we read the letters my great-grandmother wrote to her family in the early twentieth century.

At first, I wasn't really eager to spend an hour reading yellowed letters in a difficult handwriting. I'd already heard stories about my colorful Great-Granny; that was enough. Besides, I had other things to do. But I went for Mom's sake, so we could pare down her closet clutter and save only the important things.

As we read the letters to each other, I began to appreciate my great-grandmother's humor, struggles, shortcomings, wisdom, creativity and faith as she labored through some of life's most difficult circumstances.

The stories I'd heard really hadn't told me much about her. Yet by reading her letters, her words to her children, she became real to me.

I find my Granny Hour has reinforced something I know in my heart, but often fail to practice: I can hear stories about God, and I can read devotions and books about Him. But until I get into His Word, His letters written to us, His children, I can't really know Him.

Father, as I read Your Word, reveal Yourself to me, so I can know You better and love You more. —MARJORIE PARKER

MON
21

THE LORD HEARS WHEN I CALL TO HIM.
—Psalm 4:3 (RSV)

THIS PAST SUMMER I worked as a college intern for U.S. Senator George Allen of Virginia. Mostly I did boring clerical-type duties—answering the phone, data entry, things like that. But occasionally I got the chance to see history.

One such occasion came on a particular morning when the buzz on Capitol Hill was about an annual fundraising gala called "The President's Dinner." Somehow I got offered a free ticket. Since they normally cost two thousand five hundred dollars apiece, I was pretty excited.

The dinner turned out to be everything you'd expect. There were lots of important people, lots of tuxedos and a small serving of filet mignon for everyone. The president gave a speech about the progress of his administration and received a long standing ovation.

Afterward, I noticed booths set up all over the room where attendees were lined up to get their photo taken under a sign that said "President's Dinner." Figuring these photos were only available to those with VIP tickets or those who forked over an additional sum of money, I left the conference center and headed back home on the Metro. To my surprise, I discovered the next day in the office that those photos were actually free for anyone who had a ticket!

My feelings at that moment were similar to those I had experienced on a beach retreat for a group of guys from my college. During a late night discussion by the ocean, one of my friends was talking about his prayer life, and it struck me that I had always viewed the power of prayer just as I viewed those photos—something available only to super saints or to those with seminary degrees. But that night on the beach, I realized that prayer is a gift offered to anyone in God's family, including me. It's free and available just for the taking.

Thank You, God, for hearing my prayers. —JOSHUA SUNDQUIST

TUE

22

BEFORE HONOUR IS HUMILITY. —Proverbs 15:33

I OFTEN BEGIN my American Literature class by telling my students about Phillis Wheatley, a little girl who arrived in Boston in 1761 on a slave ship. Naked and toothless, she was nonetheless purchased by a prominent Boston couple who taught her to read and write, and who later set her free. Phillis fell in love with America and with God, being baptized at the Old South Church during the Great Awakening.

One day young Phillis sent a poem of praise to Gen. George Washington, whom she much admired. Washington wrote back to tell her how much he liked the poem and invited her to his headquarters for a visit.

Three months later, Phillis met with the general, who gave her a half-hour of undivided attention. The image of this fragile woman sitting with the strong, six-foot-three general is to me the essence of America.

Phillis had no way of knowing that Washington would soon defeat the most powerful army in the world and become the first president of the United States. And Washington had no idea that he was talking to the first female African American poet. The two of them were just mutual admirers, enjoying the pleasure of conversation.

To see people as people, without regard for background, appearance or rank, is, I think, the heart of humility. It's a quality Jesus Himself demonstrated when He put together a team that included lowly fishermen and a tax collector. Everyone I meet has something special for me to admire, if I will look for it.

Happy birthday to George Washington, and thanks for the lesson in meekness.

Thank You, God, for all the people who saw something worthwhile in me, something that I didn't see. —DANIEL SCHANTZ

A VERY PRESENT HELP

SOMETIMES WE DON'T truly understand the depth of our faith until it's tested. Over the next three days, join Carol Kuykendall as she discovers the glimmers of hope that shine through even the darkest night. —THE EDITORS

DAY ONE: DEEP ROOTS

WED
23

"BUT BLESSED IS THE MAN WHO TRUSTS IN THE LORD. . . ." —*Jeremiah 17:7 (NIV)*

WHEN MY HUSBAND LYNN suffered a major bleed in his brain a few months ago, family and friends gathered at the hospital while he had emergency surgery. Six hours later, the doctor emerged to give us a report.

"There's been extensive brain damage," he began, "and the next few days will be critical. . . ." He talked on, but I hardly heard him. I remember little except the faces of the people around me—people who offered comfort with their presence and people I could count on to tell me what I needed to know.

Later that evening, a dear friend hugged me. "Everything in your life so far has prepared you for this moment," she said gently. Her words sounded odd at the time, but they kept coming back to me over the next few days, as Lynn's condition worsened and he was rushed back into surgery again; as he was placed on life support in a drug-induced coma in the ICU; as we feared the outcome of his extensive brain damage.

In the midst of those realities, I saw how so many of life's circumstances had prepared me for this moment: the strength of our thirty-six-year marriage; the physical nearness of our adult children, who offered emotional support; and most especially, the roots of our faith that had grown deeper into the truth of God's promises.

My friend's words remind me of all the ways God provides for us. He knows the end from the beginning, and weaves the circumstances of our lives together to deepen our trust in Him and strengthen us for the future.

Father, the longer I live, the more I see how You connect everything that has gone before with everything that comes after . . . and everything works together for good. —CAROL KUYKENDALL

DAY TWO: A FLOWERING OF HOPE

THU
24

WE WILL TELL THE NEXT GENERATION THE PRAISEWORTHY DEEDS OF THE LORD, HIS POWER AND THE WONDERS HE HAS DONE. —*Psalm 78:4 (NIV)*

OUR CHILDREN and their spouses gathered at our house during those days when my husband Lynn was in a coma on life support. When they were young and my own faith was growing, I remember wanting to plant hope in their hearts. So I did what most parents do: We said bedtime prayers. I played praise songs really loud, especially in the car. I also had what they considered an annoying habit of writing Bible verses on sticky notes and posting them on the refrigerator door or their pillows or the bathroom mirrors. As they grew up and left home, I often wondered if anything on those sticky notes stuck.

But during those long days of waiting and wondering about Lynn's future, the most amazing thing happened: Sticky notes with Bible verses began to appear on the refrigerator door—in the kids' handwriting. As they drove me back and forth to the hospital, they played praise music in the car—really loud. And every night before I fell into bed, they prayed with me, when I felt too tired to pray for myself. They planted hope in me during those fearful days of waiting and wondering.

Father, I am so grateful that hope planted in the lives of our children comes back to us. —CAROL KUYKENDALL

DAY THREE: FIRSTFRUITS

FRI
25

AND A LITTLE CHILD WILL LEAD THEM.
—Isaiah 11:6 (NIV)

WHEN MY HUSBAND LYNN finally came out of his coma, he could talk and respond to us, but he had no movement on his left side. He couldn't move his fingers or hand or leg or foot—not even a twitch. The doctors and nurses cautioned us about getting our hopes too high about his chances for recovery. But we couldn't hold our hopes back.

"Dad, move your finger," the kids coaxed, "like this!" And they'd wiggle a finger close to him. No response. "How about your toes?" No response.

Finally, our son Derek and his wife had an idea. They brought their ten-month-old Gabriella to the hospital and held her up outside Lynn's window. When she began clapping gleefully for her *Opa*, he vowed to learn to clap again like Gabi.

Over the next few days, he struggled. Then he was able to move a finger. Then, haltingly, his hand. And one morning when we walked in, he clapped—just like Gabi. Within a week, he was wheeled out of the ICU and sent to a rehab facility. Two weeks and lots of hard work later, he walked out of there on his own and came home to continue his recovery.

Today he is back at his law office part-time, and in response to every step of progress he makes, we all clap—just like Gabi.

Father, thank You for the children who are sunbeams of hope on our lives.
—CAROL KUYKENDALL

EDITOR'S NOTE: A month from today, on Good Friday, March 25, we will observe the thirty-fifth annual Guideposts Good Friday Day of Prayer. We'd like you to join us as we bring our hearts before the Lord in praise, petition and intercession. Send your prayer requests to Good Friday Day of Prayer, 66 E. Main St., Pawling, NY 12564.

SAT
26

But he was pierced for our transgressions, he was crushed for our iniquities; the punishment that brought us peace was upon him. . . .
—*Isaiah 53:5 (NIV)*

ONE SATURDAY MORNING, my husband Whitney breezed into the kitchen, holding out a hymnal. "I forget how this song goes, and in an hour I'm supposed to lead it at the men's Bible study. Will you sing it with me?" he asked, looking at his watch.

I frowned. *I'd rather eat that hymnal than sing right now* is what I wanted to say. Last night I'd relived a wrong done to me a few years earlier. I'd stumbled out of bed dragging resentment like a ball-and-chain. But Whitney didn't seem to notice my pain. And of all the songs. . . .

"Please . . . if you just get me started I know I'll remember the tune," Whitney said.

"Okay," I mumbled. He sat next to me, and I led in a cracked, unhappy voice.

> *Beneath the cross of Jesus I fain would take my stand,*
> *The shadow of a mighty Rock within a weary land. . . .*

The powerful old hymn pulled at my resentment. I pulled back. *But I was wronged.*

"I got it," Whitney said, launching into the last verse:

> *Upon that cross of Jesus mine eyes at times can see*
> *The very dying form of One Who suffered there for me. . . .*

Those words I'd sung all my life drew across my resentment the picture of Jesus hanging on the Cross, looking at me with redeeming love. I began to cry.

"Is something wrong?" Whitney asked, closing the hymnal. My tears turned to laughter. In his obtuseness, my wonderful husband had inadvertently led me to the one place of peace. Surrender at the foot of the Cross. I bowed my head and prayed:

Lord Jesus Christ, Lamb of God, have mercy on me. —SHARI SMYTH

SUN

27

AND OF ALL THAT THOU SHALT GIVE ME I WILL SURELY GIVE THE TENTH UNTO THEE. —Genesis 28:22

MY FIRST REAL JOB came in my thirteenth summer. Brown McMillan, a local contractor and family friend, asked me if I wanted to work. "Yes, sir," I answered, not because I liked work, but because I liked the idea of getting paid.

Before I knew it I was up at dawn and getting a ride to Mr. McMillan's rural job site. All day I hauled heavy loads of mortar in a wheelbarrow, hoisted big boxes of nails up a ladder, and ran back and forth retrieving tools. By quitting time I was the dirtiest, smelliest, most worn-down kid you ever saw.

Friday at quitting time Mr. McMillan drove me up to the country store to meet my mom. As I got out of the truck, he handed me a crisp one hundred dollar bill! When I got into Mom's car I showed it to her. "Wow, Brock!" she said. "Just think, on Sunday you can tithe big time!"

I gulped. Already I was feeling pretty attached to that one hundred dollar bill, thinking of all the things I could buy with it. Then I thought of all the things God had given me: my parents, my friends, even people like Mr. McMillan. As my grandmother Bebee said, "Brock, you can never outgive the Lord."

The next morning Mom drove me to the bank to break my one hundred dollar bill, and that Sunday morning I put ten dollars in the offering plate.

A lot has changed in my life since my thirteenth summer, but Bebee's wisdom still rings true, not just about the money I tithe but whatever I dare to offer. You can never, ever outgive the Lord.

Father, when I remember how good You've been to me, how could I ever think of holding out? —BROCK KIDD

MON

28

ALL THE WAYS OF A MAN ARE CLEAN IN HIS OWN SIGHT, BUT THE LORD WEIGHS THE MOTIVES. —Proverbs 16:2 (NAS)

OUR FAMILY POSSESSES an odd trait: The backs of some of our heads are as flat as a wall—no pretty round curve whatsoever. My mother passed this flat-headedness right down to my brothers and me and to one of my children. But I didn't realize I had it for quite some time.

I was newly married and choosing a new hairstyle. The hairdresser said that she'd have to be careful to cut the layers to flatter the back of my head.

"What are you talking about? What's wrong with the back of my head?"

"Well, it's sort of flatlike." From behind me, she looked at my eyes in the mirror with a smirk.

"I didn't know I have a flat head," I said as I felt my head. "My mother never told me. She has one."

She studied my problem area and fluffed my hair. "There's nothing you can do to fix a flat head! That's for sure."

When I got home, I studied the back of my head in a mirror. Sure enough—flat as a frying pan. My husband confirmed the news. "Yeah, I thought you knew it."

"How would I know? I've never seen the back of my head!"

Twenty-five years of marriage have passed since that revelation in the salon. My head's still flat, but I've finally grown to see some unappealing hidden traits in my attitudes, too. I can be stubborn in areas in which I should surrender. I like to be right. I try to fix people. Sometimes I'm sweetly controlling. For a long time I didn't see them. And, unlike my head shape, those are things I can do something about.

Father, You help me look in the mirror of my heart. Thank You for caring enough to point out the truth. —JULIE GARMON

SEEDS OF REJOICING

I _____

2 _____

3 _____

4 _____

5 _____

6 _____

7 _____

8 _____

9 _____

10 _____

11 _____

12 _____

13 _____

14 _____

15 _____

16 _____

17 _____

18 _____

19 _____

20 _____

21 _____

22 _____

23 _____

24 _____

25 _____

26 _____

27 _____

28 _____

March

This is the day which the Lord hath made; we will rejoice and be glad in it.

—Psalm 118:24

GOD SIGHTINGS
KNOWING OUR NEED

TUE
I

As for me, I am poor and needy. . . .
—*Psalm 40:17 (RSV)*

I SANK GRATEFULLY into my seat on the plane. It was the middle one of three—the only one available at the last minute and extra expensive because I hadn't been able to book ahead. You can't foresee a crisis. Mother had fallen again, a broken hip.

I felt like an expert on crises at that point. For three months there'd been nothing but. My husband's surgery, a close friend in another hospital, relatives turning to us in a marriage breakup, others with a job loss, a temporarily homeless woman staying with us—plus the usual demands of work and family. I couldn't remember when I'd had a full night's sleep. Now, even wedged between a largish man and a woman with a baby, the four-hour flight meant a chance to sit still for a while.

The screen above the aisle was displaying the preflight video. "Fasten seatbelts . . . chairs and tray tables upright. In the event of a sudden loss of air pressure," the recorded voice continued, "a mask will drop from the overhead compartment." I pulled my paperback book from my carry-on. I'd heard the routine instructions dozens of times.

Why, then, did one phrase, as familiar as all the others, break through my inattention? "If you are seated next to someone who needs assistance, first adjust your own mask, then help the person beside you." A prerecorded public message, yet the words rang as though they came new that moment from God Himself to me alone.

You cannot reach out to others, I heard Him say, *if you yourself can't function.*

For many weeks now, I'd been refusing the provision offered me. A friend's offer of help . . . a nap . . . a take-out meal . . . daily aids I'd refused, seeing *myself* as the provider. "Father," the prayer rose from seat 32B, "You are the Provider. I, along with the others, am the needy one."

Give me the grace, Father, to recognize my need and accept Your ever-present supply. —ELIZABETH SHERRILL

WED
2

CAUSE ME TO HEAR YOUR LOVINGKINDNESS IN THE MORNING, FOR IN YOU DO I TRUST; CAUSE ME TO KNOW THE WAY IN WHICH I SHOULD WALK, FOR I LIFT UP MY SOUL TO YOU. *—Psalm 143:8 (NKJV)*

I LOVE THE FIRST few mentally uncluttered moments of morning when my thoughts, often reruns from the day before, come one at a time and stay for a little visit.

You could have corrected her a little more kindly, one thought says about my eleven-year-old daughter Deanna. I ask God to forgive me, to help me be gentler, and then promise myself I'll ask her forgiveness, too.

Why couldn't you have hugged Mrs. Doyle before leaving the nursing home? So what if it's a little out of your comfort zone? says another thought as I picture this dear lady sitting by the bed of the love of her life and husband of sixty-two years. She's waiting to see if he will pull through this latest setback after a stroke and probably wondering how she will go on without him if he doesn't. Surely a hug would have comforted Mrs. Doyle. The next time I see her, she's going to get one!

There was a time when these early morning memories would have settled on my mind like condemning black clouds and darkened my mood for days. Today I embrace them as gentle reminders from Jesus on how to live—and love—a little better.

Thank You, Lord, for the loving conviction of Your Holy Spirit. Please never stop showing me little ways to love better. —LUCILE ALLEN

THU
3

"BUT WHILE HE WAS STILL A LONG WAY OFF, HIS FATHER SAW HIM AND WAS FILLED WITH COMPASSION FOR HIM; HE RAN TO HIS SON, THREW HIS ARMS AROUND HIM AND KISSED HIM." *—Luke 15:20 (NIV)*

DAY AND NIGHT, year-round, I keep four electric candles glowing—two in the center bay window at the front of the house and two more on the windowsill in the back sunroom. They spill a warm amber glow into kitchen and porch. The houses in our small subdivision are built around an open green space, so folks on both streets can see one another's homes. From front or back, our neighbors know I am always ready to welcome my children, two of whom are currently on active duty in the military.

A few years ago a neighbor up the street whose son had just been sent to jail set a similar candle in his bedroom window. Like mine, it glowed for all the neighborhood to see. It would stay lit until his release. Over the next years I heard that while in prison, he was seeking a new way of living. I prayed for him regularly, but the candle bothered me.

"Humph!" I sniffed. "Here *my* sons are out doing helpful things and certainly deserving of lights in the window. *Theirs* is in jail for something awful. Why would they remind us of that night after night?"

Then one night it dawned on me: My candles were showing off my pride. And their candle shone forth with the love of parents who will wait and wait and then joyously welcome the one who finally returns, no matter how crooked his path has been.

God, help me remember that Your candles burn forever in the windows of heaven, waiting to welcome the prodigal home. Forgive me for being a prodigal in my pride. —ROBERTA ROGERS

FRI

4

GREAT PEACE HAVE THOSE WHO LOVE YOUR LAW, AND NOTHING CAUSES THEM TO STUMBLE.
—*Psalm 119:165 (NKJV)*

MY SON CHASE and I walked away from our townhouse. Neither of us was talking. I was terrified, unsure that I'd done the right thing. My daughter Lanea had said she wanted to be alone. "Please, just leave the house!" she pleaded, a hint of hysteria in her voice.

Earlier that day, Lanea, home on a college break, had gone to the doctor for a checkup. The doctor found a lump in her breast. A mammogram showed a large mass that needed to be removed—immediately, the doctor said. She was only nineteen!

How could this happen to my little girl? Something that I can't fix? Anxious thoughts tripped over each other in my mind. Shutting them out, I said, "It's going to be all right. We just have to trust God."

Lanea's icy voice cut through my optimism. "You don't have to trust anybody," she said. "I'm the one with the lump." We rode home in silence. Now, Chase and I were walking out the door, praying she'd be all right when we got home.

When we did get home, Lanea was smiling. "I just needed to scream at God," she said. "No matter what, I know it's going to be all right." And it was. When Lanea went to the hospital for surgery, she found herself cheering the ministers who came to encourage her.

It's been nine years since her surgery, but Lanea still tells people about the peace God gave her then. She learned to really trust Him, because she had to.

Thank You, Lord, for teaching me to find peace amidst the storms, to find my way even through the shadows. —SHARON FOSTER

SAT

5

WHERE TWO OR THREE ARE GATHERED TOGETHER IN MY NAME, THERE AM *I* IN THE MIDST OF THEM. —*Matthew 18:20*

I REMEMBER OFTEN going to my husband Norman's office whenever he needed to talk through a sermon or a speech. "Lord," he'd say, "we have this problem. You know what it is without our telling. Please guide us in the right direction. Make us receptive to Your will. We thank You for this help that You are now giving us."

Then we'd sit quietly for a while. We never concentrated on the specific problem or on possible solutions. Instead, we tried to make our minds quiet and open. Sometimes, I'd think of some appropriate phrase from the Bible, like "In returning and rest shall ye be saved; in quietness and in confidence shall be your strength" (Isaiah 30:15) and focus on that. After a while, one of us would say to the other, "It seems to me this is the way to deal with this." Or, "I believe we've been on the wrong track with this one. Perhaps we should handle it this way." It was uncanny how often the same conviction came to both of us and how often a clear line of action would open up where things were obscure before.

If you're facing a problem or a decision in your life, why not ask a friend or loved one to be your partner in prayer?

Lord, thank You for the guidance You give me through quiet prayer with my brothers and sisters in Christ. —RUTH STAFFORD PEALE

SUN 6

HOW CAN WE SING THE LORD'S SONG . . . ?
—*Psalm 137:4 (NAS)*

EVERYONE IN CHURCH that Sunday sang the opening hymn enthusiastically—everyone but me, that is. I'd woken up depressed that morning, and I didn't know why.

Halfway through the sermon, three-year-old Archer reached over and squeezed my hand. He's a live wire, decked out in cowboy boots and a fresh crew cut. He gave me a bright Sunday-morning smile, and when I simply couldn't return one, he withdrew his hand.

During the closing hymn, Archer randomly opened his songbook and nudged me, offering to share it. Matter-of-factly, I placed my hand under the book and stared down at "Whispering Hope." I'd sung the song as a child. Silently, I skimmed the sweetly familiar words:

> *Soft as the voice of an angel,*
> *Breathing a lesson unheard,*
> *Hope with gentle persuasion*
> *Whispering her comforting word. . . .*

While the congregation concentrated on the announced song, I looked over what Archer had found for me:

> *Come then, O come, glad fruition,*
> *Come to my sad weary heart;*
> *Come, O Thou blest hope of glory,*
> *Never, O never depart.*

When the congregation began the last verse of their hymn, I flipped through my hymnal to the text and sang along with everyone else—from my heart. And this time I reached for Archer's hand.

My Father, help me to keep singing and rejoicing over Your faithfulness.
—MARION BOND WEST

MON
7

FOR HE SHALL GIVE HIS ANGELS CHARGE OVER THEE,
TO KEEP THEE IN ALL THY WAYS. —*Psalm 91:11*

EVERY MORNING I get up before dawn, dress, gulp down
some coffee and then rouse Sally, my twelve-year-old
cocker spaniel, for her walk. Sally is a little slow these days, and she
takes her time before she lowers her head to receive her collar and leash.

Once we're outside, it's all business. We hit the corner deli to buy
the *New York Times* and whatever supplies are needed for the day. I'm
usually rushing because I want to get to the gym before work. Sally
doesn't dally because she knows that breakfast will be served immediately upon our return to the apartment. We are definitely on a schedule.

This morning, it was still dark. We exchanged a few pleasantries
with the deli guy, paid for our stuff and headed toward the door.
Something caught my eye—the front-page headline on top of a stack
of tabloid newspapers: "BRITNEY IN WILD VEGAS WEDDING!" As
much as I'd like to say that I can just walk past something like that, I
couldn't. The sheer absurdity of the story stopped me in my tracks.

I don't know how long I stood there, transfixed by that ridiculous
headline, but it couldn't have been more than a few seconds. Next thing
I knew, there was a tremendous commotion outside. A car had come
plowing violently up on the sidewalk—exactly where Sally and I would
have been walking on our way back to the apartment if I hadn't been
distracted by Britney Spears.

I thought of all the things that could have gone differently in the previous fifteen minutes (and what if Britney hadn't gotten married, however briefly?). To say I felt lucky would be a gross understatement. To
say I felt protected, watched over and guided, well, that's more like it.

Sally and I headed back to the apartment, a grateful spring in our
steps.

*God, thank You for watching out for me even when I'm not watching out
for myself, which is most of the time.* —EDWARD GRINNAN

TUE

8

SAY NOT, "WHY WERE THE FORMER DAYS BETTER THAN THESE?" FOR IT IS NOT FROM WISDOM THAT YOU ASK THIS. —*Ecclesiastes 7:10 (RSV)*

THE EGG WAS already cracked when I took it out of the carton. I shrugged and tossed it in the garbage. They were on sale anyway—a nickel's not worth fussing about.

Then a long-ago memory surfaced. We lived outside the city limits then. My parents raised hundreds of chickens and sold eggs in town. I recall wanting to help my father layer eggs into square crates. "Breaking one is like losing a nickel," he warned. "If you don't drop a single egg today, I'll give you a nickel when we're done."

I may have been only four or five years old, but I knew that a nickel would buy a 3 Musketeers bar, my favorite because it had three little bars each with a separate filling: vanilla, chocolate and strawberry. Evidently I didn't drop any because I vividly recall returning from town clutching the candy and my mother saying, "You can't have it now, it'll spoil your supper."

I recall smelling Mom's home-baked bread, hearing Dad's overshoes with their bent metal clasps count the porch steps as he brought in wood for the potbellied stove, then feeling the warmth on our feet pointed toward that iron heater. After supper, Dad read aloud from Hurlburt's *Story of the Bible* while Mom crocheted and I ate my Three Musketeers, one bar at a time.

"Prices have rocketed," I told my husband. "You can't buy any candy for a nickel now. Of course, wages are higher in comparison, but nothing's the same as in the 'good old days.'"

Lawrence answered, "You just told me you lost a nickel on that broken egg. Seems to me that's the same as back then. A nickel still represents a whole day's wage for a hen."

Dear Lord, every day You provide everything we need for living, yet You charge us nothing for Your services. —ISABEL WOLSELEY

WED
9

"WISDOM IS WITH THE AGED, AND UNDERSTANDING IN LENGTH OF DAYS." —*Job 12:12 (RSV)*

FOR SEVERAL YEARS I've participated in a writers' group once a month. I critique their work, answer questions and offer advice on getting published. I try to encourage the members as much as I can. They're quite prolific; they often send their work to magazine and book editors, and enter contests. Some have seen their prose in print, and others have finished ambitious memoirs they're trying to get published.

Why is this group so special? Every member is over the age of eighty. Their founder is still writing poetry at ninety-five. They inspire me because they all have dreams—of writing a good story, seeing it published and sharing it with others. And aside from the occasional jokes about fading memory and bifocals, they don't see their age as an obstacle to achieving their dreams. In fact, as each day passes, they continue to use the gifts God has given them. Age is never an issue.

Thanks to these friends, I'm filled with hope when I try to picture myself twice the age I am now. I don't fear growing older because I've seen that enthusiasm and good humor can help keep my spirit young. Also, I know that God will still have work for me. I think of others whom God put to work in their later years: biblical heroes like Noah and Moses, and more recent heroes like Mother Teresa and the Reverend Billy Graham. As my own parents continue to work and volunteer, I see firsthand that God will have plenty for me to do as long as I'm healthy and my spirit is willing to follow where He leads me.

Lord, as my body grows older, keep me young in heart, mind and spirit.
—GINA BRIDGEMAN

THU
IO

AND GOD MADE THE BEAST OF THE EARTH AFTER HIS KIND . . . AND GOD SAW THAT IT WAS GOOD.
—*Genesis 1:25*

EVERY SO OFTEN I get a letter from someone who wants to know if I think there will be dogs in heaven.

Teddy, a Welsh terrier, is my canine responsibility at the moment. I walk him, feed him, bathe him, apply nostrums that protect him from ticks and fleas and heartworm, and take him to the vet when he requires medical care. In return, he licks my hand when I give him a treat, wags his tail when I come home or when I scratch his neck or rub his belly, sleeps at my feet when I take a nap (and gets even closer when it thunders), protects the house with his barking when a stranger approaches, and obeys my commands most of the time. My wife says I'm his master, but I'm not sure. He has a mind of his own and sometimes ignores me.

I suppose that Teddy's relationship with me is not unlike mine with my Master. I depend upon God for everything, including life itself, but I don't always obey His marching orders. He gave me a mind of my own, too, and though I want to do His will, I sometimes forget, grow hard of hearing and do my own thing. Fortunately, He reminds me of who's in charge with a tug on my leash, and I'm forgiven.

Now what was the question? Oh yes, will there be dogs in heaven? Absolutely, I say. The Creator of all life must have loved dogs, so I assume He will have a place for them in eternity. And what about ticks and fleas? Teddy says no.

> *Thank You, God, for the dog whose tail teaches,*
> *We can show love without long speeches.*
> —FRED BAUER

FRI
11

CHRIST WAS ALIVE WHEN THE WORLD BEGAN, YET I MYSELF HAVE SEEN HIM WITH MY OWN EYES AND LISTENED TO HIM SPEAK. I HAVE TOUCHED HIM WITH MY OWN HANDS. . . . —I John 1:1 (TLB)

I'VE LEARNED MORE about communication from watching my student-teachers than I've learned from books. Erica, for example, is a natural-born teacher. She started a class on Jonah and the whale with a clip of a nature movie about whales, then she opened a can of tuna, filling the room with a fishy fragrance while she told the story with enthusiasm.

As she talked, she passed around a piece of wet rubber, so her students could "feel" a whale. When the story was over, she served goldfish crackers, "sea soda" and Jell-O "whale blubber." Through it all, her busy brown eyes and charming smile made her irresistible.

Children are not the only ones who need multisensory communication. When I need to contact our college registrar, it's tempting just to fire off an e-mail and be done with it. But if I really want to communicate, I go to her office, sit down facing her and spend some time. I snitch a few of the M&Ms she keeps in a jar on her desk and study her expressive face for reactions to my ideas. The give-and-take of conversation is stimulating, and I always leave her office feeling refreshed and connected, a little less lonely, and a lot more hopeful about life.

E-mail and the telephone have their place, but I need to involve all the senses in communication: the sight of a smile, the smell of cologne, the touch of a handshake and the sound of a happy laugh.

God, I am so glad You came down here where we could see You face-to-face and know what You are really like. —DANIEL SCHANTZ

SAT
12

KNOW YE NOT THAT YE ARE THE TEMPLE OF GOD, AND THAT THE SPIRIT OF GOD DWELLETH IN YOU?
—*I Corinthians 3:16*

MY HUSBAND DAVID and I were visiting in the home of a relative, a physician who had never married and had been in practice for some forty years. As we passed through his dining room, I looked around amazed. "My goodness, everything's set as though you were having a party," I said.

The mahogany table was waxed to perfection. A silver candelabrum, with fresh white candles, was polished bright. A place setting of lovely old china was laid out and a crisp linen napkin was folded carefully by the silverware.

"Actually," replied this man who never said no to anyone in need, "the table's set just for me. After a long day, it's nice to come home and be good to myself. Even if the food is take-out, I light the candles, put on some music, sit quietly and enjoy my meal."

Eating alone for many of us is standing in front of the refrigerator, shoveling cold food into our mouths. In a world set on fast forward, it seems we've lost sight of our own individual worth. We treat our bodies with disrespect. We suppress our talents.

Stop a minute and imagine that you have been selected to host a world-famous dignitary. He could have gone anywhere, had wealth, position, power laid at his feet, but he has chosen to come and reside with you.

Well, guess what? The All-Powerful, All-Wise, All-Knowing, Almighty God *has* chosen you. As you sit holding this book, you are His earthly residence. He chooses to dwell with you, to dwell in you.

So set out your best china, light candles, use cloth napkins, just for you. Treat your body as though it were God's temple, because it is. Dust off your talents, follow your dreams, God will truly enjoy seeing you strut your stuff!

Father, if I'm really good enough to be appreciated by You, I'm good enough. Thank You. —PAM KIDD

SUN

13

THE LORD HAS ANOINTED ME . . . TO GIVE THEM A GARLAND INSTEAD OF ASHES. . . .
—Isaiah 61:1, 3 (RSV)

TWO TALL SILVER vases stand behind the altar in our church. During Lent they hold only dark green leaves—no flowers—to represent the "wilderness" season of penance and preparation. We take this tradition seriously. A few years back, when St. Patrick's Day fell on Sunday, someone asked the pastor's permission to add a dozen kelly green carnations to the leafy altar bouquets. "We'd better not," the pastor said, "but they'd look great in the parish hall."

Easter morning we celebrate with banks of regal white lilies delivered to the church by a florist. But that's not all. Everyone brings fresh-cut flowers to the service, and we "flower the Cross." Blossoms in hand—azaleas, daffodils, tulips, carnations (some kelly green!)—we process down to the front of the church and fill up a chicken-wire frame about three feet high. Last year I brought purple grape hyacinth stems, enough to share with others who had forgotten their own colorful contributions. The result? A lush visual reminder of abundant and everlasting life.

Lord, prepare my heart for Your Easter blessing. —EVELYN BENCE

MON
14

IF THE LORD BE GOD, FOLLOW HIM. . . .
—*I Kings 18:21*

"PLAY WITH ME, DADDY," says two-year-old Maggie.

I put down my book, pick up Maggie and put her down on the sofa beside me. "What game do you want to play, honey?" I ask her.

"You be Maggie and I be Daddy."

"Okay, Daddy," I say.

Maggie's face lights up. "What do you want to do, Maggie?" she asks me.

"Can I watch a video, Daddy?"

"No," Maggie says, her smile widening.

"Can I play a computer game, Daddy?"

"No!" says Maggie, bouncing up and down with glee. "You cry now, Maggie," she commands me.

"*Wah, wah,*" I wail. Maggie laughs.

As I play with Maggie, it occurs to me that I sometimes play a similar game with God. How often in my prayers do I tell Him what to do? How often do I reserve a part of my life for myself and act as if it's no concern of His?

"Will you read me a book, Daddy?" I ask Maggie.

"Okay, Maggie," she says. She takes a picture book from the shelf and crawls up onto my lap. She opens the book and looks up at me as if to say, "You take it from here." There's a limit to how far Maggie's game can go.

Father, whenever I pretend that I'm the one in charge, I run into trouble. I've reached my limit; You take it from here. —ANDREW ATTAWAY

HE LEADETH ME . . .
TO FOLLOW MY HEART

TUE
15

BUT THE COMFORTER . . . SHALL TEACH YOU ALL THINGS, AND BRING ALL THINGS TO YOUR REMEMBRANCE, WHATSOEVER I HAVE SAID UNTO YOU.
—*John 14:26*

ONE SNOWY MARCH DAY I got a call from my dad, who was being treated for cancer. "Honey," he said, "my good sweater has a hole in the elbow, and I was wondering if you could help me find another one like it." I knew the sweater well. It was a V-necked cardigan, the color of pine needles, and just about as prickly. "It has to have pockets," he reminded me.

The local department stores had already switched over to their spring merchandise, so I telephoned a mail-order company. I told the clerk that my dad needed a nice sweater to wear to his radiation treatments. Later that afternoon, she called me back. "We've struck gold, Mrs. Messner," she said. "I can get you one in forest green, red, navy, chestnut brown, yellow or camel. Why don't I send them all out to you, so your dad can choose the one he likes best?"

My mind quickly began to calculate the cost of all that return postage when something I learned in nursing school came back to me. *When you're old and ill, you don't get many choices.*

When the sweaters arrived, Dad tried on the entire shipment, his eyes dancing as he fingered the soft wool and checked out the pockets. "This brown is my favorite. . . .No, I like the red best. . . .No, I'll take this yellow one. Wait until those nurses see me in it!"

Marveling over the sweaters' bargain-basement prices, I recalled Dad's stories about the hardships of his childhood and how embarrassed he'd been by the threadbare hand-me-downs he'd worn to school. I sensed another nudge, and this time I didn't waste a moment. "I have a solution, Dad. It's high time you had that back-to-school wardrobe."

Thank You, Lord, for the pure magic in store for me when I follow Your nudges. —ROBERTA MESSNER

READER'S ROOM

HOW DO YOU PICK one blessing from eighty years of blessings? But it was easy for me, because on March 18 God blessed me with my first great-grandson. There is something about a baby that makes the world and everything around it aware of the miracles that God can give us!

As I hold that new life in my arms, I know that no matter how much we foul up this beautiful world He gave us, He is still watching over us, and I thank Him daily for not giving up on us.

—*Wanda E. Brooks, Bellingham, Washington*

WED

16

I PRAY FOR THEM . . . FOR THEY ARE THINE.
—*John 17:9*

I STOOD AND STARED out of the kitchen window. The telephone was ringing, but I didn't move. I was overwhelmed by the news I'd received earlier that day. Colonel Palmertree, the ROTC commander at the high school where I teach, had told me he had a serious health problem, and I was devastated. We had begun teaching across the hall from each other ten years before, and we'd quickly become friends, sharing a firm belief in duty to our country and a love for the 104-year-old American flag that hangs in my classroom.

"Mom," my son called out, "Mimi's on the phone."

Mimi is my husband Roy's mother. I was pleased she had called. Her concern for others and her strong faith in the Lord had always been an inspiration to me. After I finished giving her the latest news about the children, I told her about Colonel Palmertree.

"I wish there were something I could do," I lamented. "I feel pretty helpless."

"Why don't we put him on the prayer line?" Mimi asked.

"What a great idea!" I replied. Over the years I had always found the prayer line to be a source of comfort. One phone call with Mimi, and my prayer request was sent to a vast network of people who took time to pray for all the concerns they received.

The next morning when I walked into the teacher's lounge at school, the colonel was sitting on the sofa. As I walked by I heard him say, "If I felt any better today, I don't think I could stand it!"

I listened to his laughter and said my own prayer of thanks.

Thank You, God, for a wise and experienced mentor who knows where the answers lie. —MELODY BONNETTE

THU
17

AND WHEN PETER WAS COME TO HIMSELF, HE SAID, NOW I KNOW OF A SURETY, THAT THE LORD HATH SENT HIS ANGEL, AND HATH DELIVERED ME. . . .
—Acts 12:11

I FIRMLY BELIEVE that God sends people into our lives to give us the help we need when we're faced with hard times and tough choices. They become our guardian angels. For me, it was Mrs. Kelly, my seventh-grade math teacher.

I had a hard time in the seventh grade. My classmates were tough kids, several of whom were older students who'd been left back to repeat the grade, and I was not about to let them bully me. One morning, I got into a fight in Mrs. Kelly's math class and was sent to the dean's office. I was angry at Mrs. Kelly for turning me in, but I was willing to listen to her a few days later when she asked me to stay after class.

"Pablo," she said, "I don't like seeing you get into trouble. I believe you have what it takes to be a good student. Let's work together to make the most of your time in school. If you get good grades in all your subjects, I'll place you in one of the top eighth-grade classes next year."

Mrs. Kelly's words startled me. I'd never thought that I was cut out for the academic track, but with her encouragement I decided to give it a try. I worked hard in all of my classes and stayed out of trouble. When the school year ended, Mrs. Kelly kept her promise: I was promoted to a top-ranking eighth-grade class, and I had developed the skills I'd need for success in the future.

Lord, thank You for the guardian angels who have made a difference in my life. And help me to make a difference in the lives of those around me.
—PABLO DIAZ

FRI

18

Even the night shall be light about me.
—Psalm 139:11

I JUST COULDN'T get into my workout that morning. Even the proximity of other early-risers jogging or lifting weights didn't motivate me. My mind was on some hard decisions I was having to make at work, decisions that would have dramatic and long-reaching effects on the whole staff. *How can I know the right thing to do?* Finally, I stepped off the treadmill and, pulling on my sweatshirt, headed outside. Maybe the fresh air would help clear my head.

It was still dark as I turned into the subdivision adjacent to the health club. Stars, brilliant in that predawn moment, filled the sky. A tiny sliver of buttercream moon looked down on me. I walked at a brisk pace past brick houses and well-kept lawns, my breath making little puffs in front of me. A few porch lights glowed, but it was actually darker than I thought it would be.

I made my way down the deserted street, mentally chewing (again!) on my problem at work. Then, suddenly, my path was filled with bright light. I looked up. It was a motion-sensitive light on one of the garages. I smiled at the puddle of light as I moved forward.

A few houses further down the street, it happened again. Light. Just when I needed it. I kept walking, moving forward, waiting for the light to reappear. And it did. Again and again.

Back at my car, I was feeling better. My decisions were not as overwhelming as they seemed. All I had to do was move forward. And trust the light of God's wisdom to guide me at just the right moment.

All-knowing Father, direct my decisions. Purify my intentions. Let me be guided by Your light! —MARY LOU CARNEY

SAT

19

Verily I say unto you, Inasmuch as ye have done it unto one of the least of these my brethren, ye have done it unto me. —Matthew 25:40

SOME YEARS AGO, my wife Kathy and I attended a meeting in New York City. At the time, we lived on a small farm in Pennsylvania, and visiting the "Big Apple" was a bit daunting to us.

We boarded a bus that took us to the Port Authority Bus Terminal in the heart of town. The terminal was crowded with commuters, traveling families and street people. All the things I'd ever heard about the dangers of the city swirled through my mind. It was too much for this country boy, and I couldn't get out of there and to the safety of our hotel fast enough.

We enjoyed the meetings and our stay in the city, but I was uneasy when it was time for us to go back to the terminal to catch our bus for home. As we waited there, I gathered our bags close to us and watched the crowd warily. When I had to leave Kathy for a few minutes, I warned her not to speak to anyone. But when I came back, I was surprised to see her smiling and talking to a scruffy-looking old man. When I saw him giving something to Kathy, I hurried over and sent him on his way. Then I asked Kathy what the old man had given her. "Only this," she said, handing me a crumpled piece of paper. On it was a name and address.

"That poor man never gets any mail," Kathy said, "so he gave me his address. We're going to send him a card."

Father, help me never to overlook the opportunities You give me to minister to others' needs. —TED NACE

AT THE FOOT OF THE CROSS

THERE ARE TIMES in all of our lives when hope is hard to come by. Julia Attaway went through such a time last year, and this Holy Week she invites you to join her as she follows Jesus to the place where Easter truly begins—at the foot of the Cross. —THE EDITORS

PALM SUNDAY

SUN
20

THE CROWD SPOKE UP. . . ."HOW CAN YOU SAY, 'THE SON OF MAN MUST BE LIFTED UP'? . . ."
—*John 12:34 (NIV)*

I SIT IN THE DARK living room with my cup of decaf, absorbing the quiet of the early morning. My soul aches. How did my family come to be in this place of pain? Over the past eighteen months, my son John has gone from being a charming child to being a behavioral nightmare. We have tried every approach we can think of to help him. Discipline of any sort drives him into uncontrollable rage; mercy is not much more effective. Months of trying to deal with the situation have worn us all to a frazzle, and by now Andrew and I are angry and easily irritated.

What has gone wrong? Why has this happened? Why can't I make it better?

These questions resonate so loudly in my heart that I stop for a long while to listen to them. I have heard them before; it takes me awhile to figure out where. They are the questions of those who followed Jesus on the road to Golgotha. The disciples knew this heartache. Mary knew this torment. I am not the first to cry out, "Why him? Why me?"

I meditate a bit on the anguish of Jesus' followers as they went from proudly following their Lord on Palm Sunday to trailing after Him as He stumbled down the road on Good Friday. How great it must have been to see Christ acclaimed as king that Sunday! How grand to be known as one of His followers! And then . . . oh, the grief and shame of it all!

Lord, I want more than to cast palms before You. Bring me with You all the way to Calvary. —JULIA ATTAWAY

MONDAY IN HOLY WEEK

MON
21
"Yes, Lord," she told him, "I believe that you are the Christ, the Son of God, who was to come into the world." —John 11:27 (NIV)

I HAVE PRAYED and prayed and prayed for things to get better. They haven't. Last night John's rage was so intense we had to pin him to the bed for three full hours. Today I am sore, both physically and emotionally. I don't understand what is going on. I don't know why God doesn't seem to be listening to my pleas.

Getting no response when I am pleading, crying on my knees to God is hard. Very hard. I wonder why God remains silent. He promised not to give me more than I could bear, but the combination of John's wretchedness, my misery and God's silence is very close to my definition of unbearable.

I stop to ponder what Scripture says about God's silence and turn to the story of Lazarus. While Lazarus lay dying, Martha did what she ought to do: She turned to Jesus. Jesus knew that Martha was worried and grieving; He knew her need for Him was real. Yet He did not come.

Martha did not know why, but she didn't wonder about it. Martha didn't second-guess herself, fearing she had not asked Jesus in the right way. Martha did not give in to fears that she had too little faith. She simply trusted that Jesus would respond in the way He deemed best. Her words to Him when He finally arrived were a clear declaration of faith: "Lord . . . if you had been here, my brother would not have died. But I know that even now God will give you whatever you ask" (John 11:21-22, NIV).

This gives me hope, and a model for prayer. Silence from God tells me I have to trust in God's will, which is manifested in God's time. If He wants me to wait and trust, that is what I must do.

Lord, You are king even of my anguish. Let me serve You in and through it. —JULIA ATTAWAY

TUESDAY IN HOLY WEEK

TUE
22

"A WOMAN GIVING BIRTH TO A CHILD HAS PAIN BECAUSE HER TIME HAS COME. . . ."
—*John 16:21 (NIV)*

IN RARE MOMENTS of quiet, I gaze into my son's eyes. In them I no longer see the lucid glow of childhood. Instead there are ferocious dark clouds of anger, which part occasionally to reveal a fog of pained confusion. I feel as if I have lost my child.

We have had to curtail many extracurricular activities because John's behavior is so erratic. We still see his good friend Matthew once a week. I also take the kids to ballet class. It is a long trip—two subways and a bus—but the effort is worth it. Ballet is the one place John's eyes regain their former luster. Seeing him happy for even an hour a week helps me hold on.

Searching for more hope, I reread the Passion in the Gospel of John. This time I'm deeply aware that the disciples did not know how things would turn out. They lived through the events of Holy Week without knowing that Easter lay in wait. If I grieve over my son, they grieved more fully over Christ. Yet surrounded by danger and consumed by fear and anxiety, they still held on.

I decide it is not an accident that Scripture tells us that the way of the Cross contains times of not knowing what will happen, times of incomprehensible pain. Jesus asked His closest friends to go through this. He is asking it of me.

Jesus, let me be patient with not knowing and not understanding. When I must wait, let it be in Your loving arms that wait for me on the Cross.
—JULIA ATTAWAY

WEDNESDAY IN HOLY WEEK

WED
23

AND WHOSOEVER SHALL EXALT HIMSELF SHALL BE ABASED; AND HE THAT SHALL HUMBLE HIMSELF SHALL BE EXALTED. —*Matthew 23:12*

MY SON IS withdrawn, dull-eyed. Andrew thinks John is depressed, and I agree. It's time to get help. This is a hard step for us:

We like to think of ourselves as competent and capable, not as failures who can't guide a six-year-old through his troubles. But we have held on to our pride too long already.

I bring John in for a full medical and psychiatric exam. Turning my son over for professionals to evaluate is rough. I do not want to cede what little control I have.

It strikes me that this feeling is not new. All too often when I finally, fully turn something over to God, it has my claw marks on it. I hold on, I waffle, I give some but not all. Today I hunt through Scripture for a better understanding of what it means to give to Christ completely. This time it's Mary with her alabaster jar of nard who gives me insight (Matthew 26:6–13).

Truthfully, I've never made a material sacrifice for God as generous as Mary's gift. I'm not sure if I even own anything that is worth an entire year's wages. Yet Mary gave her whole nest egg of nard to Christ without being asked.

Judas was partially right: It was an extravagant gift. What he didn't grasp was that the cost was not to be counted in silver but in love. Christ saw first and foremost the lavish outpouring of Mary's heart. She anointed the king of love with her love, in preparation for His entry into His kingdom.

I want to love my family that way. I want to love Christ as Mary did. But I know such extravagance can't exist when I insist on being the one who is in control of my life. To love Christ fully, I must first remove the stopper of pride from my heart.

Oh, teach me to love with extravagance, my Lord! —JULIA ATTAWAY

MAUNDY THURSDAY

THU
24

"*COULD YOU NOT KEEP WATCH FOR ONE HOUR?*"
—*Mark 14:37 (NIV)*

THE ANGRY STORM was over, and John snuggled quietly next to me on the sofa. I asked him what set off his massive temper tantrum this time. "It wasn't because of anything, Mommy. I thought it would be fun to make you mad."

His words hit me like a punch in the gut. I listened to their echo for a full minute. I could see the ray of hope: John was speaking in trust and innocence. But I also felt stupid and hurt. Perhaps the bulk of my six-year-old's behavior problems was my own fault. A howl went up inside me. What kind of child finds it fun to provoke his mother?

I put John to bed quietly, then considered what to do. Among the mixed feelings swirling inside me, resentment was gaining the upper hand. *I ought to pray,* I thought. But I didn't want to. *I ought to pray,* I thought again. But I wanted to indulge my feelings instead of turn them over to God. I went to bed.

Andrew roused me, asking, "Are you going to pray with me tonight?"

"No," I said, and went to sleep. Like the disciples in the garden, I was more concerned with my own sorrow than with Christ's.

Lord Jesus, forgive me when I wallow in my suffering instead of uniting it to the healing power of Yours. —JULIA ATTAWAY

GOOD FRIDAY

FRI
25

SURELY HE HATH BORNE OUR GRIEFS, AND CARRIED OUR SORROWS. . . . —Isaiah 53:4

WE LEARN THAT there is no organic cause to John's rages: no brain tumors, no rare diseases. That means it's an emotional disturbance, though we still don't know what kind. This is helpful information. But I have reached the end of my emotional reserves.

"Oh, dear God, stop this! Help me!" I moan. I'm tired of being kicked at, punched and spat upon. We have tried so hard to be faithful, and I am in anguish, not understanding what has gone wrong.

Tonight fear and pain have pushed me to cry for help. I'm utterly desperate for a break, but sense that none is coming. I feel helpless, pinned to the situation. Laid flat, I grieve over my son and our family life.

Somewhere in the peripheral vision of my mind, I see Christ on the Cross. A momentary light twinkles, and by it I see that the agony to which I am pinned is my cross. In the midst of my pain I dimly grasp that even here—especially here—He is with me; I am not alone.

Lord Jesus, the greatest good in the world came through Your suffering. Help me become more like You through mine. —JULIA ATTAWAY

EDITOR'S NOTE: Join Guideposts today for our annual Good Friday Day of Prayer. Today and every day, Guideposts Prayer Ministry prays for each prayer request by name and need. Join us at www.dailyguideposts.org to request prayer, volunteer to pray for others or contribute to support our ministry.

HOLY SATURDAY

SAT
26

"WHOEVER HAS MY COMMANDS AND OBEYS THEM, HE IS THE ONE WHO LOVES ME. . . ." —John 14:21 (NIV)

I NOW KNOW I am not the cause of my son's troubles. In my frustration, however, I sometimes contribute to them. Since I cannot fix John, I decide to focus my efforts on eliminating my increasingly unholy responses to his behavior.

This is hard work. It is the work of detachment, of relearning to love John in the biblical sense: with my actions, rather than with my feelings. Like faith itself, love is only peripherally a matter of sentiment.

Do I really have faith? How can I know? I reread Jesus' words to His disciples after the Last Supper, where He comforts their troubled hearts. Over and over He says that the sign by which they will know they love Him is if they keep His commands. And his foremost command is to love one another as He has loved us. I am determined to do this with John.

I sit my son down and tell him I love every atom in his body, and nothing he does will ever change that. I say it must be scary to feel so out of control, and even scarier to have the power to make grown-ups upset, too. I tell him I know he is hurting inside. I know he doesn't want things to be this way. I don't want things to be this way. God doesn't want things to be this way. So even if it seems that I am his enemy, he and God and I are all on the same side. That is a powerful alliance. Together we can conquer this darkness.

I see a glimmer of hope in John's eyes. Could it be a reflection of the spark of faith that sustained the disciples that long, dark Saturday while Jesus lay in the tomb?

Lord, I said yes to You long ago. Hold on to me now in this darkness while I wait for the courage to repeat it. —JULIA ATTAWAY

EASTER

SUN
27

PRAISE BE TO THE GOD AND FATHER OF OUR LORD
JESUS CHRIST! IN HIS GREAT MERCY HE HAS GIVEN US
NEW BIRTH INTO A LIVING HOPE THROUGH THE
RESURRECTION OF JESUS CHRIST FROM THE DEAD.
—I Peter 1:3 (NIV)

BALLET HAS BEEN a good thing for John. Tonight he and I are back-stage at a theater in New York City, awaiting his cue to go on in the Arabian dance scene of *The Nutcracker*. He has a small role as a page.

At the moment things are tense: One of the other children in the scene has decided she hates her costume and is refusing to go on. The principal dancers confer in whispers, frantically figuring out how to modify the dance to use one less child.

John's eyes fill with tears. A last-minute change is a hard thing for almost anyone, and this is only his third time on stage.

"I can't do it!" John whispers. "I can't do it if Sophia doesn't go on!" I put my hand gently on his shoulder. "Sure you can! Take some deep breaths and say a prayer. You can do all things in Christ." His eyes close; his lips move silently.

Nine months ago John could not reply to a simple request without attacking. Tonight he is facing a theater of four hundred people and a challenge that would be stressful for many adults. I send up a silent prayer of my own.

My little boy straightens his shoulders, grips his prop and steps out onto the stage. He moves smoothly to position and executes his part flawlessly. Head high, John walks steadily back to the wings. Then he flings himself into my arms and goes entirely limp.

My eyes well up with tears of pride. My heart is fit to burst with thankfulness. I don't understand how God did it, but He has rolled away the impossibly heavy stone and instead of death there is life.

Jesus, in You all *things are risen! Hallelujah!* —JULIA ATTAWAY

MON
28
AND AFTER THESE THINGS I HEARD A GREAT VOICE OF MUCH PEOPLE IN HEAVEN, SAYING, ALLELUIA; SALVATION, AND GLORY, AND HONOUR, AND POWER, UNTO THE LORD OUR GOD. —*Revelation 19:1*

IT'S EASTER MORNING, and my dog Shep and I are as usual out at dawn and into Central Park. The rain has stopped, and the morning air is fresh and tingling. Shep runs freely and keeps an eye on me to make sure I don't stray. We go under the Winterdale Arch and climb the hill. Nobody around—it's too early. We pass the two statues before the Delacourt Theatre—one of Romeo sweeping Juliet into his arms, and the other, wind-blown Prospero and Miranda looking seaward in *The Tempest*—and head to the Turtle Pond. The turtles are swimming and they move their heads out of their shells, begging.

"*Woof! Woof!*"

Shep barks on cue, as he does every day at this juncture. I throw him his biscuit and one to the turtles, who paddle madly for the prize. An egret flies over the pond, white against the blue sky, and just then I hear glorious voices. I run around to get a better view and, gazing upward, I see Belvedere Castle, stately and grand, and before it the Pavilion, where, upon its mighty stone steps, a choral group—fifty, maybe sixty, men and women—are greeting the sun with the good news that the Lord has risen: "Hallelujah! Hallelujah! Hallelujah!"

Shep and I walk around the Great Lawn, passing two or three dog walkers, and now with "Praise be to God" within me, I shout, "Happy Easter!" to them. "Happy Easter, Shep! Happy Easter, world!"

Hallelujah! Hallelujah! Hallelujah! —VAN VARNER

TUE
29
NOW OUR LORD JESUS CHRIST HIMSELF . . . ESTABLISH YOU IN EVERY GOOD WORD AND WORK. —*II Thessalonians 2:16–17*

WHEN I VISITED my daughter Tamara's family in Barrow, Alaska, the spring whaling season was keeping the Eskimo village busy. Subsistence hunting was how many in this town of several thousand bordering the Arctic Ocean survived. *Umiaks*, small ribbed boats covered in sealskin, sat offshore on the Arctic ice, flying the captain's flag if the crew had been successful.

One cold overcast afternoon, I watched a flurry of activity from Tamara's apartment window. A forty-six-foot bowhead whale had been hauled onto the edge of the ice two miles out. Men and women bundled in parkas were loading supplies on sleds and towing them behind snowmobiles to the site. It would take the village several days to harvest the *muktuk* (blubber) and meat from the whale. I longed to ride with them and see this unusual event, but I felt hesitant.

Tamara knew I wanted to go. Before I could protest, she dragged her arctic gear from the closet, zipped me into it and pointed me out the door.

I walked to the beach and asked two young men if they had room for me on their sled. They showed me how to sit holding on to the side ropes, and we bumped over the rough trail until the ice ended. Beyond us the blue-gray water stretched to the far horizon. Huge and black against the snow-covered ice lay the whale that would provide food for the villagers.

Later, I hiked back to town with the villagers across the same rough trail—keeping an eye out for polar bears. "I am walking on the Arctic Ocean," I kept telling myself. "This is unbelievable!"

It was an unforgettable experience, and it happened because Tamara thought I could do it. She pushed an undecided me out the door and pointed me in the direction of an amazing adventure.

Thank You, God, for the people in my life who get me moving in the directions I ought to go. —CAROL KNAPP

WED
3O
CREATE IN ME A CLEAN HEART, O GOD; AND RENEW A RIGHT SPIRIT WITHIN ME. —*Psalm 51:10*

THERE'S A GARDEN HOE in our laundry sink this morning, the blade beneath the faucet, the handle propped against the wall. I've left it there to remind me of what it taught me.

I'd gone out to the garden earlier than usual because I couldn't focus my mind during my quiet time. Prayer wouldn't come; the Scripture passage seemed miles away from my concerns. So I'd put the Bible down, picked up the hoe and headed outside.

I'd finished weeding the flower bed and was running water over the hoe in the sink when I recalled another hoe, another sink. When I was eight or nine, I'd gone out with my father to his prize rose garden. In ten minutes, he was soaked with sweat from the humid Kentucky heat. When he was finished, he gratefully carried his hoe into the cool basement of our home in Louisville and washed the blade in the laundry tub.

"Keep your tools clean, Johnny," he said. "They'll lose their sharpness if you let them stay soiled."

Now, as I let the water run over my own hoe, I remembered an argument I had with my wife Tib the night before over some silly, minor thing. I can't even recall what it was, only that I'd exploded.

And this morning in my quiet time God seemed far away. Of course. I'd lost my temper, shouted. There was spiritual soil on my soul. No wonder the Word didn't speak to me.

I put the Bible down and went looking for Tib, to set things right.

Preserve me, Father, from the self-righteousness and pride that close my ears to the Voice that never shouts. —John Sherrill

THU
31

I remember the days of old; I meditate on all thy works; I muse on the work of thy hands.
—*Psalm 143:5*

I was ten years old and standing with my father on an ancient cobblestone street in Jerusalem. An aged and stooped Bedouin came up to us with a handkerchief in his hand. Opening the handkerchief, he showed my father a dozen old coins. Dad bought them as souvenirs and gave them to me.

That was forty-three years ago. For decades the coins have been stashed away, forgotten, in a box of old keepsakes in the top of my closet. Forgotten, that is, until I recently pulled the dusty box from the shelf in a fit of spring cleaning.

Holding the timeworn coins in my hand, the memory of the old man and my father came flooding back. Selecting a large silver coin, I took it to a friend who is a classics professor. He told me it was a Greek drachma minted in 250 B.C. Though the value of the coin is modest, the renewed memory is now a treasure, a window into time.

I took the coin to a skilled jeweler and had it set into a necklace for my wife Beth. Now it is her favorite piece of jewelry. Our children think of their grandfather each time the necklace is worn. And I am proud of a memory saved from oblivion.

Father, may I enrich the present day with treasures from the past. Amen.
—SCOTT WALKER

SEEDS OF REJOICING

1 _____

2 _____

3 _____

4 _____

5 _____

6 _____

7 _____

8 _____

9 _____

10 _____

11 _____

12 _____

13 _____

14 _____

15 _____

16 _____

17 _____

18 _____

19 _____

20 _____

21 _____

22 _____

23 _____

24 _____

25 _____

26 _____

27 _____

28 _____

29 _____

30 _____

31 _____

April

But I will hope continually, and will yet praise thee more and more. —*Psalm 71:14*

GOD SIGHTINGS
THE MASTER PLAN

FRI

1

"BEFORE I FORMED YOU IN THE WOMB I KNEW YOU. . . ." —Jeremiah 1:5 (RSV)

WHEN OUR GRANDDAUGHTER Kerlin phoned from Nashville, Tennessee, to say that she and her husband Jordan were expecting a baby, I was as excited as a great-grandmother-to-be should be.

"As soon as we learn the sex," Kerlin said, "we'll let you know."

This was a new dimension for me. When my children came along, you could only guess at an unborn baby's gender. They, in turn, expecting their own children, had opted not to know. Five months before the due date, Kerlin called with the news that she was carrying a boy. It was no longer "when it's born," but "when he's born."

Soon Kerlin and Jordan chose a name. Somehow, awaiting Adin Marshall Richter was different again from waiting for "the baby" or even for "him" to come. He had an identity, a name to sew on a blue blanket. I even wrote him a letter: "Dear Adin . . ."

The birth was still four months away when they set the date for his baptism. "We thought you'd like to make plane reservations ahead," Kerlin explained.

So much advance planning, so many details already decided—how strange it all seemed to me! Strange . . . and troubling. "Is it right, Father," I prayed, "to know so much so far ahead?"

I knew you, the answer came at once, *before you were born. Before you were conceived. Before the mountains and the seas were in place.*

Five months too long to plan ahead? For an awestruck moment I had a sense of the unimaginable vistas of time as matter was flung into space, and galaxies formed, and the components of the earth were forged in exploding stars. How far ahead did God plan for the creation of life . . . of humankind . . . of you and me?

Take away my fears for the future, Father. It is already in Your care.
—ELIZABETH SHERRILL

EDITOR'S NOTE: What kinds of "God sightings" have you experienced this year? Please take a few minutes to look back at what you've written in the "Seeds of Rejoicing" pages, and let us know how the Lord is working in your life. Send your letter to *Daily Guideposts* Reader's Room, Guideposts Books, 16 E. 34th St., New York, NY 10016. We'll share some of what you tell us in a future edition of *Daily Guideposts*.

SAT
2

FROM THE LIPS OF CHILDREN AND INFANTS YOU HAVE ORDAINED PRAISE. . . . —Psalm 8:2 (NIV)

OUR SON RYAN was a sophomore in high school, and this was his first big social event. A young lady, a member of the ROTC, had invited Ryan to be her guest at the Junior Military Ball. The escorts would wear their best attire for the occasion. Many, we learned from the grapevine, would be renting tuxedos for the evening.

"Mom, Dad, that's not necessary," Ryan said. "My old suit will do just fine, fresh from the cleaners." Ryan would never ask for anything that would stretch the family budget. But at the same time, his mother and I knew in our hearts how much he wanted that tuxedo.

Rosie and I talked it over. We called the rental outfit to get a price, then listed all the other things we could put the money toward: a family vacation, the leaky roof, our measly retirement fund. We debated and we debated.

We rented a smart black tuxedo.

The night of the ball, Ryan put on the tuxedo and paraded in front of the mirror, smiling from ear to ear. "Thank you, Mom and Dad," he said, standing tall. "I won't ever forget this." He went out our front door a confident young man, knowing his parents' gesture showed their pride in him.

Lord, we pray that our son will praise You for all Your blessings to him, including the blessing of his parents. —DOLPHUS WEARY

SUN

3

"Be strong and of good courage; be not frightened, neither be dismayed; for the Lord your God is with you wherever you go."
—*Joshua 1:9 (RSV)*

WHEN CHOOSING a boarding school, our older son Will declared that he didn't want to go to a church-affiliated school. No mandatory chapel. No Bible classes. "There are some excellent schools in our denomination," I pointed out.

"He's looking to do things his way," Carol explained. After all, for fourteen years he'd gone to church almost every Sunday morning with us. Now he wanted to spread his wings. "He's pretty good at making decisions on his own," she went on. "We need to trust his judgment in this."

So off he went to New Hampshire to an excellent school. For that first year we got e-mails and phone calls about his friends, his classes, his extracurricular activities. But no reports on any Sunday worship services. On Parents Weekend we went to chapel on our own. He slept in.

But then a curious thing happened. In his sophomore year he announced that he'd found a local church with services on Wednesday at midday—"so I won't have to get up early." He volunteered for community service. He brought cookies to their Maundy Thursday evening dinner. And one Sunday he called and said, "I heard the best sermon this morning. The Bible verse was just what I needed to hear: 'Be strong and of good courage; be not frightened, neither be dismayed; for the Lord your God is with you wherever you go.'"

I don't know what decided Will to reacquaint himself with church— whether it was a tough Latin class or the memory of a habit from home. But I'm glad he's sorting things out on his own. In the meanwhile, it's not just Will I'm learning to trust.

God, we give You our children. They have been Yours all along.
—RICK HAMLIN

MON

4

PRAISE THE LORD, O MY SOUL. . . .WHO SATISFIES
YOUR DESIRES WITH GOOD THINGS SO THAT YOUR
YOUTH IS RENEWED LIKE THE EAGLE'S.
—*Psalm 103:1, 5 (NIV)*

I'VE EARNED MY LIVING in a very different way in the last five years. In the past I had a full-time job with a salary and benefits. Now I do projects for groups from time to time and have to manage my own salary and benefits. This new arrangement, though scary at times, left my wife Joy and me free to travel to many parts of the world as volunteers working on interethnic reconciliation and ministering to medical needs. But this past year, some of my clients went out of business and I was faced with having almost no income for a time.

When it became clear the way forward was not going to look like the path behind, Joy and I took some days off to visit Alaska and think through the future. One of our stops was the Raptor Center in the town of Haines. There we came across a beautiful bald eagle that could not fly and was reduced to hopping around on the ground, eating what was thrown into his cage and drinking from a metal bowl. We asked the center staff about him and were told he had come to them injured. When he healed, they were concerned that he had forgotten how to hunt in the wild and might starve if they released him, so they clipped his wings. I watched him for several moments, saddened at how small his life had become.

Watching that eagle told me something about my career problem, too. If you're an eagle, don't settle for hopping on the ground, no matter how easy getting the groceries becomes. Besides, losing a few pounds would look good on me.

Lord, let me always look to You and live up to my potential, not bound by my fears. —ERIC FELLMAN

TUE

5

"BEFORE THEY CALL, I WILL ANSWER; AND WHILE
THEY ARE STILL SPEAKING, I WILL HEAR."
—*Isaiah 65:24 (NAS)*

AS I TUMBLED the wet laundry into the automatic dryer, my thoughts went back to a windy spring day more than forty years ago. Awkwardly pregnant with our second son, I nevertheless toted a heavy wicker basket full of wet clothes out to the wash line. *Squeak, squawk, squeak*, the pulley protested each time I pinned another garment to the line. The noise attracted the attention of a telephone repairman high up on a pole across the back lane, and we exchanged a neighborly wave.

I continued to hang out the wash. Bend and stretch, bend and stretch. Next to a row of embroidered tea towels and snowy pillowcases, five white shirts were soon billowing in the breeze. If there was anything my husband Leo liked better than putting on a fresh white shirt every morning to go to his teaching position, it was getting into his old work clothes after school to garden—the soil underneath the clothesline was soft and black.

As I made lunch for our toddler son, I could hear the clothes snapping in the wind on the line outside, then suddenly, silence . . . ominous silence. Looking out the kitchen window, I groaned, "Oh no!"

The clothesline had broken, and most of my snowy white wash had fallen onto the garden plot, where the wind was playing "crack the whip" with the loose ends of the line.

I wearily pulled on my rubber boots, picked up the clothesbasket and trudged back outside. Coming around the corner, I was startled to meet the telephone repairman face to face.

"Saw the whole thing happen, ma'am, so I came down the pole to give you a hand. Free service and lifetime guarantee!" he grinned, pulling a pair of pliers from his leather tool belt. With a few deft twists, he quickly mended the broken clothesline.

Forty years later, as I stand here folding a pile of laundry, I think about that kindly repairman so unselfishly giving of himself to help a stranger in her plight. It reminds me of another "Free service and lifetime guarantee"—God's profound promise. He anticipates our needs and comes unbidden to help us splice the breaks and put the broken ends of life together. Sometimes we just don't recognize Him in the hard hat and coveralls.

Thank You, Lord, for sending kind people to help me when I have been in need. —ALMA BARKMAN

WED

6

FOR, LO, THE WINTER IS PAST, THE RAIN IS OVER AND GONE; THE FLOWERS APPEAR ON THE EARTH. . . .
—*Song of Solomon 2:11–12*

SINCE MY WIFE Shirley and I have been wintering in Florida, we've missed the harbingers of spring—such things as snowdrops that sometimes peek out from blankets of snow, and crocuses, those fragile sapphire and purple blooms that silently trumpet warmer days ahead. I'm tempted to call summer-heralding flowers *prescient*, the fancy word for foreknowing, but a teacher once told me to be careful of giving plants and animals human characteristics. "Steer clear of anthropomorphism," he cautioned. Of course, that instructor would have advised against "presuming the hidden hand of God" behind phenomena of nature, too, but I don't have any trouble with crediting God with creating such beauty or orchestrating when flowers bloom. His timing is always perfect—for flowers and for us.

Anyway, my everlovin' and I always head north in time for one of our favorites, daffodils. They were budding, and a few were open, when we got to Pennsylvania last week. Today, I went out to greet them despite a chilly nor'easter that soaked my coat and blew off my hat. Wordsworth immortalized this spring beauty, you'll remember:

> *I wandered lonely as a cloud*
> *That floats on high o'er vales and hills,*
> *When all at once I saw a crowd,*
> *A host, of golden daffodils;*
> *Beside the lake, beneath the trees,*
> *Fluttering and dancing in the breeze.*

Dancing daffodils? My professor would never have approved of such humanization. Me? I think I should emulate daffodils and do more dancing in celebration of good things to come—even when the wind and rain try to dampen my spirits.

> *Teach me, God, to drink deep from life's fresh spring,*
> *To discover the sweetness You placed in everything.*
> —FRED BAUER

THU
7
FOR WE ARE LABOURERS TOGETHER WITH GOD. . . .
—I Corinthians 3:9

SINCE I MOVED from Guideposts to work at a Christian book club, I've missed the wonderful feeling of opening the daily packages of sweaters knitted by our readers for the Guideposts Sweater Project. They are so beautiful, made in all kinds of colors and each one the product of a different imagination. I also miss the notes tucked into them and the occasional phone call seeking advice on how to cast on the sleeves or what kind of yarn to choose. I like to talk to other knitters.

Just recently I met a knitter in the airport lounge in San Antonio. I thought I recognized the familiar shape of her knitting. "What are you working on?" I asked.

"This is a kid's sweater," she replied. "I knit for Guideposts. They go to children around the world."

I was thrilled. "I do that, too!" I exclaimed, holding up the half-done back of the bright purple sweater I was knitting. I was explaining how I knew about the project as the boarding announcement came. By then we were already deep in conversation about how many stripes looked best, different sizes and where the need was greatest. We were still talking as we walked down the Jetway.

The conversation reminded me that the work of the Guideposts knitters was going on all around the country even as we talked. We two were part of a dedicated multitude bringing warmth and the love of God to chilly children all over the world, one garment at a time.

Lord, send Your blessing on the work of these many hands. And may the lives of children everywhere be healthy and happy. —BRIGITTE WEEKS

FRI
8
BE NOT HIGH-MINDED, NOR TRUST IN UNCERTAIN RICHES, BUT IN THE LIVING GOD, WHO GIVETH US RICHLY ALL THINGS TO ENJOY. —I Timothy 6:17

THE WINDOW in my office is large and odd. The bottom of the window is six feet off the floor; through it, I can see the tops of the buildings across the street. That view, however, is slowly fading:

Five plants (two jades, a begonia, a Christmas cactus and one defiant pothos plant) are creating their own little hothouse. The pothos alone has curled vines that reach twenty feet when unfurled.

Knowledgeable people have told me to cut them all back—it's not healthy to have massive plants in smallish pots. I listen politely, then ignore their sound advice. The pothos and one jade have followed me from office to office for nearly twenty years. They have witnessed hundreds of late nights, thousands of mistakes, endless sighing, occasional victories, maybe a nap or two. We have an understanding: I feed and water them and provide as much sun as Pittsburgh will allow; in exchange, they absorb my exhaled breath and bad vibes and give me life's oxygen.

I'm childish enough to think that living things—plants, pets, people—thrive on simple kindnesses. A little water, some food, understanding, sunshine, company, patience, some soil to call our own, plus a little help from heaven above—that's all we need. At least it works for my pothos.

Lord, when I start confusing my wants with my needs, remind me of that pothos. —MARK COLLINS

SAT
9

"*EACH OF YOU MUST RESPECT HIS MOTHER. . . .*"
—*Leviticus 19:3 (NIV)*

ON THE ANNIVERSARY of his mother's death, my husband Robert became aware that he had not fully completed the task of grieving for his parents. We'd learned in our hospice training that delayed grief is not unusual and needs to be faced, so Robert decided to honor his parents by making a trip through Kansas. He invited me to accompany him.

We visited the important places the family had lived throughout his life with them. At each home, he took pictures and shared memories with me. It seemed we were outside of time, as I imagined the young couple with their new baby, the birth of Robert's sister Carolyn, the children's growing-up years and their move into a new home after the children were gone. At the end of a long Saturday, we went to the retirement home where Lola and Floyd spent their last years and came to the end of their lives.

The next morning we visited the cemetery. Robert had potted some of the flowers he'd grown in our Colorado garden, which he placed by his parents' headstones. Then the two of us knelt and said prayers of thanksgiving for their lives and for the many tangible and intangible gifts they had given him. We said a regretful good-bye and ended our time there with a long hug.

The trip was very healing for my husband, and it blessed me with a deeper sense of closeness to this tenderhearted man who has chosen to spend his remaining years with me.

Whether or not your parents are still living, perhaps you will consider honoring them in some concrete way. You will be blessed beyond measure.

Heavenly Parent of us all, may I think of some loving way to honor my parents this day. —MARILYN MORGAN KING

SUN
10

NOT BY MIGHT, NOR BY POWER, BUT BY MY SPIRIT, SAITH THE LORD OF HOSTS. —*Zechariah 4:6*

ONE SUNDAY at church the children's lesson was an overview of the life of Jesus. As a response, I asked the children to paint or draw a scene from His life. Most of the drawings were straightforward and easy to decipher. But Ethan's drawing left me puzzled.

In brown colored pencil he'd drawn the open tomb. But instead of Jesus, a beefy man in blue jeans stood there, flexing his muscles. "Can you tell me about your picture?" I asked Ethan.

"Oh sure," he said, pointing to the man in blue jeans. "This is Jesus coming out of the tomb. He won."

Then I remembered that in the lesson I'd said that when Jesus came out of the tomb, He'd won a victory over our greatest enemy, death. And to Ethan's seven-year-old eyes, how else would Jesus conquer than by brute force?

What Ethan will learn in time, and what I need to remember in my own struggles, is that the strongest "muscle" of all is love. It was love—made perfect in weakness on the Cross—that defeated death and brought Jesus out of the tomb a winner.

Father in heaven, Yours is the power and the glory forever. Amen.
—SHARI SMYTH

MON
11

"RETURN TO ME WITH ALL YOUR HEART. . . ."
—*Joel 2:12 (NAS)*

SPRING DIDN'T HOLD much promise for me. It seemed that one of my sons had turned his back on God and was headed full steam in the wrong direction. I'd tried praying, Bible reading, counseling with friends and talking to him. Nothing seemed to be helping him turn around. Everything looked dismal.

My husband Gene, picking up on my mood, said, "Let's walk down to the lake. Some Canada geese have been visiting. I've been feeding them every other day for more than two weeks." Silently we walked hand-in-hand to the lake. Gene had grabbed a sack of cracked corn in case the geese happened to be there. Just before we reached the water, we saw and heard the geese soaring overhead—in the wrong direction.

"Hey, guys!" Gene called loudly, cupping his hands to his mouth. "You're missing dinner. Come on back. Turn around."

I couldn't help but smile at the way Gene pretends the geese, ducks and an occasional heron understand him. We stood still, watching their perfect V formation sailing almost out of sight.

At first I thought it was my imagination. But, no, the lead goose turned and the others followed. They did a perfect U-turn high above and returned to Gene's call. They all touched down in the water and hurried toward the bank where their trusted friend waited.

Lord Jesus, if wild geese can return when called, surely sons can, too. Please call his name. —MARION BOND WEST

TUE
12

LET US THEREFORE FOLLOW AFTER THE THINGS WHICH MAKE FOR PEACE. . . . —*Romans 14:19*

I WAS PRETTY PROUD of myself when I took my car in for an oil change last week. *Now that's off my mind,* I thought. And it was—until on the drive home from work the next evening, dark gray smoke started pouring out from under the hood of my car.

"Hey, lady," another driver shouted at me, "your car's burning up!"

I was already swinging over to the side of the road. "I see it, I see it!" I muttered.

When I popped open the hood, I saw that the oil cap was missing. The mechanic had forgotten to put it back on. I drove the rest of the way home—I had no idea that wasn't a good idea—and worked myself into a state of anxiety.

They'll tell me it's my fault, I thought. *They'll tell me they can't fix it. I'm probably ruining the engine by driving it. I'll have to take them to court.* By the time my imaginary fears had the judge holding me in contempt for not checking my car before I got into it, I knew that I had to pray. *God, thank You for keeping me safe. Now please keep me sane! I need Your help to deal with this situation calmly.*

The next morning, at eight o'clock sharp, I called the oil-change place. One hour later, a young man in a blue uniform showed up at my front door and I got a sincere apology, a thorough engine checkup and a coupon for a free oil change.

"I was afraid the manager would fire me on the spot," the mechanic said as he cleaned up. "I sure would like to thank you for being so calm about this."

I smiled as I remembered my panic and anger and fear. "I had to ask for some help staying calm," I admitted. "And I appear to have gotten it."

Today, Lord, let me come to You with my worries. —LINDA NEUKRUG

WED

13

O LORD, HOW GREAT ARE THY WORKS! AND THY THOUGHTS ARE VERY DEEP. —*Psalm 92:5*

"NAME A PLACE you've never been," my stepfather Herb asked one day as we were talking on the phone, "a place you'd really like to go."

"Why, the Grand Canyon," I answered without hesitation.

A few days later my mother and Herb called again. "Guess where we're taking you for your birthday?" my mother announced. "The Grand Canyon!"

On the flight to Arizona, I boned up on the history of the canyon. It was created, I learned, by a massive land collision over two billion years ago, which drove enormous mountains six miles up into the sky. Then millions upon millions of years of water erosion cut down deeper and deeper into the canyon, giving it its present appearance. Today it is 277 miles long, eighteen miles wide and a mile deep.

When I stepped off the plane in Phoenix, I was ready. Equipped with lots of information and a good camera, the Grand Canyon was mine! We drove the last leg of our journey in a rented car. At last— quite suddenly—we were there. After miles and miles of desert land- scapes, we were parked at the first lookout point. I rushed from the car to have my first look.

Once the canyon was in view, I stopped short. My first inclination was to throw away my camera. It seemed a sacrilege to think I might capture even an inch of the miracle that stretched out before me. What I saw could never be printed on paper or stuck in an album. It was beyond any words I could hope to write.

Before me, plainly, simply, lay the majesty of God, bigger, more beautiful and much more powerful than anything I could imagine. God's thoughts, the Grand Canyon told me, are very, very deep and very, very wide. With the Psalmist, I could sing, "Before the mountains were brought forth, or ever thou hadst formed the earth and the world, even from everlasting to everlasting, thou art God" (Psalm 90:2).

Thank You, God, for sending me to the Grand Canyon where I could know this for myself. —PAM KIDD

THU

14

"SO IF YOU ARE OFFERING YOUR GIFT AT THE ALTAR, AND THERE REMEMBER THAT YOUR BROTHER HAS SOMETHING AGAINST YOU, LEAVE YOUR GIFT THERE BEFORE THE ALTAR AND GO; FIRST BE RECONCILED TO YOUR BROTHER, AND THEN COME AND OFFER YOUR GIFT." —Matthew 5:23-24 (RSV)

I ALWAYS THOUGHT this Scripture meant that it was my job to make sure reconciliation happened before I could be worthy to worship. But what to do when I didn't feel reconciled to a person after confessing my sins against him or her?

"I don't think Jesus wants us to *force* a reconciliation," a friend suggested, "but instead to try to give the injured person his or her dignity back."

"How?"

"Well," my friend said, "when someone hurts me, I feel awful, like I've been devalued, my dignity as a human being discounted. So when I've hurt someone, I say something like, 'I can imagine how much what I did must have hurt and embarrassed you, and I feel sad about doing that. I'm sorry.'"

I wondered where my friend got the idea to console people instead of trying to get them to forgive you.

"The prayer of St. Francis," my friend revealed. "'Help me to seek not so much to be consoled as to console, to be understood as to understand, to be loved as to love.'"

Lord, forgive me for being so focused on winning people's forgiveness that I overlook the effect of my sins on them. —KEITH MILLER

FRI
15

I CAN DO ALL THINGS THROUGH CHRIST WHICH STRENGTHENETH ME. —*Philippians 4:13*

FOR ME, wrestling down all the information for my income tax is an annual trauma. It was my husband's job when he was alive. A civil engineer with a mind given to detail, he kept meticulous records in his spidery handwriting. He laid out our financial life in a twenty-five-column ledger that was daunting, to say the least.

The first year the job fell to me, I stared at the long-neglected bank statements and the mess of papers that had collected on my desk. Where to start? Math was not my favorite subject, and even now I have to think twice before remembering that seven times seven equals forty-nine. In fact, there's only one thing about math that to this day I remember without fail and that's "Fair Try" Willis.

His students never knew him by any other name. We'd groan when he passed out a pop quiz, for surely we'd fail. "Give it a fair try!" he'd boom out. "A fair try, that's all I expect." Mr. Willis was generous with his grades and gave extra points to those who he thought had diligently wrestled with a problem and tried their best to solve it.

Here goes. I sat down at my desk. I prayed for strength and comprehension as I slowly went through the accounting steps that my husband had set up over the years. It didn't come easy. Then, when I was at my wit's end trying to make sense of the dollars and cents, I heard "Fair Try" Willis say, "Give it another try!"

Now I take one day a month to balance the bank statement and enter the credits and debits in my twenty-five-column ledger. It's a drag, but with a fair try I'm getting it done. Extra points for me.

It is such a good feeling, Lord, to accomplish what at first seems to be the impossible. —FAY ANGUS

HE LEADETH ME . . .
TO BE AN ENCOURAGER

SAT
16

A WORD APTLY SPOKEN IS LIKE APPLES OF GOLD IN SETTINGS OF SILVER. —*Proverbs 25:11 (NIV)*

IT WAS her T-shirt that caught my attention. I was having lunch alone in a local steakhouse when a teenage girl came stomping in behind a man who appeared to be her father. As they placed their trays on the table in front of me, I read the neon green lettering on her black shirt: PRETEND I'M NOT HERE. THAT'S WHAT I'M DOING.

But as my eyes traveled upward to braces and a sprinkle of acne, I noticed the most gorgeous auburn hair pulled back into a ponytail. *If she didn't have such an attitude, I'd compliment her.*

Just then, I sensed a prompting: *Do it anyway. You'll pass her on your way to the salad bar. It won't be so hard. Her T-shirt is a cry for help.* And before I lost my nerve, I tapped the girl on the shoulder and heard myself stammer, "You have the most beautiful hair." She glared back at me, and words I never planned rolled off my tongue. "You must hear that a lot."

"No, never," she answered, a startled look on her face. And then she smiled—a sweet "I forgot I'm wearing braces" smile. Her dad looked on, positively beaming. When I returned with my salad, the two of them were adding sweetener to their iced teas, words tumbling out in a flurry of conversation. As I listened to their laughter from the table behind them, I prayed:

Lord, help me never to be fooled by a message on a T-shirt.

—ROBERTA MESSNER

READER'S ROOM

I'M A NATURE PERSON, and I've watched the beauty of winter snow and enjoyed the golden finches at a feeder outside our family room window. Now that spring is here, hearing the mourning doves again calms me. And seeing the robins hopping through the yard and the spring flowers popping through the ground gives me new hope. I love the sound of trains, and when I hear a train whistle, I pray, "Thank You, God, for the train whistle I hear, a testimony of Your providence and love for me."

—Nila Benci, Streetsboro, Ohio

SUN

17

THE MOUTH OF THE JUST BRINGETH FORTH WISDOM. . . . —Proverbs 10:31

DAVID WAS ONE of my Sunday-school students years ago, and one day he entered the class beaming with joy. He had been selected to deliver the oration during the playing of "The Battle Hymn of the Republic" at the band concert that spring.

One week later, David was less joyful. "Mr. Greene," he said, "my mom says my speech isn't right. I've practiced, but she isn't satisfied. She says something's wrong."

I spoke to her after Sunday school and she said, "Maybe you could come by the house and help him. The concert is only one week away." I agreed to try.

When I dropped by his home, I found David in his room, sitting on his bed. He turned on his record player, and we listened to the hymn and the oration that went along with it. The presentation was clear, moving and patriotic. Rather a big undertaking for a fifth-grader.

I asked him to record his recitation, so he could listen to it. But this time he played back his tape with the professional recording. The results were startling. He could tell clearly what he needed to do to sound like the recording. David listened carefully, slowed down his speech and smoothed out his presentation. On concert night, he was superb.

It seemed to me that David solved the problem himself. He is now married, with two lovely children, yet on every Christmas card, he thanks me. In a recent speech at his church, he began, "I want to thank Oscar Greene for teaching me something so long ago."

But you know what? All I did was sit and listen to him. It wasn't much, but it seemed to mean the world.

Thank You, God, for giving me the chance to help by hearing.
—OSCAR GREENE

MON
18

NOT THAT I COMPLAIN OF WANT; FOR I HAVE LEARNED, IN WHATEVER STATE I AM, TO BE CONTENT.
—*Philippians 4:11 (RSV)*

WHEN OUR FAMILY lived in New Zealand, I wasn't sure what I missed most: my clothes dryer, dishwasher or central heating. After rushing outside to rescue a load of clothes from a rainstorm—and burning a pot of pasta in the process—I decided it was the dryer I really missed.

The next morning I battled a black mood while running a load of laundry and listening to my preschooler's favorite music tape for the umpteenth time. When the washing machine spun to a stop, I scooped the wet clothes into a wicker basket and called, "Elizabeth, want to come outside with me?"

"No, I want to build with my blocks."

"Okay. I'll be back in a few minutes." I left her banging her blocks to the "Hokey Pokey" and headed for the yard. *Ah, silence.* As I pinned the clothes on the line, I heard the soothing sound of a little brook gurgling nearby and the chirping of birds. Stretching a sheet across two lines, I glimpsed the azure sky dotted with cotton ball clouds and felt the warmth of the sun, which had not yet penetrated the house. "Thank You, Lord," I whispered.

Then I laughed. What I had considered a burden—going outside to hang up the laundry—turned out to be a blessing, forcing me outdoors to soak in nature's sounds and sights. And when I stepped inside, I brought the sunshine with me. I sat down on the floor to build a tower with my daughter, and we sang a chorus of "The Wheels on the Bus" along with her tape.

Is there a burden in your life that could be a blessing? For me it was a day without a dryer.

Lord, help me accept the trials in my life and see Your goodness.
—MARY BROWN

TUE
19

WHOM HAVE I IN HEAVEN BUT YOU? AND EARTH HAS NOTHING I DESIRE BESIDES YOU. —*Psalm 73:25 (NIV)*

THE CHEST PAINS started around noon. *What's this?* I wondered. *Indigestion before I even eat lunch?* The discomfort persisted all day and into the night. Next morning, it had settled into a dull, deep ache, a pressure that made it hard to breathe. By midmorning, with no letup in the pain, I did the only sensible thing: I went to the Internet and typed, "heart attack symptoms." Turns out I had several of them.

Which is how—via the emergency room—I came to be lying in a hospital bed. Lots of tests were scheduled for the morning. I had already had an EKG . . . and three nitro pills. I was on oxygen. My purse and jewelry had been sent home with my husband. I had no makeup, no hair dryer, no cell phone, no briefcase. Everything that was *me* had been stripped away. I was just the patient in Room 3303. I stared at the blank TV, but I couldn't bring myself to turn it on.

"I wish I had a Bible," I said aloud to the white walls. On impulse, I pulled out the top drawer of my nightstand and found one waiting. I opened to the Psalms and began reading. Then I turned to John 14.

And by the time they brought my lunch tray, I knew that the *essential* part of me was still intact. My faith. My optimism. My belief in God's abiding presence.

P.S. My heart turned out to be perfect. A viral infection in my lungs had been the cause of my pain.

Thank You, Father, for Your Word and Your abiding presence—whether I'm in a church, a boardroom or a hospital room. You are what matters most! —MARY LOU CARNEY

WED
20

I WOULD NOT WRITE . . . BUT I TRUST TO COME UNTO YOU, AND SPEAK FACE TO FACE. . . . —II John 12

"E-MAIL'S DOWN!"

I must have heard that message three times the other morning between the elevator and my desk. Hanging up my coat, I could only sigh in resignation as I glanced at my barren computer screen. When it would be fixed was anyone's guess because, well, e-mail was down and no one could communicate. No matter. It would probably be back up by lunch.

Noon came and no e-mail. By three o'clock, the tech department's "help desk" was no longer even answering its phones. I threw up my hands and stalked down the hall to deliver a manuscript to an editor to whom I would have normally e-mailed my suggestions. I just hoped she could read my handwriting. "Oh, who's that?" I asked, noticing a snapshot of a newborn on her bulletin board.

"That's my nephew!" she said proudly, pulling out some more pictures from her desk.

"Wow, your first one?"

"Yep."

"Congratulations. By the way, nice work on this story."

"Thanks."

I walked back down the hall wondering when the last time was I'd stopped by her office. It struck me how nice it felt just to hand something to someone, have a look at a bulletin board and exchange a few words. It's become entirely too easy, I decided, for people to avoid actually talking to each other. Yes, a lot of our technology shrinks the world and makes it easier for us to communicate. But it can also make it easier for us not to communicate. And that's shrinking the world too much.

By the time I got back to my office, I hoped my computer screen was still blank. Thankfully, it was.

God, don't let me forget that people are more important than technology. Maybe that's what You're trying to tell me when the e-mail crashes.
—EDWARD GRINNAN

THU
21

THERE IS PRECIOUS TREASURE AND OIL IN THE DWELLING OF THE WISE. . . . —Proverbs 21:20 (NAS)

EARLY ONE MORNING I arrived at my friend Scarlett's house with a heavy heart. Life seemed off track, out of control. I'd allowed my worry to overshadow my prayer time for weeks.

I let myself in her front door. "Be right down! Grab some coffee! I put out a mug for you!" she hollered from upstairs.

Scarlett and I meet for simple things—coffee, long walks and to get acquainted with each other's children. The thing I love most about Scarlett is her daily passion for God, even though her life is far from carefree. Scarlett often grabs my hand and prays out loud no matter where we are or what we're doing. Once she began praying as we ran laps around the mall parking lot. It didn't matter that we were covered in sweat and wearing tennis shoes. We didn't even close our eyes.

Sitting down with my cup at her kitchen table, I noticed Scarlett's brown leather Bible lying open to Proverbs 21. Scarlett reads the matching chapter of Proverbs for each day of the month, and today was April 21. Quickly, I flipped through the worn Bible. Smiley faces, exclamation marks, colored markings and notes crammed the margins. I ran my hand over the pages, soft from hundreds of touches.

"Hey, girl. You ready to walk?" Scarlett pulled her long hair into a quick ponytail.

I slid the red ribbon marker back to Proverbs 21. "Always ready to walk with you, girlfriend."

Father, thank You for the people who draw me back to the richness in You. —JULIE GARMON

FRI
22

"HE HAS GRANTED US NEW LIFE TO REBUILD THE HOUSE OF OUR GOD AND REPAIR ITS RUINS. . . ."
—*Ezra 9:9 (NIV)*

I LIKE TO WALK my dogs along a country road that leads down to a reservoir near my home. A lot of other people like to walk and drive there, too, and unfortunately some of them leave their trash behind. It's sad to see such a lovely area cluttered with cans and food containers, so I got in the habit of picking up things, stuffing them into my pockets and putting them into my trash bags when I got home.

One evening, I saw a man coming toward us on the other side of the road. He kept stopping and walking off into the field to pick something up. As he got closer I saw that he was carrying a plastic shopping bag. *He's picking up trash, just like me!* I thought. *What a good idea to bring a bag!*

It turned out that he was collecting aluminum cans for a recycling program at his church. "We get paid more than fifty cents a pound for these things," he said, holding up the bag, which was almost full. "It's a great way to make money for some of our programs—and clean up the roads at the same time!"

I've always been a recycler, but it never dawned on me that it could be profitable. Now we have a program at my church, too, and it's bringing in much-needed money. It's also getting us out for some much-needed exercise. And the road leading down to the reservoir looks a lot better these days. Now, when Suzy and Tara and I go for our walk, I can't help but think that only God can bring something so worthwhile out of trash.

Dear Lord, on this Earth Day, help me to work with my neighbors to preserve the beauty of Your creation. —PHYLLIS HOBE

SAT
23

"ASK AND IT WILL BE GIVEN TO YOU; SEEK AND YOU WILL FIND; KNOCK AND THE DOOR WILL BE OPENED TO YOU." —*Matthew 7:7 (NIV)*

A FEW YEARS AGO a friend gave me a gold cross hand-crafted by her mother. I treasured that cross and took special care of it.

Then one day I couldn't find it. I made a careful search for it, but to no avail.

The missing cross weighed on my mind for weeks, until one Saturday I decided I'd look for it and wouldn't give up until I found it. That morning, as I finished my prayers, I reached for pen and paper and wrote a letter to the Lord, reminding Him how much I loved the cross and asking Him to help me find it. After I'd written two pages, I put aside the prayer letter and began my search.

The logical place to start was my jewelry box, even though I'd looked there many times before. I opened it and removed all the necklaces. There in the back was the cross. I was stunned. After weeks of worry and fruitless searching, I found it in the first place I looked.

I clenched the cross in my hand, closed my eyes and prayed a prayer of thanksgiving. Then I heard an answer in my heart.

"Debbie," the voice said, "all you had to do was ask."

God, I don't know why I turn to You as a last resort when You should be the first one I seek. Every time I wear this cross, remind me of Your faithfulness. —DEBBIE MACOMBER

SUN
24

FOR FROM YOU THE WORD OF THE LORD HAS SOUNDED FORTH. . . . —*I Thessalonians 1:8* (NKJV)

BEING A PREACHER'S SON in the 1940s and '50s had its perks. One of them was getting to ring the church bell on Sunday morning.

The bell rope felt as thick as a camel's leg to my small hands. Often I'd need my father's muscular, furry arms to get the heavy bell moving, but then the weight of the bell would lift me high in the air with each ring. "Riding the bell" was more fun than a circus. I was only supposed to ring it about ten times, but if no one was watching, I could stretch that to twenty.

As the powerful bell echoed through the streets, I felt like the most important person in the world. I was the apostle Paul, sounding out the Gospel to the Gentiles, or Simon Peter, preaching to Pentecostal masses. What I was doing was just as important as my father's sermon or my Sunday-school teacher's lesson. And during worship, when we sang,

"Ring the bells of heaven! There is joy today, for a soul returning from the wild," the congregation was singing about me, of course.

As long as I can find a way to express my faith in God, there is hope for the future. It may be a letter to the newspaper editor over a moral issue, or wearing a T-shirt that says I LUV JESUS or reading a Bible story to my granddaughter Rossetti. I find deep satisfaction in sounding forth the good news that God is alive and heaven is waiting for us.

Father, thank You for helping me to get the bell started. I will always ring it with pride and joy. —DANIEL SCHANTZ

MON 25

I AM BRINGING ALL MY ENERGIES TO BEAR ON THIS ONE THING: FORGETTING THE PAST AND LOOKING FORWARD TO WHAT LIES AHEAD.
—Philippians 3:13 (TLB)

THE GAME WAS on the line when my grandson David, eleven, came to bat in the top of the ninth inning. There were two outs and a runner on second base, and his team was behind by one run. I held my breath as David fouled off the first pitch, swung at and missed the second, took a ball low, and fouled off the third ball. Then he drilled a high fastball past the diving first baseman, batting in the tying run. He stole second and ended up scoring to give his team a 13–12 victory. I don't know who was more excited, David or his cheering grandma!

But the next game was different. David batted 0 for 2, and had trouble getting the ball over the plate when he pitched. He was pulled from the game in the fifth inning, and his team was knocked out of the tournament.

Still, my young grandson is able to keep baseball in perspective: The main thing for him is doing his best and having fun. He accepts his successes and failures, his wins and losses, for what they are—an inevitable part of the game. He did the same thing after the loss as after the win: He practiced batting to improve his skills. That's a pretty good example for living life, wouldn't you say?

Lord Jesus, thank You for loving me just as much when I strike out as when I hit home runs. —PENNEY SCHWAB

TUE

26

CAST THY BREAD UPON THE WATERS: FOR THOU SHALT FIND IT AFTER MANY DAYS. —*Ecclesiastes 11:1*

THIRTY YEARS AGO I lived on a houseboat on the Hudson River at the 79th Street marina. For four of the happiest years of my life I saw the waters flowing by in tidal propriety. I named my boat *Ashland*, because it was also the home of my dog Clay, and Henry Clay, for whom he was named, lived on a Kentucky estate called Ashland.

Ashland was thirty-two feet long and came equipped with a living room, galley, bunk and bathroom. From November to the end of March, we were locked in the marina. Come April we were freed, and away we went, south to the Statue of Liberty or north via the Harlem River to Long Island Sound. We even ventured—once—past the Verrazano Bridge into the Atlantic Ocean. There was always adventure for my friends and me.

In the winter we were warmed in our snug quarters by propane gas. I can still see the ice covered with snow just beyond our bow and hear the snap of the ice floes as they roared past, presaging spring.

I remember the day that Arthur Gordon, who had just assumed the editorship of *Guideposts* magazine, lounged on deck and suggested, "Why don't you come in for half a day?" Gradually, at first reluctantly, then with increasing zeal, I exchanged my role as roving editor for a full-time job at Guideposts. That meant little time for Ashland.

Clay and I came ashore to where I live now. Clay died in time, and I have another dog, Shep, who must wonder, as we come off the Henry Hudson Parkway at 79th Street, why I always say, "Godspeed, *Ashland*, wherever you are."

And, lest I forget, Lord, Godspeed to those who are blessed enough to sail on her. —VAN VARNER

WED

27

I SOUGHT THE LORD, AND HE HEARD ME, AND DELIVERED ME FROM ALL MY FEARS. —*Psalm 34:4*

MY DAUGHTERS Lindsay and Kendall gave me an unusual present on my fifty-something birthday—a gift certificate to get my ears pierced. For years I've resisted getting them pierced, even though my daughters and most of my friends have pierced ears. "I don't like the thought of getting two more holes in my head," I rationalized. "Besides, I've got plenty of clip-on earrings." But I rarely confessed the real reason: I was afraid of the pain.

"Mom, let's just do it," Lindsay told me as we sat at the kitchen counter.

"Yeah, Mom, pierced ears are cool," Kendall added. She knew she was hitting a vulnerable spot. I dread the thought of growing hopelessly uncool and stodgy as I get older, and I count on my daughters to tell me what's cool.

"I don't know. . . ." I hesitated.

Just then my son Derek walked in. "Maybe you're right, Mom. At your age, why bother?" His comment sealed my resolve.

"Get the car keys and let's go," I said with finality.

Soon I found myself sitting in the middle of a busy mall where shoppers could stop and watch a nervous, middle-aged lady get her ears pierced. First the technician carefully marked an X on each ear lobe, then picked up the piercing gun and with a quick *pop, pop,* she was done. She gave me a handheld mirror, and I could hardly believe myself. I had pierced ears!

"Wow," I said, grinning. "Let's go celebrate!"

Father, I know pierced ears don't have a thing to do with my "cool quotient" in Your eyes, but thank You for daughters who care enough to help me not to stay stuck in my fears. —CAROL KUYKENDALL

THU
28

AND YE SHALL HEAR OF WARS AND RUMOURS OF WARS. . . . —*Matthew 24:6*

IT SHOULD HAVE BEEN the perfect way to start the day: Get up early, catch the news while the coffee perks, then take my Bible onto the side porch for my quiet time in the predawn hush.

Why, then, was my mind whirling with negative thoughts? Negatives in the news, of course, there always were. Another country facing famine or civil war, a soldier killed somewhere, a foster child abused. The news gave me plenty of needs to take to God out there on the porch, but my prayers didn't seem to climb as high as the treetops.

Some time later, at a conference in upstate New York, I was getting a prebreakfast mug of coffee in the hotel lobby and listening to the news blaring from the lobby TV. That's when I spotted my old friend Andrew Foster, pastor of the Church of the Ascension in New York City, who was attending a conference at the same hotel. We exchanged how-are-you's, and for once I told him. "Oh, you know, there's so much trouble in the world I don't even know how to pray anymore."

"I used to fall into that trap, too, but no more," said Andrew. "I've put myself on a strict news fast until noon."

A *news fast*. How those two words have changed my life! I do, of course, have to know what's going on in the world, but the world can struggle along without me until noon.

Today, on our side porch, I listen to the birds, feed a chipmunk, read Scripture and wait till noon to catch up with the latest tragedy. The news is neither better nor worse for my fast, but by starting the day with the calm that comes from listening first to God, I cope more successfully with my own problems and see more clearly my role in the larger problems around me.

Thank You, Father, for granting me time each day to look at the world from the perspective of eternity. —JOHN SHERRILL

FRI
29

IN HIM WAS LIFE, AND THE LIFE WAS THE LIGHT OF MEN. THE LIGHT SHINES IN THE DARKNESS, AND THE DARKNESS HAS NOT OVERCOME IT. —*John 1:4–5* (RSV)

OUR FIRE-PIT circle began when we were building our home in the country. We used it to burn scrap lumber. Then we added three large boulders, a picnic table and camp chairs, and before long most of the neighborhood came drifting in to sit by the welcoming flames and chat. Late nights around the fire became opportunities to ask heartfelt questions, share our faith and listen to problems.

One evening Ryan—a teenage neighbor who'd had a few run-ins with the police—came swooshing across the grassy field on his bicycle and parked beside me at the fire. I had sent him cookies, with a note saying I was just down the street if he ever wanted to talk. Now here he was in the darkness, lit up by a spray of shooting sparks, opening up to me about his life.

"I wish I could talk to my dad about things," he said, "but I'm too nervous."

"Maybe we should invite your dad to our fire one night," I suggested. "It would be easier to talk to him here."

Ryan liked the idea, and two nights later his dad showed up. The three of us had a wonderful conversation. After that, Ryan came often to the fire. It was giving him what he really needed—love and attention from people who viewed him with respect.

Yes, our fire circle began as a place to get rid of scrap wood. Somewhere along the way, Jesus the Light transformed it into holy ground.

Lord, whether we're gathered around a fire in the country or clustered on a city stoop beneath a streetlight, come among us to do Your holy work.
—CAROL KNAPP

SAT
30

"I THE LORD BRING DOWN THE TALL TREE AND MAKE THE LOW TREE GROW TALL. . . ."
—*Ezekiel 17:24 (NIV)*

WE LIVE in a high mountain desert. Juniper and piñon trees struggle to grow here. Stunted cottonwoods hug the arroyos and a few ponderosa pines survive on the higher ridges. We have tried many times to coax various deciduous trees to grow in our nutrient-poor soil. We planted two ash trees in the fall of 1993, and to our delight they survived the winter. We watered them and dreamed of someday sitting beneath their shady branches.

We also got a new pup that fall. For some reason, Jordan decided that one of our ash trees needed to be eaten during its first spring; I came home from work one day and saw him happily chewing on our future leafy shade. I put chicken wire around the still-healthy trunk, but that evening I saw Jordan lying next to the chicken wire, chewing on the trunk of our ash tree.

Eleven years later the ash tree that Jordan chewed down to its roots is twice as tall as the unmolested tree. Neither of them provides much protection from the sun yet, but the one favored by Jordan is large enough for him to lie in its shade on a hot summer day.

Looking at it, I think about my own spiritual growth. My faith was strong when I was a child, but then it was cut down to the roots for twenty-five years. Since then, I've suffered through some rough, dry patches. Sometimes I feel so far behind friends who never seem to have struggled. But now I see it's those very trials that have made me strong, like my ash tree spreading its shade.

Dear God, be with me as I grow toward You. —TIM WILLIAMS

SEEDS OF REJOICING

1 _____

2 _____

3 _____

4 _____

5 _____

6 _____

7 _____

8 _____

9 _____

10 _____

11 _____

12 _____

13 _____

14 _____

15 _____

16 _____

17 _____

18 _____

19 _____

20 _____

21 _____

22 _____

23 _____

24 _____

25 _____

26 _____

27 _____

28 _____

29 _____

30 _____

May

Let all those that seek thee rejoice
and be glad in thee. . . . —*Psalm 40:16*

SUN

I

ALL THY CHILDREN SHALL BE TAUGHT OF THE LORD;
AND GREAT SHALL BE THE PEACE OF THY CHILDREN.
—*Isaiah 54:13*

MY SON Chase stands over six feet tall. Looking at him, his beautiful ebony skin contrasting with the pale colors of his blue-and-white choir robe, my heart aches with pride at the man he has become. He's much younger than the other choir members and the only African American.

My daughter Lanea and I are visiting the church Chase attends each Sunday. He sings, and they pay him a small honorarium. It's an answer to prayer. "Please, Lord, find Chase a church home while he's away," I prayed as he packed his things to leave for school. "And he needs a little pocket change. And, oh, by the way, does he know the Lord's Prayer by heart?"

My son hugged me and smiled down at me. "I know the Lord's Prayer, Mom. Relax."

Before he was conceived, his father prayed for a son who'd look just like him, and Chase came into being, a gift from God. After his father died, I worried and prayed that Chase would not become a statistic. An African American, father deceased, no male role models in the home, being raised by a single mom—it all added up to disaster. So I prayed. When pneumonia threatened his childhood, I prayed. When a snowboarding accident and peer pressure threatened his teens, I prayed.

Chase has survived, flourished and is now enrolled in the North Carolina School for the Arts in Winston-Salem, where he's studying opera. As I listen to the choir, I can hear his powerful sometimes tenor, sometimes baritone voice rising above the others. He's singing the Lord's Prayer. And I know that all my prayers have been answered.

Thank You, Lord, for being a father to the fatherless and a husband to widows. —SHARON FOSTER

GOD SIGHTINGS
ANSWERING PRAYER

MON
2

[God] IS ABLE TO DO EXCEEDING ABUNDANTLY ABOVE ALL THAT WE ASK OR THINK. . . . —Ephesians 3:20

"PLEASE PRAY that I can find the right place for my mother," my friend Denise asked when she had to move her mother from the house in Brooklyn where she'd lived for thirty-six years to an assisted-living facility.

"The problem," she told me, "is Muffy."

Muffy was a Brittany spaniel. "Mom's had so many losses—Dad, my brother, most of her friends. Muffy is her lifeline!"

And that created a dilemma. Some of the places Denise visited had a no-pets rule. At others, the problem was the health-care aides her mother would need. They were allergic, or fearful, or from cultures where animals were never brought indoors.

At last Denise located an attractive retirement community where, she was assured, the dog would be welcomed by all concerned. Over a strenuous weekend, Denise got her mother and belongings moved to her new home, only to have the aides refuse to enter the apartment with the dog there. Denise was frantic, taking weeks off from work to provide her mother's daily care.

What about those prayers? I wondered. Why had faith and effort resulted in such a wrong choice?

But as it turned out, they hadn't.

Bringing Muffy back from his morning walk one day, Denise noticed a man helping his wife from a car into a wheelchair beside a pile of suitcases. Seeing the dog, their faces lit up. "A Brittany spaniel!" the man exulted. "We haven't seen one since ours died last year. Looked just like this one!"

"Does he live here?" the wife asked hopefully. "Would you bring him to visit us now and again?"

It even "happened" that the apartment they were moving into was directly across the hall from Denise's mother—and the man handled his wife's care himself. Muffy lives with them now, and Denise's mother visits him and her new friends every day.

Father, I'd forgotten that Your answers to prayer always encompass more than just the needs I know of. —ELIZABETH SHERRILL

TUE

3

HE THAT BELIEVETH SHALL NOT MAKE HASTE.
—*Isaiah 28:16*

"LOOK, DAD!" I rushed outside when I heard eight-year-old Andy's yell. He was pointing to our rundown garage. Wedged high in the vines covering the east wall was a small basket of twigs and grasses, the nest of some unknown bird.

I hoisted Andy up and together we gazed at three squirming balls of fluff. "No doubt about it," I said. "They're robins!"

Over the next few weeks we watched the mother swoop down on her young ones, dropping worms into their gaping beaks. Then one day my older son John came to me with a sad look. "They're gone, Dad. I think they've flown away."

We missed the robin family more than we had expected. Watching the miracle of new life helped us to feel closer to nature and to God. When the birds spread their wings, it seemed as if a little light had gone out of our lives. "Let's collect the nest," I suggested, "and put it on our bookcase. That way we'll always remember the robin family."

At first everyone was enthusiastic, but soon doubts crept in. It just didn't seem right to remove this tiny home from its natural habitat. Still, I wanted the souvenir and decided to collect it next weekend.

The evening before the fated day, my wife Carol said, "I saw a robin fly over to the nest today. Do you think it could be the mother? I wonder what she's up to." Puzzled, I decided to check the nest. Three new robin-blue eggs lay inside.

"Robins," I read later in a nature guide, "have two or three broods per year." Thank God I hadn't removed the nest too soon. Nature had been given a chance to work its magic, and we were about to be foster parents once again!

Lord, teach me to pray and wait awhile lest in my haste I disrupt Your handiwork. —PHILIP ZALESKI

WED

4

HE MAKETH ME TO LIE DOWN IN GREEN PASTURES. . . .
HE RESTORETH MY SOUL. . . . —Psalm 23:2-3

TWO DAYS AGO, the cow lot behind our ranch house was a cacophony of sounds. Cows whose calves were being weaned were mooing in protest—an incredible variety of deep and high-pitched noises. On a ranch, it's called "bawling." The mothers were bawling for their babies, making such noise that if the babies were bawling back, I couldn't hear them. I felt sad for both the cows and calves, but I knew this yearly ritual must take place. It was time for the babies to grow up.

Yesterday, I looked out my window and saw the calves contentedly lying in the pasture, stomachs full of green grass, unbothered by their mothers' cries, which were only slightly less adamant than the day before. The calves had adjusted, but the adults were taking longer to get used to the change.

I've done a bit of my own "bawling" over change lately. I've been asked to take leadership positions in church and in a Bible study, and it's moved me far from my comfort zone. I've had to give up depending on someone else to feed me from God's Word and get into the Bible for myself. I've had to do things that make me anxious, like speaking to groups and shepherding others.

But you know what? God has led me to green pastures! I've had to lean more on God, depending on Him to enlighten my mind, stretch my time, and give me joy and energy when I lack it. He's sent me helpers when I needed them and even enabled me to speak before a crowd in a steady voice. I never would have experienced God's incredible empowering if I hadn't been weaned from my comfort zone.

Today, the cows are fine. I am, too.

Father, thank You for the changes that make me grow.
—MARJORIE PARKER

THU

5

BUT JESUS OFTEN WITHDREW TO LONELY PLACES AND
PRAYED. —Luke 5:16 (NIV)

AT AGE THIRTY-TWO, as I suddenly came alive in my faith, I desperately wanted to do something of value for the kingdom of God. But at that point in my life, my days and nights were filled with the always-right-now demands of home and small boys. I bought a paperback book of devotions for those precious minutes alone. And I played (and sang, too, when no one else could hear) inspirational music tapes as I cleaned house.

Yet all this was input, and I longed for some sort of meaningful, valuable output. Then someone recommended the book *Shaping History Through Prayer & Fasting* by the late Derek Prince. With joy, I realized that I could intercede for people and situations beyond my own home and friends, and that the Lord would hear me. I could actually be helping the world from my kitchen table, simply by asking my Father in faith.

Today is the fifty-third National Day of Prayer. It's a grand moment to meet with friends or your church family to intercede earnestly for our nation and its leaders, a God-blessed time when He listens for us. But if all you have today is you, take a moment, seize the day, intercede anyway. Your prayer makes a difference—in wonderful ways you may never know.

Dear Lord, hear my prayers for our nation this day. Hear our prayers whether we pray in large groups or one by one. Hear and answer.
—ROBERTA ROGERS

FRI
6

THE THINGS WHICH ARE SEEN ARE TEMPORAL; BUT THE THINGS WHICH ARE NOT SEEN ARE ETERNAL.
—*II Corinthians 4:18*

MOST OF THE pictures I have of myself as a child are stiff-backed Polaroids—the kind that were such a novelty in the early sixties when I was growing up. I still remember the excitement of watching one of these photos come into being. Take the picture, pull the film out, then wait one minute and peel away the protective paper.

I have several of these old Polaroid shots on my office bulletin board today, as do a number of my neighbors here at Guideposts who are about my age. Looking up from my computer, my eye usually comes to rest on a shot from 1966—the date is helpfully printed on the photo's white margin—of my mother and me in our backyard in Virginia. The photo has aged over the years, and the trees and grass around us are now so dark we look like we're underwater. The shots on my neighbors' walls and bulletin boards have the same greenish look to them.

I feel about these old Polaroids the way I suspect people born a little before me must feel about the black-and-white shots that have partially rescued the details of their own childhoods. The imperfections are part of their magic—a reminder that nothing lasts completely, except through the One Who saves and preserves all things perfectly.

Thank You, Lord, for the mementos that remind me of where I've been, and for the hope of heaven that keeps me going.
—PTOLEMY TOMPKINS

SAT
7

EVEN YOUTHS GROW TIRED AND WEARY, AND YOUNG MEN STUMBLE AND FALL; BUT THOSE WHO HOPE IN THE LORD WILL RENEW THEIR STRENGTH. . . .
—*Isaiah 40:30–31 (NIV)*

IT WAS EVERY ring bearer's worst nightmare.

"This is the wrong ring!" my grandfather whispered to his bride.

My fellow ring bearer and I looked at each other in shock. We had somehow switched our rings before the ceremony—thus failing at our sole duty. Nevertheless, my grandfather and his bride-to-be ignored our mistake and carried on.

The wedding itself was the culmination of a great love story. For years, my grandparents were best friends with the Rouses, another elderly couple that lived two doors away. When my grandmother and Mr. Rouse died of Alzheimer's just one day apart, my grandfather and Mrs. Rouse supported each other.

And as the months passed, the friendship grew deeper. At age eighty, they took up square dancing and memorized hundreds of calls. At a point when many would consider themselves to be just about done living, they were just getting started. It wasn't long before they announced that they were engaged to be married!

Several years later, they're still alive and in love. My grandfather competes on the national level in the Senior Olympics and, at the age of eighty-four, he lifts weights every day. He and my new grandmother teach Sunday school every week and keep the whole family in touch through e-mail.

I hope that when I get to be eighty-four I will be living half the life they do. And at the very least that I can be as understanding as they were of two ring bearers' mistakes.

God, thank You that we don't have to stop living until the day You call us home. —JOSHUA SUNDQUIST

SUN 8

ADAM CALLED HIS WIFE'S NAME EVE; BECAUSE SHE WAS THE MOTHER OF ALL LIVING. —*Genesis 3:20*

WHAT TO GET my wife Carol for Mother's Day? There was a book she wanted and a CD. The boys had made cards . . . but it'd be nice to show her how much I appreciate all that she does: the cooking, the carpooling, the shopping, supervising the homework, arranging the doctors' appointments and music lessons.

"Take the day off," I said. "Enjoy yourself."

"Really?"

"Sure. We'll be fine."

That Sunday Timothy and I did the week's grocery shopping and got dinner ready, and I supervised his homework. In the late afternoon I took him to his soccer game and brought him home. But just as we pulled into the driveway, he frowned. "Dad, I think I left my sweatshirt back at the field."

"Are you sure?"

He nodded gravely.

An hour later we returned home after searching the field in the waning light.

"Where have you been?" Carol asked.

"A little detour," I said. How to explain that the dirty sweatshirt on her son's back was part of her present? "I guess I found out how complicated your days really are," I said. "Happy Mother's Day!"

God, help me remember how much work it takes to be a mother.
—RICK HAMLIN

MON

9

AND THEIR SOUL SHALL BE AS A WATERED GARDEN;
AND THEY SHALL NOT SORROW ANY MORE AT ALL.
—Jeremiah 31:12

I AM ROMANCING the earth, cultivating, planting and coaxing from it the greening of this plot of land we call home. Running my fingers through the soil is a therapeutic balm on my heart, hurting from looking around and not finding the lanky bent-over figure of my husband weeding the beds or stretching tall to snip shaggy whiskers from the hedges round about.

Raised on the fertile plains of Canada, John knew how to woo the earth into a good harvest. Tomatoes, picked warm from the sun and sliced right into a lunchtime sandwich; peaches, persimmons and bunches of grapes, which he would preserve into jams and jellies and present as a love gift to me, his city-bred girl, who didn't know one end of a canning jar from the other. His memory lingers in the garden and is as strong and firm as each rock he laboriously moved to form the steps I tread on every day while he rejoices with his Lord in heaven. But this is a new adventure for me.

I probe and twist my tools around to yank up endless roots of crab grass that together with the ants, I am convinced, are inheriting the earth, at least in my backyard. I find nutrients carefully stacked in the garage: bone meal, citrus, avocado and camellia food. All the good stuff that makes things grow. I toss it around with the thought, *What's nourishing my soul today?*

Now I am planting a bed of flowers. Soft colors, gentle on the eye. Lavender, pink and creamy white, named *yesterday, today* and *tomorrow.*

How grateful I am for all my yesterdays. I will take pleasure in the moments of today and, blessed Lord, I rejoice in the hope of whatever is Your perfect plan for each of my tomorrows. —FAY ANGUS

TUE **10** *AND WHAT I SAY UNTO YOU I SAY UNTO ALL, WATCH.*
—Mark 13:37

"OH, LOOK," my mother said, "I think I see a deer up in the woods."

My stepfather Herb and I looked in the direction she was pointing. The three of us were on a driving tour of Arizona after a memorable visit to the Grand Canyon. On this day, we were braving the steep roads and hairpin turns of the White Mountains.

"Oh, Herb, over there, isn't that some kind of hawk?" my mother said. "Beyond those trees, could that be a coyote?"

"Gosh, Bebe," I finally said to my mother, who usually spent extended driving time listening to tapes or reading out loud from the newspaper, "where did this new interest in the great outdoors come from?"

"Well, surely you saw that sign when we started up the mountain," she answered, still peering out the window. "You know: WATCH FOR WILD ANIMALS."

I caught Herb's eye in the rearview mirror from my place in the backseat and giggled.

"I'm sure that was a coyote," my mother was saying.

Of course, the sign was meant as a warning for drivers, but my mother had turned it into an opportunity. I thought about some of the ways I could do the same.

I might respond to YIELD by resisting the urge to score a point in every conversation and listening more thoughtfully to the views of others. I could turn DRIVE CAREFULLY into a challenge to care for each fellow traveler I came across. SLOW could remind me to take time to enjoy the scenery as I pass through the seasons, and STOP might prompt me to put a halt to negative thoughts and useless worries.

Maybe Mother was the only one among us who saw where the sign was really pointing. I didn't know if I would ever pass through the White Mountains again, so I set my gaze on the deep woods that rimmed the road, watching for wild animals, too.

Father, as I pass through this world of wonder, let me watch for the signs that point me to You. —PAM KIDD

WED

11

BUT IF ANY OF YOU LACKS WISDOM, LET HIM ASK OF GOD, WHO GIVES TO ALL MEN GENEROUSLY AND WITHOUT REPROACH, AND IT WILL BE GIVEN TO HIM.
—*James 1:5 (NAS)*

RECENTLY I TRAVELED with members of our church to work for ten days in an orphanage in the high, remote mountains of Guatemala. The orphanage is primitive and has many needs. Most of the orphans had no mattresses to sleep on, so we pooled our resources and bought twenty new bunk beds and mattresses.

There was one problem, however. The bunks had to be rounded up from many small stores sprinkled across Guatemala, collected at a central place and then trucked to the orphanage up steep, mountainous roads. On the day before we were to return to Texas, the beds had still not arrived. So I began to do something that I sometimes neglect: I began to pray.

As the sun set on our final day in Guatemala, I watched the orphans eat their meager supper and prepare for another night of sleep without their new beds. I felt defeated. Then I heard the blare of a truck's air horn. Rushing to the orphanage gate, I stood in the glare of the headlights of a large delivery van from Guatemala City. Against all odds, the beds had arrived!

We stayed up all night assembling the bunk beds. As the new day dawned, we were tightening the last bolts and positioning the mattresses in place. We were physically exhausted, but our faith and our spirits had been renewed.

Father, may I not doubt Your ability to answer my deepest prayers in Your way and for Your purposes. Amen. —SCOTT WALKER

THU

12

But remember the Lord your God, for it is he who gives you the ability to produce wealth, and so confirms his covenant, which he swore to your forefathers, as it is today.
—*Deuteronomy 8:18 (NIV)*

WHEN I PICKED UP my six-year-old daughter from school, she was jumping around like a pogo stick. "Hey, kiddo," I said. "What's up with you?"

"Mommy, look!" Katherine showed me two quarters. "Nicholas *paid* me."

Boy? Money? My rather gullible daughter? All my systems went to red alert. "Paid you to do *what?*"

"Make paint for him."

"What did you use to make the paint?" I was suspicious, but then I still can't get the glue Katherine made from Play-Doh, wax and something else off one of the porch chairs.

"Just rocks and dirt." My daughter did a little hopping dance around me. "And he liked it so much that he *paid* me."

I recalled the first time I had made money. I was five, and I pulled up half my mother's flower garden and went around the neighborhood, selling the flowers (dirt, roots and all) from my little red wagon for a penny each. I had made about thirty cents before Mom caught up with me. Replanting flowers, by the way, is a lot harder than selling them.

"Good work, honey. So what are you going to buy with your quarters?" I could stop on the way home and let her get a treat for herself.

"I'm giving them to God at church," Katherine said. At my surprised look, she added, "The rocks and dirt are His, Mommy."

Heavenly Father, never let me forget that You are the source of all bounties and blessings. —REBECCA KELLY

FRI

13

Your Father knoweth what things ye have need of. . . . —*Matthew 6:8*

"WOW, BROCK! You couldn't have chosen a worse time to make a career move," one of my friends had said. His words hung over me like a dark cloud as I sat in my new office and tried to organize my desk.

God, I prayed, *surely I haven't made a terrible mistake*. The problem wasn't with the new company. It had a good reputation for service, and my job would allow me to concentrate on investment management, my area of expertise. The problem was with me.

My move happened to coincide with the most difficult time of my life. My wife and I were divorcing after less than two years of marriage. We had been in counseling from the beginning, yet even the counselor said it was time to go our separate ways. Now the pain of a failed marriage, the separation from my little boy Harrison and an endless maze of legal entanglements seemed more than I could bear. I was having a hard time just showing up for work.

That day Rob, my boss, asked me to lunch. As he slid into the booth, he said, "Don't worry about any pressure from us. Just get yourself through this. I'm behind you one hundred percent."

A week later, a note from Terry, the CEO, landed on my desk. "I know this is a tough time for you," he wrote, "but you will get through this and find happiness again. In the meantime, let me know what I can do for you."

Then a short while later another note came, this time from Ed, the executive vice president: "I know that you've gone through some difficult challenges, and I want to encourage you."

By then I was getting the message. The word from God was loud and clear: *I'm behind you one hundred percent*. He couldn't have chosen a better time to make His move.

Thank You, Father, for bringing me to a place where service is a priority, even when I'm the one being served. —BROCK KIDD

SAT

14

DON'T LET ANYONE LOOK DOWN ON YOU BECAUSE YOU ARE YOUNG. . . . —I Timothy 4:12 (NIV)

SOME OF THE KIDS at our church festival were "doing nails." At a table lined with colorful bottles sat Katie, my friend's granddaughter—without a customer. *I'll do her a favor*, I thought, and approached the booth. I glanced at Katie's garish blue-glitter nails before tentatively offering my hand for a manicure. "I'm a terrible biter, so you won't be able to do much."

"I'll fix them for you," Katie said in that way young people have of thinking everything's so easy.

I watched as she smoothed the rough edges with an emery board. "Did you ever try nail polish?" she asked.

Of course I had. "I never could get the knack," I allowed.

"I'll show you how, no problem. Pick a color." I chose a respectable burgundy. Katie used slow, smooth strokes from cuticle to tip: up one side, then the other, and a final stroke up the middle. I liked the results: immediate compliments! Every time I put a finger to my lips, I drew it back. The color deterred me. When Katie's handiwork chipped away, I bought some red polish. My technique improved as I practiced Katie's method.

Months later I ran into Katie at church. I flashed my fingers. "You did me a big favor." And it had all seemed so easy.

Lord, may I always be open to learning new lessons from the younger generation. —EVELYN BENCE

READER'S ROOM

I AM THANKFUL that I have lived in a small rural community all of my seventy-seven years. I raised four children here, and all love to come back and visit their hometown. I now live on the edge of town with farm fields around me. I love to watch the first green shoots of corn or beans breaking through the rich black soil in the spring and then watch the bountiful harvest that God has provided in the fall. My small town will be 125 years old this year, and my church will celebrate its 135th anniversary. So I know that it was people of faith who built the town.

—*Rosemary Hoberg, Sacred Heart, Minnesota*

SUN

15

THE WIND BLOWETH WHERE IT LISTETH, AND THOU HEAREST THE SOUND THEREOF, BUT CANST NOT TELL WHENCE IT COMETH, AND WHITHER IT GOETH: SO IS EVERY ONE THAT IS BORN OF THE SPIRIT. —John 3:8

EVERY YEAR my spouse and I gather for a week with some old Princeton, New Jersey, church friends on North Carolina's Outer Banks. The reunioneers are now scattered all over the country, so it's great fun renewing old ties and reminiscing.

One of our group, Steve from West Virginia, is a scientist who understands more about how the universe works than just about anybody I know. Right now he is studying tornadoes. He has also spent time investigating ocean wave action and hurricanes. In other words, he knows a lot about the wind. So when Shirley and I joined Steve and his wife Marge on a trip to Kitty Hawk one day, we were in the company of a guy who grasps, more than most, the challenges the Wright brothers faced when they tried to get a motorized plane airborne in 1903.

One of the exhibits in the museum was a facsimile of the wind tunnel the brothers built to help them understand "adverse yaw," the phenomenon that puzzlingly caused their plane to dip left when the pilot raised the left wing. "Their rudimentary wind tunnel was flawed," Steve explained, "but no one had ever built anything like it before, and it proved to be the key to their success."

The wind has been a mystery for humankind since time immemorial. Even Jesus mentioned its unpredictability when He tried to explain being born again to a confused Nicodemus: "The wind bloweth where it listeth, and thou hearest the sound thereof, but canst not tell whence it cometh, and whither it goeth." In other words, the Holy Spirit, like the wind, is unfathomable, ungraspable and unmeritable, but as real as the heart it touches.

Give us faith, Lord, to believe in things unseen,
To trust in the life-giving words of the Nazarene.
                                                —FRED BAUER

MON

16

In every thing by prayer and supplication with thanksgiving let your requests be made known unto God. —Philippians 4:6

IT SOUNDED LIKE a sick animal had taken up residence under the hood of my car that Monday morning when I started it up. *Oh no.* For a kid from Detroit, I know pathetically little about the mechanics of an automobile.

I stared at the incomprehensible array of gauges and indicator lights in the dashboard. Nothing seemed awry. Just this racket emanating from the engine. *Maybe it'll go away,* I thought desperately.

As I drove to the store to pick up a few things, I found myself begging God, "Look, I don't want to take the car into the shop this week. *Please* help me out." As soon as I said the prayer, I was embarrassed by the smallness of it. What kind of problem was this to bother the Creator of the universe with? I decided that if the engine was still bellowing when I started up the car again, I'd bite the bullet and take it in to the shop.

I bought the things I came for and returned to the car. I took a breath. I turned the key.

Ffrrumphakatatata . . .

I leaned my forehead against the steering wheel. *No telling what it will cost—parts, labor, tax. . . .*

"Hey!"

I looked up. A man was tapping on my windshield. "Sounds like your power steering fluid is low," he said. "Better check it out." Then he was gone.

I turned off the engine, jumped out and took a look. I located the power steering fluid reservoir and checked the level. He was right! At least, I hoped he was. I ran back inside the store and inquired about fluid. Sure enough, they had shelves of it at a price so low I found it hard to believe. A few minutes later, the engine was purring like a warm kitten.

All right, Lord, You win again. Who am I to say what prayers are important and what aren't? And thanks for the tip about the power steering stuff.
—EDWARD GRINNAN

HE LEADETH ME . . .
TO TRUST HIS VOICE

TUE

17

BUT THE SPIRIT ITSELF MAKETH INTERCESSION FOR US WITH GROANINGS WHICH CANNOT BE UTTERED.
—Romans 8:26

SEVERAL YEARS AGO, I found myself drawn to an exquisite quilt in an antiques shop. It was hand-pieced from cheery feed sack fabrics in the Grandmother's Flower Garden pattern. Problem was, someone had machine-quilted it in a contemporary zigzag stitch.

I purchased it anyway and brought it to show a co-worker who had just completed a quilting class. Sherry loved it immediately and volunteered to redo it. "Whoever originally pieced this quilt was a true artist," she told me. "Let me pick out that machine quilting and quilt it by hand for you." But it seemed too big a job to ask of anyone, so I brought the quilt home and stashed it in an armoire.

Soon after, Sherry went through some devastating experiences and had to give up her nursing career. One evening as I was dusting the armoire, the quilt nearly jumped off the shelf. A thought came to me: *Give Sherry that quilt.*

I gave the quilt to Sherry without even beginning to understand God's purpose. Years later, her daughter told me about the role in which that quilt had served. During sleepless nights when Sherry's problems loomed so large and she couldn't imagine a new beginning, she would pick out those contrary zigzag stitches and replace them with her perfect hand quilting. And she prayed (for the first time in her life) that she would be restored, just as the quilt would be. "If it hadn't been for that quilt and your friendship, my mother would have surely committed suicide," her daughter said.

Today, Sherry believes in God, is active in church and is building a new life—stitch by simple stitch.

Oh, Lord, sometimes Your nudges seem so small that I overlook them. Help me always to follow Your direction. —ROBERTA MESSNER

WED

18

THERE IS ONE GLORY OF THE SUN, AND ANOTHER GLORY OF THE MOON, AND ANOTHER GLORY OF THE STARS: FOR ONE STAR DIFFERETH FROM ANOTHER STAR IN GLORY. —*I Corinthians 15:41*

FIVE-YEAR-OLD MARY loves made-up stories about a little girl named Francesca who's very much like her. Francesca's life, like Mary's, revolves around her ballet classes and her friends. When she's not in school, Francesca is presiding over the Ballerina Princess Club, where her friends dress up, play games, dance and eat sweets.

Our Mary is an extrovert. Friendships are the air she breathes. She could no more go without play dates than she could go without food. She's at her happiest in ballet class, dancing and sharing giggles with a half-dozen other girls. And in that she's different from the rest of us Attaways. Athletic and outgoing, she seems to have been dropped from space into our family of bookish introverts.

And introverts we are. I've been known to walk around the block in the morning to avoid chatty colleagues in the office elevator, I find parties a real challenge, and I'm rarely found gabbing on the phone. Julia is not so bad, but when we were dating, she did ask me to come over one evening with a book to see if I could read quietly without disturbing her. Our daughter Elizabeth loves to do math problems and read, while John's favorite recreation is playing alone while listening to story tapes. We're not sure yet about Maggie.

Mary is a great joy, with her beautiful, bright smile and her energy and enthusiasm. But she's also a puzzle. Raising her requires us to stretch our minds to understand someone whose gifts and needs are very different from our own. Maybe that's why God put her in our family.

Lord, help me to value the variety of gifts that You give to those around me. And thank You for our Mary. —ANDREW ATTAWAY

THU
19
Tribulation worketh patience; And patience,
experience; and experience, hope.
—*Romans 5:3–4*

ONE NICE THING about getting old is that I no longer panic when I hear dire prophecies of the future. I've seen too many of them come and go.

Books on "the coming economic crash" have come out in every decade of my life. "Prophets" said that we would run out of food by the turn of the millennium, but instead the number-one health problem in America is obesity. George Orwell's totalitarian world of *1984* turned out to be one of the happiest years of my life. Then there was the "Jupiter Effect" of 1976, when planets were supposed to align, creating high tides and earthquakes. It didn't happen.

Now we are told that the earth has a fever, that asteroids are missing us by millimeters and that genetic engineering will give our grandkids two heads.

As my college students say, "Whatever." I've watched dangerous trends suddenly reverse. Terrible threats dissolve into thin air. New factors come into the equation. People change. Life goes on.

I remind myself that Jesus lived in a totalitarian world of mass slavery and sickness, when the life expectancy was less than forty years. On this ocean of woe, He launched His Ship of Zion, the church.

Prophecies that leave God out of the picture are always suspect with me. In every generation God has provided saviors: a Joseph, a Moses, an Esther. Perhaps someone reading these words will be the one to solve global warming or rekindle the economy. Maybe you, like Esther, have come to the kingdom for just such a time as this.

God, help me not to be paralyzed by fear, but fired into action.
—DANIEL SCHANTZ

FRI

20

WHEN I WAS A CHILD. . . . I REASONED LIKE A
CHILD. . . . I AM DONE WITH CHILDISH WAYS.
—*I Corinthians 13:11 (AMP)*

FOR NEARLY twenty-five years, I fought a deep-seated fear of being abandoned. When Jerry, my first husband, went on a business trip, I experienced overwhelming dread. When we had separate errands to run at the mall, I was reluctant to let him out of my sight. Then, in 1982, we discovered that Jerry had a brain tumor. Fear of being left alone cemented itself inside me for seven horrific months. But victory over my fear came two months before Jerry actually left this life.

It began when Jerry spoke two simple sentences: "Your father didn't want to leave you, Marion. He loved you." My father died suddenly when I was twenty-two months old. As I child, I pored over pictures of him in old family scrapbooks. My mother told me how much he loved me, carrying me around on a pillow for the neighbors to see when I was only a week old. Even so, I felt an ache in my soul when I saw my friends with their daddies.

"Marion," Jerry continued, "let me hear you say *Daddy*." I couldn't make myself do it. He kept encouraging me, and finally I whispered the word. Then I said it aloud, over and over. Suddenly, I experienced emotionally what I'd always known rationally: My father hadn't abandoned me. And Jerry didn't want to leave me either.

I was lonely after Jerry's death, but without bitterness. Jerry had been taken from me; he hadn't deserted me. God still had a plan for my life. And when I married Gene, I knew that loneliness wasn't to be a part of it.

Even all grown up, I need You, my Father. Amen.

—MARION BOND WEST

SAT

21

"WHOEVER WELCOMES A LITTLE CHILD LIKE THIS IN
MY NAME WELCOMES ME." —*Matthew 18:5 (NIV)*

ON A TRIP to Washington state, my husband Don and I stopped at Fort Columbia. The fort was built in 1904 and served as a coastal defense unit during World Wars I and II. The ocean view was breathtaking! We also prowled around an underground ammunition storage area.

We were going to skip the second bunker, but a teenage girl called from the entrance, "Were you going to look in here? My friend and I want to go in, but it looks scary. We'd feel safer with adults along." So we became tour guides, reassuring the girls about safety and giving a minilesson on coast-watching during World War II.

In 2001, I worked on a project sponsored by Kansas Health Foundation that asked children of all ages one question: "What do you need from adults to grow up healthy and safe?" More than three thousand kids responded, most talking about the crucial role parents, teachers and other adults have played in their lives.

Amy, seventeen, wrote, "I believe it is up to the older, much wiser people to lead me in my search for a safe, healthy life." Joe, twelve, urged parents to get tough: "Kids need to be nagged to do their homework, so they can get better grades." Michael, fourteen, expressed a need shared by almost every young writer: "All of the other things would be nice, but love is better."

My own children are grown, but I can make a positive difference in my grandchildren's lives as well as the lives of other children in my life. I can take time to listen, to understand and love. After all, two vacationing teenagers showed me that it isn't all that difficult!

Loving God, help me reach out in love to the children who share my world. —PENNEY SCHWAB

SUN
22
THE LORD GOD IS MY STRENGTH, AND HE WILL MAKE MY FEET LIKE HINDS' FEET, AND HE WILL MAKE ME TO WALK UPON MINE HIGH PLACES. . . .
—*Habakkuk 3:19*

I'VE NEVER enjoyed running; I was always the slowest kid in my physical education class and I dreaded the mile run. So I was surprised when my boyfriend Travis suggested I train for a seven-kilometer footrace in San Francisco. I was even more surprised to find myself accepting the challenge.

I made friends with the treadmills at the gym, and soon I was going much farther than the old dreaded mile. I almost enjoyed the exercise, but I wasn't so sure about the race.

The morning of the race was cold and unusually clear; I had to bounce around in the starting chute in order to keep warm. The race began, and I was carried along by the crowd for the first half-mile or so, until the pack spread out along the course. On I ran, past Fisherman's Wharf and up the torturous hill into Fort Mason. My knees ached and my heart was pounding.

Then I realized I'd run most of the way looking at the ground, as if I were on my trusty treadmill. I looked up from the pavement, stunned by the view. The ocean was just steps away, the sky was an incredible blue, the Golden Gate Bridge was a beautiful deep orange-red. The race was a gift. Finishing the race was not about being the slowpoke in gym class or impressing Travis; it was about challenging the body God gave me to do new things, about taking time to play in this beautiful world.

Travis met me at the finish line, as he promised. "Will you run again next year?" he asked as I collapsed into the fragrant grass on the sidelines.

"Try and stop me," I answered.

Lord, today I rejoice in this body and this world You have given us! Strengthen me as I try to take better care of both! —KJERSTIN EASTON

MON
23

I WENT BY THE FIELD OF THE SLOTHFUL. . . .
—*Proverbs 24:30*

I'D LIKE TO put in a good word for the sloth, the South American mammal that hangs back-downward from the branches of trees. It draws its name from its slowness, its indolence, but my guide in Panama, where I saw a sloth high up in a tree, said it could move with surprising alacrity from branch to branch. He said that sloths rarely descend to the ground because the peculiar conformation of their feet made them crawl with difficulty. "They're nocturnal," he said, "and are seldom seen."

But I saw one a week later. I was canoeing in a freshwater lagoon near the muddy Amazon River when a little Indian girl and her brother paddled up. The boy extended an iguana while the girl held out her hand, begging. I was astounded when I saw what turned out to be a shaggy-haired sloth hugging her waist with all four of its limbs. It turned its small round head toward me, its brown eyes looking over a snub nose. The head turned as though on a swivel—it could look either way, to the front or to the back. It reached out a paw. I offered my hand and the sloth grabbed hold of an index finger. It grasped tightly with its hooklike toes. We stared at each other. In that moment I was mesmerized. The surprising geniality of this sloth gave me visions of St. Francis, surrounded by his brothers and sisters of the forest. I felt a communion with all other animals, with nature, with God.

When, reluctantly, the sloth let go of my finger, I gave a dollar to the boy and five dollars to the girl. She'll never know what a moment her sloth had created in me.

Bless that sloth, Father, and all its fellow creatures of the jungle.
—VAN VARNER

TUE
24

FOR WHATEVER WAS WRITTEN IN EARLIER TIMES WAS WRITTEN FOR OUR INSTRUCTION. . . .
—*Romans 15:4 (NAS)*

MY SISTER Becky enjoys a measure of local fame for the dishes she brings to social gatherings. The other evening, as we sat around the table after eating big bowls of Mom's homemade vegetable soup, we got to talking about recipes.

Becky told us about the time a co-worker asked her for her Never-Fail Fudge recipe. Becky gave it gladly, stressing the importance of following the directions to the letter. A few days later, the woman told Becky that she had tried the recipe and was disappointed with the results. Becky was amazed. Never-Fail Fudge had truly never failed to turn out perfectly for her.

"Did you boil the chocolate for exactly six minutes?" she asked.

"Yes," the woman began, nodding. Then she stopped. "Well, somebody came to the door and I had to turn it off for a second, but I timed it carefully and I'm sure it was six minutes in all."

"Hmm. And you didn't use a beater, right?"

"No . . . well," her friend confessed, "just for a few seconds. I just couldn't believe you could mix it well enough just stirring it!"

"I can understand that," Becky said agreeably. She was beginning to get the picture. But the woman never did.

I only half-heard the end of Becky's story as I thought about how often I'm disappointed because I've failed to follow some simple direction for God's never-fail recipe for life, like "Trust in the Lord . . . and lean not on your own understanding" (Proverbs 3:5, NIV). Or "Be content with what you have" (Hebrews 13:5, NIV). Or "Humble yourselves before the Lord, and he will lift you up" (James 4:10, NIV). Such simple directions that, when not followed, can ruin a moment, a day, a life.

Lord, help me get the picture. When I'm disappointed with life, help me see which of your directions I've failed to follow. —LUCILE ALLEN

WED
25
GIVE THEREFORE THY SERVANT AN UNDERSTANDING HEART . . . THAT I MAY DISCERN BETWEEN GOOD AND BAD. . . . —I Kings 3:9

WHEN IT COMES to home repairs, I am no handyman. Yet I always want to try, just to see if I can help. When the water from our kitchen faucet slowed to a trickle, I was determined to do something.

I purchased replacement parts, studied the instructions and disassembled the unit. Slowly and carefully I inserted the new parts. Everything fit. I was elated. Then I turned on the faucet. Instead of a trickle, no water flowed at all.

The plumber arrived and disappeared into the cellar. After a long while, he called me downstairs, and he explained that the pipes were clogged and would have to be replaced. He even had the nerve to smile as he presented the bill: $2,366. I swallowed hard.

"Oscar," my wife Ruby said to me, "just tell me when something needs to be fixed. I'd rather hire an expert than have you botch things up."

Hiding my hurt, I returned to the study.

Two days later the new pipes were in and water from the faucet flowed instantly, easily, clearly. In the meantime I had balanced the checkbook, sent two letters to friends and done some work in the yard.

"You're such a help," Ruby observed.

"Thank you," I replied. I have my own gifts to contribute, as long as I leave certain chores to seasoned professionals.

Heavenly Father, thank You for the gifts You have given me—and others. Help me to use mine in wise ways. —OSCAR GREENE

THU

26

HE LEADETH ME BESIDE THE STILL WATERS.
—*Psalm 23:2*

LAST NIGHT, sitting on our deck, we counted six deer grazing on the mountainside facing our house. The deer, oblivious to our eyes, allowed us to watch them for a good length of time. As we sat silently in the stillness of the early evening, listening to the sounds of the little stream that runs along the edge of the mountain, I thought of that wonderful deer image in Psalm 42. Then a loud truck rumbled down the road between our house and the mountain, and the animals scampered for cover before they could reach the creek.

Like the deer longing for flowing streams, my soul has always had a deep, insatiable longing for the flowing, yet unchanging presence of God. There have been times in my life when I've known myself to be in the presence of that great Mystery, and I have drunk deeply from those clear waters. More often, though, I'm painfully aware of having let the busy rumble of life divert my awareness from the living waters of the Divine Presence. But always, always, the thirst comes back, leading me to return to the only Source that truly satisfies my soul's deepest longing.

Perhaps in the clamor of my days I could stop now and then, even for a brief moment, to still my soul and take note of God's presence, which is always "closer than breathing, nearer than hands and feet." Will you join me in doing that now?

Loving God, help me to get quiet inside for just this moment, so that I may drink from Your stream of living waters.
—MARILYN MORGAN KING

FRI
27

COUNT IT ALL JOY, MY BRETHREN, WHEN YOU MEET VARIOUS TRIALS. —James 1:2 (RSV)

MANY YEARS AGO my husband Larry's mother Enid came to visit us in Ohio for a much-needed vacation. Larry and I had made numerous plans for entertaining her—trips to museums, galleries, shopping centers, points of interest such as Serpent Mound, an ancient Indian earthworks. Instead, we spent the week confined to our home during torrential rains that dropped fifteen inches during seven days, a record for that area. Rivers overflowed; roads all around us closed due to flooding. At one point we couldn't even get out of our own driveway.

At the end of the visit, as we traveled toward the airport via numerous detours around still-flooded highways, I apologized to Enid for her disastrous vacation.

She smiled. "I came determined to have a good time no matter what happened, and so I have. If it had to rain, then I'm glad it was so memorable."

I've been helped many times since then by the memory of her positive attitude. Such as one year, when the pump on our well quit up at our cabin in the mountains when we had twelve guests under our roof. I started to panic, but Larry said, "Relax. We can carry drinking water from the lodge, and we can flush the toilet with water from the river."

Okay, Enid, I whispered to the air, *looks like we're going to have a memorable weekend.*

The pump didn't change, but my attitude did. And guess what? We had a good time.

Lord, please help me count as joy any challenge today that comes my way. Amen. —MADGE HARRAH

SAT
28

AND WHOSOEVER WILL, LET HIM TAKE THE WATER OF LIFE FREELY. —Revelation 22:17

THE SUN WAS barely up in the sky when the early birds arrived at our yard sale. A woman and her daughter looked at the chipped Mickey Mouse cookie jar and then stopped in front of the washing machine. FREE. IT WORKS read the sign taped to it.

"What's wrong with it?" the woman asked, opening the lid and look-ing in.

"Nothing," I said. "We just got a new one."

"Why get a new one if this one's okay?"

"We got the energy-saving kind," I said. There had been a great sale at the appliance store. We had been given our old machine by a friend years ago, and it seemed only right to pass it on to someone else.

"Oh," the woman said, "I've never gotten anything worth anything for free." This same sentiment, with slight variations, was repeated throughout the morning.

At lunchtime we looked over the yard at what was left. "I don't want to have to load that onto my truck and bring it to the dump," my hus-band said, nodding toward the washing machine.

"Put twenty-five dollars on it," I said.

My husband finished his sandwich, threw out the FREE sign and put up a new one: $25. Within the hour, a man in a red truck drove up. "Works?" he yelled. I nodded. The man stopped the truck, got out and took a closer look. "Would you take ten dollars for it?"

"Sure," my husband said. "Actually, if you can use it, I could let you have it for nothing."

"Really?" the man said. "This is going to make my wife's day. She's been complaining about going to the Laundromat."

"No problem," my husband said.

As the man pulled away, my husband handed me the $25 sign. "Sometimes you have to put a price on things to show their value."

Lord, please keep my heart open to the gifts that You give me. Especially those clearly marked FREE. —SABRA CIANCANELLI

SUN
29

REMEMBER, O LORD, WHAT IS COME UPON US: CONSIDER, AND BEHOLD OUR REPROACH.
—*Lamentations 5:1*

AWHILE BACK my college class reunion was scheduled on Memorial Day weekend. My husband had never been in my hometown since we've been married, so I was eager to show him around.

We first drove to our former eighty-acre property, now a park. At the entrance I told the attendant my family's name, adding, "These grounds used to be ours." I expected instant respect or at least some recognition. "That so?" he said. "You still need a pass."

Our next stop, the newspaper office. I asked for the editor and was introduced to a nice young woman. "Your plant printed the college annual when I was its editor," I said. "That so?" she answered. "That was quite a bit before my time."

On Sunday we visited the church where our family had been pillars in the congregation. Before entering the building, I bragged to Lawrence, "Dad and Mom and I helped in its construction, even nailing and painting. We all volunteered to save the expense."

Inside a greeter said, "Welcome!" He pinned "Visitor" tags on our lapels "to make sure our people will show you around," as he put it. *I know more about this place than you ever will*, I thought. Then I thought again. These are the people who'd taken up where we left off. If it hadn't been for them the church would be in ruins, our old place an overgrown jungle and my old office an empty shell.

"Thanks," I said to the greeter, really meaning it. Later I told Lawrence, "They've done well with the old town."

Father, I must remember that I'm always somebody in Your sight.
—Isabel Wolseley

MON

30

"Honor . . . your mother." —*Exodus* 20:12 *(NIV)*

I watched the miles click by on the odometer. The 250-mile trip to Mother's seemed to get longer every time I drove it. But I knew why. It was because it wasn't Mother I would find at the end of this long drive; it was her grave.

If only I lived closer, I thought as I turned off the expressway. With my sister living in Florida and many of Mother's friends aged or deceased, I knew the chances of anyone visiting Mother's grave were slim. How I longed for her to have fresh flowers and an occasional friendly voice!

I parked my car and walked toward the grave, carrying a bouquet of daisies. *What's that?* I thought. I got closer and stopped, amazed—and then amused. A huge, perfect ear of corn rested on top of Mother's headstone.

I laughed aloud. Mother's love of fresh sweet corn was legendary. She gave it to her friends; she made it for her friends; she ate it and called her friends to regale them with how good it had been. Someone had been here. Perhaps many someones.

I remembered my friend telling me about leaving stones on her relatives' graves, a sign of both remembrance and respect. Reverently, I placed my bouquet next to the corn. And awhile later, when I turned the car around for the long drive home, I felt a little better about Mother's final resting place. And about the friends who visited her there.

When my loved ones are out of my care, Lord, I'll remember that they're never out of Yours! —MARY LOU CARNEY

TUE
31

HE THAT BELIEVETH ON ME, AS THE SCRIPTURE HATH SAID, OUT OF HIS BELLY SHALL FLOW RIVERS OF LIVING WATER. —*John 7:38*

GROWING UP in the West, I knew about the Mississippi River, but I had never actually seen it. Still, the name held a certain Huck Finn appeal for me. I had always thought of it as a Southern river, so imagine my surprise when we moved to Minnesota and I learned that the "Mighty Mississippi" springs from a secluded northern Minnesota lake!

This I had to see. So on my birthday, my husband, my mother and I drove to Lake Itasca, first called Antler Lake by the Chippewa Indians. In fact, it was a Chippewa chief who ended the centuries-long search for the river's source by guiding Henry Schoolcraft to it in 1832. Schoolcraft strung together parts of two Latin words, *veritas caput*, meaning "true head," to create the name Itasca. From this hidden forested place, the Mississippi flows approximately twenty-five hundred miles to the Gulf of Mexico, bordering ten states and expanding to more than a mile in width. A drop of water takes sixty days to reach the balmy Gulf.

It was with a sense of awe that we hiked the path to the headwaters. There, over a smooth rock walkway just nine steps in length, clear water spilled from the lake to form a small creek. A hewn log a few feet away beckoned us to cross, and we did. I walked across the

Mississippi River on a log on my forty-seventh birthday! It was a good day to mark beginnings.

Remembering that experience encourages me, on days when I feel like a mere trickle of a person, when I wonder how God will ever be able to make something from my life. He took the Mississippi from shallow creek to mighty river, and He can take my trust in Him and turn it into "rivers of living water" for the good of others and the glory of His name.

O God, You are the Source of the Living Water that carries me along the course You have set for me. —CAROL KNAPP

SEEDS OF REJOICING

1 _____

2 _____

3 _____

4 _____

5 _____

6 _____

7 _____

8 _____

9 _____

10 _____

11 _____

12 _____

13 _____

14 _____

15 _____

16 _____

17 _____

18 _____

19 _____

20 _____

21 _____

22 _____

23 _____

24 _____

25 _____

26 _____

27 _____

28 _____

29 _____

30 _____

31 _____

June

Thou wilt shew me the path of life:
in thy presence is fulness of joy. . . .

—Psalm 16:11

GOD SIGHTINGS
THE BOUNTIFUL GIVER

WED

1

GIVE, AND IT SHALL BE GIVEN UNTO YOU. . . .
—*Luke 6:38*

FOR A FRIEND'S wedding, I'd agreed—with reluctance I tried to hide—to look after the groom's blind great-aunt. As I guided the old lady up the walkway to the main door of the church, I longed to be with the animated group accompanying the bride to the side entrance. What if I were stuck at the aunt's side all through the reception, too?

Once seated, however, cane safely stowed beneath the pew in front of us, the old lady turned out to be a lively companion. As we waited for the service to begin, she peppered me with questions. Was it a Gothic church? Stone! What kind of stone? Was there stained glass in the windows? Where was the pulpit located? What color was the seat cushion beneath us? Before long I was seeing the church I'd gone to for twenty years with a whole new awareness.

When someone else offered to escort the aunt to the reception, I shook my head. I wouldn't have missed her inquiring delight in the guests, the dance steps, the table settings for anything.

I wouldn't have missed the insight into God's mysterious ecology either. A very small and grudging kindness on my part had returned to me in blessing. The blind woman I'd believed I was helping had helped me to see.

Whenever I'm called on to help, Father, remind me that I can never out-give You. —ELIZABETH SHERRILL

THU

2

FOR ALL THE ANIMALS OF FIELD AND FOREST ARE MINE! . . . —*Psalm 50:10* (TLB)

"MOM, COME QUICK!" My daughter woke me by shining a flashlight in my face. It was just after 2:00 A.M., but I pulled on a robe and followed her onto the terrace. "Look," she said, shining the light up into the oak tree. "A bobcat."

There it was, stretched out lazily on a high limb, watching us with unblinking nonchalance. With pointed ears and beautifully marked brown and tan spots, it was a magnificent animal. Living as we do in the foothills of Southern California's San Gabriel Mountains, we'd had encounters with a mountain lion and a bear, but this was a first. We roamed around the garden beaming the light on it from various angles.

"Do you think it might pounce on us?" I asked.

"Not as long as we don't bother it," my daughter said. She is savvy in the ways of wildlife.

The next thing we knew a flashlight shone on us. "Everything all right?" a police officer asked. "The neighbors called about prowlers."

Katrelya laughed. "I guess we're the prowlers! Look." She pointed her light up the tree.

"How about that?" the officer said. "You want us to get it out of there for you?"

"No," my daughter replied. "These are the bobcat's mountains. We're the intruders."

Help me to remember, Lord, that mountain lions, bears, bobcats and other wildlife that sometimes go bump in the night are all a natural part of our hills and forests. —FAY ANGUS

FRI
3

LET US LOVE ONE ANOTHER, FOR LOVE COMES FROM GOD. . . . —I John 4:7 (NIV)

AFTER YEARS OF dreaming about remodeling our house, we finally knocked down the walls between our kitchen, family room and dining room. But I still have one item on my wish list: a new family table.

I want a user-friendly, sturdy table that people are drawn to, not only to eat, but to read the newspaper or have a cup of coffee or play games. I call it a family table because it's the kind of place where family "happens."

The family table of my childhood was an oblong glass table that my mother inherited from an aunt. My mother insisted it set a proper tone for our family with four rambunctious children. It was the only place where we came together regularly.

Then there was the family table we had when our children were growing up—a heavy wooden trestle table with a bench along one side so we could add people without scouring the house for chairs. Our photo albums show what happened around that table: birthday parties, pumpkin carvings, Valentine's Day dinners, science projects, love.

Now I want a family table with comfortable chairs that beckon both adults and children. I may not get my dream table for a while, so in the meantime I'm taking note of what else beckons and connects people, like our big comfy couch in front of the fireplace, a bunch of stools pulled up to the kitchen counter and, most of all, the presence of God in the words and attitudes of the people who live in our home.

Father, may Your presence bless our newly remodeled home each day.
—CAROL KUYKENDALL

SAT
4

DO I SEEK TO PLEASE MEN? FOR IF I YET PLEASED MEN, I SHOULD NOT BE THE SERVANT OF CHRIST.
—*Galatians 1:10*

"LORD, HOW DO I get myself into these things?" I asked. Trying to be the perfect employee, I'd agreed to dress up as Winnie-the-Pooh for Saturday-morning story time at the bookstore. The costume was a heavy suit with a helmetlike head and only little slits for eyes. Another employee guided me around as my "handler."

When my handler led me into the children's department, the kids who didn't run away in fear crowded around me and hugged my knees, nearly knocking me off balance.

"That's not Winnie!" one boy protested. "His fur isn't right." The boy was right. My fur was too pale, almost white, not Winnie's rich gold color.

From the sweaty confines of my suit, I heard my handler say, "That's Winnie's brother!"

"You're Winnie's brother?" the boy asked skeptically.

I nodded so furiously that I was afraid my furry head would come off. But my nod only made matters worse. Some of the kids yelled out,

"You're not Winnie?" Through my slits I could see that one was about to cry.

"No, it's Winnie!" my handler said.

I nodded vigorously again, and luckily the mother of the outspoken boy took him away.

Finally, after hugs and high-fives from little hands to big paws, I was led back to the break room. My handler laughed, saying, "I guess I was trying to please everybody—that boy by saying you were Winnie's brother and the other kids by assuring them you were Winnie."

As I gratefully removed the hot, furry, size-fifteen feet, I nodded. I'd been doing the same thing by agreeing to do a job I was clearly not suited for. From now on, I'd stick to bookselling.

God, is there someone I'm trying to please by being something I'm not? For today, let me have the courage to be myself. —LINDA NEUKRUG

SUN
5

A FLAME SETS THE MOUNTAINS ABLAZE.
—*Psalm 83:14 (NIV)*

IT WAS DAWN, and I was returning from a twenty-four-hour shift at the Missionary Ridge fire. On our way back to the Durango, Colorado, Fire and Rescue station, I stopped at the Los Ranchitos subdivision to check on the houses of three families from my church. The owners, like hundreds of others, had no idea if their homes had burned or not. I figured I would drop by on our way through town to let them know that, so far, their homes were unharmed.

One couple, Will and Barb, had parked a motor home in our church parking lot and were living there until they could either return to their home or return to the charred site where their house had once stood. When we pulled into the church parking lot, I saw several parked cars. "What's today?" asked Dave, the firefighter who had worked with me all night. "Is it Sunday already?"

"Pull in here," I said to him. "I have some good news to share." Will and Barb saw us, and Barb hugged me almost before I climbed out of our truck. Barb didn't bother to brush the black soot from her Sunday dress after she finally let go of me. "Your house is fine," I said. "We didn't lose a single home at Los Ranchitos. At least, not yet."

"I don't care," she said. "I'm just glad you're safe. We've been worried about you."

On the way back to our station, I wished that I could have shared some permanent good news with the three families, instead of just the news that their homes had survived the night. But I'd keep praying, and I was sure they would, too, during worship that morning. That's just what a church is. Not a place, not a building, but people who look after one another and care for each other even when their homes are threatened.

Dear God, thank You for my church. It's always there when I need it most.
—TIM WILLIAMS

MON
6

I HAVE SHEWED YOU KINDNESS, THAT YE WILL ALSO SHEW KINDNESS. . . . —Joshua 2:12

VAN—VAN VARNER to those of you who aren't veteran *Daily Guideposts* readers—always says that he's not a member of the Better Invitation Club. It's a moral principle, as I've come to understand, or putting the Golden Rule into practice: If someone invites you to do something, you don't ditch them because a better invitation happened to come your way.

I thought of this ten years ago when we received an invitation to Van's seventieth birthday party. What a bash it would be! Good friends gathered together to reminisce over his seven decades and cheer him on for more. "But we can't go," my wife said. We'd already promised to join several old friends at the beach that weekend. I was tempted to see if the beach trip could be rearranged, then remembered how hard it had been to schedule in the first place. Well, if anyone would understand, it would have to be Van. "Next time," I told him. "Next time," he agreed and added another of his favorite phrases: "God willing."

So for almost ten years I saved the date: June 6, 2003. This time when the invitation arrived, the decks were clear. No conflicts. Even if the president of the United States had invited us to dine, I would have refused, saying, "We're not members of the Better Invitation Club." It's a moral principle, you know, and it seems to ensure a long happy life with the very best of friends. Not to mention invitations that you'd never want to turn down . . . God willing.

Courtesy is kindness, Lord. Let me do as I would have done unto me.
—RICK HAMLIN

TUE 7

TOUCHING THE ALMIGHTY, WE CANNOT FIND HIM OUT: HE IS EXCELLENT IN POWER. . . . —Job 37:23

I WAS STANDING at an upstairs window in early June after we had moved from Alaska to Minnesota, looking out at the evening, when I saw a bright twinkle float through the air. It flashed again—and yet again. I was seeing my first firefly! I dashed outside, utterly entranced by the blinking, bobbing lights.

Since then, I've seen hundreds of these cheery nightlights winking and blinking in the Minnesota dark, and I've tried to find out something about them. Fireflies are actually beetles. And it is only the males that fly during their elaborate summer courtship. The female hides on the ground until it sees a flash pattern signaling the presence of a male of her species, and then gives a quick answering blink. There are orange-colored flashes, and double flashes, and flashes that form the letter *j*.

This amazingly intricate dance is going on around me, and all I really see is a flurry of tiny lights flitting about on a June night. There's so much I don't know about the way God puts things together in the natural world—and in my own experience.

For instance, before my husband Terry was born, his parents stopped in Spokane, Washington, on their way from Pennsylvania to Oregon because Terry's father had served on the USS *Spokane*. Why did they happen to settle there—never reaching Oregon? How was it that my father chose to take a pastorate in Spokane, moving his family from southern Idaho when I was six years old? These patterns created the possibility for Terry and me eventually to meet and begin our own version of "winking and blinking" courtship!

It's something old that I'm newly learning all the time: The intricacies of God's work in the details of life are beyond my comprehension. It only takes a blink on a summer night to remind me.

Even now, Lord, You are arranging the right patterns for me. May I respond with an answering flash of faith. —CAROL KNAPP

WED

8

AND LET US NOT BE WEARY IN WELL DOING: FOR IN DUE SEASON WE SHALL REAP, IF WE FAINT NOT.
—*Galatians 6:9*

TWO DAYS AFTER my eightieth birthday I was dining at the Silk Road Palace with my friend Daniel. After we had finished our egg drop soup and General Chan chicken, we called for the check. It came, along with the usual plate of orange slices, canned pineapple bits and, of course, two fortune cookies.

"You tell me your fortune and I'll tell you mine," Daniel said.

"Fine. You start."

"'You have great things in store.'" *Hmmm.* "What about yours?"

"'You will be successful someday.'" We both laughed. "What a time to tell me that when I have just turned eighty." I took it as a joke.

Yet somehow the fortune rattled in my mind. Just what is a successful life? How do I rate? It set me to thinking. I was rather proud of having been editor-in-chief of *Guideposts.* I never married, but my two nephews and their wives are close, as are their children, and I know I have dear friends. God has given me a strong body, strong enough to survive a stroke several years back. I don't smoke or drink. No, not a blatant success story, but a moderately successful one.

Just the same, it's set me to thinking, and I've resolved to concentrate on giving, not only of my goods but of myself. I'm going to try with what's still ahead. Who knows? Maybe I'll be successful someday.

Father, it's never too late. Help me to find the areas I need to work in. I'm ready. —VAN VARNER

THU

9

In God I trust; I will not be afraid. . . .
—*Psalm 56:11 (NIV)*

TOMMY, OUR ORANGE outdoor cat, had been gone a few days. I saw him coming out of the woods, hopping on three legs. "What'd you do to yourself?" I said, sitting on a railroad tie on the edge of our drive, waiting for him to come to me.

"*Meow,*" he cried painfully as he hopped over.

The wound, bloody and swollen, was coated with dirt and held the beginnings of infection. "This is going to hurt," I said. Tommy had come to us three years earlier as a wild kitten, and I'd won his trust. Now he was my porch buddy, climbing all over me, purring. But he'd never been to the vet. Today would have to be the day. I dreaded it, for good reason.

In a crate in the car, Tommy screeched and scratched like a wild thing. At the vet's, he peered out of his crate like a minibobcat, hissing, raising his back, his green eyes lit with fear. I left him to be neutered as well as to have his paw fixed. Hours later I brought him home, calmly sedated. Gently I laid him on a clean bed in the garage, where he slept nights. The next morning I found him cowering behind a pile of boxes. He stared accusingly.

"It's okay, Tommy," I said, approaching him. "I'm your friend." He limped away as fast as he could.

Two days went by. I was sitting on my porch, lonely without my buddy. Then I saw him coming up the sidewalk, his wound obviously better. He climbed the porch steps and slinked my way. Holding my breath, I kept reading. He leapt to the cushion beside me, I stroked his back. His quirky motor started up and he stepped into my lap. We were friends once again.

"Tommy, Tommy," I said, a lump in my throat. "Welcome back."

Lord, when trouble surrounds me, may I trust in You, rather than falling back on my fears. —SHARI SMYTH

FRI
10

"YOU WHO TRAVEL ON THE ROAD — SING!"
—*Judges 5:10 (NAS)*

MY HUSBAND LEO has a musical background, and he always encouraged our children to sing, especially in the car. At one point, he even composed a little ditty we dubbed "The Manitoba Song," and it became the toddlers' favorite. As they got older, the challenge of singing four-part harmony helped allay the many sibling squabbles that sooner or later erupted in the backseat of the family sedan during long road trips. As teenage voices began to change, yet another dimension was added to our singing.

But it was not to last. As one by one the kids grew up and moved away, six voices were gradually reduced to two—just Leo's and mine. We still sing bits and snatches of old familiar hymns as we crisscross the country to visit our offspring. Scattered across Canada, none of them were home to mark Leo's birthday this year, but they did not forget him. They even drew me into a little family conspiracy, so the minute the package thumped into our mailbox, I knew what was in it.

"Birthday present!" I called to Leo.

"Right on! Another music CD!" he exclaimed as he opened it.

He was rather taken aback to see his own picture on the cover. And that Heintzman keyboard—wasn't that our piano? Through misty eyes, he began to read the label. It featured all four children performing their own renditions of hymns, songs, original compositions and a funny arrangement of "The Manitoba Song." After forty years, hearing that little tune filter out of a CD made us both cry.

Thank You, Lord, for the growing gift of memories that enrich my life.
—ALMA BARKMAN

SAT
11

"A DISCIPLE IS NOT ABOVE HIS TEACHER, BUT EVERYONE WHO IS PERFECTLY TRAINED WILL BE LIKE HIS TEACHER." —*Luke 6:40 (NKJV)*

I WAS WAITING in Dryer's Shoes for my wife to finish her shopping. I strolled through the aisles, fingering the lustrous footwear and breathing in the fragrance of rich leathers.

Meanwhile, the manager, a big teddy-bear type, was chatting with his clerks as they worked. He laughed with them and praised them with a happy, musical voice. The clerks responded to him as if he were their beloved grandfather.

Soon my wife and I were back on the road. "You know," I exclaimed, "those were the friendliest clerks I've ever met!"

Sharon nodded. "Weren't they, though? Trying on shoes is such an ordeal, and grumpy clerks make it a nightmare, but they treated me like I was Cinderella trying on glass slippers."

"I'll bet the manager has a terrific training program," I added.

Sharon shook her head. "Oh no, I don't think it's that. It's the manager himself. Did you see the way he treats his clerks? He makes a fuss over them, laughs with them. He treats them like people rather than employees. The clerks were just treating us the way he treated them."

I smiled, thinking of all the leadership books I've read that don't mention the most important leadership quality of all—*I must be what I want my students to be.*

We are all teachers. You may be a coach, a father, a librarian, a race car driver, a mother, and everyone is watching your example.

Thank You, God, for all the people who have shown me how to live, instead of just preaching to me. —Daniel Schantz

SUN
12

This is the day which the Lord hath made; we will rejoice and be glad in it. —*Psalm 118:24*

After church, I had settled into a lounge chair on the deck, relaxing into my usual Sunday afternoon of reading the paper and dozing, when I heard the doorbell. At the front door stood my friend Sasha, with her daughter and mom waiting in the car.

"We were driving by your neighborhood and felt we should stop. Mike is in the hospital in critical condition. I knew you would want to know."

I pictured the sweet, elderly man who sang in the choir and had become dear to our family over the years. Sasha continued, "As we were heading home, I had the strong feeling I should go see him now, before I forget."

"I'll go with you!" I said without hesitating. Soon my daughter Elizabeth and I were in Sasha's van heading to the hospital. Our little parade of visitors made its way to Mike's room and found him sleeping. We whispered hello, and his eyes blinked open, then widened in surprise to see us. Mike squeezed our hands and thanked us for coming.

Back home, I recalled our pastor urging us to view Sunday not just as a day of rest but as the day of the Resurrection, and to share that Resurrection joy with others by visiting a shut-in or calling a lonely person. I had rarely followed that advice, but now I resolved to follow Sasha's example and be open to God's leading. Some Sundays, when I desperately need rest, I still spend afternoons at home, but on other Sundays God invites me to meet Him as I reach out to others.

Lord, show me how to spend this day for You and with You.

—MARY BROWN

MON

13

I WILL INSTRUCT THEE AND TEACH THEE IN THE WAY WHICH THOU SHALT GO. . . . —*Psalm 32:8*

OUR NEIGHBORS are fine people, and I especially enjoy their two boys. One day the eight-year-old called out, "Oscar, my birthday is Saturday!" I was startled to be called by my first name. Later my wife Ruby heard him address me, and she said, "It isn't right for a youngster to call you by your first name. You're old enough to be his grandfather. I'd speak to him." But I didn't because I feared there would be a misunderstanding.

Recently, I was clipping our hedges when his mother approached. "Oscar," she said, "may I ask you something? The other day an older friend was visiting, and she heard my son call you Oscar. She scolded me and said it showed disrespect. You should be called Mr. Greene."

The mother hesitated, then went on, "How do you feel?"

I explained how I had been startled at first and that I still found it disconcerting. "Thank you," the mother said. She paused, then added, "You know, I should tell you, Oscar, you're the only one who calls him Billy. Everyone else calls him William."

All at once I understood: I, too, was showing disrespect.

Now from his front porch, from his backyard and from the park across the street he shouts, "Hi, Mr. Greene!" I smile and answer, "Hi, William!" Mutual respect is everything.

Holy Father, Your lessons of tact and patience will serve me in all situations. —OSCAR GREENE

READER'S ROOM

MY HUSBAND AND I are rapidly approaching retirement and are struggling with all the changes that will come with it—selling our business, leaving our twenty-two-year-old, too-big-for-two house and many other things. As I was spending time with the Lord one day, I read a verse from the Psalms that I'd read many times before: "Your path led through the sea, your way through the mighty waters, though your footprints were not seen" (Psalm 77:19, NIV). I am claiming that verse as my anchor as we take one step at a time. I know He will lead us as we spend time in His Word and ask His direction for each step we take.

—*Marla Williams, Chehalis, Washington*

TUE

14

AND, BEHOLD, GOD HIMSELF IS WITH US. . . .
—*II Chronicles 13:12*

I DOUBT the Wisconsin schoolteacher who originated the idea of Flag Day in 1885 could have ever imagined the places he could see the flag displayed in 2005. Today I saw a flag flying on a car antenna, stuck on a store window, pinned to a man's lapel and even painted on a rock. No doubt, early Flag Day supporters would never have imagined the flag on the surface of the moon, or held aloft by six proud men, five Marines and a Navy corpsman, on the Pacific island of Iwo Jima during a world war, or raised by three New York

City firefighters amid the rubble of a place of unspeakable tragedy known as Ground Zero.

Such images remind me of the song "Ragged Old Flag" by the late country-music legend Johnny Cash. A visitor to a small town notices the disheveled courthouse flag, and he's told that the wear and tear has come from a lifetime of experience—from the hole it got when George Washington carried it across the Delaware River to the beating taken through several wars. Yet it still flies, and folks remain proud and thankful for all it represents.

When I look at the flag, I see its many threads—freedom, tragedy, joy, triumph, sorrow, independence, faith—an intricate history woven together over the course of years since Old Glory's birth. Today, as that flag flies outside my own front door, I pray that God will bless our nation with strength and endurance.

Lord, on this Flag Day, wherever in the world our flag is flying, please bless that place. —GINA BRIDGEMAN

HE LEADETH ME . . . TO HAVE A HEART FOR OTHERS

WED
15

"I AM THE LORD YOUR GOD, WHO TEACHES YOU WHAT IS BEST FOR YOU, WHO DIRECTS YOU IN THE WAY YOU SHOULD GO." —Isaiah 48:17 (NIV)

I WAS AT the drugstore, leaving some film to be developed, when the young lady at the checkout counter complimented me on my perfume. "I used to wear that fragrance," she said wistfully.

A gentle insistence tugged at me. *You've been asking God to make you more sensitive. That girl needs some of that perfume.* I'd just run into a great sale and had purchased three bottles.

Then the inner arguments started: *Surely God doesn't work like this.*

Nobody needs *perfume*. But I obeyed. When I returned to pick up my photos, I asked if the young lady was still on duty. The man at the register brought her from the back room. She had been crying.

I handed her the perfume. "I just felt like you needed this," I said.

"Oh, ma'am," she gushed, "you don't know what this means. When I was expecting my little girl, I wore that fragrance the whole time. But today's been so hard. I've been to class and worked two jobs, and I didn't know how I could make it home one more night and give her a bath and read to her." A smile spread across her face. "When I smell this perfume, I'll remember how much I wanted her."

Dear Lord, help me to be mindful of Your nudges and let go of my limited expectations. —ROBERTA MESSNER

THU

16

I, EVEN I, WILL SING UNTO . . . THE LORD GOD OF ISRAEL. —Judges 5:3

YEARS AGO, I went on a mission trip to the Philippines. The heat, mosquitoes, hard work and lack of sleep were intense. A handful of us ministered to people who were desperately poor but wondrously receptive to the Gospel. Our leader, Ben Barredo, possessed a steady, persistent faith that even the most difficult circumstances couldn't shake.

One hot night we were with four or five hundred people in a public square near Bacolod City. Families with small children had walked the dusty roads most of the day to attend. Ben had finally acquired a film projector—he'd prayed for one for years—but just as he was about to show *Peace Child*, a drizzle began to fall. Quickly, Ben took off his shirt and covered the projector. Then, looking toward heaven, he prayed, "Lord God, please move that cloud over." People huddled around the precious projector to keep it dry.

To my horror, Ben looked over to me and said, "Marion, you lead the crowd in praise songs until the cloud moves."

"Ben," I answered, "I don't sing—not at all! I'm tone deaf. I can't."

"Marion," he said gently, "over here, we do whatever is necessary. God will help you. Now sing."

Hesitantly, fearfully, I began: "Praise Him, praise Him, all ye little children. . . ." The huge crowd joined in loudly. We sang for six long minutes—until the cloud moved. Hundreds of people knelt in the dirt that night to receive Jesus. And I came to a new level of trust in Him.

My Father, give me the voice to sing Your praises.
—MARION BOND WEST

FRI
17

LET THEM DO GOOD, THAT THEY BE RICH IN GOOD WORKS, READY TO GIVE, WILLING TO SHARE.
—*I Timothy 6:18 (NKJV)*

WHEN WE MOVED into our new home, the first thing on our agenda was to redo the garden in the front yard. We dug up overgrown boxwoods and ligustrum, and replaced them with colorful camellias and lantana. We even planted a holly tree. Our hard work paid off—our garden was beautiful—but we had exceeded our budget by hundreds of dollars.

The next summer, wiser about our needs and committed to staying within our budget, we mapped out a more realistic garden in the backyard. I had my doubts that it could match the fabulous garden we had created in the front yard.

"We're calling it 'gardening on a budget,'" I explained to my friend Lee.

"What a great idea!" she exclaimed. " I've got some agapanthus I've been wanting to separate. You can have as many as you can pull apart! And call my daughter Cindy. She's ready to thin her daylilies."

Jeannie and Hilly gave us Louisiana irises from their front yard, and Steve and Kathleen brought over pots of hostas and begonias. Another friend alerted us to a plant sale at a local university where the agriculture students offered great deals.

"Not only did we stay within our budget, but we now have flowers with a history," I explained to my daughter, a new homeowner. "When the time comes, I'll divide up my flowers for you, and then you can do the same one day."

Now when I look at my bucket daisies, sweet Williams and the rest of my flowers, not only do I see a beautiful garden but also the generosity of my friends who made my gardening on a budget more meaningful than I ever imagined.

Lord, what can I share with others today? —MELODY BONNETTE

SAT
18

CAN ANY HIDE HIMSELF IN SECRET PLACES THAT I SHALL NOT SEE HIM? SAITH THE LORD. DO NOT I FILL HEAVEN AND EARTH? . . . —Jeremiah 23:24

THE FOG WAS unusually thick for a mid-June morning in Tennessee. In the forest behind our home, a late-night rain had saturated the canopy of tall trees. Now the dripping leaves combined with the fog to mimic a resplendent rain forest. The branches of one tree, completely dead, were filled with hundreds of mist-coated spiderwebs, intricately spun to mesh perfectly with the tree's limbs. Normally invisible, they had been revealed by the misty fog.

"It makes you realize," my husband David said, "how many unseen things are woven around us every day of the week. Then out of the blue, some unexpected circumstance—like the fog on the spiderwebs—brings us new vision."

Later, over breakfast, I recalled a painful time when our family had been the target of a barrage of hurtful acts.

"You know, we would never have had any idea how many people loved us, if that hadn't happened," I said. "Like the fog this morning showing us things we hadn't seen before."

"Yep," David answered. "Can you imagine God, Who sees the unseen world of everything, somehow weaving all their workings together according to His plan?"

"Nice of Him to send the fog this morning," I answered. "And it's nice to be reminded that He's got us covered."

Father, thank You for these glimpses of Your omnipotence. —PAM KIDD

SUN
19

Listen to your father, who gave you life. . . .
—*Proverbs 23:22 (NIV)*

ONE DAY last year I turned around and found that when I wasn't looking, my three sons had all grown up. Jonathan, our youngest, announced that he was moving out of the house, and Nathan, our middle son, told us that he was moving to New Hampshire! No consultation, no permission requested, just announcements.

That evening as I sat by the fire, I wanted to sit all three boys down and expound a few more times on the life-lessons I'd learned the hard way, but no one was around to listen. And apparently my advice wasn't needed, because no one was asking.

A few weeks later I found out just how wrong I was. Nathan, ever the computer whiz, made me a card for Father's Day. On the cover was written, "Happy Father's Day to a dad who taught me what life is all about." Then inside came the punch line, "Could you repeat it? I wasn't listening." Below that Nathan had handwritten this note: "Thanks for always being there, Dad. And don't go anywhere, I'll be calling."

So I may no longer be the director of my children's lives, but I am a valued counselor. My new role is sort of nice: on call twenty-four hours a day for advice when a car battery fails or the water heater leaks, but not in charge of the solutions to these or life's more difficult questions. This role feels pretty good now and doesn't cost nearly as much as my original one.

Lord, thanks for the relationships I have and the roles I play. Help me to change when I need to and always to be there for those I love.
—ERIC FELLMAN

THE MYSTERIOUS GIFT

DURING THE NEXT three days, Marilyn Morgan King will reveal a series of mysterious events that happened to her last year that are so extraordinary they border on the miraculous. May your spirit be touched by the deep truth that God does, indeed, interact with us in our human lives in stunningly mysterious ways. —THE EDITORS

DAY ONE: BEHOLD THE MAN

MON
20

BY REVELATION HE MADE KNOWN UNTO ME THE MYSTERY. . . . —Ephesians 3:3

FOR SOME unknown reason, I'd been feeling a loss of confidence, and I had no idea how to deal with it. Was it a fact of aging? Could it be depression? What was happening?

One morning in the midst of my dilemma—the first day of an important retreat—I was startled awake by an image that lasted less than a second. It wasn't until the image had disappeared that I sat up in bed and said aloud, "Good heavens! That was Jesus!" I could hardly believe it, because the image was so very vivid, and though it passed in an instant, I could recall every detail.

It was not the suffering image sometimes depicted in paintings. No, this was a very masculine figure, clad in tan robes bordered in red, standing in a stream. I saw only His profile, and yet I had no doubt about His identity. He had a tall staff, not a shepherd's crook but a sturdy, rough-hewn piece of wood that was wide and flat at the bottom and tapered almost to a point at the top. He was probing the bottom of the stream.

Questions flooded my mind. Where had the image come from? What was He probing for? Why had this happened at this time? Most important, what did it all mean?

When I discussed this with the retreat leader she said, "Sometimes there are questions to which the best answer is *I don't know*. Can you accept the uncertainty and allow the questions to reveal their answers in their own time?"

I decided to try.

When spiritual questions arise, Lord, I'll simply hold them in my heart, trusting the answers to come in Your own time.
—Marilyn Morgan King

DAY TWO: A DREAM IN THE NIGHT

TUE
21

Behold, I dreamed a dream. . . . —*Judges 7:13*

I continued to hold the questions that came to me after the image of Jesus appeared that morning, but no answers seemed to come. Then, I had a dream in which the same image of Jesus reappeared.

I was in the stream with Him this time, and we were walking together in ankle-deep water. He stopped periodically to probe the ground under the stream with His staff, as in the original image. When I asked the reason for this, He replied, "I'm trying to find out where your grounding is." Then He made a strange suggestion—that I close my eyes and let myself fall backward so He could catch me. As I did this, I was graced with sudden trust. It was a safe surrender, and I did, indeed, feel secure, solid, *grounded*. Then my companion did a surprising thing. He handed me His staff!

As I wrote about it in my journal, I realized this dream was an answer to the question I had about what I needed to do to recover my self-confidence. It was also a response to my questions about the earlier image. I was filled with gratitude. What I didn't know was that there was more mystery to come.

Thank You, Jesus, for showing me where my grounding is and for demonstrating the way to self-confidence through practicing complete trust in You. —Marilyn Morgan King

DAY THREE: CROSSING THE STREAM

WED

22

WITHOUT ANY DOUBT, THE MYSTERY OF OUR RELIGION IS VERY DEEP INDEED. . . .
—*I Timothy 3:16 (JB)*

LAST WEDNESDAY I spent time on the mountain behind our home searching for the staff I had been given in my dream. I found it just as I remembered it, lying next to the stream that descends from the falls, as though it had been placed there for me.

Then, surprisingly, I found that I was lost on a mountain as familiar to me as my own breath. In my attempts to find my way, I soon came to a barbed wire fence that required me to cross the stream. As I did so, I slipped on a mossy rock and found myself ankle deep in water, just as I had been in the dream. The sun was starting to go behind the mountain, but I wasn't worried because I knew I was not alone.

I climbed out, and within a few minutes a house came into view with people on the deck. When I called to them that I was lost, a young man named Hiro came down through the brambles and led me to the house. They just happened to be there looking at the house, which was for sale, and were about to leave. As they offered to take me home, they mentioned they were a film team from California who were in Colorado to meet with a "script doctor" who lived a few miles down the road from our house. What they said next was too extraordinary to be a coincidence: "The film we are working on is about the life of Jesus."

I still can't think of this series of events I've so recently experienced (both the inner and the outer) without catching my breath with the wonder of it all.

Companion of the Way, how could I ever doubt that You walk with me, making Yourself known in ordinary and in immensely mysterious ways.
—MARILYN MORGAN KING

THU

23

ASK, AND IT WILL BE GIVEN TO YOU. . . .
—*Luke 11:9 (RSV)*

A FEW YEARS AGO my wife Tib and I took a walking tour of Oxford, England. Our guide was known as "the Major," a wizened fellow who walked with a limp, which I imagined had come from some campaign in the far reaches of the Empire.

When we reached the high point of the tour, Christ Church College, we found to our dismay that it wasn't open. We looked on as the Major held a heated conversation with the porter in the gatehouse beneath Tom Tower. A dour man in a bowler hat, the porter kept shaking his head until finally the Major limped back to us.

Seemingly unperturbed, the Major announced that we had a treat coming anyhow, a visit to one of the college gardens. But as it turned out, this was closed, too. Undaunted, the Major knocked at the door; another porter peered out with a frown that would have sent me beating a hasty retreat. "My friends have come a long way," the Major told him. "Maybe they could just have a quick look-see."

This time the guardian of the gate glanced at his watch and allowed that he'd put the sign out a bit early. "If you could leave in fifteen minutes . . ."

So we did get to see the splendid garden. Outside again, the Major said, "Never be afraid to ask. Sometimes you'll fail, sometimes you'll succeed. But you'll never know if you never ask."

I went back to our hotel that afternoon determined to be much bolder in my prayers for a granddaughter recently diagnosed with scoliosis of the spine. The prognosis was so bleak that I'd been shy in my prayers. Now I boldly asked God to give Lindsay a strong, straight spine.

Just last week I saw Lindsay—slender, beautiful and, thanks to the intercessions of many and the skill of her surgeon, walking down a beach with her back straight—and completed that prayer begun in Oxford years ago by thanking God for her renewed health and for the Major's insight.

Father, help me remember that You have instructed us to be bold in asking.
—JOHN SHERRILL

FRI

24

THOU SHALT LOVE THY NEIGHBOUR AS THYSELF. . . .
—*Mark 12:31*

I LOOK FORWARD to sitting in the whirlpool at my gym with an Englishman named Terry, who is wheelchair-bound. I've long since stopped offering to help him out of the chair.

"It's good exercise," he explains, hoisting himself into the steamy, burbling water. Terry has always struck me as quite at ease with himself and that makes it pleasant to be with him.

One day I got around to asking what he did for a living. "I own an introduction service," he said. "My job is to bring together people who might be right for each other. They can take it from there, if I've done my job."

"You must do a lot of background checking to make sure your clients are compatible."

Terry nodded. "You would think so, but that's not the real secret." He shifted in the water so that he could look at me. "First we have to find out if they are compatible with themselves.

"You see," he continued, "until a person is comfortable with who he or she is, there's no sense trying an introduction. So many people are looking for a partner simply because they don't want to be alone. We try to find people who are content with who they are."

Terry reached for his towel and moved toward his chair. Reflexively I went to help but he held up his hand. "I'm fine," he said. Then, with a touch of pride he added, "Sitting in an office in New York, I bring good people together from all over the world."

We are meant to find joy in our work by bringing something of ourselves to the process. Terry has a lot to bring. He wears a wedding ring, but I haven't gotten around yet to asking him how he met his wife. I do know one thing: Someone got lucky.

Father, only when I can love the person You've made me am I ready to love another. —EDWARD GRINNAN

SAT
25

NOT WITH EYE-SERVICE, AS MEN-PLEASERS; BUT AS THE SERVANTS OF CHRIST, DOING THE WILL OF GOD FROM THE HEART. —*Ephesians 6:6*

MY FATHER raises Missouri Fox Trotter horses. These beautiful animals were developed in the rugged Ozark hills during the nineteenth century by settlers who needed easy-riding, durable mounts that could travel long distances. They were invaluable to country doctors, cattlemen, law officers and tax assessors in the days before improved roads and cars. Today, the Missouri Fox Trotter is a registered breed, highly sought after by riders who appreciate their characteristic "Fox Trot" stride, and each horse is worth thousands of dollars. Yet they live out their lives unaware of the great value people have placed on them.

One afternoon, as I was leaving Daddy's farm, I pulled up outside the fence that surrounds a large pasture and studied the young colts. It was a hot, dry day, and little whirlwinds of dust swirled around them as they pulled large mouthfuls of hay from the feed bin. Two of the colts were playing a game of tag, chasing each other across the pasture, over a small rise and then back again. The strenuous workout lathered their necks and backs with patches of sweat, turning their coats a wet brown.

Closer to the fence, a third colt wallowed back and forth on the soft ground, hooves in the air, luxuriating in the feel of the sand in his coarse hair. As I watched, he stood to shake himself free of the grit, sending grains of sand scattering in every direction. His companions had wandered away to drink from the trough of cold water near the gate, and he soon followed.

The horses were not showy or exotic looking; nothing visible to the eye distinguished them as special or exceptional, yet because of the service they could provide to riders, they had great value.

How wonderful, I thought, *to be like the Missouri Fox Trotter! With no showy talents or gifts, but valued instead for whatever service I might provide to others.*

Father, humbly I seek to do Your service! —LIBBIE ADAMS

SUN

26

"SIX DAYS YOU SHALL LABOR, AND DO ALL YOUR WORK; BUT THE SEVENTH DAY IS A SABBATH TO THE LORD YOUR GOD; IN IT YOU SHALL NOT DO ANY WORK. . . ." —*Exodus 20:9–10 (RSV)*

"COME ON," a young acquaintance named Bobby challenged, "give me one good reason I should have to take a whole day off every week and do nothing when I have so much to get done."

"The Sabbath law doesn't say to do nothing, just not to work. Think of the law as similar to the instructions in an owner's manual for a racing car. The rules keep us from crashing and burning. Real life just works better when we keep the Sabbath, for instance, than when we don't."

"Why?"

"You're a serious weightlifter, Bobby. But do you lift every day?"

"Of course not. I take a day off after exercising any part of my body. I work upper body on Monday, skip upper body Tuesday, and work upper body again on Wednesday. . ."

"Why not work your upper body every day?"

"Because," Bobby explained patiently, "working a muscle tears it down. Your body needs time off. And muscle growth actually takes place while you're resting."

"So maybe our spiritual lives grow on our Sabbath days off from work—just like our muscles do."

Dear Lord, I am grateful for Your laws and guidance, which help us to grow. —KEITH MILLER

MON
27
A TIME TO KEEP SILENCE, AND A TIME TO SPEAK. . . .
—Ecclesiastes 3:7

OUR MINISTRY Mission Mississippi sponsors a program called "Two and Two Restaurant Day," which encourages couples to invite a couple of a different race out to dinner. The other day, I got a call from a local businessman, who wanted to tell me about his remarkable experience with the program. He and his wife and children had invited James Meredith, the first African American student at the University of Mississippi, and his family to have dinner with them.

"Dolphus, I wanted this time with James to ask him to forgive me for my silence. I told him that I was a student at Ole Miss at the same time that he was. I was like the majority of the students: We wanted James to be there, but we stood back and said nothing.

"I said, 'James, I am asking you to forgive me, not because of all the troops on the campus, not because I was involved in all the rioting, shooting and bombing that took place on the campus. I was not responsible for any of those things. I want to ask you to forgive me for my silence.'

"When I had finished talking, James and his wife and family reached out and forgave me."

As I hung up the phone, I praised God for this man's courage in confessing his sin of nearly forty years ago, and for the grace of forgiveness that he had experienced so powerfully. And looking into my own heart, I asked myself, *How often am I silent when I ought to be speaking up and speaking out?*

Lord, please teach me when to speak and when to be silent. Forgive me of the many times I've been silent when I know that You wanted me to speak. —DOLPHUS WEARY

TUE

28

"MY FATHER IS THE GARDENER." —*John 15:1 (NIV)*

I LIKE GARDENS—not *gardening*. I am good at planting, usually in a rush of adrenaline brought on by seed catalogs with blossoms bursting off the page. But when the blush of the moment fades, I tend to forget about my flowers. And as time goes by, weeds grow and my garden begins to look, well . . . ragged.

My friend Desila, on the other hand, likes gardening. Her beds are beautiful, her blossoms huge and richly colored. So I had to laugh the other day when she showed up with something for my flowerbed—a flat, gray stone that read: MY GARDEN WAS AT ITS BEST LAST WEEK. SORRY YOU MISSED IT.

I think the rock was meant to motivate me to take better care of my flowers. But it's done more than that. It's made me think about the way people perceive my actions, too. That moment when I'm short-tempered with a waitress, the times my driving gets too aggressive, the laugh I have at the expense of someone else. These things don't occur often—but when they do, I want to say, "Wait! I looked better last week when I was doing church volunteer work. When I was letting that hassled mother in front of me in the grocery store line. You should have seen me when. . . ."

My well-placed stone reminds me that life, like gardens, requires ongoing care. And you never know who's looking to see just how well you're blooming!

Master Gardener, weed from my life all that is ugly and selfish. Let me grow strong and tall in the beauty of Your love. —MARY LOU CARNEY

WED
29

AND GOD CREATED GREAT WHALES, AND EVERY LIVING CREATURE THAT MOVETH, WHICH THE WATERS BROUGHT FORTH ABUNDANTLY, AFTER THEIR KIND, AND EVERY WINGED FOWL AFTER HIS KIND: AND GOD SAW THAT IT WAS GOOD. —*Genesis 1:21*

CONSIDER THE SMALLEST of feathered things, the hummingbird, like the one that just buzzed me so angrily I thought it would tear my ear off. It must be a male—no female would fly that recklessly and aggressively. I watch him slam into warp speed to challenge another hummingbird.

A most amazing being, the hummingbird, with a heart the size of a freckle, a heart that beats ten times faster than ours does. They fly faster than I drive, and they can fly backward, and they can fly hundreds of miles in a single flight without pause for rest or restaurant, which I cannot do.

They gleam and delight, they are shards of all the colors there are, they have a vast wild courage that I have to admire even as I worry about the end of my ear. Would you barrel headlong at a being a thousand times your size?

It may well be, as my biologist friends tell me, that the hummer is probably defending his territory, the slice of the world he claims as his own, but I wonder if his ambition is not as large as his bravery, and he fires himself at the incomprehensibly large to measure its mystery, to assert his character, to understand himself in some hummish way I'll never know. So we all launch ourselves at the Maker, hoping to see and smell and sense and feel and hear and touch that which we can only dimly comprehend; we pray; and we attend to the smallest of feathered things, invented by the coolest Engineer there ever was.

Dear Lord, please just let me see the shards of Your creative zest clearly.
                                                            —BRIAN DOYLE

THU
30

WHO SHALL ASCEND THE HILL OF THE LORD? AND WHO SHALL STAND IN HIS HOLY PLACE?
—*Psalm 24:3 (RSV)*

THE VIEW DOWNRIVER from Nankoweep is one of the most photographed and familiar in the entire range of Grand Canyon pictures. The river curves gently from one side of its bed to the other, tucking wide sand beaches into the curves, until its serpentine path vanishes behind a rock wall several miles away.

I first saw this view myself on my third or fourth river trip. That was the first time I'd climbed the steep, pebbly trail to the set of Anasazi granaries tucked under the lip of the Tonto platform. The climb, though relatively short, is almost vertical. I would take three or four steps, then have to stop and breathe for a while before I could take three or four more. Boatmen and other passengers breezed past me; most had reached the top while I was still laboring along about halfway up.

It would have been really easy to give up and return to the boats, where some passengers who accepted their limitations better than I did had decided to remain. I was sorely tempted. I was much more couch potato than camper, despite my addiction to the river. My cardiovascular system was accustomed to digging in its heels when I couldn't find a parking place close to the mall entrance. This was a lot worse than that.

And then Dwight, one of the boatmen who had delayed at the boats for quite a while before he started hiking, caught up with me and dropped his pace to mine. I moved for him to pass me, but he shook his head. "The view is good the whole way up the trail," he said. "We'll get to the top together."

It still took me a long time. But I enjoyed it a lot more, because I no longer thought of the journey as keeping me from my goal; I thought of it as part of my goal. And the view *was* good the whole way up.

Lord, when I'm spiritually out of shape, give me the strength to keep climbing toward You, three or four steps at a time. —RHODA BLECKER

SEEDS OF REJOICING

1 _____

2 _____

3 _____

4 _____

5 _____

6 _____

7 _____

8 _____

9 _____

10 _____

11 _____

12 _____

13 _____

14 _____

15 _____

16 _____

17 _____

18 _____

19 _____

20 _____

21 _____

22 _____

23 _____

24 _____

25 _____

26 _____

27 _____

28 _____

29 _____

30 _____

July

Happy is that people, whose God is the Lord. —*Psalm 144:15*

GOD SIGHTINGS
A CHANGE OF DIRECTION

FRI
1

THERE IS A WAY THAT SEEMS RIGHT TO A MAN, BUT IN THE END IT LEADS TO DEATH. —Proverbs 14:12 (NIV)

COMING BACK from the post office today I almost ran over a turtle. She was in the middle of the road as I turned into our street—a large handsome Eastern box turtle, plodding determinedly toward the intersection with busy Route 133. I managed to miss her, but the next driver might not be as lucky. And if she went any farther. . . .

I couldn't stop here at the corner or on the steep hill. I pulled into our own driveway, then ran back down the hill. The turtle had nearly reached the larger road.

I picked her up, surprisingly heavy in my hand. As I carried her up the hill, four long scaly legs curved up around the carapace and claws raked my hand. Neck extended, she regarded me with cold, prehistoric fury.

There's a swampy woods at the far end of our street, with berry bushes in the clearings. *Turtle heaven*, I thought. I carried her there and set her down. For perhaps three minutes she surveyed her new surroundings. Then slowly, deliberately, she started back in the precise direction she'd been headed when I picked her up.

Three times I turned her around, hoping the advantages of the new location would dawn on her. Unerringly, each time she resumed the route that would take her to Route 133 and disaster.

I walked back home with a new understanding, not of turtles, but of God's patience with all His stubborn creatures. How many times in my life has He stooped, picked me up, turned me around and pointed me in a new direction? How many times have I struggled to return to my own agenda, unaware of Whose hand had barred my way?

Turtles can't change, Father, but people can. Help me ask when my plans are interrupted, "What better one do You have for me?"
—ELIZABETH SHERRILL

SAT
2
AND HE WALKED IN THE WAY OF HIS FATHER ASA AND DID NOT DEPART FROM IT, DOING RIGHT IN THE SIGHT OF THE LORD. —II Chronicles 20:32 *(NAS)*

MY HUSBAND RICK and I are total opposites. He doesn't make lists, wear a watch or scribble notes in a calendar as I do. We're building a log house, and I've tried to get him to see the benefits of organization. "Don't you think we could stay on target better if you'd just jot down priorities? Here, I made you a list."

"Nope. I don't need to write things down. I know what's important."

Last Saturday, I followed Rick and Thomas, our eleven-year-old, out to the pickup truck in the steamy morning heat to offer suggestions. They were headed out to work on the house.

"Did you remember to pack the cooler? Y'all are going to want drinks."

"Yep, we have everything we need, don't we, buddy?" Rick stuck his baseball cap on crooked and made a goofy face at me.

"Thomas, watch for snakes. Don't go near that creek!" I hollered through the passenger door window, tapping to get their attention.

My two workmen came home way after dark, filthy and tired. Rick took off his big work boots and headed for the shower. "Mom, you won't believe how much we got done today," Thomas said, still standing on the porch.

"For real? Tell me. I want to hear everything."

"Well, after we cleaned up the yard real good, we sat on the back deck and Dad prayed. He thanked God for the land and for our new house and for helping us work."

"He did?" I stared at his muddy face and serious brown eyes, and felt ashamed for all my pushing. "I guess Dad carries his priorities list around in his heart."

Father, I've been wrong. My ways aren't always best. Let Thomas follow after his dad's priorities. —JULIE GARMON

SUN

3

It was good of you to share in my troubles.
—*Philippians 4:14 (NIV)*

THIS YEAR, Dad and I were the only ones in the family getting ready to watch the Independence Day fireworks. As we headed outside, the phone rang. Dad carried the cordless phone with him, happy to hear from Mom, who was in Washington state, trying to sort through the house she had inherited from Grandma Ellen. I slid the glass balcony door open and stepped into the summer evening. The fireworks were just starting, so Dad said good night to Mom and joined me, leaning against the balcony railing.

When the horizon fell silent and dark, and we started to notice the mosquito bites and the evening chill, I reached for the sliding glass door. "Dad, did you lock the balcony door?"

"Why, is it stuck?"

The door wouldn't budge! As Dad pulled at the door, I peered over the side of the balcony. I was pondering how best to get the neighbors' attention, when Dad remembered the cordless phone in his pocket. We could phone for help! It seemed silly to call the police for something like this, and we were sure the fire department had its hands full with fireworks. So we called Mom. She started calling around from Washington, trying to find someone nearby to come to our rescue. After several tries, she finally reached Walt and Marlene, good friends from church who had a spare key.

About ten minutes later Walt pulled up, shouted a cheerful hello and let himself in. He was laughing as he tugged the sliding glass door open, saying, "Your cats must have locked you out!" We thanked him, and I said, "So much for celebrating 'independence'—we sure needed you! Thank goodness we reached Mom, too. Why, if we hadn't had that phone. . . ."

"But you had the phone," Walt winked, "and everything is fine."

Lord, friends and family are among Your greatest blessings. As I celebrate the independence of our nation, thank You for my dependence on them.
—KJERSTIN EASTON

MON

4

*He hath sent me to bind up the brokenhearted,
to proclaim liberty to the captives, and the
opening of the prison to them that are bound.*
—Isaiah 61:1

GETTYSBURG, PENNSYLVANIA, lies about two hours south of our summer home, and not long ago I toured the famous Civil War battlefield. It's hard to imagine the ferocity of the fighting that went on there on the first three days of July 1863, but it's not difficult to picture the scene on July 4, "four score and seven years" following the signing of the Declaration of Independence.

On the Fourth of July, the day following the battle, Gen. Robert E. Lee and what was left of his army began their return to Virginia. Confederate casualties numbered twenty thousand, many of them incurred in Pickett's famous charge up Cemetery Ridge. The high ground occupied by the North had been an advantage; still, Union losses numbered eighteen thousand, and though Gen. George S. Meade followed Lee's troops south, it could not have been with great enthusiasm. The battle had left both sides exhausted and discouraged.

A little more than four months later, President Lincoln traveled to Gettysburg to dedicate the battlefield to the soldiers who had paid the ultimate price. Though he told those gathered there that "the world will little note, nor long remember what we say here," he was wrong. His words still ring like the bell that first sounded liberty in Philadelphia. Historians note that the speech he wrote in Washington and revised on the train was not the same as the one he delivered. The spoken version added two words: *under God.*

That significant phrase came in the final sentence of his address: "that we here highly resolve that these dead shall not have died in vain—that this nation, *under God,* shall have a new birth of freedom—and that government of the people, by the people and for the people shall not perish from the earth."

God, we thank You for our country free.
Teach us the duties and costs of liberty.
*—*FRED BAUER

TUE

5

HE SATISFIETH . . . THE HUNGRY SOUL WITH GOODNESS. —Psalm 107:9

I WAS THINKING dark thoughts as I walked past what had always been my favorite patch of woods. The acreage had been scalped, leaving only raw dirt and little yellow markers dividing the land into tiny lots. The woods had long been deemed common property to be enjoyed by those of us who had cabins by the lakeside. Now, all that was left of the tall trees was a broken promise. With the inequities of the world weighing heavy in my heart, I prayed, *Oh, Father in heaven, why can't the world be fair?*

I stopped short. He'd heard this all before.

Okay, God, I don't need to spend this time whining. Show me something good.

Ahead, a glint of sun caught my eye. I focused there and saw a fat blackberry hanging from a briar on the side of the road. I stepped closer, thinking of my stepfather Herb, who would be visiting that day. He adored blackberry cobbler. I hurried back to the cabin for a bucket, walked back to the briar and picked that one berry. With a *plop*, it fell into the empty bucket.

I looked deeper into the undergrowth. There was another berry, then still another. Soon I was surrounded by bushes and briars. Standing in the glaring sun, wet with perspiration, I inspected the bushes as a sweet breeze wafted in from the lake and cooled me down. Then, my eyes fixed on a mother lode of shiny, ripe blackberries.

Soon my bucket was full to overflowing. On the way back to the cabin, I forgot to notice the ruined woods. I was thinking ahead to the look on Herb's face when I pulled that cobbler, brown and bubbly, from the oven.

God, I am hungry for hope. Show me something good today.

—PAM KIDD

WED *HE WILL TEACH THE WAYS THAT ARE RIGHT AND BEST*
6 *TO THOSE WHO HUMBLY TURN TO HIM.*
       —Psalm 25:9 (TLB)

WHENEVER WE VISIT my husband's parents near Lake Erie, my daughter Maria spends hours digging at the beach, piling up mounds of wet sand, and building tunnels and castles. A princess lives in one and her friends in another. Their activities keep Maria busy for a long time.

Lake Erie waves aren't huge, but they're big enough to wipe out a tiny shorefront village. "Start building a little farther away from the water," I told Maria one time, but she assured me everything would be okay. But soon the waves got bigger. "Mommy, Mommy, oh no!" she cried as water lapped the edges of the princess' castle. "Do something, Mommy!" But I couldn't keep the next wave from washing away Maria's afternoon of work. I hugged her tightly and told her we would build another castle together. Still, it hurt, especially since I'd told her not to build so close to the water.

I thought later that Maria's cries to me are similar to my own cries to God when I go my own way, forgetting His gentle guidance. I'm reminded of a work project that I took on, thinking I'd make some quick money, even though in prayer I'd felt a nudge to decline. But I confidently said *yes*, and then regretted it when the job caused a lot of aggravation. Of course, I ran to God in prayer to fix my mess. Thankfully, He didn't scold me and say, "I told you so." He wrapped His loving arms around me and gave me the strength to finish the job.

Open my ears, loving God, so that in prayer I might not only speak but also listen. —GINA BRIDGEMAN

THU *EVERY CREATURE OF GOD IS GOOD. . . .*
7 *—I Timothy 4:4*

I'VE ALWAYS THOUGHT the world was divided into cat people and dog people. Carol was one of the former, and I was definitely one of the latter. I loved big dogs with wagging tails, and she loved furry, purring kittens—a standoff. The best solution for twenty years of marriage was that we owned neither dog nor cat.

Then our friend Mary Alice rescued an eight-month-old kitten on a subway platform in Harlem. "He's very pretty," she told Carol. "Long, fluffy, gray hair with neat white paws." The problem was that Mary Alice couldn't keep him. Would we be interested?

"No," I said. "I don't want some beast meowing around the house, sitting in my lap when I'm trying to work, begging to be petted."

"Mary Alice asked if we could just take him for a couple nights until she finds a home for him."

"I suppose so."

Can you guess the rest of the story? The cat—christened Fred because he was found on Frederick Douglass Boulevard—has become my great pal. Delighted, I wake up to Fred licking my ear. I eat breakfast with him at my feet. When I come home at night, he's the first one to greet me. "Meow, meow," he says. *Play with me!* And I do.

The scariest thought is if I had clung to my preconceived notions, I would never have known the pleasures of working at the computer with a purring cat in my lap. All I needed was a little nudge.

Now I wonder, though, what would Carol—and Fred—think of adding a mutt to our ménage?

Open my eyes, Lord, to the beauty of all Your creatures.

—RICK HAMLIN

FRI

8

"I HAVE BEEN VERY ZEALOUS FOR THE LORD GOD ALMIGHTY . . . I AM THE ONLY ONE LEFT. . . ."
—*I Kings 19:14 (NIV)*

PROBABLY YOU'VE often heard how, of all the people in the United States, only one does all the work. If not, here's how this fanciful figure is calculated: Add up the number of unemployed—retirees, babies, those in school, prison, hospitals, etc.—then subtract this total (supposedly 249,999,998) from 250 million, the number of people in the United States. This leaves only two: you and me. *I'm* doing all the work; *you're* just sitting there reading this.

This conundrum came to mind the other day when I read the story of Elijah, the Old Testament prophet who raised the ire of Queen Jezebel. Elijah was so afraid of Jezebel, he ran and hid in the wilderness, then sat under a juniper tree feeling sorry for himself while self-righteously telling the Lord how much he had done for Him. Elijah had forgotten to add in the number of enemies from whom God had protected *him*: kings, jealous leaders, Baal-worshipers, etc. He concluded his "poor-me" litany, "*I* am the *only one* left, Lord, who does Your work."

God's answer to Elijah was quick and brief: "I have seven thousand followers. Get up and I'll show you some of them."

Well, Elijah isn't the only one who's ever had a case of the "poor me's." I, too, am quick to note and add up those I think are idle: "Lord, nobody else teaches junior-high school." "Nobody else visits old Mrs. James." "Nobody else services the communion table." Then I conclude, "Everyone else just sits. I'm the only one left to do all Your work." I must remember to check my arithmetic.

Lord, teach me to see what You have for me to do and not look around at what I think others have not done—or should do. —ISABEL WOLSELEY

SAT
9

THEN OUR MOUTH WAS FILLED WITH LAUGHTER. . . .
—*Psalm 126:2 (RSV)*

WHILE WATERING my husband Gene's three beloved tomato plants, I discovered that some of the tomatoes were missing. To my horror, I spotted Lovey, one of our dogs, chewing on a tomato! Just then, Red Dog came trotting up proudly holding a nice-sized tomato in her mouth. "*No!*" I screamed, but both dogs continued devouring their newfound treats.

When Gene came out later to admire his tomatoes, he stooped down for a closer look. "Marion! Who's been picking the tomatoes?"

Looking in the other direction, I mumbled, "The dogs."

"What?"

"Just the green ones." I tried to smile.

Not even a hint of a smile from my husband. I quickly explained, "Well, they do look exactly like the green tennis balls we throw for them to retrieve, and they probably figured. . . ."

"What are you going to do about it?" he said.

Right then Lovey came up to offer Gene a tomato she'd dug up from its hiding place, and I sashayed back into the house and considered bolting all the doors. A few moments later in the kitchen, our eyes met for what seemed like forever. "Normal dogs don't eat tomatoes off the vines," he explained grimly.

Don't laugh, Marion. This is serious business. "I know, I know. . . ."

I thought I glimpsed a hint of laughter in Gene's eyes. I ventured a half smile, and so did he. I snickered. Then my husband started laughing out loud, and I fell over onto the kitchen counter, laughing helplessly.

Father, one of Your most remarkable gifts is laughter—especially in marriage. —MARION BOND WEST

SUN
10

REMEMBER THE SABBATH DAY, TO KEEP IT HOLY.
—*Exodus 20:8*

EACH YEAR my father and I set aside a week in summer for some far-flung adventure. We have explored parts of Alaska, Colorado, New Mexico and Maine. Camping, hiking and fishing, we detach ourselves from the stress of everyday life and draw closer together as father and son. And surrounded by the great outdoors, we're reminded of God's gifts. For us, this time is sacred.

But then all too soon the outings are over and we are flying back to Tennessee. We're caught up in our work and the pressures that go with it, but we're better able to keep them in perspective because of our time far away in the great outdoors.

Recently, though, I realized that every week offers a similar opportunity. As a preacher's kid, I remember scoffing at the Sabbath day commandment (while being shepherded to church every Sunday). But those weeks in the wild with Dad have taught me differently. More and more I consider every seventh day as the sacred space that puts the rest of my week in perspective. Without a sermon to guide me, a slice of wisdom from the Bible to teach me and a silent moment to think about God's goodness, I'm afraid I'd begin my week stale and uninspired.

It would be like a summer without getting away.

Father, let me honor You not only on Sunday but in every glimpse of Sabbath You send my way. —BROCK KIDD

MON

II

"I PRAY ALSO FOR THOSE WHO WILL BELIEVE IN ME. . .
THAT ALL OF THEM MAY BE ONE. . . ."
—John 17:20–21 (NIV)

I AM UP early after a restless night's sleep. My head hurts, and my heart is in that fog of unease that creeps in after anxious dreams. I've prayed and turned over the day to God, but I'm still not at peace.

I know why. Today when I drop off the kids for Veggie Tales camp, I'm going to run into some moms I'm not yet ready to see. A year ago I was deeply hurt by them during a disagreement at Bible study. Though we remain outwardly gracious toward each other, nowadays we can hardly be called pals.

It's frustrating that my former friends are not interested in what I think, or why. I sometimes lie awake at night trying to figure out the perfect one-liner that would enlighten them. Fortunately, I know it's my wounded pride and not the Holy Spirit that prompts those thoughts. I wait as patiently as I can for the Spirit to tell me if and when to speak. I assume that the right time won't come until I can speak with utter charity, so it probably won't be today. I sigh and try praying some more.

My prayers are interrupted by the kids, who bounce out of bed excited about seeing their friends at camp. They are too young to know about fractured fellowship; they only know about friends and being friends with Jesus.

Friends with Jesus. The answer to my prayer nearly knocks me over. I am friends with Jesus. These women are friends with Jesus. From Christ's perspective that means they are not my *former* friends, because we are united forever in Him.

I smile and get the kids ready to go. There are friends to see, through Christ's eyes.

Lord Jesus, feeble, foolish and sinful as we are, in You we are perfectly one. —JULIA ATTAWAY

TUE **12** AND THE LORD GOD FORMED MAN OF THE DUST OF THE GROUND, AND BREATHED INTO HIS NOSTRILS THE BREATH OF LIFE; AND MAN BECAME A LIVING SOUL.
—*Genesis 2:7*

THE CREW SNAPPED to attention as Nancy Reagan took her place with the dignitaries on deck. She had come to Norfolk, Virginia, to put into commission the aircraft carrier named in tribute to her husband, President Ronald Reagan. The ship was home to six thousand sailors, carried more than eighty aircraft, and with two nuclear reactors, could operate for twenty years without refueling. "I have only one line to say," Mrs. Reagan said as she waved to the cheering crowd. "Man the ship and bring her to life!"

"Aye, aye, ma'am!" the captain responded as he gave the salute. Sailors rushed to their posts. Anything that whistled, whistled. Anything that turned, turned. The USS *Ronald Reagan* had come alive and would stay "at ready" until the day she was retired.

Watching TV coverage of the ceremony, I was reminded that God used only one line to bring us to life: "Let us make man in our image, after our likeness" (Genesis 1:26). He set into motion the amazing spins and whistles of all that we are—body, mind, soul and spirit. With the Scriptures as our compass, empowered by the energy of the Holy Spirit (not for a twenty-year refueling, but for eternity!), our earthly vessel is "at ready." We are commissioned into the service of our Commander in Chief until, in His good time, we, too, are retired from duty.

Lord, through quiet waters and stormy seas, You are Captain of my soul.
—FAY ANGUS

WED **13** DO NOT FORSAKE YOUR FRIEND AND THE FRIEND OF YOUR FATHER. . . . —*Proverbs 27:10 (NIV)*

OUR TRIP TO Alaska last year was the first time my wife Joy and I had taken a vacation together without any kids along or any obligations to see family or friends along the way. Just the two of us with our backpacks and Inland Marine ferry tickets.

One afternoon we rented a car and drove north out of Juneau along the coast highway. Because Juneau is on an island, the road is only forty miles long, but ten or fifteen miles out of town it feels very remote. The day was clear and bright, with temperatures in the high seventies, and the views of the sound were incredible. About two miles from the end of the road, we saw this sign: TRAVEL BEYOND THIS POINT NOT RECOMMENDED. IF YOU MUST TRAVEL PAST THIS POINT, DO THE FOLLOWING:

- EXPECT EXTREME COLD AND SEVERE WEATHER.
- CARRY COLD-WEATHER SURVIVAL GEAR.
- TELL SOMEONE WHERE YOU ARE GOING.

We took one look at our shorts, sandals and T-shirts and started to laugh. Then we drove to the end of the road, got out and walked to the beach to watch the sunset.

After some jokes about "severe weather," we began to talk quietly about the many changes and challenges we faced in the days ahead. With an impish grin Joy finally said, "You know, maybe we're worried because we forgot to tell someone where we were going."

It was all too true. Mostly because of my ego, we had not told anyone about our struggles. We were carrying the load alone. Right then, we decided to confide in a few close family members and friends when we returned home. That made all the difference in the weeks and months to come.

Lord, help me to keep remembering that all the survival preparations in the world can't make up for having friends to help on the journey.
—ERIC FELLMAN

HE LEADETH ME . . .
TO SPREAD THE WORD

THU
14

YOUR WORD IS A LAMP TO MY FEET AND A LIGHT FOR MY PATH. —Psalm 119:105 (NIV)

LAST SUMMER at a book convention, I stood in line for an autographed copy of *101 Amazing Things about God* by

Marsha Marks, a flight attendant who after September 11 found herself wondering about the reality of God in everyday life.

As Marsha handed me my book, she asked, "Did you fly here?" When I told her yes, her face lit up. "I just had an idea!" she exclaimed. "Let me give you a copy to give to your flight attendant on your trip home."

I accepted the book, but as the flight attendant worked the aisles of my plane, reminding everyone to buckle up and place their trays in an upright position, I began to have second thoughts. *I don't know about this, Lord. I'm not ashamed of You or anything, but I don't even know this lady. What if she's offended?*

When the flight attendant came down the aisle to collect empty soda cans, I finally summoned enough courage to approach her. To my surprise, a look of pure delight crossed her face. "What a lovely gesture," she said. "I can't wait to take a look at it." Before we landed, she'd shared several entries with other passengers, explaining, "A fellow flight attendant wrote this book and sent it to me through the lady in 4D."

Since that day, I've often thought of Marsha Marks. She possessed a unique opportunity to touch her fellow flight attendants, and when God nudged her, she didn't question Him; she got to work.

Lord, there's nothing like Your Word to light my way. Help me to listen to Your nudging to share it with others. —ROBERTA MESSNER

READER'S ROOM

GOD HAS BLESSED ME with a little log cabin in the Wildcat Valley and a loving husband to share it with. We are surrounded by the beauty of nature, God's creations. Nature has taught me about living and dying, about being reborn and rejuvenated, about the power of prayer and Divine guidance. God has blessed me with a loving family and many caring friends who have supported me through hard times. We gather and pray for each other on a large stump on the side of a ravine. And God restores our faith, hope and peace, helping me to live each day with an open and grateful heart. —*Joanna Bordner, Cutler, Indiana*

FRI
15

IF RICHES INCREASE, DO NOT SET YOUR HEART ON THEM. —Psalm 62:10 (NKJV)

"TURN HERE," my wife Sharon urged. "Let's stop and see Juliette." We were vacationing in Georgia. "Juliette is the home of the restaurant that was used as the Whistle Stop Cafe. You know, in the movie *Fried Green Tomatoes.*"

Expecting the usual tourist ambush, I was surprised to find a quiet village hidden in the countryside near the Ocmulgee River spillway, where old men sit below the spray, smoking their pipes and casting for catfish. Each modest house has its own garden of green tomatoes and its own peach tree. The sign on the cafe says, FINE FOOD AT FAIR PRICES.

Inside, the restaurant looks just as it must have fifty years ago. The floor appears to be the original oiled wood, and the walls are cluttered with old photos and collectibles. The only sign of fame is a poster of the actress Jessica Tandy.

"These tomatoes are scrumptious," Sharon noted. "Crunchy on the outside, juicy on the inside, just like they're supposed to be." The bill was twelve dollars, and eight others shared the dining room with us. The whole experience was peaceful, pleasant, almost mystical, and I hated to leave it for the busy highway.

The Whistle Stop Cafe reminds me of the people I most admire: colleagues and friends who have distinguished themselves, yet have stayed true to their sense of service. They're the kind of people who will help you move a piano or mow your lawn while you're on vacation. They have the spirit of Jesus, Who left the wealth of heaven to serve the poor of Palestine. I would like to be more like them.

God, help me to see through the glamour of the world to the true riches of service. —DANIEL SCHANTZ

SAT
16

MAKE SURE THERE IS NO ROOT AMONG YOU THAT PRODUCES SUCH BITTER POISON.
—Deuteronomy 29:18 (NIV)

THE WEEDS in my rock garden have been especially pesky this year, in spite of my efforts to pluck away at the problem.

"You can't do it that way," a gardener-friend told me as she watched me casually pull a couple of weeds from a bed of bright yellow marigolds. "You've got to dig down deeper and get the whole root system, or that same weed will just keep reappearing year after year." She then rummaged through my basket of garden tools, pulled out a long weed digger, plunged it into the dirt next to a weed and dug the weed out, along with a clump of dirt. "This is how you get to the root of the problem," she said, sounding like some wise weed philosopher.

Her words got me to thinking about some of the pesky weeds in my life. Take procrastination, for instance. On some days, I have a bad habit of putting off the most important tasks that I must tackle. Finally, I force myself to start the project, but in a couple of days procrastination crops up again. If I stop and dig deeper around the edges of this habit, I find that it is rooted in a fear that I won't do a good job or that I won't adequately meet someone else's expectations. What if I dig out my fear of failure and surrender it to God in prayer?

Thanks to my weed philosopher, my garden is starting to look a little better—and so is my life.

Father, help me get to the roots of my problems and surrender them to You in prayer. —Carol Kuykendall

SUN
17

"You feed them. . . ." —Mark 6:37 (TLB)

RETIRE? How could I retire with the state of the economy what it was, taxes rising and Social Security dwindling? With retirement, my gross income was reduced to one half of what we were struggling to live on already. Besides, I was still paying off a mortgage and was behind in my taxes.

I went over the numbers in my head again and again, and just couldn't make them work. The greater our combined income, it seemed the less we had to spend. My biggest fear was having to reduce our weekly pledge to the church. Having served on the vestry, I understood how important support was. What could I do?

One Sunday I stumbled into church, my mind too filled to listen. The first readings swept by me like a speeding car. Then came the Gospel. St. Mark spoke of Jesus addressing the five thousand until almost dusk. The disciples came to Jesus because there was nothing to eat. But His command was very clear: "*You* feed them." The puzzled disciples found five loaves and two fishes. Jesus blessed the fish and broke the bread, and amazingly enough, there was enough for all.

That resolved it: I had reached my decision about retirement and my tithe. I spoke to my boss about retirement and, within the week, an unexpected check arrived with just enough to pay off my taxes. All the rest of the year, even though my income was reduced by half, there was a sizable increase in the money I had to spend because my expenses were greatly reduced.

I have remembered those words from Mark ever since, putting aside my church pledge first. Each year that amount has increased. So have my blessings.

Good Provider, You ask us to trust You and show the first effort. Then You guide and support us. —OSCAR GREENE

MON *PRAY FOR EACH OTHER. . . . —James 5:16 (NIV)*

18

FOR MORE THAN a year, I had prayed for my father-in-law. First, that his medical tests would come back with good news. Then after he had been diagnosed with colon cancer, I prayed for good doctors and sound treatment. After intense, extended chemotherapy, I prayed that God would give Dad the strength he needed to keep fighting the disease. And, finally, on a gray morning in March, I stood shoulder-to-shoulder with other family members around his hospital bed and prayed that God would end his suffering and take him home to heaven.

Several months after his death, I often caught myself starting to pray for Dad, only to realize there was no longer any need. Every time this happened, I felt helpless all over again. Then, one Monday as I was on my way to work, I found a way to put those Dad-focused prayers to good use.

That weekend my mother-in-law had cleaned out Dad's closets—a painful but unavoidable task. She had taken his clothes to the church resale shop I passed every day. Handsome suits, crisp white shirts, almost-new shoes, a stack of gently faded denim jeans. *Who will buy these things? Who will wear them?* I decided then and there that I would pray for those men who would. I'd pray that some of Dad's honesty and candor, some of his love for country and family, some of his unflagging faith would also become part of their lives.

So these days when I'm prompted to pray for Dad, I pray instead for whoever is walking in his shoes—or wearing the tie I bought him last Christmas.

You hear all our prayers always, Father. Help us to be open to new ways to pray for each other. Amen! —MARY LOU CARNEY

TUE
19

COME YE, AND LET US GO UP TO THE MOUNTAIN OF THE LORD . . . AND HE WILL TEACH US OF HIS WAYS. . . . —*Isaiah 2:3*

ONCE A YEAR I make it a point to climb Monument Mountain in Great Barrington, Massachusetts. The views are impressive, and so is the lore connected with the rocky summit.

In 1850, two great American writers met there for the first time. Nathaniel Hawthorne hiked up the north side and Herman Melville ascended the south trail. They celebrated their rendezvous with a picnic lunch that was rudely interrupted by a tremendous summer thunderstorm. The authors took shelter in a cave, where they passed the time vigorously debating the great ideas of the day. Was mankind doomed to sin? Did science and technology offer a better future or were they to be feared? Could one man ever be allowed to oppress another?

The other day I made my annual pilgrimage. It was a hot, sticky day, but conditions improved a bit when the trail wound into the tree cover. I stopped to fill my water bottle from a quick-moving stream running down a crevice, then pushed on. Finally, I scrambled up some boulders to the top, where I could look out over the Berkshire Hills.

Melville and Hawthorne must have sat very near here and enjoyed their abbreviated repast. That reminded me. I pulled a sandwich out of my pack, ate slowly and thought about the two writers. They had debated the great ideas of the day, and those questions hadn't changed very much in a century and a half. We still struggle with sin, science raises as many questions as it answers and men continue to oppress other men, often horribly. And maybe that's what I needed to know: We continue to battle those ancient human failings, hoping that we become not a perfect race, but a better one in the sight of God.

Lord, I climb mountains so my ears can be a little closer to Your lips. Please help me to find answers. —EDWARD GRINNAN

WED
20

THE LORD SHALL BLESS THEE. . . .YEA, THOU SHALT SEE THY CHILDREN'S CHILDREN. . . . —*Psalm 128:5-6*

"MOM, OUR pregnancy test is positive!" our daughter Brenda told us on the phone last March. This would be her first baby, due on Thanksgiving Day.

Two months later, at the end of May, my husband opened his birthday card from our daughter Tamara and out dropped a baby shoe! This was her unique method of letting us know when she's pregnant. So far, we had collected three small shoes, so now we were adding a fourth for Tamara's baby due in mid-January.

After another two months, our daughter Kelly and her husband invited us to dinner at a local restaurant. Scrawled in crayon on the paper tablecloth beneath our menus was this message: "Kelly is pregnant!" Her first child would be born in early March. Our trio of daughters expecting babies together—we couldn't believe it!

Next, Tamara phoned from her Arctic Ocean home to tell us they were adopting a newborn Eskimo girl named Ruby Dawn. Now we had one "just arrived" grandchild, plus three more on the way!

This cluster of family birth announcements recalled a typo I'd made several years ago. While writing a friend about my "empty nest," I inadvertently typed, "empty next" instead. It was a prophetic mistake: God always has a "next" for me. And it's astounding how *empty* climbs to *full* again, when His hand is tipping the pitcher.

Father, I rejoice with You in the wonder of seeing my children's children. Fill me with anticipation for the many satisfying "nexts" You have for me.
—CAROL KNAPP

THU
21
A MAN'S MIND PLANS HIS WAY, BUT THE LORD DIRECTS HIS STEPS. —*Proverbs 16:9 (RSV)*

IF YOU'VE EVER driven out of town in your car, I'm sure you are familiar with Road Trip Rule #1: You will always arrive an hour late. It doesn't matter how early you intend to leave or how good your directions are, you will be late.

Which is why this particular day was so amazing. An out-of-town meeting lasted half as long as I had expected, and I was on the road to Charlottesville, Virginia, for a doctor's appointment ahead of schedule. But as I cruised down the freeway fantasizing about how to kill a few hours upon my arrival, I noticed the road signs were indicating Washington, D.C. instead of Charlottesville. I was on the wrong road! Road Trip Rule #1 had caught up with me, and now I wondered if I'd make my appointment at all.

When I finally arrived at the hospital parking deck, I had to wait in my car while a man flagged down a motorist in front of me. He gestured angrily at a prehistoric minivan with its hood popped up. After the motorist moved on without giving assistance, I was the next obvious target. Sure enough, the man needed a jump start and could I please help him?

I looked at my watch nervously. Would I have time? To my amazement I would. For the jump start and my appointment. *Perfect timing*, I thought. But it wasn't exactly mine.

Thank You, God, that Your timing is perfect. —JOSHUA SUNDQUIST

FRI
22
JUDGE NOT ACCORDING TO THE APPEARANCE, BUT JUDGE RIGHTEOUS JUDGMENT. —*John 7:24*

WHEN MY FRIEND Naomi and I arrived in Barcelona, Spain, we walked into the youth hostel slumped under the weight of our bags. I couldn't wait to drop my backpack and settle in, but the dim fluorescent lights in the dreary lobby made me hold on to my belongings even tighter. *Maybe we should have spent some extra money on a* real *hotel*, I thought. But we had no extra money, and the reservations were already made.

We got our keys from the front desk and walked to the room we'd be sharing with four strangers. *What am I doing?* I thought as we walked through the dark hallway. *Who knows what kind of people they'll be?* We opened the door and there was our room—tiny, colorless and crammed with prisonlike bunk beds. "Home sweet home," I moaned, as I sat on the bare, flimsy mattress.

One by one, our roommates arrived as we made our beds with our own colorful sheets. As they introduced themselves, my fears were slowly calmed. They were interesting and friendly, and came from places like Canada, Australia, New Zealand and England. When the last bed was claimed, the room bubbled over with life, and my dread had given way to excitement.

Throughout the week we visited the sights together, fumbling with tourist maps and instant cameras. Late at night we'd return to our room and snuggle into our sleeping bags—laughing and talking like one big slumber party. It was hard to believe that I'd walked into that experience clutching my belongings in fear.

Lord, thank You for the new experiences that help me grow, even if they look a little daunting at first. —KAREN VALENTIN

SAT
23

"SEE, I HAVE REFINED YOU, THOUGH NOT AS SILVER; I HAVE TESTED YOU IN THE FURNACE OF AFFLICTION."
—*Isaiah 48:10 (NIV)*

"THERE'S A FIRE in the Gap!"

The phone call came at about ten o'clock on a Friday evening. Rushing to our porch windows we saw a dull red glow on the east side of Kern Mountain just north of where Route 211 wound up through Virginia's New Market Gap. Unusually high winds were forecast and, indeed, already blowing in from the northwest.

By midnight I was stunned to see a molten red-orange glow on our side of the ridge. By 2:00 A.M. it had become a string of fiery pearls laid on the dark velvet of the mountainside. Pockets of fire glowed like suns between the black silhouettes of oak and chestnut trees.

Slowly, the fire burned its way downhill and uphill. By Saturday night it was a glowing red strand looping from north to southeast. Two hundred and fifty acres had been scorched. An old Sikorsky H-34 helicopter hauled buckets of water five miles from a farm pond and dumped them on the leading edges of the flames. From our porch, it looked like a mosquito spitting at a dragon. Yet, after two days, with the help of a Hot Shot team from California and the Park Service firefighters, the fire was contained. By Sunday night only smoldering ash was left. Our friends' homes nestled on both flanks of the mountain were safe.

Upset at the loss of acres of trees and plants, I wondered why the firefighters had not been more aggressive. Then I recalled what I'd heard on a TV program just two days before the fire: A forest fire is not all bad. Deadwood stands of blighted chestnut trees need to be burned out. The sturdier or healthier deciduous trees have thick bark; they may scorch on the outside, but they don't die. Burning pines drop their cones and the seeds nestle into the newly enriched soil. The root systems of many plants are not affected by fire burning off the tops. In a few years, healthy new growth will replace a forest grown too dense. The mountain will be better, healthier, even more beautiful. And the deer and bears and peregrine falcons will have even finer places to roam.

Lord, You burn out the deadwood in my life and plant the seeds of fresh, new growth. Thank You for Your refining fires. —ROBERTA ROGERS

SUN
24

HOLD THESE VIRTUES TIGHTLY. WRITE THEM DEEP WITHIN YOUR HEART. —*Proverbs 3:3 (TLB)*

LAST JULY my husband Don and I decided to combine a business meeting in Portland, Oregon, with a trip to Mount Hood, then a drive down the coast. The meeting ended at noon Saturday, giving us time to walk through Portland's colorful and fragrant rose gardens before spending the night on the outskirts of the city.

I called around to check service times at United Methodist churches in the area, and Sunday morning we headed for the one we'd decided to attend. The only problem was that we couldn't find it!

Finally, with ten o'clock approaching, we stopped at First Baptist Church in Gresham. It was great! The music was upbeat and lively, the sermon provided sound biblical instruction, the people were friendly and welcoming, and no one minded our casual dress.

The most lasting "take-home," however, came from the rainbow-hued banners—deep purple, ruby red, bright blue—that adorned the sanctuary walls. Each banner was appliquéd with a "rule" for Christian living—a reminder that following the Lord doesn't stop when we leave the church parking lot. The banners read:

JOYFULLY PRAISE GOD
ENCOURAGE ONE ANOTHER
STRIVE FOR MATURITY IN CHRIST
USE OUR GIFTS TO SERVE
SHARE THE GOOD NEWS

I wrote them down, but didn't notice until we were in the car that the first letters of the banners spelled out JESUS. The name was a visual reminder that He wants to be Lord of my life every day—at work in my office, participating in a business meeting, doing laundry at home or enjoying the fragrance of a Peace rose while on vacation. Surely His name is the best thing of all to take with us as we go out into the world.

Lord, help me keep my eyes, thoughts, words and work focused on You as I travel through life. Amen. —PENNEY SCHWAB

MON
25

AND NOW THESE THREE REMAIN: FAITH, HOPE AND LOVE. BUT THE GREATEST OF THESE IS LOVE.
—*I Corinthians 13:13 (NIV)*

I WAS VISITING my daughter Laura on Whidbey Island in Washington, where she was a part of the AmeriCorps community service program. I wanted to feel close to her, and yet not be too much of a mother—I didn't want to be a walking suggestion box. More than that, I wanted to be able to put aside the differences we have in our outlooks on life.

Laura met me at the ferry, her long dark hair and sparkling blue eyes standing out in the crowd. We hugged and laughed, then roared away in her noisy pickup. As we talked, I swallowed hard at some of her free-spirited opinions.

We stopped to walk a trail she'd helped build. At the entrance was a kiosk she'd built and painted. "I hurried to get it finished before you came," she said. On it she'd painted a colorful outdoorsy scene with an enormous sun pouring down over all.

"It's beautiful, Laura," I said.

She always did favor the sun, even as a small child. As we walked the trail, I told her a story about her childhood. *Does she even want to hear this?* I wondered. But when I finished, she said, "Mom, thank you. I like it when you tell me things from back then. No one else can give those things to me but you."

The whole week was like that, a twining of old and new. At week's end, when we parted at the ferry, she said, "I love you, Mom. You'll always be my mother."

We laughed and hugged tight. "I love you too, honey," I said. "I'll be praying for you."

"I'm glad," she said. I could tell she meant it.

As the boat pulled away from its moorings, I waved at Laura, feeling the strong sunshine of her grown-up love—and the grace that allowed me to get out of the way to receive it.

Lord, help me to keep letting go of my daughter, while holding her in prayer. —SHARI SMYTH

TUE

26

THE LORD SHALL GIVE THEE REST FROM THY SORROW, AND FROM THY FEAR. . . . —*Isaiah 14:3*

THE ELDERLY WOMAN sitting next to me had never flown before and was clearly frightened. She was giggling to keep from crying. As the jet engines thrust us down the runway and into the air, she buried her face in her hands, covering her eyes. She would not look out the window. She stared straight ahead, refusing to gaze at the bright sky, the cumulus clouds, the beauty of the green, mottled earth far below.

Cautiously, I began a conversation. I joked and asked her if she would risk just one peek out the window. She twittered and nervously shook her head. "No," she replied. "If I don't look at it, it ain't there." And she didn't.

After we landed, I watched my new friend walk off the airplane. She heaved a huge sigh of relief and broke into laughter. She had survived the flight. It's a shame she didn't enjoy the journey.

Father, give me the courage to face my fears. —SCOTT WALKER

WED

27

"EVERY PLACE THAT THE SOLE OF YOUR FOOT WILL TREAD UPON I HAVE GIVEN YOU. . . ."
—*Joshua 1:3 (NKJV)*

"SO WHY DID you move to Chicago?" There's something in the voice, the tilt of the head, the raising of the brow of the people who ask me this question that tells me they're sure they'll be getting me to confess my deepest secrets.

I tell them that I was raised in Illinois, and I say it as though I have an irrevocable right to be here. Then I square my shoulders, because this is, after all, the City of Broad Shoulders, and tell them that I love the city, that I've always wanted to experience living right in its heart.

I love hearing the stop-and-go, the rush and horns of traffic far beneath my window. I love the sound of the el train that's my lullaby at night and my alarm clock in the morning. I've enjoyed eating crabs in Maryland, quahogs in Rhode Island and boiled peanuts in North Carolina, but I've found gastronomic fulfillment in Chicago. Smoked sausages, pickles, catfish . . . finally I'm amongst my people; I've found my way home!

Then I share the one thing I most appreciate: When I go for walks now, I'm not pacing on a track or strolling in a park. When my feet hit the pavement, my exercise has a purpose. Now when I walk, I'm going someplace, and what a joy it is!

Lord, bless my footsteps and let me be a blessing wherever I go. And thank You for the place I call home. —SHARON FOSTER

THU

28

I HAVE GONE ASTRAY LIKE A LOST SHEEP; SEEK THY SERVANT; FOR I DO NOT FORGET THY COMMANDMENTS. —*Psalm 119:176*

LAST SUMMER, my wife Sandee and I spent our twentieth anniversary in Wyoming with college students. I was teaching a study session outside Yellowstone National Park. Here's my diary of Day One:

10:00 A.M. Start hike on Crazy Creek Trail.

10:45 A.M. Lose all ten students, who have dispersed in random groups throughout the Absoroka Mountains.

11:00 A.M.–4:00 P.M. Frantic worry.

4:00 P.M.–4:15 P.M. Everyone located.

Great start, *eh?* I'm eternally grateful for the happy ending, but how could eleven reasonable, educated folks get lost so quickly?

Back at the camp, I was too annoyed to celebrate our anniversary. I lay in bed that night, in the midst of one of the world's most beautiful parks, next to one of the world's most beautiful women, and it occurred to me how often Sandee and I have lost each other, wandered off by ourselves, never noticing we had left the path.

What a dangerous journey marriage can be, how easy it is to lose our way. You'd think we'd know these woods by now, but I've seen how that presumption can hurt you—suddenly you're alone and nothing is familiar. You're left with only the sun, the moon, the stars—heaven itself—to find your way back.

Happy anniversary, Sandee. For our twentieth anniversary, I'm supposed to buy you china, but how about paper instead—like maybe a map?

Thank You, Lord, for our marriage. And if we start to get lost in the woods, put us back on the right road. —MARK COLLINS

FRI
29
"DO NOT STORE UP FOR YOURSELVES TREASURES ON EARTH. . . . BUT STORE UP FOR YOURSELVES TREASURES IN HEAVEN. . . . FOR WHERE YOUR TREASURE IS, THERE YOUR HEART WILL BE ALSO."
—*Matthew 6:19–21 (NIV)*

"I'LL DO THE BATHROOM," I said to my sister Maria. Maria had been taking care of Aunt Lillian for the last year or so, and although they had gone through some of her belongings before she died, the house was full of the accumulation of a lifetime.

My sister had been far closer to my aunt, and I scanned the rooms for personal things that I imagined would be difficult for Maria to throw away—Aunt Lillian's toothbrush, bar of soap, clipped coupons. In the closet, I stumbled upon boxes and boxes of photographs and greeting cards: anniversary cards, Valentines, the sympathy cards from 1981 when my uncle died.

We had been cleaning for an hour or so when one of my aunt's visiting nurses knocked on the door. She was driving by when she noticed my sister's car, and she'd stopped in just to say hello. Over graham crackers and tea, Maria and the nurse shared stories about the final months of my aunt's life.

Sunlight streamed in through the window, and the things in the drawers of Aunt Lillian's desk, the magazine-filled bookshelves, the closets became simple objects, flat and one-dimensional when held against the memories in the voices of Maria and the nurse. Memories—like faith and the warmth of the sun, the things our hands can't hold—are what our hearts hold on to.

Lord, help me to remember that my belongings are only borrowed for use while I'm here. It's love that's everlasting. —SABRA CIANCANELLI

SAT
30

BE STILL, AND KNOW THAT I AM GOD. . . .
—*Psalm 46:10*

I WAS RUSHING down the rain-swept freeway with my son Julian in tow when I noticed that he was particularly quiet in the backseat. I looked at him and saw him staring out the window. The poor kid had nothing to do!

It occurred to me that my cell phone had games. "Look, Julian," I said, "you can play games on my cell phone!"

"Okay," he said without much enthusiasm.

Later, as the car was filled with the thin beeps of the cell-phone game, I looked out at the view from the freeway. Massive storm clouds were still unleashing torrents of rain, while in the distance three spectacular bolts of sun broke through the clouds.

I looked back at Julian. He was staring intently at the cell phone's tiny screen, ignoring the magnificent display just outside his window. Why did I work so hard making sure that he was entertained? Why couldn't I have just left him the space to sit quietly and enjoy the beauty around him?

It occurred to me that there are so many activities in our family's life that none of us has much time to simply sit and reflect. Besides work and school, there are soccer, dance class, art class, speech class, vacation Bible school, swim lessons, working out, church activities . . . the list goes on and on. Then there's the entertainment that fills up whatever time's left over, the TV and the DVD player and the computer games—and now, even games on the phone.

Somewhere in all this we'd lost the quiet spaces that God can fill up with the beauty of a storm.

Lord, help me make time for quiet reflection. —DAVE FRANCO

SUN
31

WITH THEE IS THE FOUNTAIN OF LIFE. . . .
—*Psalm 36:9*

ON THE GROUNDS OF Christ Church on Quaker Hill in Pawling, New York, there is a beautiful little fountain. During my service as interim pastor of that church, I enjoyed walking past its sparkling waters. Whenever I arrived at the church, I'd flip the on-switch, then wait as the water was pumped up from a container to the fountain's highest tier and sent skyward as a spout, splashing down into the first basin and overflowing into the basin below.

One day as I entered the churchyard, I saw that the fountain wasn't working, even though the container had water in it. Although my mechanical skills are limited, I went back to the electrical system and turned the main breaker off and on. But the fountain did not start.

As I looked at the fountain more closely, I saw a small sign that read, "If the container is not completely full, the fountain will not operate." Sure enough, as soon as I filled the container all the way up, the water began to pour forth from the fountain.

It works the same way in life, I thought. If I'm half-hearted about my spiritual life, it affects everything I do. But when I allow my life to be filled to the brim with Christ's love, I can be a blessing to all, like that sparkling fountain.

Lord, I love You with all my heart. May my fountain of life sparkle with Your living waters. —TED NACE

SEEDS OF REJOICING

1 _____

2 _____

3 _____

4 _____

5 _____

6 _____

7 _____

8 _____

9 _____

10 _____

11 _____

12 _____

13 _____

14 _____

15 _____

16 _____

17 _____

18 _____

19 _____

20 _____

21 _____

22 _____

23 _____

24 _____

25 _____

26 _____

27 _____

28 _____

29 _____

30 _____

31 _____

August

Hope we have as an anchor of the soul, both strong and stedfast. . . .

—*Hebrews 6:19*

GOD SIGHTINGS
LOOKING WITH LOVE

MON *Do not hide your face from me. . . .*
—Psalm 27:9 (NIV)

I

I'D BROUGHT MY three-year-old granddaughter to the beach. Lugging blanket, umbrella, plastic pail and shovel, a thermos of lemonade and a picnic basket, I found an inviting stretch of sand and gratefully laid down our gear. For me it was a welcome break from weeks of pressure, finishing one demanding assignment and launching another.

For a blissful hour we were absorbed in constructing an improbable castle with an elaborate canal conducting seawater to our moat. We ate our lunch and were collecting shells to beautify the castle walls when I noticed one of our sandwich wrappers blowing away.

"We don't want to mess up the pretty beach," I said as I started after it. *This will be a little environmental lesson for her.*

I hadn't gone thirty yards when a wail stopped me. "What's the matter, honey?" I called back.

"I couldn't see you!"

"But . . . I'm right here!"

"I couldn't see your *face*."

Wrapper and ecological education abandoned, I went back to where a little girl stood with a bucketful of shells and eyes full of tears. *My face!* I thought. She'd seen what I was *doing*, but that wasn't enough. She needed my face turned toward her, telling her, "I see you. I'm attending to you. I care."

Maybe, I thought as we alternated slipper shells with scallop shells on the grand gateway to our castle, *that's my trouble, too. Maybe I've been so busy asking what God wants me to do that I've failed first of all to seek His face, to start each day with a relationship, to ask to hear not His orders, but just that He loves me.*

Your face, Lord, I will seek (Psalm 27:8, NIV).

—ELIZABETH SHERRILL

TUE
2

"WHOEVER WELCOMES ONE OF THESE LITTLE CHILDREN IN MY NAME WELCOMES ME. . . ."
—*Mark 9:37 (NIV)*

SOME THINGS never change. Saturday I noticed neighbor girls, Cynthia and Katrina, jumping rope to the same silly rhymes I learned forty-five years ago, four hundred miles north of here. From behind my screen door, I watched, wishing myself one of them—going on ten instead of fifty. As I walked upstairs to get dressed for a dinner gathering at my friend Betty's, I thought, *Oh, to be a kid again, before adult responsibilities crowded in.*

At Betty's, the age-perspective changed. I was the youngest of her six guests. And she topped the list at age eighty-five. Before dinner, the conversation turned briefly to the spiritual connection between body and soul. Betty took the floor. Her aging body may have slowed down, but—she pointed to her heart—"Inside here I'm the same kid I was seventy-five years ago, the girl who climbed trees and chased around the yard."

Yes! I silently agreed. *That child within me, she's there. To be happy she just needs to feel welcome inside my adult skin. She's feeling cramped. She wants to be out skipping rope—and there's no good reason she's not.*

So on Sunday evening I pushed open the screen door and asked Cynthia if I could take a turn . . . thirteen jumps. Monday night, twenty. Today I'm on my way to buy a jump rope.

Someday I may not be physically able to skip rope, but even then I'll remember that some things never change—like the presence of that child within me, who never grows old but needs to feel welcome in my heart.

Lord, when You walked this earth You welcomed the children and the childlike into Your life. Help me to make room for that child in myself.
—EVELYN BENCE

WED
3

THEREFORE CONFESS YOUR SINS TO ONE ANOTHER . . . THAT YOU MAY BE HEALED. . . . —*James 5:16 (RSV)*

IT WAS HAPPENING again today, the shyness I used to feel when walking into a roomful of people. I thought I had outgrown it. I knew a lot of the people in the room, but I felt vulnerable and withdrawn.

We were there to share the problems and joys we had in trying to live for God. I knew that in the process of sharing, I might discover the reason for my irrational shyness. But I didn't want to confess that I was afraid.

As the meeting began, one man admitted that he kept neglecting his family and forgetting about God because he was so wrapped up in his business. "I haven't had time to pray regularly, because I've been thinking almost totally about myself," he said. "This morning I realized that I'm not much, but I'm about all I ever think about." We all laughed. The man shook his head, and laughed with us. "When I walked in today, I didn't want to tell you. But I'm sure glad I did."

My stomach churned in the silence that followed. Then I said, "I've been feeling miserable the last few days. I didn't have a clue as to what the problem was till just now. I'm not sharing my real problems with anybody." I went on to tell them about my uneasiness when I walked into the room, and about similar fears I had had as a boy. As I talked, I began to see what had brought back those scary feelings: "Earlier this year, I made a commitment to do some writing, and now the deadline is here. I haven't done this sort of writing in a while, and I'm afraid I won't be able to do the assignment well. And when I came in here, all I felt was the old shame and fear of not being good enough."

As soon as I got those words out of my mouth, the fear was gone.

Lord, thank You for leading me out of my self-centeredness and bringing me peace. Amen. —KEITH MILLER

THU
4

"RETURN TO YOUR TENTS WITH GREAT RICHES. . . ."
—*Joshua 22:8 (NAS)*

WE MET JOE at a northern Manitoba, Canada, campground, where he liked nothing better than to go fishing with his Labrador dog Goldie. They were easily recognized out on the lake, Joe in his outboard with Goldie braced at the front of the boat, ears flapping in the wind and nose pointed toward the open water. Returning from a day's fishing, they often stopped by our campsite, Joe for a cup of coffee and Goldie for a stale biscuit or two.

One morning I peeked out the window of our camper just in time to see Joe and Goldie silhouetted against the first streaks of sunrise as they pulled away from the dock. *This must be the day he plans to portage three miles into Brad Lake for some choice pickerel.* Joe had explained how a canoe could be pulled over the rough terrain on a cart equipped with bicycle wheels. "A lot easier for an old guy like me," he said.

All that day I kept thinking of Joe and his dog out in the wilderness at Brad Lake. As twilight crept in, I began stoking up the campfire. Suddenly Goldie bounded up to greet me. "Where's Joe?" I asked. She looked back toward the dock and cocked her ears.

Squinting into the gathering dusk, I saw Joe plodding up the hill toward us, carrying something in his hands. "For you," he said simply, as he presented me with a bouquet of very rare, very lovely pink lady's slipper. "I found them at the far end of the portage."

Lord, may I always take into account the sacrifice that enriches each gift I receive. —ALMA BARKMAN

FRI
5
A WISE MAN WILL HEAR, AND WILL INCREASE LEARNING. . . . —Proverbs 1:5

WE RECEIVE a weekly publication that guides us through the many choices now available on satellite television. One column in particular, in which celebrities answer questions about themselves, always fascinates me. The questions are the same each week, and range from "What is your most prized possession?" to "What's the title of the book you are currently reading?" The answers are as different as the personalities themselves, colorful, creative, candid or elusive.

The last question on the list is "What three words best describe you?" Most of the answers are alike and complimentary: funny, thoughtful, happy, outgoing, lovable, talkative, intelligent, careful, devoted. When I asked myself the question, I patted myself on the back, describing myself as "honest, compassionate and loyal."

I had gotten so used to reading three positive adjectives in answer to that question that I was completely taken aback one week when Jerry Lewis, who is widely known and loved for his charitable activities, used these three words to describe himself: "Room for improvement."

I felt a bit chagrined at the complacency of my own answer. I decided to take a more realistic look at myself, and finally came up with the three words I hope will best describe me from now on: "Willing to learn."

Father, I know I can't grow and mature spiritually if I'm content to rest on my laurels. Help me remember that I can always find room for improvement if I'm willing to learn. —LIBBIE ADAMS

SAT

6

THE EARTH BRINGETH FORTH FRUIT OF HERSELF; FIRST THE BLADE, THEN THE EAR, AFTER THAT THE FULL CORN IN THE EAR. —Mark 4:28

ANY REAL GARDENER would look with dismay at the pathetic plot of land I have claimed for my garden. A small patch of dirt in our apartment complex, abandoned by the professional gardener, surrounded by buildings, it gets little light and less love. One spring day on a whim, I planted some basil and tomato seedlings there. To my amazement they grew, and by summer I had four ripe tomatoes and enough basil for a small batch of pesto. Not bad.

The next year I planted some snapdragons and anemones and added parsley and mint to the basil and tomatoes. The mint came back the next spring of its own accord and the parsley did fine. In the fall I put down some tulip bulbs so I'd have a spring and summer garden. Sure enough, they popped up and flowered in April, just in time for Easter. That spring I put in some carrots, beans and zucchini. Alas, the beans never appeared and the carrots were no bigger than a thumbnail, but we cooked two zucchini one August night. And I added more tulips that fall, dreaming of a Rembrandt landscape on an eight-by-six plot of earth.

"For all your efforts, we have the most expensive tomatoes in all of New York City," my wife says. She's right. I could get something at the corner deli for a fraction of the price and effort. But these tomatoes (and parsley and mint and tulips) are mine. I have watched them survive attacks by rodents, insects, cats, heat waves and drought. It's my project with God. Out of a patch surrounded by concrete, a bit of nature flourishes. And I have never taken a tomato, tulip, carrot or zucchini for granted since.

Thank You, God, for Your bounty. —RICK HAMLIN

SUN
7

DON'T SCOLD YOUR CHILDREN SO MUCH THAT THEY BECOME DISCOURAGED AND QUIT TRYING.
—*Colossians 3:21 (TLB)*

I'D BEEN HAVING a difficult day, and in every mistake I heard a message of failure. Work returned for improvement: *You'll never get it right.* Losing my temper with the children: *You're a lousy mother.* Groceries partly put away and no dinner ready: *You plan your time so poorly.*

Rummaging in a box of old toys for something to entertain then-one-year-old Mark while I cooked, I found a little blue car. Suddenly I remembered our daughter Elizabeth pushing it along a wooden bench in the tiny church we attended while living in New Zealand when she was three years old.

One Sunday she wandered from our pew to the open door and began singing loudly about the bees buzzing outside, causing all heads to turn. After the service, an elderly woman with regal posture, elegantly attired in a green silk dress, approached us. I feared she would reprimand Elizabeth for disturbing everyone.

Instead, smiling, she sat next to Elizabeth, and in her proper British accent asked her name. "And how old are you?" Elizabeth held up three fingers. "Just three! Goodness! It is difficult for someone just three to sit so quietly." Elizabeth nodded solemnly.

"But, my, you *are* learning, aren't you? And please keep singing. We so enjoy your lovely voice!" She rose and patted my arm. "She's delightful. She's trying. Each week it will get easier."

As I brought the blue car to Mark, I resolved to be easier on myself and the children. And I could hear dear Mrs. Holland cheering me on: "Keep trying. Each day you'll do better. You *are* learning."

My patient, loving Father, help me to pour out encouragement on everyone around me, even myself. —MARY BROWN

MON
8

OLD THINGS ARE PASSED AWAY; BEHOLD, ALL THINGS ARE BECOME NEW. —*II Corinthians 5:17*

AT OUR LAKE COTTAGE in Indiana where my paternal grandmother and grandfather first summered almost a hundred years ago, there are many artifacts that have been handed down to me . . . an old kerosene lamp decorated with hand-painted roses, iron tongs that were used to carry ice to the wooden ice box, an oak chest with an oval mirror that someone decided to paint white. When the chest started to come unglued and began to fall apart, I resolved to save it from the trash pile and have it restored.

When I told our youngest, Daniel, about my project, he volunteered. Patient and meticulous, he has made several pieces of furniture and restored others, so I hoped he could save the chest. But after he got it stripped down to the bare wood, I saw why it had been painted: It was ugly. The top was gouged and discolored, some of its drawers were scratched and scarred, and the brass handles tarnished and dented. I was ready to admit defeat, but not Daniel; he was sure he could bring it back to life.

He replaced the veneer on top, sanded the drawers until the imperfections vanished and polished the brass handles until they shone like new. Last, he applied an oak stain and clear varnish. When I saw it, I couldn't believe my eyes. The chest will be returned in all its grandeur to the cottage next summer, ready for another generation or two.

Seeing what Daniel did with that piece of furniture reminded me of what God can do with people. He can forgive us of any sin—sand away our scars and imperfections, if you will—and transform us into new creatures. That's how amazing His grace, how glorious His love.

> *Thank God that with Him sin knows no size,*
> *That His forgiveness can take us to paradise.*
> —FRED BAUER

TUE
9

"THE LORD WILL NOT ABANDON HIS PEOPLE. . . ."
—I Samuel 12:22 (NAS)

I SPOTTED the black dog lying in the shade in our yard as I returned from the mailbox on a hot August day. She gave me that unmistakable "I've been abandoned" look, and I went over to her and took her head in my hands: beautiful face, shiny coat, good teeth, gentle but obviously frightened, thin, no collar. I knew my husband Gene wouldn't even discuss taking in another stray. "I'm going to try to find you a home," I promised. Gene and I were due at an exercise class, and I could only hope she would wait for me to return. "Stay," I told her. She seemed to understand.

At the exercise class, I begged people to take the dog. When I asked a man named Jack Brown, he said, "Well, sure, if Mary Jo says it's okay." I practically did cartwheels over to his wife. Mary Jo had heard only part of my story when she stopped me and said, "We'll take her. I'll pick her up in two hours."

On the way home, I told Gene about my success. "You hit the jack-pot," he said. "Dr. Brown is a retired professor of veterinary medicine."

When Mary Jo drove up, she got out of her car, plopped down on our cement driveway and looked the black dog in the eye. "Hi, girl," she said softly, and her new friend put one paw on Mary Jo's shoulder and wagged her tail. "Oh, she's so much bigger than I thought," Mary Jo said. "We want a puppy."

My heart fell, but I managed to thank Mary Jo for driving all the way across town.

"Oh, we're going to take her!" Mary Jo said, changing her mind. "The only kind of dogs we've ever had are abandoned ones. Her name is Frances. Come on, Francie." The dog, her head held high, stepped up into the front seat of the red car just as though she'd been doing it all her life.

Lord, seeing Francie rescued reminds me of that day years ago when You showed up in my life and refused to abandon me.

—MARION BOND WEST

WED
10

"BUT A SAMARITAN, AS HE TRAVELED, CAME WHERE THE MAN WAS; AND WHEN HE SAW HIM, HE TOOK PITY ON HIM." —*Luke 10:33 (NIV)*

I WAS TIRED. For seven hours, we had been clearing fire-wood, wicker furniture and other flammable objects away from homes threatened by wildfire. Being on a structure-protection crew during a forest fire is neither glamorous nor exciting.

The winds shifted late that afternoon, and the fire made a run down a steep hillside, across a creek and toward three houses. The siding on one of them was already blistering when we arrived in our truck. I peeled one hose line from its bed and hurried toward the house. My partner opened the valve to fill my line; I sprayed the wood siding to cool it and then tried to cool a stack of firewood that was burning furiously only ten feet away. The siding began to crackle from the reflected heat, and I sprayed it again. I had to be sparing with our water until a tanker truck arrived. When it did, I aimed a steady stream directly at the stack of wood. The firewood scattered like bowling pins into the surrounding black landscape.

We saved all three homes. Later that night, my arms ached as I tried to repack our hose lines. I couldn't lift the heavy hose onto the bed on top of our truck. I was so tired I wanted to weep.

"Need some help?" Two strangers from another fire department hoisted the hose and began folding it neatly into place. They left before I could mumble, "Thank you."

When my partner and I collapsed on the foam-soaked front porch to eat a sandwich, I thought about the parable of the Good Samaritan. I joined the fire department to become a Samaritan. But what did I learn? That even Good Samaritans need help.

Dear God, thank You for the strangers who do not pass us by.
—TIM WILLIAMS

THU
11

I WAITED PATIENTLY FOR THE LORD; AND HE INCLINED UNTO ME, AND HEARD MY CRY. —Psalm 40:1

WHENEVER MY HUSBAND Norman and I traveled around the country for his speaking engagements, we met people who gave us new insights about prayer. One of the most unusual came from a woman in Atlanta.

She'd been worried about her son Dan, who lived far away from her. He had three young children and a demanding job that he felt locked into. He commuted to work by bus, and when he finally returned home in the evening, he often dropped into a bar before heading home to his family. He developed a serious drinking problem, and his marriage had worn pretty thin because of it.

"If only I could ride the bus with Dan and get him home safely to his family each night," the woman thought. Then she got an idea: "Why *not* ride the bus with him?"

So the next morning she got on the bus with Dan—in her prayers. She rode alongside him, sometimes reminiscing about things that happened when he was a boy and sometimes silent—just loving him and praying that he would ask for God's help. That night, when he caught the bus for the ride home, she again boarded with him, riding beside him, loving him, praying for him. Twice a day from then on, she'd remind herself, "Now's the time to ride with Dan."

Some months later, visiting her son at Christmas, she learned that Dan wasn't drinking anymore.

"You know, I have a long bus ride back and forth to work," he told his mother. "Somehow, day after day, I thought about my drinking while I was riding the bus. Finally, I made the decision to stop, and once I did, even the bar on the way home didn't tempt me."

This woman reminded me that prayer is a perfect vehicle—for commuting *and* communing. Prayer, indeed, can get you where you want to be.

Thank You, Lord, that "more things are wrought by prayer than this world dreams of" (Alfred Lord Tennyson). —RUTH STAFFORD PEALE

FRI

12

AS SOON AS JESUS HEARD THE WORD THAT WAS SPOKEN, HE SAITH UNTO THE RULER OF THE SYNAGOGUE, BE NOT AFRAID, ONLY BELIEVE.
—*Mark 5:36*

WHEN I BECAME the Louisiana Teacher of the Year, I had various duties to fulfill. Meeting all the other teachers of the year in Dallas would be fun. The National Teachers Forum sounded like an exciting opportunity. Traveling to Washington, D.C., and meeting the president was something I looked forward to. But going to International Space Camp was not something I wanted to do. *I don't really like science anyway,* I told myself. Deep down, though, I knew the real issue: I was afraid.

At church one Sunday the pastor spoke about the impala, a slightly built African antelope. It can make a leap as long as thirty feet and as high as ten feet, but can be held in by a three-foot fence. Why? Because the impala will not jump when it cannot see where it will land.

I knew then that I had to go to space camp. I couldn't deprive myself of this new experience because of my fear. *Lord,* I prayed, *give me a courageous spirit, one born of Your faith.*

I returned from space camp a glorious new me. I'd been strapped into a gyroscope and tumbled every which way. I'd been harnessed onto a pulley and slung down a cable into a man-made lake to simulate a real splashdown. I'd even been the pilot on a simulated shuttle flight, and I had experienced weightlessness.

I learned quite a bit during space camp, but the realization that God is more interested in our growth than our comfort was indeed my biggest accomplishment.

Thank You, Lord, that unlike the impala I can make a leap of faith.
—MELODY BONNETTE

SAT

13

SUFFER THE LITTLE CHILDREN TO COME UNTO ME, AND FORBID THEM NOT: FOR OF SUCH IS THE KINGDOM OF GOD. —*Mark 10:14*

LAST AUGUST, my wife Rebecca and I were having lunch in a seafood restaurant built on a pier that stretched out over Long Island Sound. Seeing a single gull floating just below us, I tore off a piece of bread and tossed it into the water. But even as I did so, I realized I was being impolite. *I guess they don't want me luring in a cloud of seagulls to a place like this.*

For the rest of our meal, I watched the bird floating on the water, wishing I could give it something else to eat but keeping myself from doing so for propriety's sake. Then, as we were paying our check, a very young girl passed by our table, a plate of leftovers carefully balanced in her hands. The gull and I both watched her as she walked to the edge of the pier, paused for a moment, then threw the contents of her plate out onto the water. The gull flapped over to the floating bits of food, letting out a squawk as it did so. Instantly, half a dozen more appeared out of nowhere, ready to eat. The girl beamed, clearly delighted with her feat of magic. The correct thing to do? Probably not. But just the right one all the same.

Thank You, Lord, for the moments of innocence and spontaneity that break in and surprise me just when I need them.
— PTOLEMY TOMPKINS

SUN
14

AND I HEARD A GREAT VOICE OUT OF HEAVEN SAYING, BEHOLD, THE TABERNACLE OF GOD IS WITH MEN, AND HE WILL DWELL WITH THEM, AND THEY SHALL BE HIS PEOPLE, AND GOD HIMSELF SHALL BE WITH THEM, AND BE THEIR GOD. *—Revelation 21:3*

WHEN I WAS a child, our family worshipped at the Primitive Christian Church, a Spanish-speaking congregation. On Sundays, we wore our best clothes and walked to church no matter what the weather—rain, snow or sunshine. Along the way, we would meet up with other families marching down the streets. It seemed like the whole community was going to church.

Services were long, but never boring. On Sunday evenings our pastor opened with a call to worship followed by a hymn, "Holy, Holy, Holy, Is the Lord of Hosts: The Whole Earth Is Full of His Glory." As I sang, the music and lyrics lifted my spirit and opened my heart to see the invisible. I imagined God descending from heaven into our little church and sitting on one of the empty chairs on the pulpit with the minister. When the hymn ended and the pastor said, "God is with us," the church seemed to be filled with God's glory. Truly, God was with me, and no matter what problems I had to face during the week, I'd be okay.

Today, I drive to church and the services are shorter, but I still have that wonderful feeling I had when I was a child—that God is with us, to comfort and to strengthen us, no matter what burdens we bear.

Thank You, Lord, for the childhood church that taught me to connect with You through worship. — PABLO DIAZ

READER'S ROOM

MY DAUGHTER SUFFERED a miscarriage of a baby she and her husband had desperately wanted. When she became pregnant again, I prayed at every opportunity for her baby. While I was mowing my lawn, a thundershower came up, and I stopped mowing and sat on the porch, waiting for the shower to pass. Closing my eyes, I lifted my daughter and her baby to God and asked Him for reassurance—a sign that all would be okay. When I opened my eyes, I saw the most beautiful rainbow. I felt God's presence and reassurance so very strongly—His promise through the rainbow that everything would be all right. I see that rainbow every time I look in my granddaughter's eyes. —*Lee Ann Fuller, Pryor, Oklahoma*

MON
15

IF WE HAVE BEEN UNITED WITH HIM LIKE THIS IN HIS DEATH, WE WILL CERTAINLY ALSO BE UNITED WITH HIM IN HIS RESURRECTION. —Romans 6:5 (NIV)

IT WAS THE highlight of my trip to Rome: St. Peter's Basilica. "And that is the Pietà," said our guide, gesturing toward the far wall where Michelangelo's famous sculpture stood. I stared at Mary holding the body of her son, newly taken down from the Cross. The piece seemed to glow with a light that came from inside the marble. I was drawn to it with a force I could barely contain.

Leaving the tour group, I headed for the small altar in front of the work. Before I got there, I began to cry. Such passion! Such sadness! And yet the look on Mary's face . . . what was it? Sorrow, certainly, but something else, too.

I knelt and lifted my head for a closer look. Mary cradled Jesus, his adult body sagging in death across her lap. Was she remembering the times she had cradled him as a boy?

I became aware of a shoulder touching mine. I looked into the face of an Italian woman about my age. Our eyes met. She was crying, too. She reached for my hand, and together we prayed. I looked full into the face of the Mary, and suddenly I recognized what the look on her face was. *Hope.* She knew that evil would not have the final say. She knew it as surely as she knew her own Son.

Even in the midst of tragedy and sadness, You, Jesus, are our hope. Because You live, we can live, too. Hallelujah! —MARY LOU CARNEY

HE LEADETH ME . . .
TO REPAIR RELATIONSHIPS

TUE

16

A BROTHER IS BORN TO HELP IN TIME OF NEED.
—*Proverbs 17:17 (TLB)*

MY BROTHER Robert went off to college when I was twelve, and ever since it's seemed as if we were generations apart. As the years went by, Robert juggled his roles as dad, teacher, soccer coach, weekend pastor and hospital chaplain, while my life as a nurse and perennial patient kept me busy. I'd undergone almost twenty surgeries for tumors caused by neurofibromatosis while Robert was healthy. Sometimes I didn't think he understood.

Last year, when I had surgery to remove yet another tumor, Robert offered to drive me to my postoperative visit. I turned him down at first, but as I was preparing to leave I couldn't help thinking, *He wants to help and you won't let him.* When I called him, there was excitement in his voice. "I'll be there in fifteen minutes," he said.

Robert dropped me off at the clinic door and went to find a parking spot. "We got more tumor out than ever before," my doctor told me, "and I have a gut feeling you're not going to need any more surgeries."

When I left the doctor's office, I dashed into an open elevator and went down to the lobby to look for Robert. I spotted him pushing his way through the revolving doors and ran toward him. Then I hugged him for the first time I could remember. "I just got the most wonderful news. And I have you to tell it to!"

As we drove home, Robert told me about all the prayers he'd sent heavenward for me, prayers I'd known nothing about. Then he caught me stealing a look in the visor mirror, patting my eye that was now opened fully, no longer bulged with tumor—smiling without pain. His voice broke as he spoke: "You haven't had much good news, have you, Sis? I'm so happy about today."

How many precious moments do I miss, Lord, because I ignore Your nudging? —ROBERTA MESSNER

WED
17

AND GOD SAID, LET THERE BE LIGHT: AND THERE WAS LIGHT. AND GOD SAW THE LIGHT, THAT IT WAS GOOD. . . . —Genesis 1:3–4

"THANK GOODNESS you came." A hand tugged on my arm as I walked wearily into the darkened lobby of my apartment building.

New York City was in darkness: no traffic lights, no refrigeration, no elevators. So there in the lobby was my friend Elizabeth with no train to take her home. I'd spent time after work checking on my colleagues and buying flashlight batteries. So Elizabeth had been waiting there in the darkness for more than an hour, wondering if I'd ever come.

Together we faced the next challenge: I lived on the ninth floor and the emergency lights in the narrow staircase had long since gone out. We walked up flight after flight of stairs in the dark, losing count of the floors with no way to check. Suddenly, I lost all sense of time and place. All I could think of was the darkness and where the next step was.

I gave a small cry of fear, and Elizabeth reached back her hand. We went up more steps, hand in hand in the darkness. "Where are we?" I gasped. "This is scary."

"Don't worry," Elizabeth said firmly, "there will be light."

And immediately familiar words echoed in my mind: "And there was light."

Seconds later a voice from somewhere above us said, "Come on up. I'm on nine and I've got a flashlight." And there was light.

Thank You, Lord, for so often and in so many places sending light in the darkness. —BRIGITTE WEEKS

THU

18

Except ye . . . become as little children, ye shall not enter into the kingdom of heaven.
—*Matthew 18:3*

MY EIGHT-YEAR-OLD granddaughter Saralisa spent some time with us last year. The first thing she wanted me to do was to go to the creek with her. It's just across the road from our house, so hand in hand, we danced and skipped our way there.

Oh, the sound of the flowing water! It's the most beautiful music I know. I sat on the bank as Saralisa took off her shoes and socks and stepped into the cool stream. The morning sun was shining in golden patches, causing the mica at the bottom of the clear water to sparkle like pure gold. Saralisa had brought along a small skillet with which she "panned for gold," just as her grandmother had done more than sixty years ago.

Suddenly, I was a child again! With only a little hesitation, I took off my shoes and socks and joined in the fun. Of course we both knew it wasn't real gold, but that didn't matter one bit. Our true gold was in the pine-scented mountain air, the sunshine, that inimitable sound and the feel of the cool water over our bare feet.

Thank You, God! I thought to myself. *For this moment in all eternity, this seventy-two-year-old grandmother is a child again. Time, like an artist on the brink of creation, stands still. And ringing down the centuries, I hear those precious words, "And God saw every thing that he had made, and, behold, it was very good" (Genesis 1:31).*

Dear God, may I make time to be a child today, letting in all the wonders of Your great creation! —MARILYN MORGAN KING

FRI

19

"I tell you the truth, the Son can do nothing by himself; he can do only what he sees his Father doing. . . ." —*John 5:19 (NIV)*

ONE SUMMER long ago, I worked for my father as a member of a rough-and-tumble railroad maintenance crew. It was a traveling crew, and I soon found myself more than a thousand miles from home and from Dad.

One night we pulled into a little Louisiana town rather late, and the only place open was a bar. I'd been raised pretty strictly, but I was eager to try my first whiskey and find out what all the fuss was about. I ordered a drink and was just raising it to my lips when the roughest guy in the crew slapped it out of my hand and across the room. "You can't drink that," he said. "You're John Fellman's son." I was furious. Even a thousand miles away, Dad was still running my life.

All that summer, whenever cigars were passed around or the language got rough, the refrain was the same: "He can't do that. He's John Fellman's son." I hated being John Fellman's son.

Then one morning we faced a particularly hard task and that same tough guy said, "I guess we'd better finish this before the weekend. That's what your dad would want." It hit me that these men respected my dad deeply and that respect was reflected in their work—and in their care for his son. That day I stopped hating being John Fellman's son.

Last year, my father died. He had been ill for some time, and his deep faith had led him peacefully from this life to the next, but his death was a blow more severe than any I'd known before. But I knew I'd get through it the way I'd gotten through all of life's challenges since that summer more than twenty years ago—doing my best to be John Fellman's son.

Lord, thank You for giving me a father who set an example for me. Help me to pass on his legacy. —Eric Fellman

SAT
20

Give thanks unto the Lord. . . .Remember his marvellous works. . . . —*I Chronicles 16:8, 12*

A sweltering Saturday morning in August seemed like a great time to visit one of Phoenix's newest attractions, the WaterWorks at Arizona Falls. It's a grand name for a simple idea—use the water from the Arizona canal running throughout the city to create several cascading waterfalls and a hydro-generator to power homes.

The temperature was already 108 degrees, and my children Ross and Maria couldn't wait to bolt from the hot car and stand close to one of the big falls that drops water twenty feet into the canal below. The slightest breeze sent cool, wet sprays into their sweaty faces. Over the roar of the water I could hear Maria's delighted squeals.

I closed my eyes and leaned closer to the railing, feeling the gentle mist on my face. How strange that only the week before we had been on vacation in San Diego, two cool, breezy weeks with the Pacific Ocean right outside our door. Yet on days when we visited the Balboa Park museums or Seaworld, we didn't even stick a toe in the water. Now, back in dry Arizona, we'd made a special trip to bask in the coolness of a man-made waterfall. How easily and quickly we had taken for granted God's fabulous gift of the ocean.

But it's not just the ocean. I have only to look around each day to see God's other gifts I take for granted. I live in a peaceful neighborhood, my family is healthy, my husband's job is secure—to name just a few. What that tells me is simple: When I'm talking to God, I need to say thank You more often.

Help me every day to truly see and enjoy all You have given me, Lord. And thank You. —GINA BRIDGEMAN

SUN
21

GOD IS A SPIRIT: AND THEY THAT WORSHIP HIM MUST WORSHIP HIM IN SPIRIT AND IN TRUTH. —*John 4:24*

MY MOTHER HAS two cousins—a brother and sister— who live in a farming community in South Dakota. Elmer is eighty-five, Frances eighty-three. They live together in the same small white house that they grew up in.

My husband Terry and I always stop and visit when we pass through their town. Frances has battled cancer for several years and wears a wig to hide her baldness. She walks with a halting step caused by nerve damage from her chemotherapy.

Elmer has looked out for Frances throughout her illness. He's a tall, broad-shouldered man, whose thick white hair is usually in need of combing. He loves to paint and read. Last summer Elmer seemed thinner, and his conversation wasn't as animated. He seemed to have trouble concentrating. When we asked him what was wrong, he said only, "Things could be better."

My mother and I visited Frances and Elmer last fall. It was a Sunday morning. I suggested that Mom play the little organ that always stood silent in a corner of their living room. Maybe some old hymns would lift their spirits. Elmer slid onto the bench beside Mom to play. As he finished each song, I read its familiar words aloud from the hymnal. Behind her glasses, tears welled in Frances's eyes.

Elmer wanted to sing. His voice cracked on the high notes, and he stopped in places to weep over the words. I laid my hand on his bony shoulder and gave a gentle squeeze.

The music wasn't professional in that South Dakota living room; the organ had no pipes; the windows held no stained glass. Yet all I could think was, *This is church. God is right here, right now.*

In that moment it seemed as if an unseen hand reached out and gave my shoulder a gentle squeeze, too.

Lord God, Who never forsakes me, wherever I worship You, let it be from the heart. —CAROL KNAPP

MON
22

NOW THE LORD GOD HAD FORMED OUT OF THE GROUND ALL THE BEASTS OF THE FIELD AND ALL THE BIRDS OF THE AIR. . . . —Genesis 2:19 (NIV)

NOW THAT WE'VE moved back to my husband's family ranch, the kitchen window is one of my favorite lookouts. The southwest view is of rolling pastures and wheat fields, with a dirt road cutting a dusty path up the hill to the horizon. I see horses and cattle grazing, wildlife of all kinds flying or scampering. I've watched stormy weather blow in and unhampered winds rearrange leaves and piles of hay.

This August morning, I'm watching some unusual immigrants for this north Texas area: egrets, fluttering to their daily landing spot beside the grazing bulls. Many settle on the grass beside the huge animals' feet, waiting for them to kick up insects as they walk. Others line the fence, watching.

As I look across the pasture, I laugh out loud. Three egrets have perched on a bull's back as he lies in the grass, their white feathers and long necks in stark contrast to their host. The bull appears hospitable to his odd guests. He lies quietly, soberly chewing, his tail swishing. I wonder what he's thinking. Does he know the birds will keep the bugs from bothering him?

Watching the bull, I begin wondering: Am I as hospitable to the stranger who comes into my space? Do I sit quietly and listen to the new ideas brought in by a new church member? Do I welcome the friendship of a new acquaintance not quite like me?

I tend to be set in my ways, and I like to be in control of things. I'm also a little shy and reluctant to get out of my comfort zone. But I've decided to try to emulate the bull and the egrets. They've shown me I can work the bugs out of almost anything if I partner with others.

Father, forgive me for my reluctance to try new things and forge new relationships. Help me to welcome whatever You send my way.

—MARJORIE PARKER

TUE

23

"YOU WILL HAVE NOTHING TO FEAR. . . ."
—*Isaiah 54:14 (NIV)*

"MISS, CAN I PAY YOU for this book?" The little boy's insistent tone jogged me back to reality—my usual spot at the cash register—and out of the world of worries I'd been in.

One of my new duties at the bookstore was to suggest a dozen books to the members of a reading group, and the prospect filled me with fear. *I'm not all that well-read in fiction. What if they don't like any of the books? What if my mind goes blank when addressing the group of fifteen women? Maybe I'll call in sick that day.*

The boy—a five-year-old with his father standing close behind—smiled as he pushed a book toward me, followed by a few crumpled dollar bills and some quarters and pennies. I glanced at the book—it was about astronauts—as I rang it up and, glad to have a distraction from my whirling thoughts, said, "That looks interesting!"

"It's about the *moon*," the boy said.

"Would you like to go on a spaceship?" I asked him.

He looked frightened, and taking a step backward, clutched his father's arm. "*Now?*" he asked.

His father and I exchanged an amused look. "No, not now," I told him. "When you grow up."

He looked skeptical until his father added, "I'll go with you, okay?"

"Okay!" he said.

Wasn't I being as silly as that small boy to worry about a project that was far in the future? I had two months to plan calmly and practice my talk. And just as the youngster felt secure with his father right there behind him as a loving, encouraging presence, I, too, had a loving Father Who would be with me no matter where my job took me.

Father, be with me today, tomorrow and throughout the future as I venture into the unknown. —LINDA NEUKRUG

WED

24

THE LORD WILL SURELY COMFORT ZION . . . HE WILL MAKE . . . HER WASTELANDS LIKE THE GARDEN OF THE LORD. . . . —*Isaiah 51:3 (NIV)*

ONE SUMMER MORNING I took a walk along a dirt road in the Catskill Mountains of New York where banks of wildflowers grew along the verge. I got my field guide out of my backpack and identified a few: chicory, smart weed, bladder campion, aster. One particular sentence in the guidebook intrigued me: "Wildflowers thrive in disturbed soil."

I looked out over the sunny meadows and, sure enough, only an occasional Queen Anne's lace poked its umbrella head above the waving grasses. But here at my feet scores of flowers grew in the inhospitable debris of gravel and grit pushed aside by road scrapers. The soil's very lumpiness must help to capture rain and wind-blown seeds.

There are seemingly infertile areas in life, too, I thought—memories pushed aside as too painful, too embarrassing, like the memory of my first day in junior high school. Three older boys picked me up, set me on a drinking fountain and turned on the water, then followed me through the halls telling everyone that I'd wet my pants. To this day the memory stings, and I'd long ago pushed it aside as too distressing and useless. And yet, ever since then, I've found myself befriending anyone who's being picked on.

Perhaps, I thought as I resumed my walk, I should take a second look at these areas of "disturbed soil" in my life. Perhaps God doesn't see them as worthless scrapings from yesterday, to be pushed aside. Perhaps He's saying, "Ah, just the place for flowers to bloom."

Father, help me see pain and put-down as a place where You intend to plant a garden. —JOHN SHERRILL

THU

25

PRAISE YE HIM, SUN AND MOON: PRAISE HIM, ALL YE STARS OF LIGHT. —*Psalm 148:3*

I STOOD in a long line at the Griffith Observatory in Los Angeles to view the planet Mars. From August through September 2003, it was closer to the earth than it had been in sixty thousand years! Astronomers predicted it would not be this close again until the year 2281.

A family from Bangladesh was behind me; just ahead were two young Korean women who had grown up in Australia; and down the line was a friend whom I had watched emerge from her childhood of Suzuki violin lessons and recitals to become an accomplished artist. The wait became a people-enrichment time, all of us cross-culturally united as we anticipated a planetary encounter.

Then came the main attraction: Mars, the red planet. To my eye, it was peach, a dazzling peach with the south polar ice cap a luminous arc, and the shadow of a dark rift clearly visible. Mesmerized, I went from reflector to refractor telescope, then round again, anxious to absorb the image of that glorious light in the sky. So fantastically far away and yet, suddenly, visually so close.

It was almost midnight by the time I got home, where I could clearly see Mars moving with the turn of the Earth across the picture window in my bedroom. Like a jewel in the darkness, it bid me a bright good night.

Oh, Lord, my God, I bow in awe and gratitude that in all the Universe You make the frail human heart Your home. Come in today; come in to stay. —FAY ANGUS

FRI

26

BLESSED ARE THEY THAT MOURN: FOR THEY SHALL BE COMFORTED. —*Matthew 5:4*

"WHERE'S THE BIG ONE?"

I was walking my cocker spaniel Sally on West 29th Street early one bright August morning when this woman—a stranger to me—spoke.

"I'm sorry?" I responded quizzically, pulling Sally back a bit as she dutifully sniffed the woman's toes.

"The big white one. I never see him anymore."

I looked more closely at her. No, I didn't know her.

But I certainly knew whom she was talking about: Marty, my big yellow Lab. He was more white than yellow, though, like the inside of a banana peel.

"I miss him!" the woman said.

So did I. My wife Julee and I had recently put our beloved Marty down because of cancer. We'd had a sundown gathering in our backyard in the Berkshires, where he loved to run and fetch and nap. Sometimes I'd catch him sitting there just looking around. I knew he was thinking, *Man, this is great!*

His vet, Dr. Ray, came over to the house that night. We all sat with Marty. Said our good-byes. Told him what a good dog he was (mostly). And peacefully, Marty was gone. After ten years. Just gone.

I explained this to the woman who had stopped me. She leaned over to stroke Sally's ears. "You poor thing, you. You must miss him." She straightened up again. "I saw him every day. He was so big. He was a part of the neighborhood." She put her hand on my arm. "Tell your wife I'll pray for her. I know that dog will leave a big hole." Then she was on her way in the sunny morning.

Big dogs do leave big holes. But don't all dogs do that? They're all big when they go.

God, thank You for giving me Marty. He's Yours again now.

—EDWARD GRINNAN

SAT **27** "GOD OPPOSES THE PROUD BUT GIVES GRACE TO THE HUMBLE." —*James 4:6 (NIV)*

I RESTORE antique quilts as a hobby, and when my mother asked me if I would repair a quilt that a friend had made for her, I agreed.

Mom brought the quilt over, and I watched in silence as she spread it out. The quilt contained no batting or quilting, and the colors of the cheap polyester patchwork nearly fried my retinas. It had to be the ugliest quilt in the universe.

"She made it all by hand," Mom said.

I felt like saying, *Someone should have slapped some handcuffs on her.* Aside from its sheer ugliness, I hated working with polyester. Still, it was for Mom, so I reluctantly began repairs.

I was surprised, however, to discover that while the fabric was ugly, the handiwork was not. The patches had been cleverly assembled, and I was hard-pressed to match the fine needlework. But why would such talented hands produce this disaster?

My curiosity made me call Mom, who told me about her friend. After losing a leg to diabetes, sewing had been a way for the elderly lady to pass the time. Because she was poor, she made quilts out of her old clothes. "I know it's not as nice as the ones you make," my mother said, "but whenever I look at it, I can see her sitting in her wheelchair and smiling as she stitched on a bit of fabric."

Feeling ashamed but newly inspired, I finished the repairs. "Who do you plan to leave this quilt to, Mom?" I asked when I returned it.

She chuckled. "Who would want it?"

I looked at the most lovingly made quilt in the universe and smiled. "Me."

Almighty God, teach me to see the beauty in all things, not just those I value. —Rebecca Kelly

SUN
28

He has made us competent as ministers of a new covenant, not of the letter but of the Spirit. . . .
—II Corinthians 3:6 (NIV)

WHEN MY HUSBAND Don and I arrived for dinner with our friends Ruby and Dennis, their porch was piled high with strange objects. I spotted a couple of shiny swords, a helmet and several odd-looking costumes. "Bible school leftovers," Ruby explained. "I still need to sort through them and store the things we'll need next year."

As the director of the summer Bible school at her church, Ruby had spent hours studying the material and recruiting volunteers. Young people collected prizes and treats for the students; adults sewed costumes, located props and helped coach the drama that made the Bible story come alive for a new generation. The Bible school was a tremendous success. Sixty children participated, many of them kids who were learning about Jesus for the very first time.

Ruby shrugged off my congratulations. "Everything went right because everyone pitched in and helped," she said. "Well, almost everyone. One man thought Bible school meant that children would sit still and read the Bible. Someone else thought we didn't spend enough time on memorization."

"You know how it is," I said. "Some folks resist anything that's new or different."

"Yes, but their opposition makes it difficult to attract young people to Jesus," Ruby answered.

Her comment lingered long after the meal was over. I gave lip service to packaging the message of God's unchanging love in fresh ways, but I had more trouble with the shiny new wrappings than I cared to admit. I liked the old familiar hymns; the guitar-and-chorus services preferred by my grandchildren left me cold. I liked church at eleven o'clock on Sunday mornings, even though my son Michael and his wife Jerie found meaning in a 6:00 P.M. contemporary service. My husband enjoyed multimedia; I found it distracting. Perhaps, my reluctance and silent disapproval were keeping others from experiencing the Lord. I needed to remember that ministry was about Christ, not me.

Thank You, God, for Ruby and for all who minister Your Spirit-covenant with each generation. —PENNEY SCHWAB

MON
29

SHE GOT HIM A WICKER BASKET AND COVERED IT OVER WITH TAR AND PITCH. THEN SHE PUT THE CHILD INTO IT, AND SET IT AMONG THE REEDS BY THE BANK OF THE NILE. —Exodus 2:3 (NAS)

"I DON'T NEED any help from y'all. I'm paying for my own college. I've gotten a full-time job. This way, you can't keep butting into my life." Our stubborn daughter packed up her clothes without looking up. "Don't worry about helping me with anything anymore. I can do it myself."

I hugged her stiff body good-bye and didn't walk with her to her car. I didn't trust myself. I thought I might race the car down the driveway, begging her to come back.

For weeks, my thoughts went over that scene, reliving it from every possible angle. I worried about all the things that could happen to her and all the bad choices she might make. One morning, alone in my house, I finally got real with God: "Could You please show me how to let her go? I'm miserable. I'm allowing this to ruin my life."

A Bible story came to me—the incredible faith of Moses' mother. To save her son, she had no choice but to trust God completely and let him go. Knowing all about the dangers of the dark Nile—crocodiles, drowning, starvation—she still turned him loose in his little handmade basket. And I bet that sweet mama let her son go with hope.

Father, I place my grown-up baby down in the Nile. Only You can follow her along the riverbank. —JULIE GARMON

TUE
30

AND THERE IS A FRIEND THAT STICKETH CLOSER THAN A BROTHER. —*Proverbs 18:24*

OVER MY DESK there's a framed, blown-up copy of a poem that appeared in *The New Yorker*. It is called "The Morning Track," and it bears an inscription in ink: "For Van, his poem, August 30, 1953." The poet is Edward Parone, and he gave the framed poem to me on my eightieth birthday. But why, you must wonder, did he say the poem was mine? Well, come back with me fifty-two years precisely.

I was thirty that year and just as mad about thoroughbreds as I have been all my life. I went up to Saratoga Springs, New York, where, for the month of August, the horse reigns supreme at the Saratoga Race Course. I was up before dawn one morning and went to the backstretch where stable hands were busily mucking out stalls, feeding and caring for their charges as they had been doing for more than a century. I was headed for one stable and one horse, Mr. Vanderbilt's great Native Dancer. I watched, starstruck, as the gallant gray was led out, saddled, and with an exercise boy went out to speed around the track and back.

Later I told Eddie about seeing Native Dancer and the glories of the morning. He, unknown to me, composed a poem: It is all there, with the beauty that I felt, but he put it into words: the humming of the grooms, the "light mist of dawn rolling with the horse's breath," the "smoke of fires built for water-and-hand warming," the colt coming from the track "snorting at the groom's caressing, cool hand. *Easy, easy, baby boy.*"

To this day I get goose bumps when I look up at the poem and feel that morning all over again. I thank God for the poem, but more for a half-century of friendship with Eddie.

Keep Your caressing, cool hand on him, Father. —Van Varner

WED
31

He that hath a bountiful eye shall be blessed. . . . —*Proverbs 22:9*

Often, on our early morning walks, I pray for a man I never met. He died long before I was born, and I know only two things about him: His name was Percy Warner, and because of his dedication and his family's generosity, more than two thousand acres inside the Nashville city limits were set aside in 1927 to be used as a park. Mr. Warner's park lies just beyond our neighborhood, giving my husband David and me a perfect place to refresh our spirits when things get hectic.

Percy Warner Park offers hills and valleys, clover-strewn meadows and deep woods. Today as I walk down a narrow road that cuts through the woods, the sunlight filters through the trees and finds a single dandelion. I stop and wonder as a sunbeam transforms it into a silver globe. Just being here in the midst of all this amazing beauty energizes me for the work that waits at home.

Better yet, anytime I come here, no matter what the season, I find myself chatting quite naturally with God. And today, as the birds call out and the last of the jasmine and honeysuckle bloom, the air is heavy with His presence. No wonder I'm often moved to offer yet another prayer of thanksgiving for Mr. Warner's bounty.

Father, open my heart and my hands so that I may also be Your bountiful child. —Pam Kidd

SEEDS OF REJOICING

1 _____

2 _____

3 _____

4 _____

5 _____

6 _____

7 _____

8 _____

9 _____

10 _____

11 _____

12 _____

13 _____

14 _____

15 _____

16 _____

17 _____

18 _____

19 _____

20 _____

21 _____

22 _____

23 _____

24 _____

25 _____

26 _____

27 _____

28 _____

29 _____

30 _____

31 _____

September

Let the field be joyful, and all that is therein: then shall all the trees of the wood rejoice. —*Psalm 96:12*

GOD SIGHTINGS
THE FATHER'S GIFT

THU
1

AND MY GOD WILL SUPPLY EVERY NEED OF YOURS. . . . —Philippians 4:19 (RSV)

WE WERE NEARING the end of a year's experiment in trusting God for everything. For twelve months, my husband and I had been volunteer teachers in East Africa, watching God supply transportation, housing, medical care, schools for our three children. How could I ask Him for something as trivial as a pair of dress-up shoes?

Muddy roads had long since ruined the only pumps I'd brought. I'd taught my final seminar in sneakers. But now we'd been invited to a farewell tea by the first-ever African bishop of a Ugandan diocese. And while I had a black dress that would do, to show up in soiled sneakers would surely look like disrespect.

Even prayer can't arrange this! I thought despairingly. I'd already been to every shoe store in Kampala. My narrow AAAA foot was hard to fit even at home; the narrowest size I'd found here was D.

The day before the tea I stopped to buy candles and rice at the tiny shop near our house. The "store" was just a counter facing the red-earth road, the stock on shelves behind it. As I'd done everywhere, I asked the Pakistani owner-clerk if he knew anyone who sold shoes. The elderly man leaned over the counter and stared for a long time at my sneaker-clad feet.

Turning around, he began pulling things from his shelves: a machete, a bolt of cloth, a can of kerosene. *He didn't understand me,* I thought.

At last, from the very back of the top shelf he drew a shoebox. Blowing the red dust from it, he lifted the lid. Inside was a pair of black pumps. There on the road I pulled off my sneakers and tried them on. They fit as though they'd been made for me. As, of course, they were—in a world where our God is also our Father.

Teach me to turn to You, Father, not only with big needs but with the small ones, too. —ELIZABETH SHERRILL

FRI

2

"In your unfailing love you will lead the people you have redeemed. In your strength you will guide them. . . ." —*Exodus 15:13 (NIV)*

I WAS HURRYING along Washington Street in downtown Boston when I had to stop for a traffic light. A car pulled up with a well-dressed couple seated inside. "Sir," they asked, "could you help us? Could you direct us to a nearby hotel?" I had driven through the area countless times, and I knew there was a hotel nearby. But I had never paid attention to exactly where it was, and it was hard for me to direct them through the winding streets. They looked at me with disbelief and fatigue when I told them I was unable to help them.

A few days later, my wife Ruby and I visited my Aunt Ruth in Williamstown, Massachusetts. She begged us to stay the night, but instead we were adventurous and drove up to Vermont. As darkness fell, we sought a motel. It was a holiday weekend, and NO VACANCY signs were everywhere. We headed back to Greenfield, Massachusetts, and stopped at the first motel we saw.

I got out of the car and went into the motel office, but when I asked for a room, the clerk shook his head no. My heart fell. We were exhausted, and the drive home would take hours. As I turned to leave, the clerk said, "Wait a minute. There's a new motel seven miles north of here." He called—there were vacancies—and made a reservation for us.

We reached the spanking-new red-brick motel and checked in. After a shower, we relaxed and chatted. Then the faces of those two tired and disappointed travelers in Boston flashed into my mind. I had not been able to help, but tonight a stranger had reached out and helped me willingly. At that moment, I vowed to learn to navigate the streets in Boston, no matter how winding.

Dear Father, help me to be a guide to others, in the world and in Your Word. —OSCAR GREENE

SAT

3

When I consider . . . the work of thy fingers. . . . —*Psalm 8:3*

IT WAS EARLY September and I was far away from home, vacationing in northern Maine. As evening settled across the countryside, I was walking along the edge of a conifer forest that

SEPTEMBER

bordered a field of oats. The sun was going down across the wide horizon in an orange blaze that gave the oat field a vibrant golden glow. In
the distance was a small town perfectly placed in the landscape.

And yet, as I tried to shake the clutter from my mind, I wondered
why I couldn't lose myself in the peace of the place. I knew that the
moment I got home the stresses would hit me and all the problems life
dishes out would be waiting. As an investment adviser, I could already
feel the crush of responsibility for my clients. My three-year-old,
Harrison, meant the world to me, but life as a single parent was daunting, to say the least.

In the midst of this pristine beauty I prayed, *Father, fill my soul with
the calm of this landscape.*

In the stillness I waited. No connection. I still felt small and alone.
Then the words of Psalm 8:3–4 came to me, committed to memory at
the insistence of some long-ago Sunday-school teacher: "When I consider
. . . the work of thy fingers, the moon and the stars, which thou hast
ordained; What is man, that thou art mindful of him?"

Slowly, as the sun went down, my spirit rose. Even though conflict
seems to be built into our nature, and life never falls into perfect order
like this rural setting, still I was important to God. The words of the
Psalm made the connection for me.

*Father, even when I stray from You, I thank You for always being mind-
ful of me.* —BROCK KIDD

SUN
4

*HEAR MY PRAYER, O LORD, GIVE EAR TO MY
SUPPLICATIONS: IN THY FAITHFULNESS ANSWER ME,
AND IN THY RIGHTEOUSNESS. —Psalm 143:1*

WHEN MY HUSBAND Larry and I traveled through
Ireland, I lost the habit of spending time each day in prayer. After all,
there was so much to see, so much to do!

Then we visited the ruins of Mellifont Abbey, established by
Cistercian monks nine hundred years ago. A damp, bitter wind tore at
my jacket as the guide led us along the cloister walkway that circled the
inner courtyard. The guide explained to us that the Cistercians were an
austere order dedicated to silent prayer. The monks had paraded in a
line round and round this courtyard, hands folded, eyes down, praying
for eight hours every day.

"What about bad weather?" I asked as I clutched my jacket closer.

"Well, the walkway had a roof over it then," the guide said. "But, of course, the wind cut right through these open arches."

I envisioned the monks marching past, their robes billowing in the gale. *If those monks could pray for eight hours a day under such conditions,* I thought, *then surely I could pray for fifteen minutes.* And what better place to start than the walkway of a Cistercian abbey?

Father, please give me the strength today to ignore the distractions that keep me from spending time with You. —MADGE HARRAH

MON

5

WHATEVER YOUR HAND FINDS TO DO, DO IT WITH ALL YOUR MIGHT. . . . —*Ecclesiastes 9:10 (NIV)*

RIGHT AFTER my kids returned to school, I volunteered to alphabetize and photocopy more than five hundred forms that parents had filled out to create an emergency phone calling system for grades prekindergarten through twelve. Thousands of pieces of paper and several days later, my feet hurt and my back ached from standing at the copying machine, and still the job wasn't finished. As the machine whirred nonstop, I thought about all the people who have such jobs, particularly those whose often unnoticed hard work makes my day easier.

The thought returned the following Sunday morning when an usher handed me a church bulletin, thirteen pages of not just hymns and the order of service, but announcements and a calendar—everything I needed to know for the week ahead. A prayer suddenly rose up in me: *God bless the hands that created this.* A few days later, I awoke early and suddenly remembered I'd volunteered to bring food for a school meeting. I quickly dressed and raced to a nearby bagel shop, where someone had been up since 4:00 A.M. making bagels. *God bless the hands that created these,* I silently prayed as I carried a fresh dozen out the door.

So many people toil anonymously to contribute to the smooth rhythm of modern life. I'm offering a prayer of blessing and thanks for all those who make getting through every day a little easier.

Lord, strengthen and inspire those who may work unseen, but certainly are not unknown to You. —GINA BRIDGEMAN

TUE

6

A SOFT ANSWER TURNETH AWAY WRATH: BUT GRIEVOUS WORDS STIR UP ANGER. —*Proverbs 15:1*

MY FIVE-YEAR-OLD-GRANDSON Cameron was ready for his first day of kindergarten. I phoned my daughter Jenny after she dropped him off to catch the school bus.

"How did it go?" I asked. I knew Cameron was eager to start school, but both Jenny and I had our worries about our little Cam riding the big scary yellow bus on his own.

"Another boy spat at him," Jenny told me and then went on to explain the circumstances. Both boys were in line waiting for the bus when some kind of disagreement broke out. Apparently the other boy didn't get his way and spat at Cameron.

My heart sank. I asked Jenny how she had handled the situation, since she was standing right there.

"I didn't need to do a thing. Cameron took care of it," Jenny explained. "He looked the boy directly in the eyes and said, 'If you do that, you can't be my friend.' By the time the bus arrived Cameron had a new friend. They had their arms around each other and were the best of buddies."

I was proud of my grandson's response to mistreatment, but at the same time I was reminded of how often I'm tempted to retaliate in kind when I feel wronged. Jesus calls me to live a life of love; my grandson gave me a beautiful example of how.

Dear Lord, help me always to follow Your—and Cameron's—example and turn aside anger with love. —DEBBIE MACOMBER

WED

7

BE JOYFUL ALWAYS; PRAY CONTINUALLY; GIVE THANKS IN ALL CIRCUMSTANCES, FOR THIS IS GOD'S WILL FOR YOU IN CHRIST JESUS. —*I Thessalonians 5:16 (NIV)*

"GOOD MORNING!" I heard as I walked through the breezeway on my way to the office. Kim, one of the curriculum specialists in our school district, walked over to greet me. "How was your summer?" she asked.

"Too busy," I replied. "We had a demanding production schedule here at work and home life wasn't much better. With all of our children and grandchildren close by, not to mention our new house and the new gardens we put in, we stayed really busy. I haven't had a moment's rest!" I moaned, shaking my head. "I've got to interview the superintendent this week, edit a school special and tape a Louisiana Purchase Bicentennial Celebration at an elementary school. I'm exhausted, and my week has just begun!"

"Isn't it wonderful to have such a full life?" Kim asked, smiling broadly as she turned to leave.

Her positive response caught me off-guard. I was reminded of a quotation by nineteenth-century author Charles Kingsley that I'd taped onto my bathroom mirror during my hectic days as a young mother returning to college: "Thank God—every morning when you get up—that you have something to do, which must be done whether you like it or not. Being forced to work and forced to do your best will breed in you a hundred virtues, which the idle never know."

"Kim," I called out with a renewed sense of gratitude and a whole new outlook, "to answer your question, yes! My summer was great, and life is wonderful!"

Lord over all of us doers, may I always have an attitude of gratitude.
—MELODY BONNETTE

THU
8

O THAT THOU HADST HEARKENED TO MY COMMANDMENTS! THEN HAD THY PEACE BEEN AS A RIVER.... —Isaiah 48:18

MY MOTHER and I have not lived near each other for more than twenty years, so when she comes to visit it's always an occasion. I've found, though, that as she grows older, it gets harder to say goodbye. Maybe deep down I'm wondering if we're seeing each other for the last time.

This year she visited me for her eighty-first birthday. Her health is good, and we enjoyed many activities together. But when it came time once again for the airport farewell, I held on to her so long that she finally said, "You have to let me go."

And that's when I recalled the biblical imagery of "peace like a river." I used to wonder why God compared peace to a river because I've seen some very turbulent ones. Then one day I really studied a river and saw how *peace* and *river* connect. The river might cut new channels, it might twist and turn, but it keeps moving ahead. Its peace comes from that forward flow.

Mom had her life to live, her friends waiting, her service for God in her small north Idaho community. I had the same in Minnesota. Our forward courses were diverging, yes, but I could be thankful for the days they had intersected.

I drove home from the airport that day, not looking back in sadness and tears and wanting to reclaim what was behind. Instead, I felt carried forward on a current of peace that was taking me exactly where God wanted me to go.

Father, help me flow freely forward, moving in Your current of peace.
—CAROL KNAPP

FRI
9

HOPE DEFERRED MAKES THE HEART SICK; BUT WHEN DREAMS COME TRUE AT LAST, THERE IS LIFE AND JOY.
—*Proverbs 13:12 (TLB)*

ALL MY LIFE I've longed to own a little red pickup truck, but I could never afford it on my teacher's salary. "Besides," I admitted to my wife, "I don't actually *need* a truck—I have nothing to haul."

One day, on my way home from work, I spotted a small, red '89 Dodge Ram 50 truck sitting on the Common Sense Cars lot, with $600 printed in large white numbers on the windshield.

This is no showpiece. It has more dents than the moon. At 170,000 miles, it uses oil and it struggles to reach fifty miles per hour in a tailwind. It's fully equipped with nothing, not even a radio.

Then why do I love it so much? Because it's red and it's mine. I paid only four hundred dollars for it, so I don't need costly insurance. I don't worry about it getting dinged—one more dent would never be noticed. And, to my amazement, I've found a thousand things to haul.

I was wrong. I *need* this truck. Something deep in my soul needed proof that dreams can come true this side of heaven, if I'm willing to modify them a bit. When I reduce my dreams to their absolute essence, there is hope.

It reminds me of a friend of ours who wanted a baby more than anything in the world, but couldn't get pregnant. Now she and her husband are the happy parents of a little girl, adopted from Taiwan.

What's your dream? If you're willing to settle for its essence, you may find that somewhere on this side of the rainbow, skies are blue.

Lord, I love You for giving me this truck, at last. —DANIEL SCHANTZ

SAT
10

THE LORD IS GOOD TO THOSE WHO WAIT FOR HIM. . . . —Lamentations 3:25 (NAS)

I DON'T LIKE waiting for anything. I abhor waiting rooms or recipes that say, "Wait about two hours and. . . ." I pace the floor waiting for phone calls to be returned, or even for our daily mail delivery.

My husband Gene moves at a different pace. He's methodical, sure, careful . . . and *slow*. Everywhere we go, no matter how hard I try to slow down, I end up sitting in the car and waiting for him. We start out the door together, and then he disappears and I sit in the car and fume, and even if I don't complain, my grim face gives me away when he finally arrives. It makes us both miserable.

One of my friends has a photograph of a magnificent rose hanging in her home. It was taken by Everett Saggus, a widely acclaimed photographer who lived in Elberton, Georgia, where I grew up. He had wanted to take a picture of a rose just as it opened in the very early morning. Getting to the garden before sunrise hadn't been good enough for Sag. He spent the whole night by the rose bush, waiting and watching. His amazing patience paid off: He not only captured the pale yellow rose as it opened, he actually caught the dew as it fell onto the thirsty flower. I visualized him crouched there in the dark, chilly hours waiting quietly, doing nothing except waiting—absolutely nothing.

A few days after I heard the story of the rose, Gene and I were leaving on a short trip. As usual, I found myself in the car nearly ten minutes before Gene arrived. This time, though, I began to fill my waiting time with prayer. *Father, thank You for my husband. Thank You that I have someone to wait for. . . .* I wasn't finished thanking God when Gene opened the car door and sat down, smiling. I smiled back. Maybe it's never too late to learn to wait.

Teach me more about the quiet power in waiting, Father.
—MARION BOND WEST

SUN
11

PUT YOUR HOPE IN GOD. . . . —Psalm 42:5 (NIV)

"WHAT IF THIS happens again?"

That's the fearful question I carried around in my heart after my husband Lynn suffered a cerebral hemorrhage that threatened his life and required two brain surgeries before he recovered earlier this year. It's the same question many of us ask after something fearful happens in our lives.

As I remember back four years ago to the terrible day that terrorists attacked our country, I ask myself:

What if . . . terrorists strike again?

What if . . . another plane gets hijacked?

What if . . . something like this happens to me or someone I love?

As I ask myself these questions, I remember what I kept repeating when similar "What if . . . ?" questions plagued me after Lynn's brush with death. For every "What if . . . ?" question, God gave me an "Even if . . ." answer:

Even if . . . I have to face my worst fear, God is still in control.

Even if . . . things don't turn out the way I want, God's love is still sufficient.

Even if . . . _____, God's promises are still true.
(WRITE YOUR FEAR IN THE BLANK)

For every "What if . . . ?" fear, Father, remind me of your "Even if . . ." promise. —CAROL KUYKENDALL

MON
12

GOD IS NOT ASHAMED TO BE CALLED THEIR GOD: FOR HE HATH PREPARED FOR THEM A CITY.
—Hebrews 11:16

I LOOK OUT my office window to the north and see the silvery Art Deco spire of the Chrysler Building rising above the East Side of Manhattan. To the west, I see the Empire State Building, so close I have to lean way back in my chair to view its celebrated pinnacle, the other side of which I can admire from the sidewalk in front of my apartment in Chelsea, on the West Side of town. These two skyscrapers remind me a little of church steeples, even though the huge buildings, full of law firms and advertising agencies and high-powered marketing companies, aren't remotely sacred in the traditional sense.

When I go home to Franklin, Michigan, to visit, I love to see the simple white church steeple on the Franklin Green pop into view above the trees. When I come home to New York, the Chrysler Building greets me from the distance before the highway sweeps me under the East River and up into the streets of Manhattan. If I'm coming from the west, I see the Empire State Building miles before I see anything else.

Strange how things made of concrete and glass can make my heart beat faster. Yet they do, every time. Which is why I know that I truly love this city in the deepest part of me, where things of earth can become something close to sacred. It is the holiness of familiarity, of God's presence in the enduring particulars of our lives. It is home.

Father, You create for all of us a place in this world that we love, and through that love we grow closer to You. —EDWARD GRINNAN

TUE

13

FOR WHERE YOUR TREASURE IS, THERE WILL YOUR HEART BE ALSO. —*Matthew 6:21*

I'M CURLED UP in the big old chair by the fireplace in the cabin next door to our house, with my notebook on my lap. It's my time to be alone with God for a day, so I've come to this place made sacred by years of prayers.

It will be a day of gratitude for the richness in my life—my beloved husband Robert, my children, grandchildren and now four new little great-grandchildren; my longtime friends in Nebraska and the newer ones in Colorado; for the many caring readers who write me letters of encouragement, as well as those who are appreciative but don't write. I thank God for the ponderosa pine that seems to bow to me as I look out the front window; the blue spruce I watched my grandfather plant in the 1930s that now towers over the house; for the crispness of morning and the cool night breeze, for potatoes and milk and carrots and cheese; for shimmering aspens that wave to me, and the creek across the road that is God's music; for the living art of white clouds changing form against a lucid blue sky; for. . . .

As I continue my list of treasures, the words stop. I find myself in wordless prayerfulness that will be with me throughout the day as I write in my journal, do a bit of dusting, fix and eat lunch, and just rest in the silence and love of God.

I invite you to find twenty or thirty minutes sometime before the sun sets on this day to sit in a quiet place, kick off your shoes and your cares, and join me in gratitude in companionship with our special friend Jesus. I'll meet you there!

Holy Friend, we've come here to thank You for _____.
(FILL IN THE BLANK)
—MARILYN MORGAN KING

WED 14

FOR AS IN ADAM ALL DIE, SO ALSO IN CHRIST SHALL ALL BE MADE ALIVE. —I Corinthians 15:22 (RSV)

IT WAS TIME to say good-bye. My good friend John was in the final stages of cancer. In a few moments I would leave South Carolina to return to Texas. I knew we would not see each other again on this side of eternity.

How do you say farewell? How do you simply stand up and walk into the night? Sitting by John's bedside, I suddenly thought of the silver cross I had worn around my neck for years, a reminder of my faith in difficult times.

I took off the cross and put it in John's hand. "This cross has been special to me for a long time," I said, "and I want you to have it. I can't be here with you in the days ahead. But maybe this cross can remind you of the faith that we share together. A faith that believes that God can take death and change it into life."

John started weeping. I did, too. But the gift of the cross was right. Sometimes our words cannot express our deepest thoughts, our strongest emotions. Sometimes we must rely on symbols.

A few weeks later, John died. But he left the cross for his wife to wear, a promise that they will meet again.

Father, may I believe that, as a nameless person once said, "Death does not extinguish the light. Rather, it puts out the lamp because the dawn has come." Amen. —SCOTT WALKER

READER'S ROOM

OUR CHURCH IS LOCATED on a hillside overlooking a busy intersection. There's a lighted cross on the church that can be seen from the road. One day I pointed out the cross to my five-year-old granddaughter Eliza. "God made the cross light up," she said. Practical me replied that the cross had electric lights on it.

"No, Grammie," Eliza said. "God makes the cross light up because of the love in His heart for us."

What a wonderful blessing these young ones are for us, and what wonderful teachers of God's truth.

—*Carol A. Talvola, Beaver Falls, Pennsylvania*

THU

15

PRAY WITHOUT CEASING. —*I Thessalonians 5:17*

WE ARE FOUR DAYS into our homeschooling schedule, and the kids are edgy with the change in routine. Most of the testing in our little school is currently being done by my offspring, as they try to figure out what, if anything, they can get away with. The next couple of weeks will simply be a bit bumpier than usual, so I've been making a concerted effort to stay patient and calm.

My main strategy is to pray hard in hundreds of two-second snippets throughout the day. It surprises me how well this works. It also surprises me how tiring it is.

Sadly, the reason I'm exhausted is I'm not accustomed to praying this way. I'm not in the habit of sending up a prayer before responding to each problem and irritation. I usually *try* to be patient: I bite my tongue, grind my teeth or find quiet ways to smother my annoyance. Still, sometimes my vexation builds to the bursting point, and when I finally do end up praying, all too often it's not to ask for grace but to say I'm sorry.

Jesus didn't tell us to put up with others as He put up with us; He *loved* people no matter how beastly they were. I'm not quite sure how He did that, so I'm asking Him to show me. These days, when I feel annoyance building, I try to turn to God. The simple act of asking for help is often all it takes to turn me away from the temptation to let my anger smolder.

It takes only a moment to substitute "Come, Holy Spirit, and guide me" for the other less charitable thoughts that pop into my mind. I'm hopeful that with practice it will become a habit.

Teach me, Lord Jesus, how to turn constantly to You. —JULIA ATTAWAY

FRI
16

BUT YOU ARE TO HOLD FAST TO THE LORD YOUR GOD. . . . —Joshua 23:8 (NIV)

FINALLY THE PEOPLE helping me restore my 1931 Model A Ford—Henrietta by name—finished their work, and I carefully hauled it home on a huge rented trailer. This deluxe four-door sedan has a new roof, new mohair upholstery, new floor covering, new door panels, new chrome door and window handles, new engine block, new radiator and, to top it all, a paint job as bright as the sun that stood still over Joshua. The body is a classy forest green with black fenders and offsetting apple-green wire wheels and trim.

I couldn't wait to take the kids and grandkids for a spin in my prize. They'd heard me brag about this gem of engineering, styling and reliability. But they were less than respectful. When the time came, I stepped on the starter and prepared to give them an automotive thrill. Henrietta issued several heartfelt groans and a *chitty chitty bang bang* of blue smoke, but wouldn't start. The battery was charged, but something was amiss, and I was unable to locate the problem. Redfaced, I called in an expert. His verdict: The car was not adequately grounded. And he was right. After sanding the battery posts and replacing cable wires, the problem was solved, and my detractors got a ride they will not soon forget.

Now, what's the moral of this story? If I asked my wife Shirley, she would probably say it proves that "Pride goeth before a fall." But I see more application in the car's grounding problem. When I become detached from my heavenly Father, a cocksure prodigal son who acts as if he can operate entirely on his own, I soon learn the folly of not staying in close touch with the One Who has promised to direct my path. We all need to be spiritually grounded, well connected to our Power Source. Otherwise, like Henrietta, we may do a lot of sputtering, but go nowhere.

> *Lord, teach us humility, how to lean on You.*
> *How to see ourselves from Your point of view.*
> —FRED BAUER

HE LEADETH ME . . .
TO SHOW MY
APPRECIATION

SAT
17

SPEAKING THE TRUTH IN LOVE, WE WILL IN ALL THINGS GROW UP INTO HIM WHO IS THE HEAD, THAT IS, CHRIST. —*Ephesians 4:15 (NIV)*

I WAS HELPING my sister to re-cover her sofa and had underestimated the amount of upholstery fabric we needed—again. The last time, I'd misjudged the fabric for the back cushions by a half yard. I'd telephoned Joan at the fabric store to see if she would check the remnant room. Now I'd run short on the checked fabric I was using for the cording. I only needed a fourth of a yard, but without it her sofa wouldn't have the look we wanted.

"We just cut the last of that bolt," Joan said, "but I'm sure there was a good quarter yard left. Let me check for you." She returned to the phone with good news and offered to put the fabric in the mail so I wouldn't have to drive to the store. "There's no charge," she assured me. "It was such a small amount, they were going to toss it."

Let her supervisor know what a good employee she has. The thought seemed to come out of nowhere, but it felt like the most important thing in the world—far more crucial than getting the fabric I needed. Yet what difference could a few words possibly make?

"Could I speak with your manager?" I asked confidently.

"Sure," Joan answered, but there was panic in her voice.

"I just wanted you to know how helpful Joan has been to me." I told the manager. "She's an absolute joy."

I didn't think much of my comment until I read the note from Joan that was pinned to the fabric when it arrived in the mail. "I can't thank you enough for the kind words. Work has been tense lately, and a few days ago a customer misunderstood something I said. Your words really smoothed things over for me."

Show me, Lord, when one of Your children needs a compliment, and help me speak the freeing truth in love. —ROBERTA MESSNER

SUN
18

"I AM WITH YOU AND WILL WATCH OVER YOU WHEREVER YOU GO. . . ." —*Genesis 28:15 (NIV)*

EVERY WEEK I tell a Bible story to my first- and second-grade Sunday school class. They sit in a semicircle around me, and I can often see their reaction to the story I'm telling in their faces. One Sunday, I was telling the story of Jacob and Esau, twin brothers who couldn't get along. As an adult, the wily Jacob tricks his aged, blind father Isaac into giving him the birthright. Too late, Isaac discovers the deception and wails with grief. Finally, Isaac dies, and Jacob has to flee his beloved home to save his life.

As I was moving the figure of Jacob across the flannel board, I noticed tears in six-year-old Daniel's eyes. I wanted to reach out and comfort him. But I didn't know what was upsetting him, so I went on with the story, making a mental note to talk to him later.

"Jacob went far into the lonely desert. It was pitch dark. A million stars sprinkled the sky. He lay down on the cold sand with only a stone for a pillow. With all his heart he wished he weren't alone. He fell asleep and had a dream."

On the board I placed Jacob's ladder, brilliant with angels climbing up and down. It filled the whole flannel board, and the children gasped with delight. "Who else do you think was on the ladder?" I asked, waiting for the answer "God."

Daniel's hand flew up. "Isaac!" he said.

Isaac on the ladder, reaching down from heaven to comfort Jacob. It was a new, wonderful and entirely possible idea to chew on. And the other astounding thing to me was the change in Daniel. His whole demeanor brightened as if he'd been given a ladder out of despair.

God of Abraham, Isaac and Jacob, thank You for reaching down to meet me in my need. —SHARI SMYTH

MON
19

LOVE YOUR ENEMIES, BLESS THEM THAT CURSE YOU . . . AND PRAY FOR THEM WHICH DESPITEFULLY USE YOU. . . .
—Matthew 5:44

ODD WHAT CAN get me riled up. For months I seethed with rage at the mere mention of a certain political figure. I flew into a fit at his remarks in the newspaper. I bored my friends to tears with my tirades against his policies. I could bring any dinner party to a halt with my views.

So one Monday morning when I had to change my password on the computer, I was surprised to find myself thinking of this person. You see, my password is always the name of someone I need to pray for that month. But . . . pray for my archenemy? Pray for my political nemesis?

I winced and entered the name. And for the next month I prayed for him. I still got riled up at the mention of his name—still argued with his comments in the newspapers—but as the month wore on, I started thinking about why he believed in what he believed. And how he'd come to those decisions. I won't go so far as to tell you that I'll vote for him. But at least I understand.

Odd what prayer will do for you. It can even turn an enemy into a friend.

Dear God, give me words for the hardest prayer of all: to learn to love.
—RICK HAMLIN

TUE
20

TO THE PRAISE OF THE GLORY OF HIS GRACE, WHEREIN HE HATH MADE US ACCEPTED IN THE BELOVED. —Ephesians 1:6

ON A SEPTEMBER afternoon I stopped at a store to buy a school folder for my daughter. As my eyes searched the folders, my ears were tuned to a conversation between two young moms.

One was telling the other about her son's game a day or so before. He was devastated because the coach hadn't allowed him to play. Her mother's heart ached, even as she comforted him and assured him there would be other opportunities. The two friends talked on about the pain of seeing their children suffer and then, before parting ways, the mother of the overlooked athlete summed up the issue with one sentence that echoed in my head for days: "I'm just praying that he won't receive rejection."

Receive rejection . . . .

At the age of nine when my best friend Mary found another best friend; when a newcomer to the ministry I worked with was given the position I felt should have been mine; when I wasn't among the handful of people chosen to be at a close friend's bedside when she died from cancer; at those times and so many more, I received rejection. By the time I heard about God's love and acceptance, the wounds had become my weapon—I had learned to reject before I could be rejected.

But that day at the store was the beginning of the end of the power I'd given rejection in my life. In addition to a shiny, green folder for my daughter, I came home with a prayer that I pray every time I feel rejected:

Father, thank You that I don't have to receive rejection because Jesus received it for me on the Cross. —LUCILE ALLEN

WED
21
HEAR THE VOICE OF MY SUPPLICATION, AS I CRY TO THEE FOR HELP, AS I LIFT UP MY HANDS TOWARD THY MOST HOLY SANCTUARY. —Psalm 28:2 (RSV)

THIS SEMESTER has a new twist: Aileen. She's the interpreter for my hearing-impaired student Justin. So as I lecture, from the corner of my eye I can see Aileen's flying fingers make sense out of my words. Sometimes Justin nods ever so slightly, acknowledging receipt. What an amazing, mysterious dance.

I also use my hands to converse, but with less sophistication and less certain results. I fold my hands, put them close to my face and whisper the contents of my heart.

I don't always know what happens after that. Sometimes, in moments of doubt, it feels as if I'm emptying my soul into the ether. But, like Justin, I keep coming back to learn what it is I don't know. And occasionally there's a reward: Justin nods, and I see the light bulb go on above his head.

I've had moments like that, too—but it's not a light bulb, exactly, more of a lick of flame—when suddenly, just for a split-second, I feel as if I understand the Almighty, in many mysterious ways, in many languages, spoken and otherwise. And like Justin, I nod my head—no, bow my head—not to acknowledge receipt, but in profound humility.

Lord, thank You for those special moments when You seem so close, and even more, for keeping me praying when You don't. —MARK COLLINS

THU
22

THE LORD IS MY HELPER, AND I WILL NOT FEAR WHAT MAN SHALL DO UNTO ME. —*Hebrews 13:6*

LAST YEAR MY DOG Suzy found a homeless kitten in the fields near our home, and the little fellow grew up to be a strong, healthy member of our household. So, a few weeks ago, when Suzy suddenly wanted to leave the road and plunge into the fields, I thought perhaps another animal needed help. "Okay," I said, "find it."

I held on to the leash, but had to run to keep up with her. She was very excited and began to circle an area. Then she stopped and lowered her head toward something in the deep grass. It moved, and I realized, too late, that it was a young skunk. Poor Suzy got sprayed, not badly, but enough to make her and the rest of us uncomfortable for several days.

Suzy's experience is something I can appreciate. I welcome the opportunity to help people, but every now and then I rush to the side of someone who doesn't need me at all, and doesn't hesitate to tell me so. The anger and resentment hurts. But in time the hurt wears off, just as Suzy's special aroma did.

If I want to help others, I have to risk rejection. On the other hand, I just might rescue a kitten who needs a good home.

Lord, give me a spirit of gratitude for all those who have helped me, and strengthen my willingness to help. Amen. —PHYLLIS HOBE

FRI

23

"Now come and have some breakfast!" Jesus said. . . . —John 21:12 (TLB)

SOME OF MY fondest memories center on something so ordinary I take it for granted: a cup of coffee. My dad, an early riser, made a pot and drank it while he waited for the rest of us to struggle out of bed. Occasionally I'd get up and join him at the table. Sometimes we talked about my 4-H animals or school, but mostly we just sat in comfortable silence. I'll never forget how grown-up I felt the first time he poured me a cup of coffee instead of a glass of milk!

During my teen years we showed cattle at fairs several weeks a year. Nickel cups of coffee helped me forget my self-consciousness and strike up conversations with other teen exhibitors.

As young mothers, my friend Glenda and I watched our friendship and our children grow over coffee. We talked about important matters and trivial ones—our relationship with God, our families, even our mutual anguish over the first gray hair (hers) and the first wrinkles (mine).

During a time of farm troubles, my pastor provided spiritual counsel as well as a mug of steaming coffee when I practiced the organ before church. Our family was lingering over coffee after a meal at Cattleman's Café when daughter Rebecca announced that, after two surgeries and years of infertility, a baby was on the way. Through the years, I discovered that the joy of companionship was a special blessing from God.

I'm old enough now to know it wasn't the coffee that created magical moments and helped me through tough times. No, the deepening of relationships, spiritual growth, and wonderful memories came from the camaraderie and self-revelation that seem to happen when people share a drink or a meal.

Perhaps that's why Jesus began His public ministry at a wedding feast and ended it by preparing a simple seaside breakfast for His disciples.

Thank You, Lord, for all that You give us in the breaking of bread.

—PENNEY SCHWAB

SAT

24

. . . To prepare God's people for works of service, so that the body of Christ may be built up until we all reach unity in the faith and in the knowledge of the Son of God and become mature. . . . —Ephesians 4:12–13 (NIV)

OUR YOUNGEST SON Jon, almost twenty, had spent three months in the Southwest climbing, caving and canoeing down the Rio Grande River. When he returned home, Jon and I decided to explore a new stretch of the Shenandoah River in Virginia from our canoe.

As we loaded our gear and prepared to set off, Jon said, "I'll take the back, Dad." The back of the canoe is the control position. You steer from the back, deciding the course and avoiding the obstacles. As a father, I had always taken the back position and, with it, the responsibility for finding the safe route and keeping our feet dry. Giving up that role was tough. I had no idea if Jon could handle it or how rough the waters might be. But I kept my mouth shut, and we started off.

Soon worry changed to wonder as Jon skillfully negotiated the river, exhibiting his mastery of everything I had taught him—and more. By the time we rounded the last bend, I was swelling with pride. Jon was doing so well at something I loved so much. For the first time I had a glimpse of the future, which will be marked with many moments of wonder at what this young man, whose diapers I once changed, can do.

The joy I felt that day gave me an idea of how our heavenly Father must feel when we do the things He's taught us: love our enemies; care for widows and orphans; live in the light of the power of His Son. He forgets all the messes of the past and says to all who will listen, "That's My child!"

Lord, thank You for staying beside me as I grow up in You.
—ERIC FELLMAN

SUN

25

O Israel, return unto the Lord thy God. . . .
—*Hosea 14:1*

LORD, I PRAYED AS I stood at the head of the stairs, *if You want me back here, You're going to have to give me the courage to take the first step*. Slowly, I started down the steps that led to the room where the prayer group met.

Years ago, I'd walked down those steps every month for prayer and reflection with people trying to live the Gospel more deeply and more faithfully. But after a while, as my circumstances changed, I'd dropped out. I missed the fellowship of the group and I'd prayed about returning, but I was busy with family and church commitments. And besides, I was embarrassed.

I took a seat in the back of the hall and tried to seem inconspicuous as I gazed around, looking for familiar faces. *Over there—that gray-haired lady. Could that be Edith?*

My heart was racing as I walked up to her. "Hello, Edith," I said. "It's Andrew. Do you remember me?"

My face reddened as she looked at me. *I knew this was a bad idea!* And then she smiled. "Andrew!" she said. "It's good to see you! Welcome back!" And she took me around the room to see other old friends: Bob and Lilly and John and Josephine.

"I'm so glad you're back," Josephine said. "I pray every week that God will bring back the members who've dropped out. And here you are!"

It's been three years since that day, and I've become a regular again in that basement meeting room, thanks to warm hearts, welcoming smiles and two answered prayers.

Lord, thank You for Your love, which will not let me go.
—ANDREW ATTAWAY

MON
26

EVEN WHEN I AM OLD AND GRAY, DO NOT FORSAKE ME, O GOD. . . . —*Psalm 71:18 (NIV)*

WE WERE MOVING my mother from her Connecticut house of forty years into a retirement community nearby. She hadn't balked at selling and giving away and cleaning out. In fact, she seemed fairly cheerful in accepting that in her eighties she couldn't keep up the house and yard anymore.

"I don't mind this move," she told me. "It's the next one I dread. That will be the one to the nursing home, I'm afraid."

Mom was wrong. Her next move, after recuperation from colon cancer at ninety-one, was to private care in Virginia a few miles north of me. Then she moved, at ninety-two, to a fine assisted-care facility in Pennsylvania. But that was too far away, so at age ninety-three, we moved her to another assisted-care place near us. She had now had three "next" moves, none of them to a nursing home.

In the meantime, however, Mom took out her dusty faith and began to reassess it. She decided really to believe that God loved her, personally; that the Bible's teachings on eternal life were accurate and that Jesus really was the Savior; that in trusting Him she would find the ultimate confidence for her "next" move. With joy, I watched my mother come to a peace about death and dying—the peace that passes understanding, the peace Jesus alone gives.

Mom has not made her ultimate "next" move yet, but now she faces it as a woman of faith, with anticipation and without fear.

Lord of all life, thank You that no one is ever too old to come to You in new or increasing faith. —ROBERTA ROGERS

TUE
27

HIS CHILDREN SHALL HAVE A PLACE OF REFUGE.
—*Proverbs 14:26*

I WAS SURE life couldn't get any more complicated, as I set out that early fall morning to face a barrage of commitments in a town three hours away.

Within minutes, I was on the Natchez Trace Parkway, a 444-mile stretch of road that runs through pristine parkland. The parkway offered the quickest route to my destination. And though the scenery on the Trace is fantastic, I was too worried to enjoy the view.

God, I'm so discouraged. I'm always letting others down. Why can't I be better? Why am I afraid?

My prayers grew more desperate. My mind was brimming with failures and fears like a pressure cooker about to explode.

Then up ahead, I noticed a flock of wild turkeys grazing by the side of the road. A mother deer and her fawn caught my eye to the left. Out the sunroof, I spied a soaring hawk.

God? Are You listening? Why can't I let go of these burdens? I'm scared about the future....

Then I recalled a moment from my childhood: my father pushing my swing skyward. He was pushing hard, but I wasn't afraid because Daddy and I had a special word. When I'd had enough, all I had to do was say, "Calf rope." Then he'd slow down the swing and I'd jump safely into his arms.

I looked in the rearview mirror. No cars in sight in either direction. Then I rolled down all the windows and opened the sunroof, took a deep breath of fresh cool morning air and yelled, "Calf rope, God. Calf rope!"

I laughed out loud as all my worries flew out the window and straight to Him.

Yesterday and tomorrow are Yours, Lord. I'm going to enjoy today, do as much as I can and trust the rest to You. —PAM KIDD

WED
28

FOR I TESTIFY THAT THEY GAVE AS MUCH AS THEY WERE ABLE, AND EVEN BEYOND THEIR ABILITY. ENTIRELY ON THEIR OWN, THEY URGENTLY PLEADED WITH US FOR THE PRIVILEGE OF SHARING IN THIS SERVICE TO THE SAINTS. —*II Corinthians 8:3–4* (NIV)

I SERVE on the boards of directors for many worthy organizations—too many, I sometimes think. So when I walked into a board meeting of Educating Africans for Christ, a group that seeks to help Africans get the training they need to minister in their own countries, I asked myself, *Why am I on this board?* My question was quickly answered as the founders and two board members told us about their recent trip to Kenya.

They talked about the schools they had visited and about a village where a group of ladies had a cottage industry sewing all kind of things from clothing to little whatnots. They told us how eager the people they met were to serve the Lord and how hungry they were to do things for themselves. These Kenyan people needed more tools, so they could do a better job; they wanted partnerships with Christians in America who would help them continue to develop; they wanted more education, so they could better serve their people. Educating Africans for Christ is a small ministry, but it's doing what it can to help make all this possible.

The impatience I'd felt when I walked in had turned to joy. *How blessed I am*, I thought, *to be able to extend my prayers, my arms, my support and my encouragement all the way to Africa! If that means a little more work for me, so be it.*

Lord, help me always to seek ways to be a blessing to others.
—DOLPHUS WEARY

THU

29

THE WORD OF GOD IS LIVING AND ACTIVE. . . . IT JUDGES THE THOUGHTS AND ATTITUDES OF THE HEART. —*Hebrews 4:12 (NIV)*

I'M NORMALLY A placid, get-along-with-everybody person. Someone even told a mutual acquaintance, "You can never get into an argument with Isabel. She won't fight back." No one disagreed.

But that self-image suddenly changed one day when my best friend and I had a sharp disagreement. I told her I was right. And why I was right. And that others agreed I was right.

Later I learned that indeed I *was* right. It was obvious to everyone. And all those others made a point of commending me for having been right. The trouble was, I didn't feel any better about it. In fact, I felt worse.

Lord, I prayed, *You knew I was right. So why do I feel terrible now?*

I stewed about it for several days, then I finally sensed His answer: "*Yes, you were right. It was your attitude that was wrong.*"

Instantly I knew why I had felt so uneasy, so unsettled. I might have won a little victory in a difference of opinion, but I had lost in the realm of friendship. I might even have lost a dear friend.

With that, I apologized to her. "My attitude was so wrong. Please forgive me."

She did. Our warm relationship was restored.

What a relief! What difference did it really make whether I was right or wrong? I asked myself. *The important part is that nothing's between my friend and me.*

All of this happened several years ago, and you know what? I no longer remember what the argument itself was about. It had seemed so important, so all-absorbing at one time. Not now.

Thank You, Father, for reminding me that letting people know I love them is far more important than letting them know I'm right.
—ISABEL WOLSELEY

FRI
3O

THIS IS HOW ONE SHOULD REGARD US, AS SERVANTS OF CHRIST AND STEWARDS OF THE MYSTERIES OF GOD.
—*I Corinthians 4:1 (RSV)*

"BRAD, DOESN'T THIS bathroom smell awesome?" I exclaimed. It had just been cleaned and they'd used something that smelled good, which was unusual.

My friend from the third floor of my college dormitory looked at me strangely, perhaps wondering what kind of person would get excited about the olfactory elements of a public restroom.

"Actually," he said, "I have no sense of smell."

"What?" I asked in disbelief.

"Yeah, I was born that way."

I was at a loss for words.

"Weird."

He smiled.

"So what's it smell like in here?"

"Pineapples."

"Oh . . . well, what do pineapples smell like?"

I was stunned. How do you describe scent to someone who has never smelled? It's simply impossible. How could I help him imagine the smells of Thanksgiving dinner, an ocean breeze on a warm summer day or even a clean bathroom? I couldn't find the words. It would be like trying to explain how it is possible that God has always existed, or how our souls will be able to live forever, or how an invisible Spirit can dwell in a physical being. Some things are mysteries, impossible to explain.

"It's fresh," I began, "like a spring rain."

For a friend I could try.

God, allow me to trust that You're in charge of the mysteries I can't explain. —JOSHUA SUNDQUIST

SEEDS OF REJOICING

1 _____

2 _____

3 _____

4 _____

5 _____

6 _____

7 _____

8 _____

9 _____

10 _____

11 _____

12 _____

13 _____

14 _____

15 _____

16 _____

17 _____

18 _____

19 _____

20 _____

21 _____

22 _____

23 _____

24 _____

25 _____

26 _____

27 _____

28 _____

29 _____

30 _____

October

Thy testimonies have I taken as an heritage for ever: for they are the rejoicing of my heart. —*Psalm 119:111*

GOD SIGHTINGS
HEART SPEAKS TO HEART

SAT
1

EVEN AT NIGHT, MY HEART INSTRUCTS ME.
—*Psalm 16:7 (NIV)*

I WAS NOT looking for God when I went on the Internet, I was looking for information about my arrhythmia. Many tests, many changes in medication had failed to halt the episodes of irregular heartbeat. It was just part of the melancholy business of getting old, I'd concluded.

Under "National Heart, Lung & Blood Institute" my search brought up a beginner's Q&A list: "What causes arrhythmia? What happens in the heart during an arrhythmia? Is the condition dangerous?"

Halfway down the list was a term I hadn't seen before. "What is heart block?"

I stopped, alerted as though I were about to learn something important. "Heart block is a condition in which the electrical signal cannot travel normally down the special pathways to the ventricle." The words described a medical problem, but they seemed to me to say more. In someone with heart block, the description went on, the signals may be (1) delayed, but all get through, (2) delayed, and only some get through, or (3) completely interrupted.

Father, I prayed, *I don't know about the medical side, but how this describes my spiritual life! Like the heart's electrical impulses, which fire scores of times a minute, Your signals are sent without cease. When I fail to receive them, it must be because of the blocks I've placed in Your path. Sometimes I receive Your messages tardily, sometimes I grasp only part of them, sometimes I miss Your signals altogether.*

Old age, for instance, I thought as I got up from the computer. *Is my grumbling blocking what You have to show me about this season of life? About the new awareness that comes with a slower pace? About the perspective of the past on the issues of today? About holding a great-grandson in my arms?*

Open Your clear pathway, Father, within my heart.

—ELIZABETH SHERRILL

SUN

2

THEREFORE ENCOURAGE ONE ANOTHER AND BUILD EACH OTHER UP. . . . —*I Thessalonians 5:11 (NIV)*

ON WORLD COMMUNION SUNDAY, our grandson Shawn came with us to church. Eleven years old, he looked handsome in his fresh-pressed chinos and sport shirt. He was very proud that this would be his first opportunity to take communion at our church. I thought back to when I first took this step in my faith in Williamstown, Massachusetts, in 1932.

I was wearing my first suit, a secondhand garment my mother had bought from a peddler who visited us regularly. My Aunt Lillian had taken it in so it wouldn't fall off my thin fourteen-year-old frame, and for the next few years she would take it out as I grew into it. She'd been less successful with the white shirt that hung crooked across my shoulders under the tie I'd carefully knotted. But I didn't care. I was so proud to have reached this milestone in my life. I had studied the church's teachings and the Bible and had read how Jesus instituted the communion service so that we would always remember Him. I walked up to the altar that day thinking I'd never be the same again.

More than seventy years have passed since that day, but I have never lost that sense of excitement. The clothes have changed (I finally grew out of that secondhand suit) and my situation has changed (I've been able to buy plenty of brand-new suits), but every time I receive communion, I thank God for the presence of Jesus in my life.

"Do this in the remembrance of me," Christ said, and for nearly two thousand years, people have followed Him.

Now it was Shawn's turn.

Heavenly Father, what an honor it is to be welcomed to Your table.
—OSCAR GREENE

MON

3

GOD HAS GIVEN EACH OF US THE ABILITY TO DO CERTAIN THINGS WELL. . . . —*Romans 12:6 (TLB)*

MY DAUGHTER Amy Jo had passed the bar exam, and she and I had driven down to Indianapolis for the swearing-in ceremony. After today, Amy Jo would be licensed to practice law in the state of Indiana—to stand before judges and plead cases, to write briefs and give counsel, to protect people unjustly accused, to "defend the Constitution of the United States against all enemies."

A gavel pounds and the court is called to order. The judges file in—their billowing robes somehow even blacker than the sea of business suits that surrounds them. The soon-to-be lawyers shuffle in, pausing at the microphone to say their names to the judges before whom they will practice. They are nervous, serious, well-groomed. Finally, Amy Jo appears. She's easy to spot: blonde, beautiful, poised—and seven months pregnant. Her black jacket buttons spread neatly across her wide belly. Inside, my grandchild is also a witness to this auspicious event. "Amy Jo Redman," she says confidently into the mike. I smile, remembering the ten-year-old girl who asked one rainy afternoon, "Mom, do you think I'm smart enough to be a lawyer?" My answer: "Certainly!"

Later, I applaud (perhaps a bit too loudly) along with other proud families. Someday, my grandchild may wonder if he or she is good enough or bright enough or talented enough to follow a dream. When that time comes, I'm sure Amy Jo will know just what to say. She is, after all, pretty smart.

Every good and perfect gift comes from You, Lord. Thank You for dreams—and for the intelligence and perseverance to pursue them. (And thanks for soon-to-be grandchildren, too!) —MARY LOU CARNEY

TUE
4

KEEP THY FOOT WHEN THOU GOEST TO THE HOUSE OF GOD, AND BE MORE READY TO HEAR. . . .
—Ecclesiastes 5:1

CARRYING THE TORAH through the congregation before it is read on the Sabbath is an honor given to people who have something to celebrate. The first time I was invited to do this, I walked slowly up and down the aisles of the synagogue, holding out the velvet-mantled scroll for the congregation to touch. But I wasn't thinking much about the honor that had been bestowed on me—I just didn't want to trip. You see, it's a very bad thing to drop a Torah. Everyone who sees it fall is enjoined to fast for forty days in atonement. Who wanted to be responsible for that?

Years later, when I'd grown rather blasé about this walk with the Torah, I was asked to carry it on the first day of Rosh Hashanah, the start of the High Holidays. There were about a thousand people in our synagogue. The aisles were mobbed, and the crush of bodies as people reached out to touch the scroll buffeted me from side to side. I locked my hands on the Torah and hugged it against my body, determined to protect it. Finally, I felt the true honor of my position: to be a guardian of the Torah, not merely of the physical object, but also of the words inside it.

Please let me remember that the reminder of You, God, is not the essence of You. —RHODA BLECKER

WED

5

THEY KNEW HE WAS RUNNING AWAY FROM THE LORD, BECAUSE HE HAD ALREADY TOLD THEM SO.
—*Jonah 1:10 (NIV)*

"MOMMY, ASK where Mary is!" my four-year-old's voice piped from the hedge. I obliged, and Mary popped out of a small hideaway, laughing.

"Here I am!" she crowed, and ran ahead to the next break in the foliage. For some reason the hedges that line one apartment building on our block have narrow slabs of cement jutting into them every fifteen feet, and these paved areas create little alcoves. Mary loves hiding in them.

She's not the only one. Maggie, at twenty-one months, toddles into each and every break in the hedge as soon as Mary has vacated it. Then it's her turn to call for Mommy, and I loudly wonder, "Where's my Maggie?" With a gurgling laugh she runs out on to the sidewalk, imitating her big sister, saying, "He-yam!"

Yesterday morning while we were coming back from the corner grocery store, Maggie began the hiding game. The game only lasts four or five rounds; the hedges at the north end of the building have died out, leaving bare dirt for the last thirty feet. So I was surprised to hear Maggie a bit later calling, "Mommy! Mommy!"

Turning, I saw her standing on a cement slab in the barren area, facing the building. It was the same set-up as all the other hiding places, except there wasn't a leaf within five yards of her. It was all I could do to keep from laughing. *Silly Maggie! If she can't see me, she thinks she's hiding.*

I know I've done the same thing with God. I run and hide in a barren place, ending up with my face to a brick wall. Then because I can't see God, I naively assume He can't see me or isn't calling my name.

Oh, silly Julia!

Lord, when I try to hide from You, help me turn to see Your loving eyes.
—JULIA ATTAWAY

THU
6

"MY BODY ALSO WILL LIVE IN HOPE."
—*Acts 2:26 (NIV)*

"YOUR SON JEREMY'S been in an auto accident. Come to the emergency room," said the voice on the phone.

My husband Gene and I rushed to the hospital, more than an hour away. Jeremy, severely depressed, had been in two other accidents recently. "He has a broken right hip and two bad breaks in his left femur," a doctor explained after sewing up Jeremy's face. We left the hospital about one o'clock that morning as Jeremy slept soundly following surgery.

Two days later, another call came from a different hospital. "Come now," we were told. Jeremy's twin brother Jon had been admitted in serious condition with a rare bacterial infection. The hand surgeon explained that he could lose fingers, his whole hand, his arm or even his life.

Back at home one day after visiting both my sons, I was overwhelmed with fear and discouragement. I'd planned to ignore the mail, but a lumpy envelope addressed in a child's handwriting caught my eye. It was from my nine-year-old pen pal Avie.

Inside was an ordinary stone, covered with a scrap of green-and-white-checked cloth and tied with a bright green ribbon. "This is a prayer rock, Miss Marion," Avie wrote. "Put it under your pillow tonight and it will remind you that nothing is impossible with God." I put the stone under my pillow and, amazingly, that very night my discouragement lifted and I began to hope.

After surgery, Jon went into intensive care and remained in the hospital for eleven days. He may need more surgery someday, but he's alive—with two hands. And his brother Jeremy seems to be viewing life differently—with hope.

Father, let me never forget that hope sometimes comes in unusual ways.
—MARION BOND WEST

WHEN LIGHTNING STRIKES AGAIN

IN *DAILY GUIDEPOSTS*, 2000, Marci Alborghetti shared the story of her battle against melanoma—and her fears. Five years later, a routine biopsy again shook her life to its roots. Join Marci for the next week as she discovers the God Who is stronger than any storm. —THE EDITORS

DAY ONE: A BOLT FROM THE BLUE

FRI

7

HEAR MY PRAYER, O LORD, AND GIVE EAR UNTO MY CRY; HOLD NOT THY PEACE AT MY TEARS. . . .
—*Psalm 39:12*

"JUST WHEN everything is going fine, life can surprise you."

As I stared at the doctor who'd found and treated two melanomas on my skin six years ago, everything seemed to slow down. His voice. My pulse. Time. My fast-paced life had suddenly reverted to slow motion.

No. I'd passed the "five-year" mark with no new cancers. *No.* This was just another of a dozen routine biopsies I'd had every year since the original cancers had been removed. *No.* I'd adopted an exercise and diet regime that rivaled any top athlete's. *No.* I'd married and started a new career since that day more than six years ago. *No. No!*

Quietly, slowly, I asked him if my husband Charlie could be called in from the waiting room. When Charlie arrived, the doctor explained that there was no reason to panic. My previous lesions had been successfully treated in the earliest stage through removal; in effect, cured. He anticipated the same would be true now. The plan was now to conduct a series of weekly biopsies on any suspicious-looking moles until we'd had enough clean reports to satisfy the doctor.

All I could think of was that the first biopsy had been taken just before Labor Day six years ago, and today was the Friday of the Columbus Day weekend. And now, every holiday between now and New Year's—including my favorite, Christmas—would be ruined.

Charlie held my hand and kept his eyes on me. I was numb. I'd heard it all before. *Been there, done that.*

Oh, Lord, do I have to do it again?

Father, preserve me from self-pity. —MARCI ALBORGHETTI

DAY TWO: RETREAT

SAT

8

HE SAID TO HER, "GO UP IN PEACE TO YOUR HOUSE. . . ." —I Samuel 25:35 (RSV)

MY VOICE WAS shaking when I called my sister Lori from Charlie's cell phone in the car outside the doctor's office. It was already twilight. We'd planned to visit Lori and her husband Bob after the "routine" biopsy report. When I told her the news and tried to beg off, she commanded gently, "Come."

She had tea waiting for me when I arrived and hugged me a moment longer than usual. She said nothing of my news, and for an hour I retreated into a semblance of normalcy as Lori and Bob and Charlie and I talked about their newly renovated kitchen, our recent purchase of a waterfront condominium, the Indian summer weather, my work and her young students. There was nothing false or uncomfortable in this hour. I even laughed once or twice.

When we got ready to leave, Lori drew me into the sunroom, apart from our husbands. As she embraced me, I knew my brief respite was over and I whispered, "Who will take care of Charlie?"

"You will," she answered firmly, displaying the same unwavering faith she'd revealed six years ago. "God won't leave him without you."

Jesus, Lord, help me embrace life's simple joys as You did, even in the midst of pain. —MARCI ALBORGHETTI

DAY THREE: A NEW PRAYER

SUN

9

"WITH GOD ARE WISDOM AND MIGHT; HE HAS COUNSEL AND UNDERSTANDING." —Job 12:13 (RSV)

AS I DROVE home from my sister Lori's house in the early October dark, our conversation stayed in my mind. We had touched on the one difference that would make this new battle with cancer both easier and infinitely more difficult: Charlie.

Six years and one month ago, I was alone. Not lonely, and certainly not desperate for a spouse. Indeed, at the ripe old age of thirty-six I was happily convinced that I would live a contented single life, enjoying my family and friends, my regular jaunts to Maine and Key West, my books and my work. And when I got the news about cancer back then, I thought, *I've had a richer, fuller life in thirty-six years than most women enjoy in twice that time.* And then I went off to Key West and relied on God and that joyful place to renew my spirit. My prayer then was, "Please heal me, Lord, and let me embrace Your will."

Within a year, I'd met Charlie, and after a resistant period of disbelieving astonishment that he not only loved me but didn't want to change me, I was overwhelmed by a love that surpassed anything I'd ever imagined.

Now, suddenly, I had everything to lose.

And I had a new prayer: "Please heal me, Lord. And let Your will be that I am not separated from this man, for I cannot even imagine heaven without him. Surely You did not wait all this time to bring us together, only to tear us apart now.

"And, Lord, who would take care of him?"

Father, gently teach me—again—to make seemingly impossible leaps of faith. —MARCI ALBORGHETTI

DAY FOUR: DELAYED REACTION

MON
10

BE NOT FAR FROM ME, O GOD; COME QUICKLY, O MY GOD, TO HELP ME. —Psalm 71:12 (NIV)

THE DAY AFTER I got the news that my melanoma had recurred, I woke up at dawn with the whole weight of what was happening crushing the breath out of me. For the first time I began to sob. My husband Charlie woke up and held me as I cried.

"How am I going to do this again?" I asked. "How can I wait for report after report, week after week, never knowing what the next one will bring? What if I don't have enough left deep down inside to face this?"

"You do, you do," he murmured. "Everything will be all right." He was still saying it when I finally cried myself out and fell asleep.

When I woke again, the short October day was nearly half over. My eyes were glued shut with dried tears as I lay quietly, listening to Charlie moving around downstairs. My meltdown had forced me to face a brutally difficult issue: The faith that had deepened and strengthened six years ago would have to grow deeper and stronger. But how?

I'd always objected to the notion that God targets us for pain or trial. Yet, I'd believed that every bad thing that comes is an opportunity to draw closer to Him, to depend more upon Him, to need Him and to love Him.

And this is what I still believed . . . I just wasn't sure I could feel it. "Lord, I can't get there alone," I whispered. "Please send help."

Then Charlie walked into our room. "I've been busy," he declared with a surprisingly luminous smile. "We're going to Key West the first week in December. I made all the arrangements."

Jesus, my Lord and Brother, speak to me of faith in the voices of those around me. —MARCI ALBORGHETTI

DAY FIVE: THE FAITH BEYOND FEELINGS

TUE

11

SHE ANSWERED, I DWELL AMONG MINE OWN PEOPLE.
—II Kings 4:13

DURING MY FIRST bout with cancer six years ago, it had taken me months to reach out to others, and I still wasn't good at it. So between trips to the doctor for surgery and reports, I began contacting friends, many of whom had come into my life since my last melanoma experience.

As October crept by, prayers poured in by e-mail, regular mail and phone. I started attending monthly healing services at a local church and often found myself engaged in faith discussions with the pastor and other participants. I even started calling a prayer line recommended by a friend and was astonished at how comforted I was by the prayers. And after a few biopsies came back clean, I even dared allow myself to look forward to Key West.

Still, I struggled with what I perceived as the lack of depth in my faith. I wanted to feel honestly that whatever happened, I would trust God and accept His will. But I didn't know how to accept His will if it meant death and separation from Charlie. The harder I fought for acceptance, the more impossible it seemed to achieve.

One day, during our weekly fellowship, Sylvia, a precious friend and prayer partner, told me, "Our God is not a God of unfinished business. Everything God does is good." At first, I wanted to argue with her. I wanted to ask her how she could feel that way. But then I realized that you can't argue with feelings. Nor can you force them.

I had always relied on God as my comfort and divine companion. Perhaps it was time to stop arguing with Him and rest in that wondrous love.

Father, let me feel Your arm round my shoulder—where it has always been—as I stumble along this rocky path. —MARCI ALBORGHETTI

DAY SIX: FACING DOWN FEAR

WED
12

"For I know the plans I have for you," declares the Lord, "plans to prosper you and not to harm you, plans to give you hope and a future."
—*Jeremiah 29:11 (NIV)*

IN NOVEMBER, after several blessedly benign biopsies, a small patch on my chest showed the beginning of a new melanoma. "Look," the doctor said, "this has not even fully developed into a new melanoma. We caught it at the perfect time. I'll just recut to make sure we have all clean flesh."

Strangely enough, I didn't panic. The next day Charlie and I canceled Key West, promising ourselves to make the most of the holidays at home. Then we sat down to talk. For over a month we'd been on automatic pilot, going to and from surgeries, changing bandages, without talking much about what was happening. What was there to say, really? But now, with the new "baby" melanoma, it was time. Together, knowing we had a consultation scheduled with our doctor, we faced some difficult questions. Should I be hospitalized for multiple biopsies? Was this the beginning of many new melanomas? Did the fact that they'd been found on my skin mean that they were lodged in my organs? Why now, after over six clean years? Should we change our plans to travel extensively over the next few years? The list was extensive, and though Charlie worried I'd be more frightened by confronting all this directly, I felt relieved. Perhaps I had learned that I could pray for healing *and* acceptance . . . and open myself so that God could provide both.

The day we went for the consultation, I stood in front of the refrigerator to read the magnet my wise and faithful friend Ruby had given me. "'For I know the plans I have for you,' declares the Lord, 'Plans to prosper you and not to harm you, plans to give you hope and a future.'" Even gloomy old Jeremiah prophesied good things from God; surely I could hope for the same.

Lord, let me never fear to seek the information that helps illumine Your will. —MARCI ALBORGHETTI

DAY SEVEN: NEW SCARS, NEW HOPE

THU
13

WAIT ON THE LORD: BE OF GOOD COURAGE, AND HE SHALL STRENGTHEN THINE HEART. . . . —Psalm 27:14

MY DOCTOR'S answers had been very encouraging. By early January, after undergoing a biopsy nearly every week since Columbus Day, he said I could take a break. He'd removed enough suspicious moles and felt my body deserved a rest. *What about my spirit?* I wondered. Would that heal as well? And would it take as long as the scars that now crisscrossed my back, chest, leg and arm?

The scars unnerved me. Though I thanked God there were none on my face, the three on my upper chest distressed me. Despite the winter weather, I tortured myself by pulling out my summer dresses. Many were from Key West, sundresses that would show the scars. Grief filled me as I riffled through them, and tears pricked my eyes when I came to the sleeveless, deep violet dress my husband Charlie had bought me in San Francisco. I'd never had anything so elegant, and now I couldn't imagine wearing it.

Charlie walked in on my pity party. He went back out and quickly returned with a handful of pins. "Try the dress on," he said. It was the last thing I wanted to do, but he insisted. He pinned each one, pulling it up at the shoulders, and then gathered them together for the seamstress at the dry cleaners.

"It's too expensive," I protested. "Some of those dresses are ancient. They're not worth it." He looked at me until further argument died on my lips.

I understood. *I* was worth it. To him. To God. I had a new life to live now. It wouldn't be as comfortable as the old one. It wouldn't look the same. It wouldn't feel the same. But just as I would eventually wear these remade dresses, God would remake me. Not on my schedule. On His.

Father, guide me as I strive to "wait on the Lord" . . . calmly, quietly, trustingly. —MARCI ALBORGHETTI

FRI
14

*I PRAY ALSO THAT THE EYES OF YOUR HEART MAY BE
ENLIGHTENED IN ORDER THAT YOU MAY KNOW THE
HOPE TO WHICH HE HAS CALLED YOU. . . .*
—*Ephesians 1:18 (NIV)*

ONE THING I've never told you about is my devotional coach.

Around the same time every year I will start to complain that I have exhausted all my ideas for devotionals and will have no other choice but to tell the editor of this book, Andrew Attaway, that I regret that I will not be turning in any material, as promised. The situation is hopeless. I'll probably never write another devotional again. I am completely convinced of this.

That's where my friend Amy steps in. "You're being foolish," she'll say, then rattle off a half-dozen things I could write about, incidents that have long since slipped my mind. What about that old classmate who called you after all those years just on the day you were talking about him? Remember how amazed you were? Or when your doctor got your tests back and everything was okay. And what about you and your nieces visiting Ground Zero for the first time? Didn't you say there was a devotional in that?

And, inevitably, she's right. My life is full of such stuff, if I just stop and look for it. In fact, everyone's is. Because it's not so much what happens to us but how it makes us see. My friend Amy manages to remind me of all the times I've felt blessed or awestruck or simply and wonderfully amazed by the moments God chooses to make Himself known in my life.

Today, let me be your devotional coach. Think of one event, one moment, where you knew for sure that God was there in the very fabric of your life. Play it over in your mind. Hold it close to you and give thanks. That's a devotional.

See? It wasn't so hard.

For all those moments when You are as close to me as my own breath, Lord, I give thanks. —EDWARD GRINNAN

READER'S ROOM

AS A LITTLE GIRL, I could never make a bed to suit my mother. No matter how hard I tried, she would always do it over. Years later, as a wife and mother, bed-making remained one of my most disliked household tasks. But now, at nearly seventy-six years of age, every day I thank God for the blessing of having to make my bed, as I know many people are confined to their beds. So every morning, I thank God for that blessing and pray I'll have to make my bed every day until He calls me home.
——*Shirley Imerti, Long Island City, New York*

HE LEADETH ME . . .
TO BE A COMFORTER

SAT

15

I WILL NOT LEAVE YOU COMFORTLESS: I WILL COME TO YOU. —John 14:18

AFTER MY MOTHER died, I did pretty well with the big events like Mother's Day and Christmas. But what I missed most were the articles and coupons Mother snipped from the newspaper for me. She had a knack for knowing when I needed one of Erma Bombeck's humorous columns or when I was about out of peanut butter or when a Dilbert cartoon would be perfect for a presentation at work.

Then fall arrived, the kind of crisp, cool day when Mother and I would sit and talk together on my screened-in porch. As the mailman drove up to my rural mailbox, I walked down to meet him, thinking a new *Country Home* magazine might take my mind off things.

Among the bills and usual junk mail was a fat envelope with three stamps on it from an address I didn't recognize. When I tore it open, some small pieces of paper fluttered out. The note inside read: "Forgive me, but I feel as if I know you from your writing in *Daily Guideposts*.

You had the devotional for today, and as I read it, I sensed God telling me that you could use a little encouragement. I'm sending along some things I thought you might enjoy."

There were coupons, a bookmark, a church bulletin and a newspaper clipping about some quilters. And, oh yes, a vintage Erma Bombeck column.

Thank You for the little things, Lord, that bring such big comfort.
—ROBERTA MESSNER

SUN

16

"AND YOU SHALL BE MY WITNESSES IN JERUSALEM AND IN ALL JUDEA AND SAMARIA AND TO THE END OF THE EARTH." —Acts 1:8 (RSV)

WHEN I THOUGHT I wanted to surrender my life to Christ, I worried about having to travel to the "end of the earth." With my luck, I'd wind up a missionary in the snake-infested swamps of New Guinea. But as I read about the lives of Augustine, Blaise Pascal, Thomas Merton and C. S. Lewis, I saw that they all struggled, too. So, finally, I surrendered.

Now I have to smile at my fear that God would dispatch me to a far-away mission field. Far away from what? Just where is the end of the earth from *God's* perspective?

The "end of the earth" may be wherever God's heartbeat is felt—the house next door, the office, at home, among our own congregation. And it just may be that God calls some of us to stay close to home and be wholly His right here at the end of the earth in Austin, Texas, or wherever you are right now.

Dear Lord, thank You for being the stable center of the universe.
—KEITH MILLER

MON

17

I WILL NEVER LEAVE THEE. . . . —Hebrews 13:5

FROM *Daily Guideposts, 1986:*

I'm writing this by the light of the clown night lamp I bought so my two-year-old granddaughter would feel safe. Dawn has never been away from her parents overnight before, but I've told her I won't leave her, and she's learned that she can trust me. . . .

My mind is filled with unknowns about Dawn's future and the world's. Like a child away from home, I sometimes long for the comfort of familiar ways. But One Who loves me has told me that He will never leave me, and I've learned that I can trust Him. That trust may be the best legacy I can give my little Dawn. Perhaps it will be a night-light for her in the twenty-first century.

My dear Dawn,

I still remember lying in bed with you that night when you were two years old and how I prayed for your future. How quickly that future has arrived! The world you have inherited is full of violence and suffering, with airplanes flying into towering buildings killing thousands, bloody wars in many parts of the world, millions of people dying of AIDS. But there are also new heart surgeries adding years to people's lives, amazing technologies allowing instant contact around the globe, a new physics that touches the realms of mystery and spirit. And most important, my dear Dawn, the same loving and changeless God is in charge, the One I trusted when you were two, the One we can trust forever.

And I will *always* believe in you.

> Much love, many prayers,
> Gram

Great Creator, thank You for being our changeless certainty in a world of unknowns. —MARILYN MORGAN KING

TUE
18

"THE CROOKED PLACES SHALL BE MADE STRAIGHT. AND THE ROUGH WAYS SMOOTH." —*Luke 3:5* (NKJV)

MOST OF MY life I've been a shade-tree mechanic, working on hundreds of cars just for the pleasure of it. Every time I tackle a new job, I'm astounded at how many costly problems could have been prevented with a dime's worth of oil.

I go to lift the hood of an old car, and the latch is rusted tight. I find spark plugs that have welded themselves to the engine and oil filters glued to the block because they were installed dry. Even worse, I've seen engines burned out because the owner forgot to add a quart of oil now and then, and I've seen transmissions that leaked a few drops of oil a day until they were bone dry and locked up.

Human relationships are a bit like cars, I think. They need a bit of the oil of human kindness if they are to last. I wonder how many marriages have died, not because of some great moral failure, but because of a thousand points of rust. How many friendships have been wounded because someone thought that brutal frankness was somehow better than gentle tact?

I know how much it means to me when a student says *thank you* or a colleague puts a snack in my mailbox. A sweet smile, a handshake, a word of sympathy—when I'm feeling a bit rusty, they keep me from burnout.

I thank You, God, for all the thoughtful people who make the rough ways of my life smooth. —DANIEL SCHANTZ

WED

19

AND THIS IS THE CONFIDENCE THAT WE HAVE IN HIM, THAT, IF WE ASK ANY THING ACCORDING TO HIS WILL, HE HEARETH US. —I John 5:14

IT WAS PROPPED up against the wall of the small room in back of the church: a new mattress with an ordinary blue covering. But we were in Cuba, and nothing was ordinary.

Earlier, our work team from Samaritan's Heart had dragged a quite different mattress from the second floor of a tiny house with a leaking roof. Our assignment was literally to raise the roof—a new roof. The old mattress had fallen to pieces as we tried to move it down the narrow stairway. A magazine with a glamorous black-and-white photo of Joan Crawford dropped from the torn lining.

Mary, our leader, picked it up. "It's dated 1940!" she said. Had the mattress lain in this low dark space for more than sixty years?

It was obvious that the parents of the family needed a new mattress. But it cost around a hundred dollars, and the maximum monthly wage in Cuba is twenty-five dollars. Even if a new mattress could be located, it would be out of the family's reach.

But two or three were gathered together that warm day in Cuba, and we needed a mattress. We went back to work, lifting up heavy concrete blocks and breaking up the rotted rafters. Then two members of the team went for water—and just happened to see a truck loaded with a single new mattress. They bargained with the driver, and finally the mattress came off the truck and into the church across the street from the house with no roof.

Later the family came over to the church. With excitement we ushered them into the room where the mattress was leaning against a wall. When the father of the family saw it, he turned and hugged me so exuberantly that my feet almost left the floor. I hugged him back and felt a tear running down my cheek. His tear.

Thank You, Lord, for miracles large and small. —BRIGITTE WEEKS

THU
20

HE CAUSETH THE VAPOURS TO ASCEND FROM THE ENDS OF THE EARTH; HE MAKETH LIGHTNINGS FOR THE RAIN; HE BRINGETH THE WIND. . . . —*Psalm 135:7*

AS A BOY, my older brother Howard was always hard to pin down. He could be building a fort in the backyard, riding his minibike down the block, racing his go-cart at the school lot or digging a tunnel in the field next door. That he managed to come home in one piece was no doubt a tribute to providence.

Age and marriage have mellowed most of us. Not Howard. He still is always on the go, almost impossible to keep track of. A competitive sailor, he participates in races all over the world. And when he's not sailing, he could easily be skiing in Canada or surfing in the South Pacific or at home in California. "Where's Howard?" is a frequent familial inquiry. My mom once told me that she never could go to bed at night until she pictured where all of us were—then prayed. Howard must be a continual challenge to her imaginative skills.

Then last year he was on the crew of Steve Fossett's sailboat *Play Station Two*, attempting a new record for circling the British Isles. Suddenly we all knew exactly where Howard was. We could log on to the Internet and watch his progress. The Web site was so precise it showed the boat every step of the four-day journey, with constant updates on the weather. We watched during the squalls, the jibes, the torturous hours when they were becalmed in the Irish Sea. And the thrilling finale when they picked up thirty-knot winds that brought them into Southampton with a new world's record.

"It must be our prayers that brought you around," I e-mailed him. "It had to be something," he e-mailed back.

Dear Lord, thanks for the technology that helps me keep in touch with those far and near. —RICK HAMLIN

FRI
21

"AH, SOVEREIGN LORD, YOU HAVE MADE THE HEAVENS AND THE EARTH BY YOUR GREAT POWER AND OUTSTRETCHED ARM. NOTHING IS TOO HARD FOR YOU." —Jeremiah 32:17 (NIV)

I DREAD NOT BEING ABLE to focus. When it hits, I can't face the work that awaits on my desk. I'll dig through boxes, cabinets and bookshelves, trying to find inspiration in places I haven't yet looked.

During a recent bout, I found myself rummaging through a box from my grandmother's house. I discovered my grandfather's immigration papers, a painted locket with my brother's baby picture tucked inside and several older editions of *Daily Guideposts*. As I picked up *Daily Guideposts, 1983*, I pictured myself, four years old, tugging at Grandma's skirt while she read this very book. I opened the book and a slip of paper fell to the floor. It was covered in familiar verses, prayers and affirmations.

When facing a tough decision, Grandma would often say, "So long thy power hath kept me, sure it still will lead me on." Every morning, when my brother and I visited, she would have us repeat, "God is with me, God is helping me, God is guiding me." When I was in high school, she moved in with our family while recovering from a fractured spine. I spent many nights helping her get to and from the bathroom and back into bed. When she was in pain, she would quote Philippians 4:13 to me, "I can do all things through Christ which strengtheneth me."

Last on this long-forgotten list was a verse she had recited to me countless times. It was in a locket she gave me and another locket she always wore, words from Matthew 17:20: "If ye have faith as a grain of mustard seed . . . nothing shall be impossible unto you."

I closed the book, placed it back in the box, then sat down at my desk to work.

Father in heaven, help me to remember that with Your help, all things are possible! —KJERSTIN EASTON

SAT
22

*WHICH WAS TURNED UNTO THEM FROM SORROW TO
JOY, AND FROM MOURNING INTO A GOOD DAY. . . .*
—Esther 9:22

MY FRIEND Christine had a cat named Fudgy for seventeen years. It seemed to me that no one ever loved a cat more than Chris loved hers. When Fudgy died, Chris agonized over whether to get another cat. She didn't want to be disloyal to Fudgy's memory.

"It's a tribute to Fudgy that you're thinking about getting another cat," I told Chris. Then I prayed to keep my mouth shut, since occasionally a friend's advice turns around and bites the advice-giver.

Christine started looking at cats. "Just looking," she said. And it was a very specific kind of cat she was looking for—a very petite tortoiseshell like Fudgy. She found a Fudgy look-alike on the Internet and went to see it. And there she fell in love with another cat—a sleek black cat named Gigi. It was like one of those movies where the girl is about to walk down the aisle to marry her boyfriend and instead falls in love with the guy who is painting the church.

"A black cat?" I asked.

"But it was so friendly," Chris said. "It put its paws on me, wanting to comfort me."

I smiled, thinking of an old saying of my grandmother's: "Man plans and God laughs."

Chris and Gigi have been together more than a year now, and again it seems to me that no one ever loved a cat more than Chris loves hers.

*God, thank You for helping me to heal today from any grief I'm feeling.
Help me to know that to get on with my life is not to be disloyal.*
—LINDA NEUKRUG

SUN
23

RUN IN SUCH A WAY THAT YOU MAY WIN.
—I Corinthians 9:24 (NAS)

WHEN CANADA'S Donovan Bailey ran the one-hundred-meter sprint in 9.84 seconds, he was acclaimed as the world's fastest man.

According to an article in the sports section of our daily paper, however, it almost didn't happen. With so many wins under his belt, Bailey had become overly confident, and before the big race he confessed he found it difficult to accept coaching and apply himself to the rigorous training such a challenge required. But he won the race, and dozens of experts analyzed the race tapes in order to ascertain his secret. The consensus? He was still accelerating when he crossed the finish line.

I have already covered well over half the miles in the "race that is set before us" (Hebrews 12:1). Sprinting is out of the question. Jogging is risky. Even a good brisk walk leaves me puffing. Today when someone asked me to serve in junior church, I felt the inclination to rest on past laurels and say, "I've done my share and more. Let the younger people do it now." And when I was encouraged to pursue an in-depth Bible study, there I was tempted to say, "That sounds like too much work. At my stage of the game I just want to enjoy life."

But like Bailey's coach, my Coach won't allow me to coast. Growing older means I have more time and resources than ever before with which to exercise the gifts God has given me. Instead of slowing down, I want to be accelerating when I cross the finish line.

God, give me opportunities equal to my strength, and strength equal to my opportunities. —ALMA BARKMAN

MON
24

IF YE FULFIL THE ROYAL LAW ACCORDING TO THE SCRIPTURE, THOU SHALT LOVE THY NEIGHBOUR AS THYSELF, YE DO WELL. —James 2:8

I LIVE IN a friendly neighborhood. Today my dog Shep and I are headed to the drugstore. Downstairs, our doorman Carlos, back from seeing his family in Trinidad, has a special hello. Shep and I walk down 81st Street and exchange *Good mornings* with all of the doormen along the way, including Tony Laguarino, who gives Shep a not unexpected dog biscuit. We round the corner of Columbus Avenue, and there in the newsstand is Riaz, as silent as ever. He is from Pakistan. I know because once he broke his silence and told me.

We start to pass the dry cleaner's, and with a "Mr. Varner, Mr. Varner!" out comes Leyda at a trot, a round tin box in her hand. I'm glad to see her because she's been away for a month visiting her old home in Lebanon. "Here," she says, "I have brought baklava from Beirut." I dig in for a piece, but she says, "Take more." As she gushes on about the blue skies and blue sea of Lebanon, she turns and notices Riaz inside his cubbyhole—"*Ah*, my friend is here, too!"—and insists that he partake of her sweets. I have seen him at 7:00 A.M. helping her lift the iron grate of the dry-cleaning establishment. "Here, have another," she says to me, and to Shep, "Not for doggies."

"Hello, Mr. Varner," says Orlando in the drugstore. "Must be time for your Coumadin refill." Shep lies at my feet while Irwin the pharmacist fills the prescription. On the way out, I get a cheerful *Hi!* from Eugene Asomanning, a smiling clerk from Ghana.

And that is how it goes in this mixed-up community of ours: the Muslim Riaz and the Christian Leyda, the Italian, Croat, Puerto Rican—you name it—all working together.

My prayer, Father, is that our neighborhood continues as it is: colorful, vibrant and at peace. —VAN VARNER

EDITOR'S NOTE: Four weeks from today, on Monday, November 22, we will observe our twelfth annual Guideposts Thanksgiving Day of Prayer. Please join us as we pray together as a family. Send your prayer requests (and a picture, if you can) to Guideposts Prayer Fellowship, PO Box 8001, Pawling, NY 12564.

TUE
25

MY HEALTH FAILS; MY SPIRITS DROOP, YET GOD REMAINS! HE IS THE STRENGTH OF MY HEART; HE IS MINE FOREVER! —*Psalm 73:26 (TLB)*

THERE IS NO doubt about it: My state of well-being is most decidedly affected by barometric pressure. On a bright, sunny day, I'm full of bounce and ready to cope with almost anything, whereas stormy weather has me drooping around, trying to conjure up energy that simply isn't there. I've spent a lifetime being "under the weather."

My mother used to put her hand on my forehead, pull out the thermometer and, unless I had a raging fever, tumble me out of bed with the cheery comment, "*Ah*, you're just a bit under the weather. Get up and get going. You'll be just fine."

Likewise, Mère Françesca, mistress of physical education at the convent school I attended, wouldn't let a bit of rain (or sleet or snow) keep us indoors. "Cold?" she'd say. "Run around. That'll warm you up." And she had us sing this ditty:

> Whether the weather be cold,
> Whether the weather be hot,
> I will weather the weather,
> Whatever the weather,
> Whether I like it or not!

These days, whenever I'm feeling under the weather, I roll out of bed and resolve to "weather it." Generally, by the end of the day, I surprise myself by how well I've coped.

On those days I droop both physically and emotionally, rev me up, blessed Holy Spirit. Strengthen and energize me. —FAY ANGUS

WED

26

HEAVEN AND EARTH SHALL PASS AWAY: BUT MY WORDS SHALL NOT PASS AWAY. —Mark 13:31

LAST YEAR, my wife Shirley and I returned to Hawaii with our kids and grandkids, and attempted to show them the places and things that were important to us when I served there in the Army in the mid-1950s.

The pineapple fields that bordered the church we attended in Wahiawa had been replaced by a housing development. The office at Tripler Army Hospital near Honolulu, where I worked, was now a patient's waiting room. And the yard in front of our apartment where Laraine, our firstborn, took her first steps is now a parking lot for McDonald's. The islands are still a magnificent place, but many of the pictures we had stored in the scrapbook of our mind were faded or missing.

Why am I always surprised by change? Like you, perhaps, I like familiar things—my eggs over easy, my shirts without fancy mono-grams, my squishy pillow to sleep on. But some day I'll lose everything I hold dear in this life. Observation should make it clear that I can't take my possessions with me. Billy Graham once reminded his listeners that he had never seen a U-haul trailer in a funeral procession.

What did Jesus tell His disciples? "Heaven and earth shall pass away, but my words shall not pass away." Now there's something to remember when I face unwelcome change.

> *Teach us, Lord, how to discern things soon past*
> *From eternal things that last and last and last.*
> —FRED BAUER

THU
27
THE MUSIC OF THE STRINGS MAKES YOU GLAD.
—Psalm 45:8 (NIV)

"MAKE SURE YOU'RE HOME by dinnertime," Julia cautioned me as I left for work. "We're having a special dinner for your birthday—with a very special dessert."

"Sure, honey," I said. "I'll be home by six." Julia is a superb cook, and I was looking forward to a delicious meal—especially dessert!

The subway was cooperative that evening, and I got home in record time. The aroma of my favorite Chinese dish, sea bass in delicate sauce, greeted me as I opened the door. After dinner, I settled back and awaited dessert. Would it be one of Julia's rich hazelnut cheesecakes? Chocolate mousse? A fruit tart? Whatever it was, it would be wonderful.

"Elizabeth has prepared a special dessert for you," Julia said. Elizabeth? I hadn't thought our nine-year-old was interested in cooking. "We need a few minutes. Why don't you sit on the sofa and relax."

I had just settled myself when the doorbell rang. It was Monica, Elizabeth's violin teacher. She was holding her violin case.

"Here's dessert!" said Elizabeth. "You sit there, Daddy, while we get ready." Elizabeth and Monica arranged the music on the music stand and took out their violins. Soon our living room was filled with the sound of their playing.

I had no idea that Elizabeth's playing could be so beautiful. I'd only heard her practicing, stopping and starting, and working hard to correct her mistakes. But now, playing in harmony and supported by the tone of her teacher's fine instrument, Elizabeth's playing was transformed.

As the little concert ended, we applauded the players. Elizabeth's eyes shone and so did mine. I'd never had a better birthday or a sweeter dessert.

Lord, following Your lead and supported by Your grace, let me be transformed into Your likeness. —ANDREW ATTAWAY

FRI

28

THEN HE TOOK THE SEVEN LOAVES AND THE FISH, AND WHEN HE HAD GIVEN THANKS, HE BROKE THEM AND GAVE THEM TO THE DISCIPLES, AND THEY IN TURN TO THE PEOPLE. —Matthew 15:36 (NIV)

WHEN I WAS nineteen, I lived alone and barely scraped by. It was scary at times, but I always relied on hard work and the Lord to provide. Disaster struck when an accounting error cut my paycheck by half, and I had to wait a month for reimbursement. The rent was due, and it took every cent I had to pay it. I was literally penniless for four weeks.

I was too proud to tell anyone about my problem, and eventually my food ran out. A week before payday all I had left was a box of spaghetti. That night I sat down and carefully divided the spaghetti into seven piles.

"Lord," I said, looking toward heaven, "if you could teach me that trick with the fishes and loaves, I'd really appreciate it."

I had scorched the only pot I owned, so I cooked the spaghetti in my copper teakettle. As I broke that day's pile in half so it would fit, tears streamed down my face. Hadn't God heard *any* of my prayers?

It seemed ludicrous to say grace, but as I repeated my comforting prayer I felt better. At least I still had *something* to eat.

After my pitiful dinner, my friend Deb unexpectedly stopped in. She had noticed that I'd been losing weight, and finally I admitted that I was broke. She called her husband, who brought over six bags of groceries for me, and made me promise never again to let pride keep me from asking for help.

That night I realized that God had shown me His bounty, not with fishes and loaves, but through the concern of a loving friend.

Father, forgive me for doubting that You always hear our prayers.
—REBECCA KELLY

SAT

29

TASTE AND SEE THAT THE LORD IS GOOD. . . .
—Psalm 34:8

IT WAS OCTOBER; my wife Tib and I were driving to a nature preserve fifty miles upstate for our annual lunch-and-leaves feast. Mohonk is so popular at the height of the autumn color that we'd made our reservation at the restaurant there back in August.

The day we'd picked was overcast, and by the time we reached Mohonk, it was raining in earnest. Since the rain showed no sign of letting up, we replaced our morning hike with a lecture by Ann Guenther, the preserve's botanist.

"There are two ways to enjoy the fall," Dr. Guenther was saying as we sat down. "You can be a gourmand—take autumn in gulps, see as much as you can, rush around to find the most spectacular sweeps of color. Or you can be a gourmet—appreciate the fine details of the season in tiny bites. An insect gall on a single twig can fill an afternoon with wonder. Try it. Take time to enjoy the gems."

That afternoon, Tib and I bought two inexpensive plastic magnifying glasses, borrowed rain slickers from the hotel and headed out. A hundred yards from Mohonk House, we examined the starburst of yellow on a witch hazel branch, admired the veins in fallen leaves, looked at moss—a forest of miniature fir trees.

Back home next morning, I was up early as usual for my quiet time. I had an ambitious project under way: to read all 1,189 chapters of the Bible in a single year. That meant more than three chapters a day. I'd soon fallen behind, and to catch up I was now racing through five or six chapters each morning.

But that morning after the Mohonk trip I changed my approach. I let a few verses speak to me. I lingered over the text, tasting, reflecting, praying—discovering the gems waiting for me under the glass of leisurely reading.

Give me a hunger, Father, for the exquisite details of Your creation and the infinite insights of Your Word. —JOHN SHERRILL

SUN

30

BUT THEY ALL ALIKE BEGAN TO MAKE EXCUSES. . . .
—Luke 14:18 (RSV)

I WASN'T CUT OUT to be a Sunday school teacher, but when the director called I agreed to substitute, just once, for a young group at our church. I arrived early to review the day's lesson one more time and set out the pictures we'd color to illustrate the point. At the end of the hour, I'd serve chocolate chip cookies. Unfortunately, I'd forgotten the grape punch on my kitchen counter. Exactly the sort of reason why I was inadequate for this job.

The children listened attentively and enjoyed the coloring project.

Then they washed down their cookies with water from the hall fountain. All except for Emily, a prim kindergartner, who ate her cookies dry. "Won't you have some water?" I asked.

"I can't drink water," she said politely. "I'm allergic."

Emily's wild excuse made me see all the more clearly that I had no business teaching Sunday school. For fifteen years I held fast to that.

Then last fall the director called. "Just one lesson," she pleaded. "I don't know whom else to ask."

"I can't teach children," I said politely. "I'm—"

I could almost hear Emily finish my sentence. I had no good reason for saying no, just a silly excuse. Emily had kept me out of Sunday school for fifteen years—and then she got me to go back.

Lord, when I'm quick to say, "I can't," help me stop and identify my "Why not?" —EVELYN BENCE

MON
31

BEHOLD, CHILDREN ARE A HERITAGE FROM THE LORD, THE FRUIT OF THE WOMB IS A REWARD.
—*Psalm 127:3 (NKJV)*

"MAMA! YOU SAY the weirdest things!" my daughter protests, and I laugh while she groans.

"What did I say so wrong?" I feign innocence, pouring it like syrup on pancakes. Lanea is now twenty-seven and I'm forty-six, but we giggle long distance on the phone like schoolgirls—schoolgirls talking way past their bedtimes. We gab each night, mostly about nothing, but each word says we love each other. Each conversation is a choice to be friends.

It was so difficult to leave her when I moved to Chicago. I packed way too quickly, laughed too loudly and left too many things behind. We drove to the airport pretending that my excitement over my move was also hers and that neither of us was fearful in any way.

We hugged good-bye at the curbside check-in, and I saw the same look on her face she's probably seen a thousand times on mine. Looking down at me from her six-foot height, her expression said, *Are you sure you know what you're doing?* When the woman checking me in told me that my flight was delayed because of snowstorms in Chicago, Lanea's doubtful expression became more pronounced. Her eyes widened and one of her eyebrows lifted higher. "I'll be okay, baby," I reassured her.

She hugged and kissed me again, waved, and then drove away, looking like a mother dropping off her child at school for the first time.

My oldest baby is grown up, and I am far away. To my mind, our separation was as much about giving her a chance at independence as any adventure I might be having in the big city. I can laugh with her now and not worry how each sentence, each word, will affect her future. Now each time I call and we laugh and giggle, she knows that while I'll always be her mother, I'm also her friend.

Lord, thank You for giving us the courage to be friends.
—SHARON FOSTER

SEEDS OF REJOICING

1 _____

2 _____

3 _____

4 _____

5 _____

6 _____

7 _____

8 _____

9 _____

10 _____

11 _____

12 _____

13 _____

14 _____

15 _____

16 _____

17 _____

18 _____

19 _____

20 _____

21 _____

22 _____

23 _____

24 _____

25 _____

26 _____

27 _____

28 _____

29 _____

30 _____

31 _____

November

And thou shalt rejoice in every good thing which the Lord thy God hath given unto thee. . . .

—*Deuteronomy 26:11*

GOD SIGHTINGS
ALL HIS CHILDREN

TUE
1

[GOD] HATH MADE OF ONE BLOOD ALL NATIONS OF MEN. . . . —Acts 17:26

ANY OF US old enough to remember December 7, 1941, can tell you exactly where we were—in what room, with what people—when President Roosevelt's voice came over the radio with the news that the Japanese had attacked Pearl Harbor. My father called us into the kitchen where radio reception was best: my mother, my nine-year-old sister, my eleven-year-old brother and me, age thirteen. I remember my sister's round frightened eyes watching Daddy's face.

"Daddy," she whispered, "are we in the war now?"

We'd heard about the war for a long time. For two years newspapers and newsreels had shown terrifying pictures of the fighting in Europe and Asia. We'd flattened our tin cans and rolled the tinfoil from our chewing gum into silver balls for our armament factories. Every week my Girl Scout troop had baked brownies to raise money for Bundles for Britain. But the war was far away, fought in places with strange names by people none of us knew.

My father looked around at us all before answering.

"We've always been in the war," he said at last. "Any war is our war."

Any war? Anywhere? Ours, too? A mysterious, unseen connection between us and everyone else? I didn't know then that this was a God sighting—perhaps my first intimation that there *was* a God. We were not a religious family. But years later, when I learned the prayer that begins "Our Father," I remembered Daddy's words: "Any war is our war." And I knew the reason why every person's suffering is also mine.

Father of us all, help me to love the brothers and sisters I have not seen.
—ELIZABETH SHERRILL

WED

2

"BLESS ALL HIS SKILLS, O LORD, AND BE PLEASED WITH THE WORK OF HIS HANDS. . . ."
—*Deuteronomy 33:11 (NIV)*

WHAT'S TAKING SO LONG? I wondered, glancing down at my watch. I am a firm believer in upholding the democratic principles of voting, but it seemed to take forever to vote.

Finally, it was my turn. I signed my name in the voting registry and listened to the worker spell it slowly. Two other commissioners repeated my name, double-checking their spelling. Another worker, who was helping an elderly gentleman figure out his voting precinct, reached behind the voting booth to reset it. I stepped in, turned to close the curtain and watched the next person in line move up to sign his name. *I guess I've never realized how much work it takes to help everybody vote,* I thought.

I cast my vote quickly and stepped out of the booth. Just then I saw a friend, working at the table across the room.

"Kristy," I said, "what are you doing here?"

"I'm an election commissioner," she said proudly from behind the table.

"I suppose I shouldn't be surprised," I stated, smiling. Kristy was a history teacher and loved teaching the political process. "Tell me why you do it."

"It's not for the money," she joked. "By the time I pay for gas, the bridge toll, lunch, snacks and taxes, I've just about spent all I'm paid. I have to show up here around five A.M., and I don't get to leave until after ten at night. I do it because I love it—and besides, democracy is worth working for."

Lord, bless all of our hardworking election commissioners today.
—MELODY BONNETTE

THU

3

BUT GOD, WHO COMFORTS THE DEPRESSED, COMFORTED US BY THE COMING OF TITUS.
—*II Corinthians 7:6 (NAS)*

I'M RATHER STOIC when faced with human tragedy, but with animals I'm emotionally about six years old. When the lupus that had attacked our beloved Red Dog grew suddenly worse, I started to grieve.

The dog had literally walked into our yard and our lives ten years ago. Incredibly intelligent and loyal, all the part-chow wanted was to be close to my husband Gene and me—touching us.

Our veterinarian had recommended that we take her to the University of Georgia School of Veterinary Medicine. The doctors there made photographs because of the rarity of the form of lupus Red Dog had. She posed willingly, wagging her bushy tail.

Her medications were enormously complicated and powerful. After a while they caused severe side effects. One day, after a year of declining health, Red Dog suddenly had trouble breathing and wouldn't get up. Gene and I took her to our vet immediately.

Words hurt too much, so mostly we talked with our eyes. For that last visit, our vet prepared a large, clean pink blanket in the corner of a familiar examining room and her assistant gently placed Red Dog on it. The four of us on the floor surrounding Red didn't attempt to control our tears.

Late that afternoon back at home, grief held me tightly. Then a delivery of spring flowers arrived. The card read, "We all loved Red Dog, too. We care deeply. Everyone at Piedmont Animal Clinic." Shortly after that, our pastor, his wife, their two children and their small dog came to sit with us. Early the next morning, a huge blue hydrangea arrived from my daughter. The card said, "Here's to Red Dog. Love, Julie."

The flowers and the company didn't make the pain go away. But the knowledge that someone cared made it easier to bear.

Lord, when someone cares—no matter what the loss—grief's hold is diminished. Show me how to care. —Marion Bond West

FRI

4

Put on tender mercies, kindness, humility, meekness, longsuffering; bearing with one another, and forgiving one another. . . .
—*Colossians 3:12–13* (NKJV)

I HAD BEEN complaining to Barb, our pastor's wife, about a lady at church I'll call Myrtle. She'd taken it upon herself to boss around a group of us who had been planning a church supper. "Myrtle is so hard to work with," I said. "It's just not right. It's not her church or her kitchen. Why can't she just let us do it the way we want?"

I figured Barb would understand. After all, she'd been dealing with Myrtle for years. Yet I was surprised by her words. "Mary," she said, "I've learned there are some people and situations I just cannot change. I can only pray for them and pray that God will help me act in a loving way and will help me control my temper."

Disappointed, I stalked away.

A couple of days later I was visiting a first-grade classroom at the school where I work. "Teacher, teacher, Heather isn't sitting at her desk. She's out of her chair!" one of the little girls cried out.

The teacher knelt by the girl's desk and said very firmly, "Emily, your job is to take care of yourself. Leave Heather to me. I'll help her do her job."

Then I remembered our pastor's wife's words: *There are some people and situations I just cannot change. I can only pray that God will help me act in a loving way.*

There are Heathers and Myrtles in this world, but the person I need to worry about most is Mary.

Dear God, grant me the wisdom to see my own faults and not to judge my brothers and sisters, for You are blessed forever. Amen. —MARY BROWN

SAT
5

HIS DIVINE POWER HAS GIVEN US EVERYTHING WE NEED FOR LIFE AND GODLINESS. . . .
—*II Peter 1:3 (NIV)*

"HERE YOU GO, Mom!" the nurse said. It was two hours after my C-section and I was about to see my son for the first time. His high-pitched cries grew louder as the nurse brought him to me. *Oh no,* I thought, *what have I gotten myself into?*

"Here's Mom," the nurse said putting him into my arms. A wrinkled red face looked up at me. As I laid his head on my chest, the word *mom* stuck in my mind. I didn't feel much like a mom. Would I be a good one? Would I have the answers, know how to stop his crying, be able to put him to sleep?

He was warm in my arms, snug in a white-pink-and-blue-striped blanket. He squinted up at me. I was so caught up in looking down at this baby I had imagined and anticipated for months that I didn't notice the silence.

"Isn't that something," the nurse said. "He hasn't stopped crying since we took him from the OR and now look at him, so happy. He knows his mama."

A calm reassurance covered me. *Trust this,* I thought. *Trust this beautiful little boy who knew you as his mother even before you did.*

Thank You, Lord, for giving me all I need to be Solomon's mom.
—SABRA CIANCANELLI

SUN
6

"AND IF YOU GREET ONLY YOUR BROTHERS, WHAT ARE YOU DOING MORE THAN OTHERS?"
—*Matthew 5:47* (NIV)

WHILE VISITING the library the other day, I picked up a book on the architecture of houses in America. One of the earliest design elements, I learned, was the porch, connecting the house to nature and the world outside. While the tall stone structure of a castle is designed to keep the world out, the porch welcomes the world to the front door. The porches pictured were wide and inviting, reminding me of the "front-porch people" I've met, whose open arms and inviting smiles seem to say, "Come and sit for a while, and we'll get to know each other."

So I ask myself, *Am I a front-porch person?* I think of the time in our Sunday-morning service when the pastor asks us to greet people around us. It's too easy to smile and say *Good morning,* without much thought behind it. Do I ever introduce myself or ask their name? Do I greet them as I would a visitor to my own front porch? Or do I smile and shake hands automatically, creating an impenetrable castle wall that sends the clear message, *Don't get any closer?*

Jesus seemed to encourage the front-porch attitude as part of what it meant to follow Him.

Welcome to my home, Lord. Welcome to my heart.
—GINA BRIDGEMAN

MON

7

THE LORD YOUR GOD HAS CHOSEN YOU OUT OF ALL THE PEOPLES ON THE FACE OF THE EARTH TO BE HIS PEOPLE, HIS TREASURED POSSESSION.
—*Deuteronomy 7:6 (NIV)*

TWO OF OUR SONS had an argument last year and stopped speaking to each other for a while. Joy and I were constantly looking for ways to reconcile them, but nothing we did worked.

Then we visited Ethiopia, and while we were there we went on a weekend retreat hosted by a wealthy couple. During the retreat, boats were available to take people out on the beautiful lake. I'm from Minnesota, so the lake was a delight to me. But not for Amelie, our Ethiopian hostess. She had been born in the desert, and she was deathly afraid of water and boats.

One afternoon her husband, challenged by my example, loaded their four kids into a small boat and headed out onto the lake. Amelie, standing on the porch of the cottage, saw them and began to cry. We tried to comfort her, but she would only say, "How can I calm down? Everything I possess in all the world is out in that little boat. What if it sinks?" For Amelie, her family was everything.

Family is more important than anything, don't risk losing it. When we got home, I decided to try out that thought on my boys. But I was only halfway through my speech when they turned to each other and laughed. "What's so funny?" I asked.

"We knew you'd have another sermon for us when you got home," they replied, "so we made up first."

Lord, help me to remember that relationships are more important than any of the other treasures You give me. —ERIC FELLMAN

TUE

8

EYE HATH NOT SEEN, NOR EAR HEARD, NEITHER HAVE ENTERED INTO THE HEART OF MAN, THE THINGS WHICH GOD HATH PREPARED FOR THEM THAT LOVE HIM. —*I Corinthians 2:9*

WHEN I WAS a child my mother made the most wonderful chocolate cakes from scratch. She used only the best ingredients: fresh eggs from

Grandmother's hens, milk right from the dairy, the silkiest cake flour, pure vanilla, rich unsweetened chocolate melted slowly in a double boiler. We waited while she brought it all together in the whirr of the mixer. Finally we moved in for a taste of thick, smooth chocolate batter.

Two of us got a beater, one a spatula, while the other four spooned up the extra batter left in the bowl. Every drop was a foretaste of what was to come: a moist, three-layer chocolate cake that melted in the mouth.

It's been many years since I've eaten the batter while waiting for the cake. But the taste of it and the yearning for the cake are still on my tongue. It calls to mind another taste that fills me with longing for heaven—the taste of joy.

It comes to me in a brilliant sunset, a soaring note in a symphony, a baby's smile, a hug from a friend, my husband's face across a crowded room. I can't summon it, I can't hold on to it, I can only receive it as a foretaste of what God is preparing for me in my real home.

Lord Jesus, thank You for foretastes of eternal joy. —SHARI SMYTH

WED
9

EACH OF YOU SHOULD LOOK NOT ONLY TO YOUR OWN INTERESTS, BUT ALSO TO THE INTERESTS OF OTHERS.
—*Philippians 2:4 (NIV)*

"WHAT DID YOU do today?" I asked my son Brett, who had called me on his way home from work. Brett was quiet for a moment before he answered.

"Raked leaves, mostly."

Raked leaves? It seemed an odd thing for him to do in the middle of the week, when he's usually busy with construction work—often supervising his crew as they tackle a remodeling job, tear off an old roof or frame up a new house. Maybe it had been at one of the rental properties he owned.

"Where?" I asked. Again, that small silence before he answered.

"Near one of my duplexes. This lady was out raking her big yard—from her motorized wheelchair. So I went and got my tractor and leaf collector and did it for her. She tried to pay me, but I told her I didn't want any money. That I was . . . well, behind on my good deeds."

If you ask me what my son does for a living, I'll tell you about his construction business, about his ambition and work ethic and attention to detail. But if you ask what makes me most proud of my son, I'll tell you a story about the day he raked leaves.

Dear Jesus, when You were among us, You went about doing good. Let us never forget to do the same in Your name. —MARY LOU CARNEY

THU   *I WILL GIVE YOU REST.* —*Matthew 11:28*

10

LORD, I'M FEELING *overwhelmed. Everyone wants something from me.*

"Come unto me, all who labor and are heavy laden, and I will give you rest."

Heavy laden. That's me. It's not just my workload; it's all the anxieties that weigh me down.

"Take my yoke upon you, and learn from me."

A yoke. How fitting for someone who feels like a big ox, slowly trudging back and forth across a field with no sense of achievement.

"For I am gentle and lowly in heart, and you will find rest for your soul."

I wish everyone were as gentle as You, God, but people can be so hurtful. Are You serious?

"For my yoke is easy, and my burden is light."

I know, Lord, You don't expect miracles out of me, just faithfulness. I do tend to take more responsibility than I should, so I'm going to turn this over to You and let You help me with my load. You'll have to empower me. I'm giving it to You.

I'm going to bed. Good night, God.

Help me through this complicated and ever-changing world, Lord, for the sake of those who look to me for help. —DANIEL SCHANTZ

FRI
11

I WILL CALL UPON THE LORD, WHO IS WORTHY TO BE PRAISED: SO SHALL I BE SAVED FROM MINE ENEMIES.
—*Psalm 18:3*

FOUR-YEAR-OLD Caleb and I were playing soldier when my daughter Rebecca called us for supper. We picked up the toy soldiers, flags, trucks and planes, then sat down at the table. "I have an idea!" Caleb said as we joined hands for the blessing. "Let's pray like soldiers!"

"How do soldiers pray?" I asked.

"I'll show you," he replied. In a slow, deep monotone, he boomed out, "God . . . is . . . great . . . God . . . is . . . good. . . ." We joined in, using our own deep, false "soldier" voices: "And . . . we . . . thank . . . You . . . for . . . this . . . food." We sounded silly, of course, and broke into peals of laughter right after "Amen."

Later, though, I thought about soldiers who pray. My brother Mike, now a retired Marine, found time during the Gulf War to pray for my family. Our father, a B-17 pilot who spent nine months in a German prison camp, wrote to our mother on April 30, 1945, that prayers had been answered: "Our camp was liberated at noon yesterday by our dear soldiers. Thank God!"

Christians disagree about whether war is ever justified and about letting children play soldier, but we should never disagree about the need to pray for servicemen and servicewomen and for veterans. And at times we'll find it good to pray like some of them, too.

O Trinity of love and power, Our brethren shield in danger's hour;
From rock and tempest, fire and foe, Protect them wheresoe'er they go.
(William Whiting, 1825-1878) —PENNEY SCHWAB

SAT
12

THEN ANSWERED PETER, AND SAID UNTO JESUS, LORD, IT IS GOOD FOR US TO BE HERE. . . .
—*Matthew 17:4*

"SHALL WE STAY in California or go back East?" I asked our family. I'd been offered a job in the New York area, and I wanted to know if they thought I should take it. There were three votes—my two kids and I—in favor of coming back to New York and one against—my wife Elba. Elba had a wonderful job in California, she was going to school, she was active at church, and she loved the warm climate. She was reluctant to leave all that for the long, cold northeastern winters.

We hadn't been back East long when Elba learned that her youngest sister Miriam had been diagnosed with a terminal illness. Every weekend, Elba traveled into the city to visit her sister. They talked about many things in their time together, sharing their hearts' deepest feelings about life, death and the hope of heaven. The two sisters laughed, played, cried and prayed together.

Looking back now, my wife understands why God brought our family back home. Her little sister needed a big sister's friendship, love and care. And Elba needed the example of her little sister's faith and courage in the face of great physical and emotional pain. "Sometimes," she said one evening as we drove home from visiting Miriam, "we find ourselves in the place we least want to be because that's where we're needed the most."

Lord, as I look around my surroundings today, open my eyes to the needs that You've put me here to serve. —PABLO DIAZ

SUN
13

"THEIR CHILDREN WILL SEE IT AND BE JOYFUL; THEIR HEARTS WILL REJOICE IN THE LORD."
—*Zechariah 10:7 (NIV)*

I LOOK FORWARD to seeing my sister and her family for many reasons, not the least of which are the lessons on God's love that Max, my nephew, is sure to teach me.

I had confessed to Max's father Tedd that I struggle with the concept of tithing. "I know that we're called to be cheerful givers," I said, "but it often seemed like a choice—tithe or help my son with his college expenses. I didn't know how to do both."

Tedd told me that he and my sister Becky had gone through the same struggle last winter. They just didn't see how they could be generous to God and still provide for their children. What they didn't know was that Max, playing nearby, had overheard part of their conversation. "What's a tithe?" he asked his father as he skipped into the room.

When Tedd explained the concept of giving ten percent of our money to God, Max was amazed. "Wow!" he said. "You mean that God lets us keep ninety percent of everything?" Then he raced away to resume his play.

Max had it right: A tithe is an example of God's generosity, not ours. Any child of God should be able to see that.

Dear God, thank You for the children who see Your love, so our hearts can rejoice in You. —TIM WILLIAMS

MON
14
HE IS A SHIELD UNTO THEM THAT PUT THEIR TRUST IN HIM. —Proverbs 30:5

TUCKING MY three-year-old son Harrison into bed was a familiar ritual. First there was the usual search for his stuffed dog Spot, then a rereading of his favorite dinosaur book—which we both have memorized by now—then his prayers. But on this particular night, after prayers, he looked up at me and asked, "Daddy, will you always protect me?" The words slammed into me like a sledgehammer.

"Of course, I'll always protect you," I said as cheerfully as I could. I kissed him good night and switched on his nightlight, a ceramic figure of a little boy on his knees praying—the same one I had as a child. As I closed his door, leaving just a crack open, I kept thinking about my answer. How could I, a single father with shared custody, possibly protect him wherever he was?

Quietly I made my way out to the back porch and found myself staring up into the night sky. Overhead I heard the clamor of the night-flight helicopter from nearby Vanderbilt Hospital. No doubt there had been some accident somewhere. It only made my worries increase.

My thoughts returned to the nightlight in Harrison's room. I remembered how as a child I gravitated to its comforting glow. No, I wouldn't be able to protect Harrison always, but I could be sure that God would always be there for him, no matter where he was and no matter how far away I was. That was a promise any father could make.

Father, help us remember that through You we are always protected.
—BROCK KIDD

HE LEADETH ME . . .
TO RESPOND WITH LOVE

TUE
15

"I WILL GIVE THEM AN UNDIVIDED HEART AND PUT A NEW SPIRIT IN THEM. . . ." —*Ezekiel 11:19 (NIV)*

SOME YEARS BACK I found myself working with an extremely difficult colleague. No matter how positive her co-workers were, she always managed to put a negative spin on things.

One afternoon, I was her target. That evening after work, I looked to the Scriptures for guidance. I heard what I'd come to know as God's voice: *You can't change her, Roberta, but you can change the way you react to her. Every time she does something destructive, counteract it with something constructive.*

I wasn't exactly sure what that meant, but whenever she blasted me, I asked God to help me think of people who were hurting worse than I was. Sometimes I'd offer to meet them in the chapel to pray on our break. And sometimes I'd take them a small gift. Perhaps a nice new pen or a book of inspirational quotes or some hand cream. And it was *fun*—so much fun that I began to keep a drawer full of little treasures for such occasions.

Then one day it occurred to me that the person who was hurting the most was my negative co-worker. So I dug through my drawer and found a package of pretty notepaper and took it to her. "You have the nicest handwriting, and I thought you might enjoy this," I said. It was the one sincere compliment I could give her.

And the most unbelievable thing happened: She wrote thank-you notes to people all over the hospital, telling them how much they meant to her. She began to change, subtly at first, and as time went on she became my coconspirator. With a little drawer of presents all her own, she began to bring help and hope to others.

Lord, help me really to listen when I read Your Word, then act as You instruct me. —ROBERTA MESSNER

READER'S ROOM

A FEW WEEKS AFTER I was laid off from my job,
I received five cards in the mail with typed labels
addressed to me. I opened the first card; inside were two
one-hundred-dollar bills. All the other cards were the same.
I'll never know whose overwhelming generosity and
unselfish kindness warmed my heart and changed my life
forever. Thank You, Father, for Your love and the blessings
You give us each day. —*Jeannie Berger, Alpharetta, Georgia*

WED

16

*IN MY DISTRESS I CALLED UPON THE LORD, AND
CRIED UNTO MY GOD: HE HEARD MY VOICE. . . .*
—*Psalm 18:6*

A MAN TELLS me a story. He was in a war, and his side
lost, so he had to leave his country and escape into the next country.
The next country was even worse. "You wouldn't believe the reasons
people were killed there," he says. "People were being killed if they
wore eyeglasses or could read. One time they killed all the doctors and
teachers. So I concluded to escape again.

"I go through the forest and I get to the border and the soldiers catch
me and they throw me in a prison. That prison was so far deep in the
forest no one even knew where it was. It was all mud and blood there.
I was blind then from the war, and I was in a pit in the bottom of the
prison. So I concluded to pray.

"I prayed for two weeks, all the time. I did not expect a miracle to
happen. No. That is not what praying is for. I was praying not to lose
hope. I was praying to be calm and accept what would be. After a while,
the soldiers let me go, and I went to a refugee camp and then I went to
another country and then I came to this country. That's a long story. In
this country, some people helped me get an operation and now I can
see.

"I still pray all the time, oh yes. I pray to be open to what is. Does
that make sense to you? I think that's what praying is for. To help you
not be closed. To be an open person."

Dear Lord, thanks for miracles, which swim around us like a trillion brilliant birds. And help me stay open, okay? —BRIAN DOYLE

THU
17

"THEN YOU WILL KNOW THE TRUTH, AND THE TRUTH WILL SET YOU FREE." —John 8:32 (NIV)

"IF MAMA AIN'T happy, ain't nobody happy."

This popular ditty lived on a magnet on our refrigerator for years. At first, I liked the message because it affirmed the positive influence I have in our family. But over time, it began to weigh me down. Was I really in charge of everybody's moods? Yikes! What an exhausting responsibility! And what a guilt-producing message for a mom who already had a tendency to accept responsibility for all sorts of things she's not responsible for.

I learned in a parenting class that when I accept responsibilities that aren't mine—when I assume it's up to me to find lost shoes or be sure my children all have their stuff before they go out the door in the morning—I keep others from accepting theirs. And if I'm responsible for keeping my children happy, they won't learn that their choice of mood is up to them.

By the same logic, my mood is my responsibility, and I need to deal with it. Maybe the words on that magnet need to be changed to something like, "If Mama ain't happy, she might need a time-out." So far, nobody's asked me to edit refrigerator magnet messages. I guess that's not my responsibility.

Father, help me to learn what I'm responsible for and what I'm not, which is a truth that will set me free. —CAROL KUYKENDALL

FRI
18

NOW YOU ARE THE BODY OF CHRIST, AND EACH ONE OF YOU IS A PART OF IT. —I Corinthians 12:27 (NIV)

MY WIFE Shirley and I deliver Meals on Wheels as the need arises, and when one of the regulars had an emergency, we were called to fill in. I had another appointment and almost declined, but something stopped me, some inner prompting, and after checking with Shirley, I agreed. An hour later we were delivering hot meals. Although this route was new to us, we found our way around and eventually reached the last subscriber—a frail widow named Ruth, who had just come home from the hospital.

"I'm as weak as a feather," she said, holding shakily on to the countertop that separated her kitchen and dining room. Shirley took her arm and helped her to a chair.

"I've gone through four days of testing, and I've been advised to see a specialist, but I'm a nervous wreck. I don't have the energy to do anything but lie down."

"Then that's what you should do," Shirley said. "You don't need to call anyone today or tomorrow. Make your appointment when you feel stronger."

For the first time, Ruth seemed to relax. She took a deep breath, and her face, which had been a roadmap of worry, brightened with a smile. A neighbor would be in later, and a nurse would be coming tomorrow, she volunteered, and she knew things would look better after a good night's rest.

"We'll keep you in our prayers," I added as we left. Out in the car, I told Shirley, "Now I think I know why we were supposed to do this route."

A month later, we delivered a meal to Ruth again. This time she jauntily met us at the door, a transformed person. She had found a specialist who had prescribed the medicine she needed, and was feeling well enough to do some gardening. "Thanks for your advice and prayers," she whispered to Shirley as we left.

> *Teach us, Lord,*
> *That every day, down every street,*
> *Come chances to be God's hands and feet.*

—FRED BAUER

SAT
19

LET THE HEAVENS BE GLAD, AND LET THE EARTH REJOICE. . . . —I Chronicles 16:31

THE NOVEMBER 2001 Leonid meteor shower was touted as a once-in-a-lifetime event. Dozens of meteors would zigzag across the sky at once, and I wasn't about to miss it. Since Minnesota's weather was unseasonably balmy, I invited all of our neighbors over for snacks around the campfire and a chance to watch the show.

What a wonderful evening of fun and friendship beside the fire! At midnight we sang "Happy Birthday" to our neighbor Steve, who turned fifty at that very moment. As our song ended, a blazing meteor streaked long and low overhead, as if meant just for him. We waited hopefully for more but saw only a handful.

By 2:00 A.M. the party had broken up, and I was left alone. Before leaving, two young neighbor boys had extracted a promise from their father to wake them at 5:00 A.M.—the expected peak of the shower—and I decided to wait up for it, too. But around 4:00 A.M., thick clouds obscured the stars. Disappointed, I doused the fire and went inside to bed.

Later I learned from our neighbor that the sky had cleared at 5:00, and he and his family had watched scores of meteors flashing through the sky like fireworks. I had wanted a grand "meteor memory" for myself, and I was disappointed.

It's true that I didn't get to see the big meteor dance, but I was wrong to think that I didn't get my grand memory. My desire for a glimpse of the nighttime extravaganza had led me to plan the campfire party. Neighbors congregated; Steve got a personalized birthday meteor; two little boys experienced a rare evening under the stars with their dad and mom.

God had created the stage and the show, while I had merely provided the chairs. Yet, together, we had drawn the people out into the autumn night to make and keep their own prized memories. And, for me, that was the grandest show of all.

Forgive my whining, Lord, and teach me to value all that You allow me to be a part of. —CAROL KNAPP

SUN
20

THE WORD OF OUR GOD SHALL STAND FOR EVER.
—Isaiah 40:8

MY BIBLE IS falling apart. And no wonder; I received it at Sunday school on September 29, 1957. With colorful plates, maps, a concordance and student dictionary complete with illustrations from ark through Zion, it was perfect for a child.

Of course, I'm no longer a kid. Over the years the inexpensive leatherette cover has broken off along the edges. The gold-leaf gilding on the title rubbed off years ago and "Holy Bible" has become a dull gray shadow. In fact, the entire front cover sloughed off a couple of months ago, taking the first forty-nine chapters of Genesis with it. I stuck it back with cellophane tape, but even that has loosened, so I keep my Bible together with a rubber band. My shabby Scriptures.

They should look a lot worse. For the first thirty years I owned this Bible, I thumbed through it only casually, mostly at Sunday school. Then a dear friend introduced me to daily devotional reading—just as I was going through a divorce with four small children to care for. Bible reading became part of my early morning routine. Over the next fifteen years I underlined and highlighted my favorite passages, all the verses that really made a difference to me. Now I wouldn't trade that Bible for a more handsome or sturdier edition. It's my constant companion, my never-failing guide through life. No matter what struggles I'm going through, I can always turn to it for the help I need.

Yes, my Bible may be falling apart, but thanks to the wisdom in its pages, I'm not!

Dear Lord, thank You for Your Word hidden in my heart.
—GAIL THORELL SCHILLING

MON
21

A FRIEND LOVETH AT ALL TIMES. . . . —Proverbs 17:17

FOR SEVERAL DAYS I'd been mulling over the question I'd been asked: "How do you know when to take someone off your prayer list?" I looked at the slip of paper in my Bible and the names that had been on it for years. I had tried to be diligent, crossing off a name when a need had been answered—when a hospitalized friend was out of the danger zone or when a marriage was no longer in trouble. But I had to admit, there were people on that list whom I hadn't prayed for in years. Why didn't I take them off? Why did I find that as hard as dropping someone from a Christmas card list?

Then one afternoon I was flipping through my Rolodex and I came across the name of a friend I hadn't seen in months. Once, in fact, during a trying time when he was searching for a new job, he'd been at the top of my prayer list. Since then, he'd found an ideal position. But how was he doing now? How was his career going? After several calls, I reached him at his new office. When we met for lunch a week later I got a complete update—and one new good reason to remember him in my prayers. "You're on my list," I said in parting.

On my way back to the office I reflected on my habits of intercessory prayer. People come and go in my intercessions, as their needs change, but when I'm current with the lives of my friends and family, I find it very easy and very natural to pray for them. My prayer list should be flexible, like a sacred circle. I update it as I hear from people. Then I pray. By praying, I keep in touch—and by keeping in touch, my prayer life improves.

Lord, I ask You to be with _____, *who is in great need today.* (FILL IN THE BLANK)

—RICK HAMLIN

EDITOR'S NOTE: Join us today for Guideposts Thanksgiving Day of Prayer. On every working day, Guideposts Prayer Ministry prays for your requests by name and need. Visit us online at www.dailyguideposts.org, where you can request prayer, volunteer to pray for others or help support our prayer ministry.

TUE

22

Vanity of vanities! All is vanity.

—Ecclesiastes 1:2 (RSV)

I'VE BEEN FEELING rather weighed down lately with family responsibilities, spending as much time as possible with a dying friend and coping with work deadlines. But tonight I remembered something I discovered several years ago, when I was feeling both burdened and somewhat depressed. I'd started reading Ecclesiastes, and it fit my mood so well that I just kept on until I'd finished the book (which is only eight short chapters). It was a healing catharsis for me then, and it had the same effect tonight.

It's the *deep honesty* of the book that moves me so much. The writer puts into words all those vague, burdensome feelings most of us have at times, about the seeming futility of earthly life and its many injustices—feelings we're afraid to speak or even admit to ourselves.

Reading Ecclesiastes is like taking hold of both ends of a battery. It's a series of shocks that makes me want to commiserate, saying, "Yeah, that's the way *I* feel, too!" Yet in the reading of it, I somehow come to a degree of acceptance of the alternating currents of life, knowing that all is in divine order, and that I can trust the great mystery of it all (see Ecclesiastes 3:11).

If you're feeling burdened or depressed, I heartily recommend reading Ecclesiastes. But I think it's *very* important to read the whole book at one sitting. In that way, you come out the other end, not dimmed out but glowing.

Thank You, Lord, for the Preacher's courageous honesty in writing the book of Ecclesiastes, and for its great truth that nothing matters but You.
                                        —MARILYN MORGAN KING

WED

23

Therefore thou shalt love the Lord thy God, and keep his charge. . . . —Deuteronomy 11:1

I SAW HIM first on the second day of his life in a hospital room, where I brought him a balloon saying WELCOME

TO THE WORLD. Later, I traveled from New York to California for his christening and accepted the responsibility of being his godfather.

I'm afraid I was weakest on the spiritual side of my charge, but as he grew up I kept a careful watch on him, making transcontinental journeys to see him at his various schools, to watch him waterskiing and playing soccer, and to have him show me the first personal computer I had ever seen. Later, when he and his mother came to New York for Thanksgiving, we started a tradition of turkey dinners at my home. His decision to go to the same eastern college from which I graduated made my watching easier. Eventually he returned to California, turned his computer knowledge into a career and got married.

Things changed as the years went by, imperceptibly and without my recognizing them. Now that I'm eighty years old, instead of my watching over him, he watches over me. It's a phone call just to say hello or a sudden (miraculous) appearance when my computer died or a surprise gift of airline tickets to California to visit his family (they have four children so far).

I believe that on one side of my godfatherhood I was pretty good, but the spiritual side worried me until last year when his mother died. When I saw him at Grace Cathedral, remembering her solemnly but rightly, I knew that my godfathering was safely accomplished.

I thank You, Father, for the privilege of being a godfather.
—VAN VARNER

THU
24

THE HEAVENS DECLARE THE GLORY OF GOD; AND THE FIRMAMENT SHOWETH HIS HANDIWORK. DAY UNTO DAY UTTERETH SPEECH, AND NIGHT UNTO NIGHT SHOWETH KNOWLEDGE. THERE IS NO SPEECH NOR LANGUAGE, WHERE THEIR VOICE IS NOT HEARD.
—Psalm 19:1–3

IT WAS A picture-perfect autumn day during a cross-country trip to my parents' home for Thanksgiving. The long drive had been fun at first, but after eight straight hours, the novelty had worn off. Now it was my turn behind the wheel. My husband promptly nodded off in the passenger seat; our two sons were asleep, slumped in back. Except for the occasional *swish* of a passing car and the *sic-sic-sic* sound of our own tires on a wet pavement, silence prevailed.

"Looks like it's just You and me awake, Lord," I whispered, not wanting to rouse the others, "and Your Word says You 'neither slumber nor sleep' (Psalm 121:4)." Even while keeping my eyes safely on the road, I couldn't help but notice the scenery alongside. "What a marvelous creation You've made!"

It was then that I saw something I'd never noticed before: Everything in nature seemed to point up to God! Trees pointed up. Grass blades pointed up. Mountain peaks pointed up. Even man-made structures—house roofs, church steeples, signboards—all pointed up. And I suddenly recalled that one autumn when I was a child, when I'd planted tulip bulbs upside down. Yet down in the dark earth, each somehow managed to turn its stem upward, breaking the soil to point toward the sky.

"Wake up!" I shouted, prodding my husband and sons. "Look at the landscape! Everything Psalm Nineteen says"—and I quoted the verse—"is true!"

This Thanksgiving I'm grateful, Lord, that You've said I'm to ask You to "Open my eyes, that I may behold wondrous things" (Psalm 119:18, RSV). Whenever I do, I'm amazed at what You've created.

—ISABEL WOLSELEY

FRI
25

TO EVERY THING THERE IS A SEASON, AND A TIME TO EVERY PURPOSE UNDER THE HEAVEN. —*Ecclesiastes 3:1*

AS A CHILD in Pennsylvania, I loved winter. So when the time came to move to Southern California, where the weather might rarely permit rain, but never permitted the rain to solidify, I decided I had to take some snow with me. The winter before I moved, I filled an empty jelly jar with snow from our backyard, the home of numerous snow angels and snowmen over the years of my growing up. I closed the jar tightly and sealed the lid with duct tape to be sure not to lose a drop. I wanted to keep my winter memories intact.

Southern California lived up to my expectations. I found a good job, a wonderful husband and lots of sunshine. Still, I made sure my jar and the memories of my childhood winters were never far from reach.

One year Keith suggested we go to the Grand Canyon for Thanksgiving, and I agreed enthusiastically. On Thanksgiving Day, it snowed. For the first time in years, real snow and I were in the same place at the same time. I danced around like a kid, and sometime during the dance, I realized that my time for memory-making was far from over. The snow hadn't gone from my life!

Back in Los Angeles, I peeled the duct tape off the jelly jar, unscrewed the lid and poured out the water. If I kept my winter memories sealed up so tight, how would I slip in the new ones?

God of childhood and maturity, You are with me in all the stages of my life, ready to surprise me in every one. —RHODA BLECKER

SAT 26

ALL DISCIPLINE FOR THE MOMENT SEEMS NOT TO BE JOYFUL, BUT SORROWFUL; YET TO THOSE WHO HAVE BEEN TRAINED BY IT, AFTERWARDS IT YIELDS THE PEACEFUL FRUIT OF RIGHTEOUSNESS.
—*Hebrews 12:11 (NAS)*

THE AIR IS thin and cold in Texas; the wind whips off the western plains, and winter fast approaches. But most important to Texans, the changing weather heralds the climax of the high-school football season.

My son Luke is a senior and plays linebacker on the varsity football team. Last night his team won the district championship. My wife Beth and I sat in the stands huddled under blankets and cheered ourselves hoarse.

Luke is tall and slender, much like his father. He is a good athlete and loves physical contact, but his size is a disadvantage when it comes to football. He's not a starter, even though he did win the Defensive Player of the Week award once this season. Because of his physical stature, he doesn't get a lot of playing time.

Thirty-five years ago I faced the same predicament. My high-school team won the district championship, but I watched most of the game from the end of the bench. I know firsthand what it is to hope, to dream, to practice hard and to be personally disappointed. Football taught me that being part of a team is more important than being an individual hero, that the real victory is hanging in there and not quitting, regardless of pain or limitations.

Last night as Luke ran off the field, he could not have been happier. He played the whole fourth quarter and made three tackles. He contributed to a team victory that required the efforts of everyone, from water boy to quarterback. Things don't get better than that!

Lord, by Your grace enable me to perform whatever tasks You ask of me for the good of Your kingdom. Amen. —SCOTT WALKER

SIMPLE GIFTS

THE GREATEST CHRISTMAS GIFT is the one God gave us in the manger at Bethlehem: the gift of Himself. As you get ready to celebrate the birth of Jesus, Karen Barber has some gifts of her own to give you. Join her for a reminder that the best gifts we can give each other are the simplest ones of all. —THE EDITORS

FIRST SUNDAY IN ADVENT:
THE ANGEL'S GIFT

SUN

27

AND SUDDENLY THERE WAS WITH THE ANGEL A MULTITUDE OF THE HEAVENLY HOST. . . . —Luke 2:13

MOM HAD JUST ARRIVED at our home for a holiday visit. As she stared at an angel ornament on my tree, she said, "My mother saw an angel when I was a girl." Then she told me this story:

"When I was young, I had severe asthma. One night I couldn't breathe. Mama was begging and praying that I wouldn't die. Suddenly she looked up in the open doorway to the hall and saw a beautiful dark-haired woman. The woman didn't say a thing. She just smiled and gave a friendly wave. Afterward Mama told me, 'I think it was an angel telling me that you would live and grow up to be a woman like the one I saw standing in the doorway.'"

Mom's story has challenged my conventional ideas about angels. Her angel looked like an ordinary person. Mom's angel didn't *do* anything remarkable; she didn't even *say* anything. Yet in the hour of deepest need, my grandmother had drawn strength and hope from this being who did absolutely nothing except stand there and wave. Sometimes the whole mission of angels is simply to appear.

Angels are spiritual beings who are invisible except when they choose otherwise; we humans are visible beings whose spiritual side is invisible until we choose to let it show. This Advent season, I can imitate the angels by letting someone glimpse my spiritual side. Maybe it will be seen as I drive to church or when I help a person in need. Maybe it will be heard when I sing a carol or write a Christmas letter telling about the wonderful things God has done for me during the past year.

This Advent, let's be angelic. Let's become visible!

Lord, I pray that Your light will so shine in my heart that it will be seen by everyone I meet. —KAREN BARBER

MON

28

AND THE EARTH WAS WITHOUT FORM, AND VOID; AND DARKNESS WAS UPON THE FACE OF THE DEEP. . . .
—*Genesis 1:2*

I FIRST CAME across the phrase *tohu va-vohu* in Professor Everett Fox's translation of the Book of Genesis. Better known to most Bible readers in the King James rendering, "without form and void," the words are the original Hebrew description of the condition of the earth at the time of creation.

I've never been much of a student of languages, but there's something thrilling to me about the way the sound of these alien words manages to conjure up the state of things before God set to building and ordering the universe. Fox translates the words as "wild and waste," emphasizing that in the Hebrew, there is a suggestion that in the course of creation God brings order out of a condition of chaos.

Tohu va-vohu. When I'm confronted with chaos in my own life— whether in the form of something as small as a messy apartment or as vast as a scene of violence and devastation on the evening news—I often find these Hebrew syllables coming to mind. To me, they serve as a reminder that all the beauty and order in the world began from an absence of those qualities, and that in every situation where chaos seems to reign, a seed of order and goodness is waiting, with God's help, to be brought forth.

Lord, send forth Your Spirit, and make a new creation from the tohu va-vohu *of my life.* —PTOLEMY TOMPKINS

TUE

29

MANY OF THE SAMARITANS FROM THAT TOWN BELIEVED IN HIM BECAUSE OF THE WOMAN'S TESTIMONY. . . . —*John 4:39 (NIV)*

I LEANED OVER my friend Tony's shoulder as he flipped through the huge photo album. Two other equally large books sat unopened and waiting by his side. With each image, I was transported back to Europe.

"Oh," I exclaimed, as Tony turned to a picture of my favorite bakery in Paris, "they make the most delicious pastries!" I could practically taste the chocolate cream.

"*Mmm*, looks good," he said, peering at the picture.

As he turned the page, he pointed to a group of people smiling at the camera. "Who are these people?" he asked. The frozen smiles on the glossy print came back to life as I remembered the laughter of that night in Spain.

"Those are my roommates from the youth hostel in Barcelona," I said. "We were trying *paella* for the first time, but we could barely eat because we were making one another laugh the whole time."

Tony opened the next photo album and was instantly awed by the pictures of enormous snow-powdered mountains. "That's amazing," he said, mesmerized by the photos. "I would love to go there."

"You should!" I urged. "As beautiful as those shots are, the mountains are even more beautiful in person. The feeling is indescribable."

By the time we got to the end of the last photo album, Tony was planning his own trip to Europe. While the photographs could never capture the essence of my trip, the images and my excitement were enough to make him want to see it for himself.

Lord, when I share my faith with others, help me inspire them to want to experience it for themselves. —KAREN VALENTIN

WED
30

THOU, LORD, HAST HELPED ME AND COMFORTED ME.
—*Psalm 86:17 (RSV)*

MOTHER WAS OLD and frail when she moved down to Staten Island, New York, to live with my brother, but she had always been so strong I assumed that she'd live for many more years. So I was unprepared when I got the call from my brother: "Oscar, it's Mother."

Ruby and I drove to Staten Island, and the next day I found myself sitting at my mother's funeral. Mother was a bright, well-educated woman. She had studied to become a registered nurse, but because of the Great Depression and the lack of opportunity in our small town, she could only find a job as a domestic. Her workday was spent in her employers' kitchens.

As I sat in the pew I wondered, had she really been happy? Did she feel fulfilled? Did she feel that service to others was its own reward? She never complained—never gave a hint of resentment. But did she wish things had been different?

Then the priest moved forward from the altar and spoke about her, calling her Mrs. Morgan (she had changed her name when she married my stepfather years before). I was taken back to the kitchens where she had worked, where she ran things with the efficiency, warmth and professionalism of a registered nurse. I thought of all those people who feasted on her rice, lima beans, French fries and chicken, and listened to her advice—all those households where she had made a difference. One woman in town was so notoriously difficult they said no one could work for her. Mother did for twelve years. And she was called Mrs. Morgan. Respected and admired, she was always Mrs. Morgan.

At once I was comforted and reassured. What might have been a job for some, Mother turned into a calling. It was not the career she planned on or studied for, but she made it something worthwhile.

Heavenly Comforter, help me make the most of all the opportunities that come my way. —OSCAR GREENE

SEEDS OF REJOICING

I _____

2 _____

3 _____

4 _____

5 ——————————————————

6 ——————————————————

7 ——————————————————

8 ——————————————————

9 ——————————————————

10 ——————————————————

11 ——————————————————

12 ——————————————————

13 ——————————————————

14 ——————————————————

15 ——————————————————

16 ——————————————————

17 ——————————————————

18 _____

19 _____

20 _____

21 _____

22 _____

23 _____

24 _____

25 _____

26 _____

27 _____

28 _____

29 _____

30 _____

December

Rejoice greatly, O daughter of Zion; shout, O daughter of Jerusalem: behold, thy King cometh unto thee. . . .

—*Zechariah 9:9*

GOD SIGHTINGS
THE MAKER'S MARK

THU
1

WITHOUT HIM WAS NOT ANY THING MADE THAT WAS MADE. —John 1:3

IT'S DECEMBER, the season of Advent, when our thoughts should focus on the coming of Jesus—as a baby in a manger and as the king of kings at the end of time. But, oh dear! With shopping and mailing and writing cards and getting the house ready for guests, I often forget the point of it all.

So as I left the house today, I murmured a quick prayer: *Don't let me lose sight of You today, Lord!*

Answers to my plea came all day long. Driving down roads recently cleared by snowplows, I recalled other obstacles also cleared away—like getting in to see the doctor whose schedule was "completely full." And I saw God as the One Who time and again has opened a way for me.

Outside the grocery store, a bell ringer stood beside a Salvation Army kettle. Jesus had compassion for the poor.

In the children's clothes section at a department store, a woman worried over the fit of a pair of boys' jeans she was sending as a Christmas gift. How perfectly God fit His gift to our need.

At the drugstore checkout counter, a manager was blasting a tired clerk for entering the wrong key on the cash register. Jesus took abuse from the authorities, too.

Let me not lose sight of You. . . . It must be a prayer God loves to answer because all day, everywhere I looked, in everyone I met and everything I saw, there He was!

This year I've remembered specific God sightings, past and present. Today He told me, "There is nothing you can see, nothing you can hear or touch, where I am not."

Enlarge my vision now and in the coming year, Father, to see You in all Your works. —ELIZABETH SHERRILL

FRI

2

THEREFORE, SINCE WE HAVE SUCH A HOPE, WE ARE VERY BOLD. —*II Corinthians 3:12 (NIV)*

"IT SEEMS that every time I take food to the homeless shelter, someone threatens me," John said to me. "But I keep going back just the same."

I'd worked in a ministry to the poor for almost thirty years. And I'd come up against some pretty dangerous folks, too. It's hard to try to help people who make you feel afraid. Why take a risk?

"What gives you the courage to keep going back?" I asked John.

"These people live a daily life of hopelessness," he said. "But God could change that. He's given me so much, including the opportunity to reach out and share His love. So I rejoice in hope. And it's hope that makes me bold."

Lord, help me to be a bold bringer of hope. —DOLPHUS WEARY

SAT

3

LET US . . . TURN AGAIN TO THE LORD.
—*Lamentations 3:40*

IT WAS QUIET behind the information desk in the bookstore where I work, and I was sorting books while mentally mulling over some big questions in my life. Where am I going? Am I on the right path? Is this job part of Your plan for me, God?

A hesitant blond boy of about four years old approached, alone. "Do . . . do you work here?" he asked softly.

"Yes, I do."

"My mommy," he said, "she got lost from me."

This happens from time to time, so I told him firmly, "Don't worry. You stay right here and we'll announce your name on the loudspeaker and your mommy will come back in a minute." I handed him some stickers and asked, "What's your name?"

He gave me a wary look. "Mommy says not to tell my name to strangers."

I hid a smile. *Okay, I'll try another track.* "Do you know your mommy's first name?" A frightened look and a shrug. I persisted, "Well, what does Daddy call her?"

"Honey," he said dubiously. Now I laughed out loud.

Getting on the loudspeaker, I announced, "The info desk has a little lost b—"

Before I could even finish, a curly-haired blonde woman rushed over, swooped the boy up in her arms and cried, "I was so worried about you!" The two of them walked away, hands tightly clasped, stickers trailing out of his back pocket.

I watched them as they left. The mother had found her child even with the small amount of information I could give. Nothing could keep them apart. Now, wasn't that just the information I needed?

God, help me to know that You are looking to help me when I feel lost, even when I don't know exactly what it is I need. —LINDA NEUKRUG

SIMPLE GIFTS
SECOND SUNDAY IN
ADVENT: THE GIFT OF HOPE

SUN

4

THEN TOOK HE HIM UP IN HIS ARMS, AND BLESSED GOD, AND SAID, LORD, NOW LETTEST THOU THY SERVANT DEPART IN PEACE, ACCORDING TO THY WORD: FOR MINE EYES HAVE SEEN THY SALVATION.
—*Luke 2:28–30*

WHEN I WAS a teenager during the turbulent sixties, my mother had a silver-haired friend named Iva. Although Iva was the product of a more formal generation, she didn't complain when our church was invaded by an assortment of hippies in faded jeans. Instead, Iva prayed, and one by one this band of noisy young people made commitments to Christ. I was one of them.

Then one Sunday, Iva's seat on the left side of the sanctuary was empty. That morning Iva had suffered a stroke and died instantly.

After the funeral, my mother told me, "Iva somehow knew that she wouldn't live to see the end result of the renewal we'd been praying for. But she always smiled and said, 'It's all right. I've seen it start. I've held the baby.'"

Mom's statement puzzled me. It was only years later that I found out what "holding the baby" meant. When Mary and Joseph took Baby Jesus to the Temple, an old man named Simeon met them. Simeon had been promised that before he died he would see the Christ. An inner sense drew him to take the baby in his arms. In the face of a helpless infant, Simeon saw the king of kings.

Advent is about the hope we allow to flow through us as we, like Simeon, "hold the baby," knowing that from these wobbly beginnings will come greater, brighter, more wonderful things. Today, I've lived nearly as many decades as Iva. Thanks to the hope she had in my small beginnings of faith, I'd like to think that I've grown into someone like her.

Father, this Advent, keep my eyes open to the signs of Your work in my life, and give me the faith and patience to allow that work to grow.

—Karen Barber

MON
5

THE LORD IS A GOD OF JUDGMENT: BLESSED ARE ALL THEY THAT WAIT FOR HIM. —*Isaiah 30:18*

WHY I HAD picked the first week in December for jury service was a mystery to me. Things were happening at work, my wife Julee was bedridden with the flu, the holidays were just around the corner, and the winter wind was raking lower Manhattan. Yet here I was, stuck in the county courthouse, waiting, waiting.

What if I got put on a case that dragged on all month? What if I didn't get on a case at all? Already I'd been questioned and peremptorily excused from one panel that was to hear a gun-possession case. A fellow jury pool member nudged me and said, "You lucked out." Had I? Frankly, I was torn. I was worried about my time, but I also wanted to serve. What was the point of showing up and waiting around day after day if it was for nothing?

I came close to getting on a couple of trials. One was a civil case that was settled at the last minute; another was a criminal proceeding from which, once again, I was inexplicably excused. As soon as I was released from jury service I complained to a lawyer friend. "I sat there all week with a million things to do and didn't even get to serve on a case! What good is that?"

My friend chuckled. Didn't I see? Just by participating in jury selection I had played a crucial role in getting a fellow citizen a fair trial, even if I wasn't chosen, and that was the whole point of our legal system. "You *did* serve," he said, giving me a pat on the back. "You showed up."

I knew better than to argue with a lawyer.

Lord, every day You use me in ways I don't always understand. Sometimes all I have to do is show up. —EDWARD GRINNAN

TUE   BLESSED IS HE THAT WAITETH. . . . —*Daniel 12:12*

6   I THOUGHT I knew about waiting. Especially December waiting. I waited in line at the post office to mail my Christmas packages. I waited my turn at the florist's. And I waited to open that big package under the tree with my name on it. But last year's Advent season was different. Our daughter Amy Jo was going to have a December baby, and waiting took on a whole new intensity.

As her time got closer, we all went on "baby standby." If I didn't hear from Amy Jo by the end of every day, I called her. I started charging my cell phone, carrying it with me and actually turning it on—three things I seldom did before baby standby. I bought and wrapped my presents early. I saved up my vacation days at work. I made sure the car had a full tank of gas. And I waited—in a more heightened state of expectancy than any I could remember experiencing, even during my own pregnancies. And on December 22, when Amy Jo gave birth to a healthy baby boy, I knew it had been well worth the wait!

This Advent, I want to remember that expectancy, the happy hope embodied in the waiting. I want to realize that this year—and always and forever—a Child is born. But only if I'm on baby standby can I really know the joy His coming brings. Only if I'm watching with breathless longing will I find my waiting rewarded with a fresh sense of wonder, with a heightened awareness of love. With *Christmas!*

I praise You, Father, for the miracle of birth and the miracle of Your love made flesh to dwell among us. I wait for Your coming. Welcome, welcome, welcome, Baby Jesus! —MARY LOU CARNEY

WED
7

I THANK MY GOD EVERY TIME I REMEMBER YOU.
—Philippians 1:3 (NIV)

WHEN I WALK into my home office each workday, I smile at the sight of the quilt that covers more than half of the far right wall. It's a crazy quilt. That means the maker didn't cut and sew a repeating pattern or even regular shapes. A crisp triangle or rectangle is the rare exception. The pentagons and hexagons are askew. Some lines are slightly curved. Some pieces are as small as one by two inches, and others are up to a foot long. It's virtually impossible to count the pieces, but I tried. About four hundred, out of maybe forty different fabrics, plain colors and plaids of mostly winter colors.

Internally the quilt has no "rule." But when it comes to the outside edge, it all ends up fit and square. It works, as a critic might say to an artist. A few years back I made a miniature crazy quilt, an eighteen-inch-square chair-seat cover. I quickly learned that the design is not as haphazard as it looks. Each piece has to fit in as a companion alongside the next.

When I walk into my office each workday, I do more than smile at the sight of the quilt blanketing the wall. I see the whole as a representation of my life, with each piece being a different sibling, niece, nephew, colleague, neighbor, church friend, college friend. . . . I can find nearly forty categories to match the forty colors. I focus on one or more of the unique quilt pieces. I think of someone that triangle or trapezoid (or indescribably unusual shape) reminds me of, and I pray for that person by name, asking God to bless him or her today, thanking God for placing that one-of-a-kind person in the colorful mosaic that is my life.

Lord, thank You for the many one-of-a-kind people You have cut and sewn into the crazy quilt of my life. It works. —EVELYN BENCE

THU

8

COMMIT TO THE LORD WHATEVER YOU DO, AND YOUR PLANS WILL SUCCEED. —Proverbs 16:3 (NIV)

I'M A CASE STUDY on how to be an overnight success in twenty years or less. It took me years of frantically pounding against opportunity's door before I sold my first novel; five long, frustrating and discouraging years.

One of the first lessons I learned in dealing with the constant barrage of rejection was the need to celebrate the small successes. My first sale was a five-dollar anecdote.

Our five-year-old son Dale was part of the Christmas program at church. His entire role consisted of reciting a Bible verse. Sure enough, when the time came, Dale flawlessly recited the verse, but hesitated when he forgot the reference. In a moment of panic he looked to me. Wanting to help, I cupped my hands over my mouth and whispered, "It's Luke. It's Luke."

Instantly relieved, Dale shouted out in a loud booming voice, "Luke Skywalker!"

This tale has long been repeated in our family, along with other Dale stories. One day I decided to write it up and submit it to a church magazine. A few weeks later, I received a check for five dollars!

I was ecstatic; I'd made a sale at last. A magazine had found something I'd written worthy of publication—worthy of payment. The confidence boost that five-dollar anecdote gave me was worth five million. I'd made a sale. I've never forgotten it.

God, thank You for the small encouragements You send into my life. Help me to celebrate the little steps I take as I trudge toward my goal.

—DEBBIE MACOMBER

FRI

9

I HEARD THE VOICE OF THE LORD, SAYING, WHOM SHALL I SEND, AND WHO WILL GO FOR US? THEN SAID I, HERE AM I; SEND ME. —Isaiah 6:8

JUST MOMENTS BEFORE leaving the house to go to my new job, my wife Nicole told me, "God gave you this job for a reason beyond work and salary. Keep an eye out for why He brought you there."

The writer I was to replace was still at the agency when I arrived, and we were to spend the week together so he could train me. We became fast friends, spending lunches together, and I shared my faith with him, answering his questions to the best of my ability. He told me that he was preparing to take a four-month backpacking trip to far-off lands and that he was packed so full he had only about *this much* space left in his bag.

Well, *this much* space looked Bible-size to me. So I called Nicole and asked her to pick up the smallest Bible she could find. That day before he left, I put the Bible on his desk.

About a month later, I received an e-mail from him. He was in the back of a rundown old camper somewhere in New Zealand, a half a world away. He was reading the Bible by flashlight. He wrote, "I find your man Matthew a most fascinating writer. I am reading with much interest. Thanks again."

God gives me many opportunities to serve and to grow. If I don't follow Nicole's advice and look for them, I wonder how many I'll miss?

*Lord, help me make the best of the space You give me to witness to You, even if it's only "this much." —*DAVE FRANCO

SAT
IO *I AM THE LIGHT OF THE WORLD: HE THAT FOLLOWETH ME SHALL NOT WALK IN DARKNESS, BUT SHALL HAVE THE LIGHT OF LIFE. —John 8:12*

SEVERAL YEARS AGO, I pastored a church in Huff's Church, Pennsylvania. One Saturday night, I went over to the church to make sure everything was ready for Sunday worship. I took our young son Joel with me to help check the candles, pull the shades, tidy up the booklet racks and make sure the bulletins were where they should be.

When we entered the church, it was so dark that we couldn't see a thing. The only light switch was at the end of a long hallway. Since I knew my way around, I started to walk quickly toward the switch. I was stopped by a frightened little voice: "Daddy, where are you? It's so dark, and I'm scared! Please come back!"

Although I was halfway to the light switch, I turned around, went back and took my son's hand. His fear disappeared and together we made our way to the switch.

There are times when the way ahead seems so dark that I can't see my way and, like Joel, I cry out to my Father in fear. And if I reach out to Him with trust, He will take my hand and lead me to the light.

Father God, with all my heart I entrust myself to You. Lead me in Your path. —TED NACE

SIMPLE GIFTS
THIRD SUNDAY IN ADVENT:
THE GIFT OF SECOND
CHANCES

SUN
11

GLORY TO GOD IN THE HIGHEST, AND ON EARTH PEACE, GOOD WILL TOWARD MEN. —*Luke 2:14*

IT WAS TWO DAYS after Christmas, and I was frustrated about how busy I'd allowed myself to become during the hectic holiday season. *I'm glad Christmas is over,* I thought as I wandered down a side street in the town we were visiting. Something about the propped-open front door of a small church prompted me to step inside. In the dim interior, a waist-high manger scene was arranged under a roof of dry palm fronds.

This is a bad place for a nativity display, I thought. *It's dwarfed by this huge stained-glass window of the Prodigal Son.*

As I stood there, more thoughts came to mind. *You're just like the Prodigal Son. You've been so worried about gifts and trips and wrapping and baking that you've squandered your Christmas inheritance.*

A pang of regret washed over me. Then the sun suddenly came from behind a cloud and blazed through the stained-glass window, making the words inscribed on the window glow brightly: "Bring forth the best robe and put it on him and put a ring on his hand."

My eyes followed the light down to the manger scene. Even though I was a prodigal child, God was still the loving Father. Year after year, He gives the gift of Christmas, beckoning me to find my way home.

Father, I'm so apt to be distracted from spiritual things at Christmastime. Help me to come to my senses and start out for home today.
—KAREN BARBER

MON
12

AND THE LITTLE ONES THAT YOU SAID WOULD BE TAKEN CAPTIVE . . . THEY WILL ENTER THE LAND. . . .
—*Deuteronomy 1:39 (NIV)*

MY WIFE Tib and I have long enjoyed a special friendship with an English couple, Ray and Jean Cripps. We got to know Ray in the sixties, when he was the publisher of the British edition of *Guideposts*, and we remained close friends until his death in 2001. We often traveled to the small blanket-manufacturing town of Witney in Oxfordshire to spend a few days with the Crippses and swap stories about our respective families.

Ray and Jean have three children, two boys and a girl; Tib and I also have two boys and a girl, born in the same order. As we came to trust one another, we began to pray about the concerns every family has. There were health questions, problematic friendships, school problems, peer pressures.

Then our practice of praying with the Crippses took a turn. Each family found—and we can't have been the first to discover this—that it's difficult to pray for our own children because it's so hard to get self out of the equation. Our children carry so many of our hopes and fears. Our reputations are bound up with them; to watch the child is to judge the parent. Clearly, our prayers needed to be more God-centered and less self-centered.

Our solution was simple: We swapped kids. The Crippses prayed for our children, and we prayed for theirs. We quickly found that the exchange gave us all a certain healthy distance from the alarms that, from too close, loomed so large. Yes, the children continued to have problems, but with the swap we and the Crippses could face those issues with more God-centered eyes.

Help me, Father, to put less of me and more of You in all my prayers.
—JOHN SHERRILL

TUE
13

"AND MY PEOPLE SHALL BE SATISFIED WITH MY GOODNESS, SAYS THE LORD." —Jeremiah 31:14 (RSV)

WHEN WE FIRST MOVED to Alaska, we lived in an older model, fourteen-by-seventy mobile home that didn't look like much. It had rickety front steps, kitchen drawers that fell out unless I balanced them with my knee, poor lighting, dark paneling and darker carpeting—pockmarked with cinder burns from the woodstove—and in the winter the water pipes nearly always froze when the temperature dropped below zero. We lived there for four years with a menagerie of dogs, cats, rabbits and a couple of litters of kittens, all of which we acquired at varying intervals, and our four kids, who came as a package deal and stayed continuously. Then we moved into another home.

Suddenly, in the new setting, it seemed the desires of my heart tumbled from every room. The house was light and airy, with sturdy upper and lower decks. Its beautiful oak kitchen had drawers that actually slid gracefully on runners. There was even a chandelier above the dining area. We more than doubled our living space. And in eight winters, the water pipes faithfully continued to deliver. It was God Who guided us to it and made it possible for us to move in. But, to be fair, it was God Who led us to Alaska in the first place and provided the affordable mobile home.

When I compare the two situations—the struggles and challenges of the first and the smoother adjustments of the second—one striking conclusion emerges: I found happiness in each home, because I had the master key. It is the key that opens doors to contented living everywhere: being satisfied with what God has given—even when kitchen drawers fall out, front steps sag and water pipes freeze.

Father, it is You Who are able truly to satisfy. Keep me content in what You give—and, yes, in what You deny. —CAROL KNAPP

WED

14

AND SO IT WAS, THAT, WHILE THEY WERE THERE, THE DAYS WERE ACCOMPLISHED THAT SHE SHOULD BE DELIVERED. AND SHE BROUGHT FORTH HER FIRSTBORN SON, AND WRAPPED HIM IN SWADDLING CLOTHES, AND LAID HIM IN A MANGER; BECAUSE THERE WAS NO ROOM FOR THEM IN THE INN. —Luke 2:6–7

MY WIFE Sandee crochets. Virtually every couch and bed in our house is festooned with afghans crafted by my wife, mostly during Pirates' games on TV. We also keep one in the van to compensate for the tepid heater.

On Christmas Eve last year, en route to my in-laws for dinner, we stopped at a red light. A young man stood in the cold with a sign: HOMELESS PLEASE HELP.

Sandee reached for her purse, I for my wallet—nothing. My wife hesitated, then reached back and retrieved the afghan.

"Hey, buddy," Sandee said, rolling down the window, "here's a blanket if you're cold."

My kids and I were silent, staring at Sandee. Each of us knew the months of work it takes to make an afghan. It's one thing to fish around for change; it's quite another to offer something you fashioned yourself—choosing the colors, the pattern, the right yarn.

What would you offer on Christmas to someone without a home—someone, say, journeying from afar, who finds no room at the local motel? Or maybe an unmarried couple, and maybe she's pregnant. Would you offer a blanket on a cold night? A place to stay? A place in your heart? Would you? Would I?

*This Christmas, Lord, help me to use my gifts to honor You in the least of my brothers and sisters. —*MARK COLLINS

HE LEADETH ME . . .
TO NOTICE THE LITTLE
THINGS

THU
15
As for God, his way is perfect. . . .
—*II Samuel 22:31*

I WAS MAKING Infection Control Rounds at the hospital where I work, when I entered a private room. A nurse was bathing a patient who had metastatic cancer and had slipped into a coma. I checked his I.V. to make sure it hadn't been in place longer than the recommended hours, part of a patient-care audit I was conducting.

As I left the room, I paused, taking notice of how the nurse had wrapped the washcloth tautly around her hand so as not to irritate her patient's crepe-paper skin. She gently washed his arm and lifted it ever so tenderly to dry it. Then she squeezed his fingertips twice, saying, "Your wife called earlier and asked me to give you the signal."

Some nurses might think such a patient was past the point of understanding words and touch and signals. But not this nurse. She had found the perfect way. For her, administering a bath was a work of art.

Later that afternoon, I went back to the nursing unit to locate her. I found her in the storage closet, gathering up supplies to insert a feeding tube into another patient. "I've thought of you all day long," I told her. "I was so touched by the loving way you cared for your patient this morning, and I just had to tell you."

She lowered her head. "Oh, thank you," she replied. "I didn't think anyone ever noticed things like that."

That's going to be one of the great joys of heaven, God seemed to say. *You'll spend the first thousand years or so finding out how by following My celestial signals, you made a difference in the lives of others.*

Lord, keep me listening to Your Voice. —ROBERTA MESSNER

READER'S ROOM

TEN YEARS AGO in December, I had brain aneurysm surgery. I don't remember my hospital stay or my coming home on Christmas Eve. But once all the medicines had worn off, I began to see everything in a new light. I noticed every little thing as though for the first time. I rejoiced in sunrise and sunset, riding a bicycle, dancing again, watching children play. It was a new beginning—a spiritual renewal. —*Mary Hinkel, Canton, Ohio*

FRI

16

LET US NOW GO EVEN UNTO BETHLEHEM, AND SEE THIS THING WHICH IS COME TO PASS, WHICH THE LORD HATH MADE KNOWN UNTO US. —Luke 2:15

THE CALENDAR still says fall, but the whistling wind today says winter, and the chill sent my wife Shirley and me inside to the closet, from which we drew several boxes of Christmas decorations. Some of the holiday items we unwrapped have been in the family for years, and they conjure up warm memories of Christmases past. Tree ornaments fashioned by the kids when they were younger than spring-time are among our particular favorites. Homely by artistic standards, these painted hunks of clay depicting camels, stars, snowmen, sheep and donkeys are heirlooms to us.

Other Christmas treasures were collected in our travels, such as the hand-carved manger scene from Bethlehem. Shirley and I visited the City of David many years ago, and while we were there, a young boy came by selling crèches carved from olive wood by him and his father. The manger and the Holy Family were obviously fashioned with great care, and we bought one of his creations. It has been a part of our Christmas décor ever since.

When my sister Joy, who is a Methodist minister outside of Chicago, saw our Bethlehem memento, she said that her family also displayed a crèche at Christmas, except theirs was different. "Several years ago the figure of Baby Jesus came up missing," she reported, "and when all our searching failed, I considered the tableau ruined. Then I had second thoughts, and put the crèche on the mantel without Baby Jesus. Christ is often missing from our self-centered celebration, I reasoned, and the missing baby reminds me that it is up to us to find Him. Not in the noisy hubbub of Christmas, but in sharing God's quiet love made manifest in the manger."

Teach us this Christmas, Lord, to listen with our heart,
To see, with spirit eyes, the true and holy part.
— FRED BAUER

SAT
17

MY GRACE IS SUFFICIENT FOR THEE: FOR MY
STRENGTH IS MADE PERFECT IN WEAKNESS. . . .
—II Corinthians 12:9

"IT'S A LITTLE scraggly, isn't it?" I said to my wife Carol as we strung garlands around the Christmas tree. Decorating Day is a big event for us and the kids, the end of a long process that begins in early November, when we drive north to the tree farm to tag our selection. This year, however, we didn't make it out until mid-December. The pickings were slim, but after some deliberation we chose a balsam fir, hauled it home and propped it up in its red metal stand.

Trimming the tree was a joyful occasion, punctuated by hot-cider-and-cookie breaks and Christmas carols. Once finished, we gathered for a moment of appreciation and prayer. Every year at this time, somebody notices something special about our tree. Maybe it is particularly tall or thick or shaped in an amusing way. One year the tree bristled with cones, as if supplying its own decorations.

But this tree just didn't measure up. It was thin and squat, with drooping branches, and no one noticed anything special. I was disappointed, and I felt the others were, too. But then Carol said, "Didn't Jesus say something about the last being first?" and someone else said, "Yes, and 'Blessed are the poor in spirit,'" and our youngest chimed in with, "I like this tree just because it's small, like me."

God had sent us this scrawny fir as surely as the splendid trees of years past. Right now He was speaking to all of us through these balsam branches.

Lord, help me to see You in the weak and plain as well as the strong and beautiful, for all declare Your glory. —PHILIP ZALESKI

SIMPLE GIFTS
FOURTH SUNDAY IN
ADVENT: THE GIFT OF LOVE

SUN

18

NOW WHEN JESUS WAS BORN IN BETHLEHEM . . . BEHOLD, THERE CAME WISE MEN FROM THE EAST. . . .
—*Matthew 2:1*

THAT DECEMBER afternoon I found an excuse to drop by my friend Nancy's office. As I said good-bye, I wrapped my arms around her in a firm hug and told her she was special. Although Nancy didn't know it, I had just delivered her Christmas present: the first hug scheduled for secret delivery by our ladies' Bible study group during the twelve days leading up to Christmas.

Nancy's world had fallen apart following a divorce, and she was facing Christmas lost in rejection and pain. When she told me, "I feel so unloved," I asked, "What makes you feel loved?" She answered quickly, "When someone hugs me, really holds me."

And that's why a hug sign-up sheet was passed around at our Bible study. Over the next twelve days, members of the group devised ways to give Nancy a hug a day. They jumped out of cars in the school carpool line, took food from our Christmas luncheon to her office, hand-delivered Christmas cards. On Christmas Eve, I clipped twelve paper dolls out of brightly colored wrapping paper, wrote a hugger's name and the date of the hug on each, added a note explaining our gift, and then delivered it along with the final hug.

On Christmas Day Nancy called me, practically shouting with joy, "I had no idea what you all were up to! It's the best gift I've ever received!"

Dear Lord, thank You for coming into our world as a tiny baby in the silence of the night to wrap us in the arms of Your love.

—KAREN BARBER

MON	AND IT CAME ABOUT THAT WHEN *Elizabeth* HEARD
19	*MARY'S GREETING, THE BABY LEAPED IN HER WOMB; AND ELIZABETH WAS FILLED WITH THE HOLY SPIRIT.*

MARY'S GREETING, THE BABY LEAPED IN HER WOMB; AND ELIZABETH WAS FILLED WITH THE HOLY SPIRIT.
—Luke 1:41 (NAS)

YESTERDAY MY WIFE Beth reminded me of a memory from long ago. Our children were little then: Drew was five, Luke was two, and Jodi was five months in her mother's womb. It was the Christmas season and we were living in Charleston, South Carolina.

Beth was sitting with Drew and Luke at a Christmas Eve worship service. Amid the candlelight and beautiful music, Luke grew sleepy, stuck his thumb in his mouth, cuddled his favorite blanket and leaned over to place his head on his mother's stomach. As Luke drifted off, little Jodi kicked inside her mother, popping her brother in the cheek. Jolted, Luke's eyes flew open and he squealed loudly, "Mama! What was that?"

For Beth this was a holy moment filled with joy and angelic laughter. As she celebrated the birth of Jesus, she felt the miracle of new life within her and heard the wonder in a child's innocent voice. Christmas became real.

In this Christmas season may you be startled awake by the movement of God's Spirit within you. May you be roused from sleep by a jolt from heaven. May you hear the voice of God in the awe-tinged voice of a child.

Father, may joyful memories and the innocence of children bring back the wonder of Christmas to me. Amen. —SCOTT WALKER

TUE
20

MAKE ME SAVOURY MEAT, SUCH AS I LOVE, AND BRING IT TO ME, THAT I MAY EAT. . . . —Genesis 27:4

SOME FRIENDS and I got to talking about the most unusual Christmas gift we had ever received. One told of unwrapping a box within a box within a box, and finding a pair of orchestra seats to *The Nutcracker* ballet. The note from her husband read, "Given on condition that you don't ask *me* to go."

When the laughter died down, I told about the year I turned fifty. The family gave me fifty different kinds of candy bars—my weakness. They went to great lengths to order Aero bars from Canada, Violet Crumbles (chocolate-covered honeycomb) from Australia and a variety of my favorite Cadburys. These were not only packaged under the Christmas tree, they were hidden all over the house so well that it was halfway through March before I found the last of them.

"My gift came during a year of tough times," another friend said. "My work hours were cut way back and money was tight. I lived on soup and casseroles unless my family invited me over for dinner. As we gathered around the Christmas tree that year, I noticed a last-minute gift being slipped under it. The gift was for me. It was ice cold. *What in the world?* I thought as I tore the paper off the rectangular box. Then I gasped. A roast beef in a shoe box! It was my best present ever."

Blessed Lord, enlarge our hearts to extend the spirit of Christmas giving, of caring and sharing all the year through. —FAY ANGUS

WED
21

HE SHALL GROW AS THE LILY, AND CAST FORTH HIS ROOTS AS LEBANON. —Hosea 14:5

AS AN EARLY Christmas gift, it didn't look like much: three brown, dried-up bulbs sitting in a dish of rocks. My friend Millie, who found so much solace in her garden, quickly explained, "They're paper-white narcissus. I just love them!"

I had often seen these tiny daffodils outdoors, bobbing in a spring breeze, but had never forced any indoors in the dead of winter. Millie coached me. "Put them in the dark for a while, so they'll grow straight. Then just keep the rocks wet." Easy enough.

I set the dish under my bed and promptly forgot about it, preoccupied by troubling thoughts of the upcoming holidays. Only one of my four children would be with me at Christmas. There wasn't much money for presents anyway: My job hunt wasn't going well, and both my computer and car transmission had collapsed in the same week. My parents weren't doing very well either. As the winter solstice crept closer, the shorter, darker days only intensified my brooding.

Two weeks before Christmas, I suddenly remembered my gift. I rescued it from under the bed and checked for damage. The water was low, but firm green stems poked from the tops of the bulbs and a tangle of roots grasped the rocks. All the plant needed was light. Unfortunately, no sunshine pierced the gray New England days. My kitchen table lamp would have to do. To my surprise the waxy spears turned toward the light. Each day I rotated the dish, until one morning the twelve-inch stalks stood straight up.

On the morning of the winter solstice, more sleet scratched the windowpane—but there was a starburst of creamy petals at the top of the stalks. Even in wan light, grasping nothing more than rocks, my narcissus bloomed on the darkest day of the year.

So can I, I thought. So can I.

Light of the World, warm me with Your hope during my darkest days.
—GAIL THORELL SCHILLING

THU
22
GOD LOVETH A CHEERFUL GIVER. —*II Corinthians 9:7*

I COULD THINK of only one reason to be glad: This was to be my last stop on this cold December day. For hours, I had driven my car, with its broken heater, from one store to the next in a frantic attempt to finish my holiday shopping.

Slamming the door of my frigid car, I headed for the store where one final item waited. Ahead I spotted a Salvation Army bell ringer. I didn't want anything to slow me down, so without even looking at him I barked a curt "No" and pushed my shoulder into the door.

"I was just going to ask if you wanted a peppermint stick," the bell ringer answered gently as I moved into the safety of the store.

All day I had hustled here and there, stretching my money to the limit as I checked each name off my list. I was tired and chilled to the bone and . . . but really, none of this could justify my rudeness to that poor man.

I quickly chose the binoculars my husband David had been wishing for and paid the cashier. Then I set my package on the counter, opened my purse and searched until I found the twenty-dollar bill I saved for emergencies. I folded it carefully. *How could I forget God's goodness?* I wondered. Here I was with every present bought and paid for, the long day was ending, my family was waiting for me at home, and I still had this twenty-dollar bill left over.

"Hey, still have that candy cane?" I asked the bell ringer, putting my money into his bucket. Then I thanked him for reminding me what Christmas was all about.

In the car, my breath was icy as I started the engine. Then something truly amazing happened: The heater roared to life. Toasty warm, I cheerfully sang Christmas carols all the way home.

How can I not give freely and joyfully, Father, knowing that I can never outgive You? —PAM KIDD

FRI
23

THANKS BE TO GOD FOR HIS INDESCRIBABLE GIFT!
—*II Corinthians 9:15 (NIV)*

IT WAS THE LAST school day before Christmas break. Just home from my school, my brother Paul was taking off his jacket.

"So what did you get?" my mom asked.

Mom and Paul had spent the previous evening at the local five-and-dime looking for a Secret Santa present. The teacher's note about the gift exchange had been lost in my brother's coat pocket and found miraculously at the last moment. It had read: "Purchase a present for a boy. Please spend five to ten dollars."

Paul and Mom had walked the aisles looking for something good and finally settled on a Duncan butterfly yo-yo. Yo-yos were the rage at school, and at seven dollars, this one was well within the suggested amount.

"So," Mom asked again, "what did you get?"

Paul opened his hand and showed her a battered miniature car, its paint worn from handling.

My mother held it in her hand. "Really?" she asked. "Who gave it to you?" She tried to cover up her disappointment. Who would give a beat-up old toy car when the instructions had clearly said, "Spend five to ten dollars"?

"Andy," Paul said, looking down at the car. "Isn't it great? It's his favorite. And he gave it to me!"

Lord, help me always to give generously and to receive thankfully—from my heart. —SABRA CIANCANELLI

SIMPLE GIFTS
CHRISTMAS EVE:
THE GIFT OF WEAKNESS

SAT
24

AND THIS SHALL BE A SIGN UNTO YOU; YE SHALL FIND THE BABE WRAPPED IN SWADDLING CLOTHES, LYING IN A MANGER. —Luke 2:12

IT WAS MY mother's first time back to church following a stroke that had paralyzed her right side. As we pushed Mom's wheelchair up the narrow side aisle, I searched for an inconspicuous spot where no one would notice her eye patch or her slouch.

Unfortunately, as Dad parked Mom's wheelchair in the aisle, the children participating in the Christmas pageant began marching up the aisle behind us. Dad had no choice but to push Mom toward the specially built plywood stage. Finally, Dad veered aside and parked Mom in the only available spot—right next to the grand piano.

As the program began, the children playing Mary and Joseph knocked on the door of a cardboard-box inn and the innkeeper bellowed, "There's no room for you here! The only place I can offer is the stable." I wondered if Mary and Joseph felt awkward and out of place as I did, with Mom sitting up front in the curve of a grand piano.

After church as I hurried Mom out, a woman stopped us, leaned down with tears in her eyes and said, "We're so glad you're back. You're such an answer to prayer."

Suddenly I remembered that many people at church had been praying for Mom. If I'd succeeded in keeping Mom neatly tucked away in an obscure corner, they might not have seen her and been able to share in the joy of her return.

Father, the cries of a newborn heralded the coming of Your kingdom; thank You for using the weak things of this world as signs of Your powerful presence. —Karen Barber

SIMPLE GIFTS
CHRISTMAS:
THE GIFT OF SURPRISE

SUN

25

And they came with haste, and found Mary, and Joseph, and the babe lying in a manger.
—Luke 2:16

IT WAS 7:30 P.M. on Christmas Eve, and our college-age son Chris, who'd just flown in from California, was going out to buy gifts for the family. "Why bother?" I told him. "You're not going to find anything. The stores are all closed."

I was still skeptical when he returned proclaiming, "Mom, I got some good stuff. You all are going to love what I got you!"

When Christmas morning arrived, we were indeed surprised by our gifts. I certainly didn't expect to unwrap a new pair of windshield-wiper blades. "I really needed these," I admitted, remembering how my windshield was always smeared.

"The gas station was open Christmas Eve," Chris said.

My husband was surprised to find a gift certificate to our favorite Chinese restaurant. Chris's brother John received passes to the movies.

I don't remember any of the other gifts we gave or received that year, but Chris's still stick in my mind—gifts I assumed would never materialize. They reminded me that the shepherds set out in the middle of the night, and followed their hearts and found Jesus. Yes, my best present that Christmas came disguised as a pair of windshield wipers. Chris's last-minute gifts showed me that a seeking spirit will always be able to find God's treasures.

Father, this Christmas as I thank You for the gift of Your Son, help me seek out the gifts and graces I need to keep growing spiritually.

—KAREN BARBER

MON

26

FOR UNTO US A CHILD IS BORN. . . . —Isaiah 9:6

I THOUGHT THAT after four children, I'd got the hang of the father-to-be business. Throughout Julia's pregnancy, I'd taken everything in stride. But then the day after Christmas, Julia, a week overdue, went to the hospital for tests. She'd been there for three hours when the phone rang.

"Hi, honey," Julia said. "They've decided to keep me here and induce labor. Call Loretta to come and stay with the kids. Bring my nightgown and slippers and my toothbrush—and a couple of apples, too. They haven't given me any lunch. Oh, and don't forget to feed the kids."

I hung up the phone, called our friend Loretta, told the kids the news, made them sandwiches, and then got Julia's things together and put them in our backpack. I was just zipping it up when I remembered the apples.

When Loretta arrived, I filled her in on what to expect. Then, feeling proud of the way I'd handled things, I threw on my coat, grabbed the backpack and headed out. Twenty minutes later, I was on the labor-and-delivery floor. Julia was sitting in a chair in the hallway, waiting for a room. "Did you bring me an apple?" she asked. "I'm famished."

"Right here," I said, slipping off the backpack. I opened it: There were some unfamiliar clothes and no apple. I looked at the backpack again. It was black. Ours was green. I'd been in such a hurry to get to the hospital that I'd taken Loretta's by mistake! Forty minutes later, out of breath and sweating, I was back at the hospital with our green backpack and apples for Julia.

Just after midnight, our baby was born. And two days later, Stephen Paul Attaway lay sleeping in an infant carrier under our Christmas tree.

Lord, Giver of all good gifts, accept the thanks of four happy siblings, one joyful but exhausted mom and a suddenly not-so-nervous dad.
—ANDREW ATTAWAY

TUE
27

THERE, IN THE PRESENCE OF THE LORD YOUR GOD, YOU AND YOUR FAMILIES SHALL EAT AND SHALL REJOICE IN EVERYTHING YOU HAVE PUT YOUR HAND TO, BECAUSE THE LORD YOUR GOD HAS BLESSED YOU.
—*Deuteronomy 12:7 (NIV)*

"DOES ANYONE ELSE have something to share?" Sean Bates, the best man, angled the microphone toward the tables where a hundred and fifty faces, softened by candlelight and glorious fall-color flowers, remained silent after his moving toast to our son John and his bride Courtney.

"I think I do," I said quietly. He handed me the mike as I rose.

Around the dance floor I saw husband and sons—Peter safe from Afghanistan and David just home from Iraq; Tom, newly married himself—and our new daughters Matti and Susan. There sat brother and nieces and nephews, cousins on both sides, friends I'd known for thirty years and some I'd known just thirty months. There were Courtney's parents, grandparents, aunts, uncles, brother, friends, neighbors. *Oh, if only I could stop it all right here—all of us safe and whole and together, laughing, dancing, rejoicing.*

"I want to tell you a 'John' story that I think is for all of us here tonight," I began. "One Christmas when he was about seven, Bill and I noticed John wandering from room to room where his brothers were playing and his grandmother and great-aunt were dozing. Then he found his dad and me and tugged us into the kitchen. In his wonderfully earnest way he looked up at us, paused, and said slowly and succinctly, 'This house is full of people I love.'

"Tonight, I think we can all say, 'This house is full of people I love!'"
I leaned over and kissed my newest daughter.

Giver of family and friends, help me to stop in the frantic pace of the holidays and thank You for a moment full of people I love.
—ROBERTA ROGERS

WED **28**   *THE CORRECTIONS OF DISCIPLINE ARE THE WAY TO LIFE.* —*Proverbs 6:23 (NIV)*

I TRIED ski racing for the first time during my junior year of high school, and it wasn't long before I was dreaming big dreams for my future in the sport. The first thing I realized was I needed to put on some muscle. At 116 pounds, I wasn't exactly what you'd call a big guy.

So I joined a gym and started working out every morning before school. Because of my high metabolism, I had to double my calorie intake in order to give my body enough fuel to build new muscle.

My discipline paid off. I put on twenty pounds of muscle in between my first and second ski season, an addition that provided much needed strength and speed on the racecourse. But the following summer I lost my focus in the gym. Six months passed and I was no stronger than I'd been before.

So I went on my computer and plotted a plan on a spreadsheet. Every workout for the next three months was planned out, right down to the last sit-up. It was hard, but eventually I started to see large strength gains.

It's the same thing with me and my faith. I can coast along through the routines of church, Bible study, and a little prayer here and there. But without active discipline, I don't accomplish anything. My relationship with God, just like my physical fitness, requires focus every day. That's where I've seen real gains.

Lord, give me the discipline I need to be the person You want me to be.
—JOSHUA SUNDQUIST

THU **29**   *THE EYES OF ALL LOOK EXPECTANTLY TO YOU. . . .*
—*Psalm 145:15 (NKJV)*

ON MY STUDY WALL hangs an enormous painting of a meadow, with windswept grasses and dancing daisies. In the middle of the meadow, a little boy in a red T-shirt is chasing butterflies with a net. I bought the painting because it reminds me of the most wonderful feeling I have salvaged from childhood—a sense of expectancy.

My mother made me a butterfly net when I was ten, and soon I was knee-deep in an ocean of alfalfa. My heart hammered in my chest. My legs were coiled springs, and my skin shivered with excitement to see what interesting creatures I could capture in my clean muslin net.

I raced through the fragrant clover, swishing the snare back and forth, then I stopped and peered into the fabric funnel. I had caught pretty bumblebees and ladybugs, bony walkingsticks and grasshoppers, soft caterpillars and tiny butterflies, scary spiders and crusty beetles.

When a yellow swallowtail caught my eye, I took chase until my legs gave out. Then I sat on a creek bank and studied a rugged snapping turtle chewing on a minnow, and a painted pheasant periscoping its head above the weeds. In the sky, great puffs of popcorn floated by on a river of blue. I could see the face of God in them, and He was smiling. When I got back home, I was still breathing hard from being in a field full of wonders all day.

I need to nurture that feeling:

- When I turn the calendar to January and wonder what the year will bring.
- When a new group of students arrives on campus.
- When I bow my head in prayer.

Lord, I look up to You as a child looks up to his father in a candy store.
—DANIEL SCHANTZ

FRI
30

BUT THOUGH GOD HAS PLANTED ETERNITY IN THE HEARTS OF MEN, EVEN SO, MAN CANNOT SEE THE WHOLE SCOPE OF GOD'S WORK FROM BEGINNING TO END. —*Ecclesiastes 3:11 (TLB)*

I'D NEVER RIDDEN a four-wheeler before. I climbed up onto the back and held on tightly to my twelve-year-old son Thomas's stomach. "Mom, just relax. You'll be fine."

"Are you sure you know what you're doing?"

"Yes, ma'am." He clicked the gear with his foot.

"Is your helmet fastened right?"

"Yes, Mom. Let's go. You'll like it."

He drove me around our wooded property. *Ah, Thomas knows me pretty well. He's not going fast.* He reached ahead and carefully pushed back tree branches so they wouldn't slap us. As Thomas headed down-hill, he drove slowly as though leading an old horse down a rocky cliff. He wound around and stopped at the little creek. We didn't talk—we didn't need to.

I relaxed and thought back over the past year. So many changes: My grandparents had both died; our middle daughter left for college. Thomas seemed to be taking charge, riding me around, leading the way. I began to trust his skills. I admired his confidence and kindness.

My thoughts raced ahead. Years ahead.

One day I'll be really old, Thomas will be grown and even have chil-dren of his own. I don't want anything else to change. Talk to me, God.

A truth came just as gently as the leaf floating down the creek. When the end comes, there will be a place prepared especially for me, a perfect place. I will love my new home even more than the majesty of these woods. No fear. Like Thomas, my Shepherd will be right beside me.

Oh, Lord, You know the outcome. You won't leave me. It's going to be good, isn't it? —JULIE GARMON

SAT
31

AND NOW, LORD, WHAT WAIT I FOR? MY HOPE IS IN THEE. —*Psalm 39:7*

THE LAST DAY of the year. It's sad to think of a year dis-appearing, but that's what was in my mind when I got up this morning. A flood of memories left me disoriented, not entirely in the present. I felt like a castaway clinging to a log floating in the ocean as I mechanically performed my morning chores. But by noon I was at the Guideposts office for a tradition more than twenty years old. When I was editor-in-chief, I always invited the entire staff into my office for a brief party—well, more like a get-together—to put a cap on the year. The present-day editor-in-chief, my friend Edward Grinnan, continues the custom.

Since I am now the editorial archivist and don't appear in the offices very often, there were many hellos and how've-you-beens and plenty of hugs and kisses. It was good to feel the warmth of the office again. About two-thirds of the staff were taking end-of-the-year holidays. The diehards who remained I had long ago nicknamed "the dregs." Among them were some people I barely knew, and this was a chance to change that, which I did while chatting, too, with the old-timers.

Sometime during the festivities, before the majority hurried away, Edward shushed the room and spoke. "We've had a good year," he said, "and I'm grateful to you for it. It hasn't been easy. We've had challenges, trauma and heartache. But rather than dwell on the past, let's welcome the new and look to the coming year with boundless hope."

Right on. The old positive thinking of Guideposts. The thoughts I should have had this morning. And that's the feeling I rejoiced in as I settled down with the dregs that afternoon, a sailor saved, hauled aboard a ship called *Hope*.

We rely on Your blessing and the expectation of future good, Father.
—VAN VARNER

SEEDS OF REJOICING

I _____

2 _____

3 _____

4 _____

5 _____

6 _____

7 _____

8 _____

9 _____

IO _____

II _____

I2 _____

13 _____

14 _____

15 _____

16 _____

17 _____

18 _____

19 _____

20 _____

21 _____

22 _____

23 _____

24 _____

25 _____

26 _____

27 _____

28 _____

29 _____

30 _____

31 _____

LIBBIE ADAMS of Richlands, North Carolina, writes, "This past year, as I groped my way through a jarring personal upheaval, I came to recognize how essential hope is to joy. Hope bolsters our confidence that the dark days will eventually pass, and that the rigors of our experiences will mold us into more insightful and compassionate people. This year, our family numbers have increased, with yet another granddaughter due for Larry and me in the spring. Somehow the continuity of life itself seems laced with hope. With that in mind, I joined a hospice this past summer as a volunteer. I wanted to offer grieving families hope that life always endures, even when circumstances might suggest otherwise."

"Rejoicing in hope" is a particularly apt theme this year for *MARCI ALBORGHETTI* of New London, Connecticut, and her husband Charlie. They're rejoicing because Marci's doctor has found no recurrence of the melanoma that had returned after six years, and they're hoping for continued health blessings. Marci is also rejoicing in her two new books for Twenty-Third Publications, *Twelve Strong Women of God: Biblical Models for Today* and *When Lightning Strikes Twice*, inspired by her series in this year's *Daily Guideposts*. By donating twenty percent of her earnings from both books to The Mothers' Union Sierra Leone Preschool Project, Marci is hoping to help rebuild an educational infrastructure devastated by recent wars. She learned about the project through Sylvia Savage, a *Daily Guideposts* reader who became a close friend. "When it comes to our life right now," Marci says of herself and Charlie, "I'm not sure what we're doing more of, rejoicing or hoping! Mostly, we are thankful that a loving God has blessed us so abundantly."

"Our life is slow-paced here in Van, our small (and I mean one-blinking-light small) east Texas town," writes *LUCILE ALLEN*. "We have to drive thirty miles for fine dining, the movies or a mall, but what we do have is family a few blocks away, a caring community of friends, and a thriving church where we're serving and growing spiritually. My husband Curtis just finished his twelfth year warehousing for Mercy Ships, a Christian hospital-ship ministry headquartered nearby. Our 11-year-old daughter Deanna and I are enjoying our fourth year of home-schooling. This year she completed the Red Cross babysitting course and immediately put it to use for MOPS, Mothers of Preschoolers. My dreams reach beyond the borders of our little town, but I'm trying to rejoice, not in fulfilled dreams, but in my hope in God, the Author and Finisher of my dreams."

"Both in serious worrisome circumstances and small, trivial irritations, I find myself grabbing hold of the promise in Hosea 2:15 (TLB): 'I will . . . transform her Valley of Troubles into a Door of Hope,'" says *FAY ANGUS* of Sierra Madre, California. "It's a lifeline that continues to pull me through the many murky waters in which I find myself floundering. Recently it was driving in the dark. My vision is not as sharp as it used to be. Maneuvering around our freeways is traumatic at best. In the evening hours it becomes a stress that plunges me into a puddle of fear. A friend pushed me through a door of hope. 'Why don't you try taking the train?' she said. Brilliant! Now I'm riding the rails to Santa Barbara, San Diego and to our beach cities. Even on short hops, such as to the aquarium at Long Beach or the Music Center in the much-trafficked hub of downtown Los Angeles, I hop on and off our local Metrolink. What's more, a blessed spin-off is the interesting people I'm meeting, and the fun I'm having as I chug-chug-chug along."

"No matter how frenetic the pace or how frazzled the parents, there's been plenty of cause for rejoicing for the Attaways this past year," says *Daily Guideposts* editor *ANDREW ATTAWAY* of New York City. "Our son Stephen Paul was born on December 27, 2003, and he's a real sweetheart—a placid, virtually fuss-free baby, alert and playful during the day and a blessedly good sleeper at night. It's amazing how our hearts have grown as each new child, gloriously unique and unmistakably him- or herself, has come into our family. Meanwhile, Elizabeth, 10, John, 8, and Mary, 6, are learning away at a furious pace in our home school. All three are continuing to study ballet. Elizabeth (as a reindeer) and John (as an Arabian page) made their stage debuts in *The Yorkville Nutcracker* last Christmas. And Maggie—now 3—continues to delight her parents and her siblings. Who'd have guessed that a 3-year-old could have a wry sense of humor? We've had some hard climbing in our walk this year as all of us—children and parents alike—seek to grow in grace. But with our eyes on the Lord Who opened His heart for us on the Cross, we go hopefully and joyfully ahead."

"I was too busy in December to have deep, meaningful thoughts about having a baby at Christmastime," writes *JULIA ATTAWAY* of New York City. "But after Stephen was born and we were all admiring him, I said, 'Can you believe God chose to be this little and helpless?'" Picturing Christ unable to even hold up His own head was mind-stretching for Julia. "Often I expect hope to be big and bright, leading me forward like the cloud led the Israelites. But the Hope of the world entered it utterly feeble and small. It's hard to trust in the smallness of Christ as well as His greatness."

"This year our family dealt with our share of uncertainties," writes *KAREN BARBER* of Alpharetta, Georgia. "Our oldest son Jeff completed his Air Force obligation, and he and his wife Leah faced relocating so Jeff could pursue an MBA. Meanwhile, our middle son Chris finished Army officer's training and awaited his first assignment, perhaps to a hostile zone. Then my 81-year-old father suffered a serious illness. As my sister Susan and I were tending to Dad's care, she told me that she'd read that the difficulties we face are like a jungle surrounding us, and that in every jungle there needs to be a paved road, a place of stability and clear ground. I realized that every morning I literally walk a paved road during my daily prayer time and that this is my stabilizing force, a changeless place where my joy and hope are always renewed in spite of the unknown future."

"Even though the years pass quickly, 'rejoicing in hope' just seems to go on and on," writes *ALMA BARKMAN* of Winnipeg, Canada. "Today I hope to bake bread, I hope the mailman delivers an interesting letter, and I hope a friend in the hospital is feeling better. In the coming week, I hope an early snowfall doesn't hinder me from picking up several women for our Thursday Bible study, that my husband Leo will be able to bring some cheer to the veterans hospital where he visits and that people will enjoy the dried bouquet I'm arranging for the front of our church sanctuary. Next month I hope to get some sewing done for a neighbor, finish a quilt and help some aspiring new writers in a workshop. And next year? Well, I hope for a nice garden, opportunities to visit family in Toronto and Victoria, and who knows what else? I just know that hope springs eternal because an eternal God gives it."

"When I was told that this year's theme was 'rejoicing in hope,' I asked myself, *How does one have hope when the world is in such turmoil?*" says *FRED BAUER* of Englewood, Florida, and State College, Pennsylvania. "My short answer is people base their hope on the Bible's promise of positive things to come. Meanwhile, we all need to wrap our earthly hopes for peace in work and prayer. Healing, I was reminded while my mother was in a nursing home recovering from a broken hip, takes time. It's not easy to be patient when one is laid low by accidents or illness—I know—but believers place their trust in the One Who pledged never to leave us or forsake us. On another level, our family hope to revisit Hawaii (where I served in the Army almost fifty years ago) was fulfilled last year, and the hope of my ever-lovin' Shirley and me to celebrate our fiftieth wedding anniversary was realized in August."

"I may have no children of my own," says *EVELYN BENCE* of Arlington, Virginia, "but I have six siblings, and I delight in the hopeful courage I see in my family's younger generation. Karin, daughter of my sister Alice, has just donated a kidney to Tracey, daughter-in-law of my sister Priscilla and mother of two young girls. A highlight of my year was helping Karin—still recuperating from surgery—host her annual backyard picnic where everyone pitched in to make a big cauldron of apple butter. Lots of peeling, chopping and stirring before we got to the *yum-yum* eating."

"It's been a happy, uneventful year for my husband Keith and me," says *RHODA BLECKER* of Los Angeles, California. "We've lived what many people would consider a dull life. We're real homebodies, and we only travel to visit places we consider home: the Grand Canyon and the monastery. Our Internet friends stay in touch regularly, and we get together with our local friends, especially those from our synagogue. We go to the movies (I cry with joy at the really uplifting ones) and rarely go out to dinner, because we love our home and our four animals (we call them our *petners*). Keith has his professional association meetings every couple of months, and I am in a critique group with other fiction writers, as well as serving on the steering committee of the Los Angeles Catholic-Jewish Women's Conference. But, really, we're not very exciting—just very contented. And because of that, we think we have very rich lives indeed."

"What can be better than seeing the world through the eyes of a child?" asks *MELODY BONNETTE* of Mandeville, Louisiana. "With three wonderful grandchildren underfoot, I'm back in that magical fairy-tale world where every day is an exciting adventure. My coloring skills have improved, my capacity to mimic all of the animal sounds in the story-books has returned, and I now have a great reason to fix an afternoon snack of raisins and apples as we watch a children's video! But the best thing of all is, like 2-1/2-year-old Indy, 21-month-old Sophia and 9-month-old Noah, I'm once again living in a state of awe, where even the bloom of a spring flower is cause to rejoice."

"As our life brings new adventures," writes *GINA BRIDGEMAN* of Scottsdale, Arizona, "God's gift of hope allows us to move forward with confidence. That's a good thing because there's always something new around our house." This year, Ross, a high-school sophomore, began driving and earned his first paycheck doing what he loves—playing music. Maria, a fourth-grader, continued dancing with a performing troupe and joined the Girl Scouts. And in June, Gina and her husband Paul celebrate their twentieth wedding anniversary. As part of a class at church, a back-to-basics study of the Christian faith, Gina gained a deeper understanding of what it means to rejoice in hope. "I learned that hope is the promise that God is good and no matter what, His love will sustain and comfort us."

For *MARY BROWN* of Lansing, Michigan, last year held unexpected sadness and joy as she said good-bye to her mom, who died of lym-phoma. "During Mom's months in hospice, our family grew unbeliev-ably close. Even in our grief, we rejoice in our hope that we will be together again one day." Elizabeth, 16, continues to play flute and piano and sing in the church choir with Mary. Mark, 11, plays soccer and bas-ketball, piano and euphonium. He enjoys "blasting" everyone by prac-ticing it as loudly as he can. Mary's husband Alex juggles physics research and teaching, and just received Michigan State University's Distinguished Faculty Award. "Alex has been my rock of support and did a beautiful job single-parenting all the weekends I visited Mom in Minnesota. After a marathon week of teaching, cooking, doing laundry and packing up everyone for the funeral, we decided he wins our Distinguished *Father* Award."

If the smile on **MARY LOU CARNEY**'s face looks bigger than it usually does, it's because this year she and Gary became grandparents. Daughter Amy Jo and son-in-law Kirk presented them with the perfect Christmas gift: a baby boy, born December 22. "His name is Drake Pennington and he is absolutely perfect!" says Mary Lou. Son Brett continues to build houses—and rebuild his motorcycle. Gary remains busy with his excavation business, as well as managing several rental units he's built. Mary Lou, working from their hometown in Chesterton, Indiana, edits Guideposts' teen magazine and www.gp4children.com. Her new picture book *Tyler Timothy Bradford and the Birthday Surprise* was released last fall. "It is, of course, dedicated to Drake."

SABRA CIANCANELLI of Pawling, New York, says, "My son Solomon turned 2 this year, and I'm still in awe of the perspective he has brought to my life. Not only have I learned a boatload about Thomas the Tank Engine and the Teletubbies, he's shown me there's always time for one more book. With Solly on my lap and a pile of his favorite books beside us, all of the day's stresses and worries disappear. 'Again!' Solly says tapping the back cover. 'Again, Mama!' And back to the book we go, just one more time." Sabra is Web editor of Guideposts Online.

"When my kids were very small, people would say, 'What joy your children must bring you!'" muses **MARK COLLINS** of Pittsburgh, Pennsylvania. "I'd smile wanly and think to myself, *I'll let you know as soon as I get a break. Just give me eight hours of uninterrupted sleep, and I promise I'll be joyful.*" Now that Faith is 13, Hope is 12 and Grace is 8, Mark says he misses those frenetic years. "Maybe the secret to joy and hope is denial and forgetfulness. You remember the good times, you look back and laugh. There's probably something divine in that." The household is still busy for Mark and his wife Sandee. "The problem is timing," he says. "As soon as I think I've figured things out—childproof caps, VCRs, kids—they change and I'm back to square one. That might be why I go to church—at least there are some things you can always count on."

PABLO DIAZ of Carmel, New York, writes, "Elba and I rejoice as we celebrate our twenty-fourth wedding anniversary this year. Our courtship began shortly after we met at a youth retreat, and it matured into a loving, caring relationship. God blessed us with two children. I am proud of our daughter Christine, who is a senior in college. Watching her grow into a mature and responsible young lady makes us very happy. Our son Paul began his first year of college. We thank God for him every day and rejoice in his accomplishments. I will always remember the telephone call years ago from the doctor who stated, 'Your wife is in high-risk pregnancy and the baby has a fifty percent chance of living.' After many prayers, several operations and ongoing medical care, Paul is thriving. In looking back, we are grateful to God for the lessons of living that we have learned as a family."

"I spend most of my waking hours hoping," says *BRIAN DOYLE* of Portland, Oregon. "Generally because, as I mutter to my three children, how can you not hope? What else is there to do with grace and courage than to hope? How can you be handed such extraordinary life and light and joy and possibility and divine fingerprints on everything and not be awash and agog in hope? And it lives everywhere: children's bemused faces, crows' amused glances, music in the morning, a kiss you never expected." Brian is the editor of *Portland Magazine* at the University of Portland. His most recent books are *Leaping: Revelations & Epiphanies* (Loyola Press), and, as editor, *God Is Love*, a collection of the best spiritual essays from *Portland Magazine* (Augsburg Fortress).

KJERSTIN EASTON is a graduate student at the California Institute of Technology in Pasadena, where she is working toward her Ph.D. in robotics. This year, her research took her to several conferences, the highlight of which was a trip to Switzerland. When she's not in the lab, Kjerstin enjoys cycling, especially along the California coast, singing with the Caltech Jazz Bands and volunteering with the Boy Scouts of America, training new leaders.

ERIC FELLMAN of Falls Church, Virginia, writes, "There were two events this past year in our household that centered on hope. The first was sad, and the second joyful. When my father died, all of us were gathered around his bed, and we held hands, sang his favorite hymn and prayed together. We were saddened to lose him, but as the Scriptures say, we 'sorrow not, even as others which have no hope' (I Thessalonians 4:13), knowing that his life continues in eternity. The event that caused great rejoicing in our family was my wife Joy graduating *summa cum laude* from a master's program in nursing as a nurse practitioner. It represents a whole new direction for us as our friendships across the globe open opportunities to serve the poor and disadvantaged together. Life after 50 is filled with hope, which in itself is cause to rejoice."

"It's good to be back with the *Daily Guideposts* family," says SHARON FOSTER. "All of your notes, prayers and e-mails touched me. The joy of the Lord is our strength, and it shows up all the time in His people. Since we last talked, my son Chase is in college studying opera—he's as handsome, wise and wonderful as ever. His beautiful, clever sister Lanea is earning her master's degree in North Carolina while working as a youth advocate. She plans to attend law school and continue her advocacy work. Please keep them both in your prayers. I've moved to Chicago, where I have a plant growing on my kitchen counter that looks like hope. Maybe love is in the air—don't gasp, just pray! I keep busy speaking and writing. By the time you read this, my fifth novel *Ain't No Mountain* should be at your bookstore."

"Our son Julian had a trying first three years in school: frustration with homework, poor test scores and anger with having to go," says DAVE FRANCO. "Our daughter Noelle, in prekindergarten, also struggled. But this past year, school suddenly 'clicked' for Julian. He's keeping up with and even excelling in most of his subjects. At the same time we decided to start Noelle in kindergarten, and she's like a new child. She's happy all the time, and so are we! Out of the blue, an unexpected blessing from our tenderhearted God." Dave, his wife Nicole and the kids live in Solana Beach, California.

JULIE GARMON of Snellville, Georgia, writes, "Hope and trust have always been difficult for me. This year, we're building the log house we've been dreaming about for twenty-five years, and I've missed out on a lot of the fun by fretting. I tend to handle people the same way—watching, wringing my hands, worrying and trying to convince them to change. In February, a friend invited me to an Al-Anon meeting. At first, I went to try to fix people and solve their addictions. After a few weeks, I began to realize the size of my own addictions—fear, worry, fixing people and control. My sweet friend—hope—is entering as I daily let go."

For *OSCAR GREENE* of West Medford, Massachusetts, things just seemed to happen last year. He was invited to the Medford Council of Churches Banquet, where he was surprised to receive the Beacon Award, which read, "In recognition of a layperson whose character, social vision and service to community life fulfill the universal motifs of Scripture." Oscar writes, "In May, my book *House of Strangers* was published, and I was asked to assist nearby university seniors in preparing papers about the Great Depression. In June, I spoke again at the Chapel in the Mountains in Killington, Vermont, and completed ten years of teaching Bible study at Grace Episcopal Church. In September, I enjoyed a book signing at the local Bestsellers Café. Days later, I purchased my first computer. Your prayers are welcomed."

"I was reading an article the other day," says *EDWARD GRINNAN* of New York City, "that claimed the current era was one of unbridled excess and self-absorption, where declining moral standards have corrupted our youth and undermined our basic values." The article was written more than two hundred years ago. "I'm not minimizing the challenges we face as a society. We've struggled against our basic human failings throughout history and, all in all, I think we've made progress, which definitely gives me hope. And that's what hope is, a conviction that tomorrow can be better than today." Last year Edward and his wife Julee said good-bye to their beloved Labrador retriever Marty, who succumbed to cancer. They still have Sally, their 12-year-old Cocker. "There's nothing sweeter in the whole world than an old dog." Edward is editor-in-chief and vice president of *Guideposts*, an old dog himself, some might say.

"By the time you read this (or at least by the date of the first devotional), I will be 50," says *RICK HAMLIN* of New York City. "Just barely. I promise not to use phrases like 'When I was your age' or 'When you get to be my age,' and I don't expect I'll be much wiser. The one thing I'm sure of is how much more there is to know about the world—enough to keep me busy for many more decades. My sons Will, 17, and Tim, 14, are very good teachers, and my wife Carol has gone back to college, so I expect she can keep me informed. Add to that all my colleagues at Guideposts telling me about music I should hear, movies I must see and books I need to read. I don't think I'll ever be completely caught up . . . but maybe by the eighth or ninth decade. There's something to hope for."

"Life continues to be good for Larry and me as we watch our children advance into mature middle age and our grandchildren grow up and marry," writes *MADGE HARRAH* of Albuquerque, New Mexico. "We're blessed by God in so many ways, including good friends and neighbors and a supportive church community. We also feel blessed still to be active in our chosen careers. Larry is a research scientist, and I'm an author of books and plays for middle-graders. Our church is small but filled with friendly, interesting people. Another woman and I teach the children's Sunday school class, which includes young people ranging in age from 3 through 16. What a challenge! Not only do I 'rejoice in hope' every day of my life, but I hope to encourage children to do that, too."

"The past year brought both sorrow and joy to our family," writes *PHYLLIS HOBE* of East Greenville, Pennsylvania. "In late June our beloved dog Suzy died. She was 11 years old, which is an advanced age for a Rottweiler, and until the day of her death she was healthy and vigorous. Suzy was the alpha animal, and my other dog Tara and my two cats Sean and Dennis were lost without her. Finally, after a month of sorrow, I decided to get a puppy. I knew it would mean a lot of work, but something told me it was the thing to do. And when I brought home a 2-month-old chocolate Labrador retriever I named Peggy, Tara immediately took over as nanny, and Sean and Dennis became their rascally selves again. The healing had begun—for all of us."

"Faith, family and humor have always been the strong foundations of my life," writes *REBECCA KELLY* of Coral Springs, Florida, "but hope is my daily companion. This year, my family and I are celebrating the completion of a project we've been working on for several years: a new church and school for our community. Just in time, too, as we're about to move upstate! We will miss our friends here, but we're looking forward to meeting new people and finding new opportunities to do God's work. The future is all about hope, and from here it looks wonderful."

"Hope springs eternal," says *BROCK KIDD* of Nashville, Tennessee, "and the truth of that old saying shines from the eyes of my son Harrison, who turned 4 this year. He's a cyclone of undiluted hope! He looks forward to every tomorrow with a delight that would make any optimist envious. Just last week he explained over breakfast, 'Daddy, when I grow up, I'm going to be a paleontologist, a football player and a zookeeper.' I find his enthusiasm contagious, and it's no wonder I usually arrive at my office anxious to jump headfirst into the day. And every day I count my blessings for making the decision to join Pinnacle Financial Partners when they first opened. The attitude there is much like my son's: full of enthusiasm and a sincere interest in the needs of every person who walks through the doors. It's wonderful to find a place in life where there's always hope—personal, professional and spiritual."

"Expectations for the family are all on track," writes *PAM KIDD* of Nashville, Tennessee. "My husband David's ministry at Hillsboro Presbyterian Church continues to inspire others, and our work with AIDS orphans in Zimbabwe is taking some exciting new turns. Our son Brock flourishes in his calling as an investment executive and delights in being a father to little Harrison. Keri, our daughter, takes great pleasure in her new role as Abby's mother, and her husband Ben Cannon is working at establishing his own dental practice. My mother and stepfather, Arlene and Herb Hester, continue to enjoy good health and contribute to causes that make life better. It's been a good year for our family. But I have to wonder if we should be extending our expectations for harmony and success out into the larger world. What if we rejected all those worst-case scenarios and presumed that God's best-laid plans were unfolding? In the year ahead, I'm going to try my hardest to expect the best not only at home but from the wide world beyond."

MARILYN MORGAN KING and her husband Robert of Green Mountain Falls, Colorado, celebrated their fifth anniversary this year, thankful for the love and quiet joy these later years have brought. As they have written in their new book *Autumn Years: Taking the Contemplative Path*, they believe this stage of life to be an ideal time for spiritual growth. Instead of seeing retirement as a time to dread, they have found it to be a time of great hope, an opportunity for developing a rich inner life as well as continuing to live with vitality and grace. "Because of writing the book, we haven't taken any major trips this year. We have enjoyed visits from my three children, ten grandchildren and four great-grandchildren, as well as Robert's son, daughter and grand-daughter. As we try to pass on to our growing families the wisdom of our ancestors, we see in them (as well as in children everywhere) the embodiment of hope for the future."

CAROL KNAPP of Lakeville, Minnesota, says, "Sequential highlights this past year include meeting my teen heartthrob Herman, of the British singing group Herman's Hermits (he's still cute!), a spring hike on the Arctic Ocean ice at Barrow, Alaska, riding a motorcycle with my husband to Sturgis, South Dakota, for the big summer biker rally, getting braces on my teeth at age 51, traveling to Alaska a second time for the November birth of our daughter Brenda's first baby, Sarah. I'm just about to head for the Arctic to help our oldest daughter Tamara as she expects her fourth child. I'll also meet our adopted Eskimo grand-daughter Ruby Dawn, 6 months old. When I return, a third daughter, Kelly, will be having her baby here in the Twin Cities—finally a grand-child in the neighborhood! Our son Phil remains a contented bachelor, which suits me fine right now."

CAROL KUYKENDALL of Boulder, Colorado, writes, "In June, my husband Lynn suffered a life-threatening cerebral hemorrhage. During the weeks that he was in critical condition, I spent lots of time in the Intensive Care Unit at the hospital, listening, watching and waiting. Feeling discouraged one day, I went for a walk and realized that I could not put my hope in the numbers on the monitors surrounding his bed, or on the results of another CAT scan, or even in the words of a doctor or nurse. I needed to put my hope in Jesus, Who is the Source of all hope. We were greatly comforted during those weeks by the presence of our children. All are married now: Kendall and her husband David, and Derek and his wife Alexandra and their baby all live in Colorado, and Lindsay and her husband Jeff live in San Diego. I told Lynn recently that I needed to write my devotionals for Daily Guideposts, and he said, 'Well, I've done my part.' He has, and we are rejoicing in hope with his recovery."

DEBBIE MACOMBER of Port Orchard, Washington, writes, "I'm pleased to be a new member of the Daily Guideposts family. When I sold my first novel, I wrote and thanked Dr. Norman Vincent Peale for the encouragement I found in his book The Power of Positive Thinking. My writing career continues, and I'm pleased to say it took me only twenty years to be an overnight success. My husband Wayne and I will celebrate thirty-eight years together this year. We're the proud parents of four and the grandparents of nine—the cutest grandkids in the universe! My father went to be with the Lord last February. I've learned valuable lessons in the art of surrendering, but I live rejoicing in hope of a big family reunion with him one day in heaven."

This has been a year of hope and healing for **ROBERTA MESSNER** of Huntington, West Virginia, as she underwent her twentieth surgery to remove tumors caused by neurofibromatosis. "At my post-op visit, when my surgeon saw that I could open my eye completely and smile," she recalls, "he hugged me so hard that it crumpled the paper in my hand into a ball." Thanks to a new procedure, they were able to curtail bleeding and remove more tumor than ever before. "When my surgeon told me that he didn't think I'd ever have to have another operation, I think I tasted fully of hope for the first time in my life."

"'Rejoicing in hope' is *exactly* where we are," says **KEITH MILLER** of Austin, Texas. "Andrea, my wife, is in remission from a serious illness, and we're living in gratitude for a whole new one-day-at-a-time chapter in our life together. We opened a Web site (www.keithmiller.com) on which we hope to help people deal with the actual issues and relationship problems that confront those who make a serious attempt to surrender their lives to God through Christ." A book Andrea compiled and edited, *The Eternal Present*, was published, and Keith hopes to complete two books: *What to Do with the Rest of Your Life: Awakening and Achieving Your Unspoken Dreams* and *The Desert Crossing: Intimacy with God in the Twenty-First Century*. "Our three children and seven grandchildren are doing well and are a large part of our grateful 'rejoicing in hope'!"

From the moment he knew he had been called to pastor two Union churches in Berks County, Pennsylvania, **TED NACE** of Poughquag, New York, has been rejoicing in hope. There, he and his wife Kathy felt God's miraculous touch through the healing of each of their newborn sons, Ryan, Joel and Kyle, from a rare blood disorder. "We really understand hope," Ted says. "Knowing that God ultimately works all things for good keeps all of us 'rejoicing in hope.' A highlight of 2004 was the wedding of our son Ryan and his beloved Jennifer at St. John's Reformed Church in Red Hook, New York, where Ryan is the pastor. Becoming instant grandparents to Mandy and Jim is another reason to rejoice." As Vice President of Ministries, Ted continues to direct the Outreach Division of Guideposts located at the Peale Center. He also hosts "Simple Living," a continuous series of daily devotionals on www.dailyguideposts.com.

LINDA NEUKRUG is nothing if not consistent. She's still living in Walnut Creek, California, still working in the bookstore and doing story time for children there on weekends. During the upcoming year, Linda intends to stop biting her nails—it's never too late to stop a bad habit, she hopes—and wants to take sign language again. Her motto for the year will be "Be kind to yourself."

MARJORIE PARKER and her husband Joe had much to rejoice in last year. In the spring, her new children's book *Assault, the Crippled Champion* came out. "Then in June," she says, "we were thrilled to gain a wonderful son-in-law, Vince Willcox, who married our older daughter Joanna. He's a dental student at the University of Oklahoma. This New Year is bringing more change as our daughter Sarah graduates from Texas Tech University and looks for a job. As we begin these new adventures as a family, we're extra appreciative of God's guiding hand." Marjorie continues to serve as church elder and is training to be a Stephen minister. She and Joe, who sings in the choir, both enjoy the chance to share God's hope with their church family. "No matter what happens, be it joys or sorrows, our hope in the Lord remains reason to rejoice."

"Each day is full of hope and rejoicing as I spend time with my family, as well as with the Guideposts staff at our New York offices in Pawling, where I live, in Carmel and in New York City," says *RUTH STAFFORD PEALE*. "One of my favorite Bible verses is 'This is the day which the Lord hath made; we will rejoice and be glad in it' (Psalm 118:24). It spurs me on and encourages me to hope that despite challenges and discouragements, the best God can give will eventually reveal itself. Difficulties do come (and I've experienced many as a mother of three, grandmother of eight and great-grandmother of eleven), but God will see me through. I believe in surrounding my loved ones with a prayer of love and hope that all will go well for them as they trust in our Lord and Savior Jesus Christ. As I watch my family grow, and our ministries of prayer and publications at Guideposts grow, too, hope and gratitude fill my heart."

ROBERTA ROGERS of New Market, Virginia, writes, "Our family rejoiced in many hopes fulfilled this past year: the marriages of my son Tom to Susan and my son John to Courtney; son Peter becoming an air traffic controller; son David going to and returning safely from Iraq; my mother Kathryn coming alive in faith at 94; my husband Bill running 180 volunteer squad calls as an EMT; a 5,900-mile car trip to Arizona and back. And we rejoice in the hope of more answered prayers in the year ahead: daughter-in-law Matti to find permanent release from an old Army neck injury; an exciting career for Tom. Most of all we rejoice in the hope that 'The word of the Lord is right and true; he is faithful in all he does' (Psalm 33:4, NIV)."

Four beautiful grandchildren fill *DANIEL SCHANTZ* and Sharon with hope: happy Hannah, scientific Silas, active Abram and reserved Rossetti, ages 6 through 12. Dan and Sharon are busy passing along to these children the lore and values they want to survive them: faith in God, and respect for family and friends. Sharon teaches the girls her homemaking arts: cross-stitching, cooking, management of a house, plus she gives lots of good advice about life. The boys help Dan in the garden, digging for new potatoes, picking beans and tomatoes, and harvesting a cherry tree for Grandma to make a pie. All the children love biking with Dan, and they hover around him when he is working on cars or building woodcrafts, asking many questions. Dan is in his thirty-eighth year of teaching at Central Christian College in Moberly, Missouri.

GAIL THORELL SCHILLING of New Durham, New Hampshire, says, "I managed to visit all of my children this year—but not all in one place. By the time Greg arrived here from California, Tom had left Boston for summer work in Los Angeles! Our family photo poses a logistical challenge. At least Tess and 4-year-old Hannah (a real ham in front of a camera) live nearby, and Trina, a senior in high school, will be living with me for one more year. Trina and I snapped plenty of photos when she bought her first car in July, then drove me around Cape Cod in it. Photos also record the most special event last year, the eagerly anticipated baptism of Trina's boyfriend Kenny. Even without film, the faith of these teens will remain in my heart forever."

"The past year held many occasions for my husband Don and me to rejoice in hope fulfilled," writes *PENNEY SCHWAB* of Copeland,

Kansas. "Caden, born to our son Michael and his wife Jerie, is now a toddler delight (and terror!) who loves playing with cousins Ryan, David, Mark, Caleb and Olivia. We're grateful for continued good health and strength. I give thanks for pastors and laypeople who hoped and prayed into existence a small missionary effort called United Methodist Mexican-American Ministries, where I've worked for twenty years. We've grown and grown, and today the agency brings hope and healing to people throughout southwest Kansas. My prayer for *Daily Guideposts* writers and readers is this: 'Now the God of hope fill you with all joy and peace in believing, that ye may abound in hope' (Romans 15:13)."

"I don't know any cause for rejoicing and hope greater than a baby," says *ELIZABETH SHERRILL* of Chappaqua, New York, of the birth of great-grandson Adin. Adin is a first name carried father to son for four generations of her family. "The first Adin, born around 1755, was a Revolutionary War soldier in Colonel Vose's Massachusetts Regiment. He was my great-great-great-grandfather, which makes this Adin his great-great-great-great-great-great-grandson." That's a cause for hope, too, Elizabeth says. "When I think how frightening and uncertain the future must have looked for that young soldier in the struggle with all-powerful England, and see his namesake born in a free America two hundred and fifty years later, I believe our future, too, is filled with promise."

JOHN SHERRILL adds a P.S. to his wife Elizabeth's biographical note by welcoming into their lives great-grandson Adin Marshall Richter. "I don't mind being a great-grandfather," John says, "but it comes as quite a shock to have a *son* who is a *grandfather*." For their vacation last year, John and Elizabeth revisited the home of one of Adin's ancestors, also a Marshall, who was at Sutter's Creek at the time gold was discovered, kicking off the famous California gold rush.

"Hope flowered in many ways for the family this year," says *SHARI SMYTH* of Nashville, Tennessee, "but especially in the marriage of our daughter Sanna Noel to Robert Glen Dean. It was a beautiful wedding with family and friends from all over the country. And Whitney and I are blessed with a wonderful son-in-law. Our son Jon has moved to Nashville and works as a chef at a fine restaurant. It's great to have him here! Wendy and Laura live in Hawaii and New York but visit and phone frequently. Our family is closer than ever, including Whitney and me. My work in children's ministry is branching out and that, too, is a joy. Something I'm learning with the gains and losses of aging is this: I have many hopes, big and little. But I have only one Hope. To be truly whole means to root all my hopes in God."

JOSHUA SUNDQUIST of Harrisonburg, Virginia, is proud to report that he completed his first year of college without failing a single class. He only skipped two lectures, a confession he always modifies with seemingly legitimate excuses. Unfortunately, he still has not found a girlfriend. Since he likes to imagine himself as a confident, handsome bachelor, Josh likes to blame this apparent lack of success on the fact that "the good girls are all taken." In other news, Josh continues to fall prey to his overachiever tendencies, spending many antisocial days and nights creating his Web site (www.JoshSundquist.com) and serving as editor of a devotional book written by young people around the world called *Forty Voices: Stories of Hope from Our Generation.*

"In my fourth year at Guideposts," writes *PTOLEMY TOMPKINS* of New York City, "I continue to be surprised by the places this job takes me. One day last fall, for example, I was driving through the suburbs of Houston, looking for George Foreman's little Baptist church and marveling at the fact that each block I passed seemed to have a church of its own. In February, my wife snapped a shot of me posing in front of a giant fiberglass dinosaur—part of the decorations at a miniature golf course—in Pigeon Forge, Tennessee, where I spoke with Dolly Parton for her summer 2004 *Guideposts* magazine story. Just the evening before, the waitress at the restaurant where we ate told us she'd been reading *Guideposts* for years. Traveling for the magazine is fun, but it's also exciting to discover firsthand what a role Guideposts plays in peoples' lives."

KAREN VALENTIN, a native New Yorker, is the author of *The Flavor of Our Faith.* She writes, "Through the process of writing the book, I never imagined how many new things I'd learn about my family and friends. Regardless of how close you are to someone you love, there's always more to discover." Karen, who taught gymnastics for ten years, is an avid traveler with a passion for singing, songwriting, languages and fine art. She's a member of Central Baptist Church, where she serves as a choir member and Sunday schoolteacher.

"You can't keep a good man down," writes *VAN VARNER* of New York City. "I kept on traveling during the year, to the Amazon, where I held the hand of a sloth (rather she took my hand and refused to surrender it), and to China for the first time—to Shanghai, Beijing and Xi'an (where the terra-cotta army is). And by the time this is published, I will (God willing) have been to Antarctica (I have flown over it, but that was a disappointing adventure) and can say that I have set foot on all the continents. The biggest news is I had my 80th birthday and my whole family attended (my dog Shep was not invited), which in entirety means two nephews and their wives and four children, including a married niece and her husband, plus a 2-year-old great-grandniece and one that was here but wasn't born until a month later. How is that for hope rejoicing?"

"This has been a busy year for my family," writes *SCOTT WALKER* of Waco, Texas. "Both of our sons Drew and Luke are seniors this year. Drew will be graduating from Furman University as a history major and anticipates going to law school. Luke will graduate from Reicher Catholic High School and is in process of applying to colleges. Our daughter Jodi will be completing the tenth grade and will be our last child living at home. My wife Beth continues to work with more than four hundred international students at Baylor University. She is uniquely gifted for this ministry and does a fantastic job of helping internationals feel welcomed and loved in America. In October, I celebrated my tenth year as pastor of First Baptist Church. Our church has begun a long-term relationship with an orphanage in Guatemala. We've also become involved in helping disadvantaged children within the school districts. And I've published a new book *Footsteps of the Fisherman: With St. Peter on the Path of Discipleship* (Augsburg Press)."

DOLPHUS WEARY of Richland, Mississippi, writes, "Our son Ryan is in the middle of his senior year at Richland High School, so Rosie and I are getting ready to experience empty-nest syndrome. Our daughter Danita is a pediatrician in Natchez, Mississippi, which is about a two-hour drive from here. Our son Reggie is working with Cellular South, a wireless phone company." Dolphus is still working full-time with Mission Mississippi and is completing his new book *I Can't Never Leave*, which is a sequel to his first book *I Ain't Comin' Back*. The proceeds from both titles will continue to go toward endowing REAL

Christian Foundation, which supports ministries in rural Mississippi. Rosie continues to serve as executive director of the foundation.

BRIGITTE WEEKS of New York City writes, "It's hard to believe that this is the tenth year I've contributed to *Daily Guideposts*. How much I've learned from this story-filled annual that is a part of so many lives! I've spent hours thinking of how to share with readers a special moment when I knew God was at work in my life. Over this decade you have written or e-mailed your reactions and shared your own experiences. I wrote about learning to knit for refugees in my childhood (you asked for the pattern, and more than 150,000 handmade sweaters for children have been shipped around the world), about my three children and about my prolonged squabble with my husband over new china (many of you were on my side!). This year will bring me my first grandchild—another of God's blessed miracles. So thank you for the stories we've shared. I'm looking forward to another decade with you."

MARION BOND WEST of Watkinsville, Georgia, writes, "This year my sons taught me more than I ever wanted to know about holding on to hope. An obscure Bible verse, Habakkuk 3:17-19 (NAS), that I've loved for more than thirty years became my Balm in Gilead. It's all marked up in my Bible, where I've prayed it, inserting my own anguishing circumstances. 'Though the fig tree should not blossom, and there be no fruit on the vines. . . .' Each time I pray through it or just read it, I can hardly wait to get to the good part: 'Yet will I exult in the Lord. . . .' I didn't want to write another book, but those verses have got me working on a new one, *Pray for Your Life*. I'm writing it for myself and for everyone who has almost given up hope, almost stopped believing, almost ceased praying—almost."

"In spite of Christ's admonitions that we shouldn't worry, I still do," says *TIM WILLIAMS* of Durango, Colorado. "Instead of 'rejoicing in hope,' I spend way too much time 'hoping to rejoice.' I hoped the melanoma that was discovered during my physical last winter hadn't spread. I didn't rejoice while I hoped—I worried. I didn't rejoice until the lymph node biopsies were clear. And again, when my oldest son was in Bolivia just as a civil war erupted, I didn't rejoice while hoping for his safety—I worried. I didn't rejoice until he was finally able to return to our country. I'm sure this year will bring many new problems, and all of them will seem worthy of worry. I pray for God's strength to rejoice during the time of hope—and then to rejoice, again, no matter how He chooses to resolve things."

"One day you can have something as innocuous as 'pay bills' on your to-do list and then the phone rings and your comfortable, routine life changes forever," writes *ISABEL WOLSELEY* of Syracuse, New York. Her granddaughter Kristen Sanford—who with her husband Keith taught at Baylor University—suddenly collapsed and died from an aneurysm. Their unborn baby, due in two weeks, survived only twelve days. Isabel's husband Lawrence Torrey, hospitalized with broken bones caused by a collapsed ladder, was unable to help. Then guardian angels arrived: A pilot friend arranged her trip to Texas, while seatmates familiar with Chicago and Dallas airports guided her through these mazes. "Our entire family is devastated, yet we have experienced the truth of 'You may not grieve as others do who have no hope' (I Thessalonians 4:13, RSV), and our faith in God's ultimate purpose remains unshaken."

"Last year we watched our children take big strides," says *PHILIP ZALESKI* of Northampton, Massachusetts. "John made the high-school varsity baseball team and Andy, still in elementary school, became an avid reader. I don't know if my wife Carol or I accomplished anything of similar magnitude, as our triumphs seem to consist in getting dinner on the table on time or finding new projects for the family to enjoy. Right now, because everyone is interested in King Arthur and Anglo-Saxon England, we're all trying to learn Old English. It's a tough language, but we have high hopes that we'll get it eventually. Hope inspires other family activities, too: growing orchids, learning piano, landscaping our backyard. We stumble a lot, but we always get up again, trust in God and forge ahead. And what a grand adventure it is!"